D1457585

THE DREAM
IN NATIVE AMERICAN AND
OTHER PRIMITIVE CULTURES

Samantabhadra, attributed to Kwan Hiu

[*see pp. 80-81*]

THE DREAM
IN NATIVE AMERICAN AND OTHER PRIMITIVE CULTURES

Jackson Steward Lincoln

DOVER PUBLICATIONS, INC.
Mineola, New York

Bibliographical Note

This Dover edition, published in 2003, is an unabridged republication of the work originally published in 1935 by The Cresset Press Limited, London, under the title *The Dream in Primitive Cultures.*

Library of Congress Cataloging-in-Publication Data

Lincoln, Jackson Steward, 1902–1941.
[Dream in primitive cultures]
The dream in native American and other primitive cultures / Jackson Steward Lincoln.
p. cm.
Originally published: The dream in primitive cultures. London : Cresset Press, 1935. Includes bibliographical references and index.
ISBN 0-486-42706-4 (pbk.)
1. Dreams. 2. Ethnopsychology. I. Title.

BF1078.L5 2003
154.6'3'09—dc21   2002041668

Manufactured in the United States of America
Dover Publications, Inc., 31 East 2nd Street, Mineola, N.Y. 11501

CONTENTS

PREFACE

ATTEMPTS to bring together branches of the sciences dealing with man, generally are doomed to opposition from the specialists of each branch. Conflicts of method and conception seem to be inevitable, but such conflicts must be resolved before it will become possible to appreciate, even remotely, man's place in human culture. Anthropology and psychoanalysis, both sciences of human nature, are often jealously kept in watertight compartments with little or no communication, and many an anthropologist will attempt to maintain this situation, even to the extent of refusing to consider a psychological study of anthropological material. "A thesis along psychoanalytic lines would not be suitable for a degree in anthropology any more than a thesis whose approach was through orthodox psychology or climatology or chemistry," is the sort of statement which illustrates this " compartment " conception of scientific research. Such a point of view can only stultify attempts to attain a more comprehensive view of the truth in a field much too vast to be exclusively monopolized by any one method of investigation. That these two sciences can co-operate to their mutual advantage has been amply demonstrated by Professor C. G. Seligman, who has clearly defined their possibilities *vis-à-vis* each other in his Huxley Memorial Lecture for 1932.

The present work, based on field and library research, is a further attempt to illustrate in some slight measure how the two sciences may supplement and control each other, and aims to supply the need of a first reference work to some of the scattered data on the dreams of native peoples.

Part III, which comprises a large body of data from

American Indian cultures, was written prior to Parts I and II, and was accepted as an M.A. thesis at the University of California. It is here re-presented with few additions and changes as necessary for constant reference.

Part of the material was assembled in the library, or collected in the field among the Navajo Indians by myself. I gratefully make the following acknowledgments for other important data :

. To Professor C. G. Seligman, who generously allowed me to sift and use much of his own unpublished material, and whose criticism and advice have been indispensable.

. To Dr. Paul Radin, who has presented a whole unpublished collection of dreams from the Eastern Woodlands.

To Miss B. Blackwood, whose unpublished chapter on dreams from the Solomon Islands I have freely quoted.

I am also indebted to Dr. O. Pfister of Zürich, for suggesting that I undertake this study, and to Mr. Lorenzo Hubbell of Oraibi, Arizona, for his assistance to me while in the Navajo country, and especially to my wife, whose active participation in the field and collaboration in critical suggestions have been a constant source of inspiration. I wish also to express my thanks to the following for permission to reprint data : The American Museum of Natural History, The Anthropos Administration and Father R. P. H. Trilles, The Columbia University Press, The Journal of American Folklore, and the Smithsonian Institute.

I wish particularly to emphasize that all psychoanalytic interpretations of dreams and other material, none of which have any pretensions of being exhaustive, have been verified by Professor J. C. Flügel of University College, of the University of London, whose experience as a trained analyst has been of invaluable assistance.

INTRODUCTION

B ESIDES bringing together material of great general interest, Dr. Lincoln has in this volume rendered a considerable service to anthropology by examining in the most precise manner one of the outstanding problems of our science, its relationship to psychology. To-day the anthropologist must be aware of current psychological theory ; he must make up his mind how far his researches should be directed by this, and on what class of material he should particularly focus his attention in order not only to test the theories of psychologists but also to further his own science. To put it briefly, how can a profitable give and take relationship between psychology and anthropology best be established at the present time?

This is a problem to which the writer of this Introduction has given much thought of recent years. Brought up in the main in the Tylorian (comparative) School of Anthropology, having thereafter gained some knowledge of and made use of the Historical School of Rivers, and of late years watched the development of the functional method, the writer has become convinced that the most fruitful development—perhaps indeed the only process that can bring social anthropology to its rightful status as a branch of science and at the same time give it the full weight in human affairs to which it is entitled—is the increased elucidation in the field and integration into anthropology of psychological knowledge. That we have not progressed further than in fact we have is probably only in part due to the relatively scant amount of material available or to any inherent difficulty which anthropologists should find in handling it. The writer hopes he is not being unfair to his colleagues, but cannot help considering that this failure is far more due to a lack of eclecticism, a determination of each exponent and adherent of a particular school to show little interest in the technique and conclusions of others. It is regrettable that there is so little tendency for anthropologists to combine the methods of different schools, or, if they do, to admit frankly what they have done.

All this must be borne in mind when endeavouring to answer the question of the relationship existing between psychology and anthropology in present-day anthropological practice. Nor must one important difference between the two sciences be overlooked, namely, that psychology in the main deals with the individual, while anthropology, apart from its physical side, in the main deals with the group. Nevertheless, certain conclusions now accepted as part of general psychology, although derived from the study of the individual, do so largely affect the behaviour of the group that they obviously concern the anthropologist even when engaged in studying groups of considerable size. It is only necessary to mention many commonly accepted conclusions as to the significance of disguised manifestations of repressed desires, as shown in dreams, neuroses, and even such apparently trivial matters as slips of the tongue. But granting that there is a wide measure of such acceptance, Dr. Lincoln has collected and examined a far larger amount of material than has previously been utilized, and may fairly claim by his investigation of American cultures to have carried further than others and to have demonstrated with greater precision the enormous part played by dreams in many primitive cultures. He has shown, to an extent that has not been hitherto recognized, the importance of the manifest content, particularly in the institutionalized—i.e. the sought, induced, or culture-pattern—dream.

Cultural images, the stereotyped images of the great cultural visions, are regarded as symbols, which not only disappear when a culture breaks down but vary with different cultures and stand or fall with them; they are in fact dependent on persistent tradition and not on anything approaching "racial memory." This is a conclusion that will be welcomed by many anthropologists, dissatisfied both with the rigidity of interpretation of some followers of Freud, and with Jung's conception of a universal unconscious and his mystic outlook.

The dream is looked upon as an intermediate stage between mental processes and cultural results, and a large part of culture is considered the direct result of the dream, due to "the equal valuation [given by the primitive] to both fantasy and the external world." Such equal valuation may be seen frequently in children, less commonly in poets and in religious mystics, who all, while to a considerable extent accepting the reality of fantasy, keep in touch with the actual world around them. Observation indicates that this is to a greater or less extent the attitude of many primitive peoples in their ceremonial behaviour.

It is then not surprising that Dr. Lincoln sees a large part of primitive culture as the result of the psychological and cultural processes behind the dream. The cultures that he has chosen to examine certainly bear out his conclusion, for among them the dream is an important element, guiding both ritual and individual behaviour. Moreover, the dream, as he says, is frequently "an intermediate stage between the initial mental process and the cultural result." This leads to the suggestion that its possible importance should not be overlooked in other societies, where the dream does not play an overt part in culture.

Dr. Lincoln's insistence that the mind assimilates new symbols to represent old primary ideas through the associative principles of similarity and identity (using to a considerable extent the mechanism of condensation), because the unconscious tends to see similarities and never differences, is of considerable practical interest. It seems to offer an explanation of a fact that every field anthropologist must have observed, namely, the far greater interest that peoples, be they primitive or advanced (the writer has found it to hold equally in New Guinea and the Scottish Highlands), take in customs and ideas similar to their own as compared with those that show a considerable difference. Here then is a contribution towards an understanding of the high emotional value which every group attaches to its own culture.

It is an interesting speculation how much earlier this book might have been written—assuredly not during the first years of our century, nor indeed during the War. In the last edition of *The Golden Bough* the only psychological principle to which Frazer could appeal in order to explain magic was that of the association of ideas (third edition, 1911, vol. I, p. 53). To-day no anthropologist would regard as adequate any explanation that did not give full weight to the emotional element. That this is so is largely due to the development of our knowledge of the psychology of emotion under the influence of Rivers, who specially stressed the importance of conflict. Since Dr. Lincoln's book is to a great extent the logical outcome of the application of this new knowledge to the problems of culture, it is not surprising that the greater part of his material is drawn from the literature of the last twenty years.

The author of this most stimulating volume has had the advantage of both anthropological and psychological training. Moreover he has been analysed. His work cannot then be taken as offering a direct contribution to the problem which the present writer discussed a few years ago in his Huxley Memorial Lecture ("Anthropological Perspective and Psychological Theory," *Journ. Roy. Anthrop. Inst.*, Vol. LXII, 1932), viz. how far may anthropologists without any special training in psychoanalysis hope to make use of current psychological theory to advance their science.

Finally, it may be well to state emphatically that *The Dream in Primitive Cultures* is not an attempt to provide additional proof of the validity of any particular school of psychological teaching, but is an honest essay in the application of psychological knowledge to some of the fundamental problems of cultural anthropology. The moral is that Social Anthropology and Psychology must work together to unravel the significance of dreams, myth, and ritual, in order to appreciate the part each has played and is playing in the development and differentiation of social groups.

C. G. SELIGMAN.

PART I

HISTORICAL REVIEW OF DREAM INTERPRETATION

THROUGHOUT the history of Western cultures in ages prior to modern science, man has continuously been absorbed in his dreams and visions, many of which he has regarded as experiences of religious significance. Seers, prophets, priests, magicians, sorcerers and professional interpreters have recorded a class of dreams which were considered the will of deity or devil, or as revelations of the supernatural. Generally they were instruments of guidance with regard to the future of individuals, nations, and to forthcoming events of cosmic importance. Kings, warriors, statesmen and heroes treated their visions with the respect and awe accorded only to manifestations of the divine powers, and the early records and traditions of all races and cultures teem with examples and interpretations of dreams and visions, whose influence on the lives of individuals and the history of nations has been far reaching.

The visions of religious significance of ancient times, however, came eventually to lose their power to compel or influence in proportion as the rational spirit of European man developed and assumed supreme control in the valuation of the inner world of man's mind and the outer world of nature and human culture. As rationalism took the place of animism, in so far as this can be said to have taken place, dreams became mere fantasms of the human mind whose meaning and interpretation varied according to the mental spirit of particular times.

Ordinary night dreams did not necessarily have any special religious significance, although in some instances in the Middle Ages these were regarded as coming from the devil. They were subject to hosts of standardized interpretations and classifications by professional interpreters, and were treated as having great importance for the guidance of the lives of individual dreamers. This class of dreams and interpretations, as recorded in the numerous and widespread " dream books," [1] also passed into the limbo of insignificance as the European mind developed the scientific spirit with reason as the supreme instrument for evaluating truth.

For a period all dreams and visions, treated as irrational products of the human mind, were no longer regarded as worthy of even the respect of investigation, or if they were accorded a passing glance it was only to depreciate their importance or to rationalize their meaning to fit in to some pre-conceived rationalistic or other viewpoint. It was not until Sigmund Freud, schooled in the observation of the processes of the mind, and trained in a rigorous method, which enabled him to regard any manifestations of mind as objective fact to be studied and treated as of the same importance as the data of any of the sciences, that the dream, in spite of its manifest irrationality, again came to be regarded as having a serious significance for man. Although no longer can it be considered an instrument of divine revelation, it has been proved by Freud to be an instrument for the revelation of human nature, and through it he has possibly discovered the key to the understanding of human culture as well.

On the basis of this newer scientific significance of the dream, the forthcoming study is an attempt to find out how far it is possible to determine accurately through the dreams

---

[1] The earliest dream book in existence from a recently translated Egyptian papyrus is supposed to date back to the Twelfth Dynasty (approx. 2000–1790 B.C.). This papyrus is regarded as enhancing Egypt's claim to be the place of origination of all later dream books (Alan Gardiner, *Hieratic Papyri in the Brit. Museum*, 3rd series, Chester Beatty Gift, Papyrus No. III (Revises), pp. 9, 22).

of primitive peoples, a few of the motive forces of human culture in some of its more primitive phases. Existing and recent native cultures still have dreams and visions of high religious significance, and interpret the ordinary individual dreams with a view to the daily guidance of life, an attitude in varying degrees similar to the treatment accorded by the early European civilizations as alluded to above. It will be necessary, therefore, only to review briefly the history of this subject in the past before plunging into the more living and hence more relevant native material.

To begin with ancient Babylon where the dream played an important part in life and religion, in the dream the deity was believed to reveal himself, declaring the will of heaven and predicting the future. The " *bârû* " or " seers " constituted a special class of priests and one of the titles of the Sun God was " *bârû-terêti*," " the seer of the revealed law." Answers to prayers were obtained by sleeping in a temple and invoking Makhir, the Goddess (or God) of dreams. A penitential psalm reads,

" Reveal thyself to me and let me behold a favourable dream. May the dream that I dream be favourable, may the dream that I dream be true. May Makhir, the God(dess) of dreams stand at my head. Let me enter E-Saggila, the temple of the Gods, the house of life."

The influence of dreams in important historical events is shown when the army of Aššur-bani-pal was encouraged to cross a river by the appearance in a vision of the Goddess Ištar, and when the order to rebuild the temple of the Moon-God at Harran was revealed to Nabonidos in a dream. In Aššur-bani-pal's library at Nineveh was a collection of books on oneiromancy or dream interpretation, which were later used by Artemidorus, the professional interpreter of Rome of the second century A.D.[1]

In early Egypt the dream, though not so important as in

[1] A. H. Sayce, Hastings' *Encyclopedia of Religion and Ethics*, Vol. 5, p. 33.

Chaldea and Phœnicia, played an important rôle.[1] The information here is still scarce owing to the need of deciphering unpublished papyri. Still it is stated that there were cases of miraculous healing obtained through dreams, and the dream in which Gods intervene were of three kinds :

1. Unsolicited dreams in which the Gods appeared in order to demand some act of piety towards themselves.

2. Dreams in which the Gods gave spontaneous warnings.

3. Dreams in which the Gods granted their worshippers an answer to a question stated.

Official Egypt admitted the method of divine warning by dreams as valid, and numerous restorations of temples and cults were the outcome of dreams regarded as the will of the Gods. An example of an unsolicited dream is the one imputed to Thotmes IV, who falling asleep during the chase at the foot of the statue of the Great Sphinx heard the voice of a God. It promised him the throne of Egypt and required him to repair the God's temple which was threatened by ruin.

What are classed as unsolicited dreams are those cases where revelation was given by a dream of the hiding-place of some wonderful chapter for use in funerary or medicinal magic, such as the traditional origin of formulæ in the " Books of the Dead," and the first medical papyri. This tradition resembles more priestly explanations of origins rather than the actual records of dreams, nevertheless, the tradition shows a tendency to look towards the dream for an explanation.

Solicited dreams were more frequent. The Kings when in a difficult situation would implore the Gods for guidance. They would go to a temple, and after prayer and sleep, a dream would answer their wishes. Cures were also obtained in this way. The story of Satui tells of Mahituaskhit going to the temple of Imuthes in Memphis, praying, falling asleep and receiving from the God in a dream a cure for her sterility. The sanctuaries for dream incubation were at the

[1] J. Foucart, *ibid.*, pp. 34–7.

temples of Imuthes (or Asklepios) at Memphis, of Thoth at Khimunu, and in Thebes, as well as the Sanctuary of Isis at Philae, and the temple now known as Sarbut-el-Qadem near Sinai for dreams sent by the Goddess Hathor, relating to the locality of turquoise mines. Often fasting took place before incubation, and magicians taught the private magic of how to evoke dreams without going to the temples, and also secured dreams by evoking the dead.

It is stated that although the interpretation of symbolic dreams in Egypt was the business of special persons, the " Masters of the Secret Things," " official dreamers," did not have the prominence enjoyed elsewhere. It is also stated that the dream was regarded as a tangible reality without mysticism and as a rule without symbolism. It was not regarded animistically as a journey of souls, but was dependent on the hypersensitiveness of sleeping man. It meant merely that the sleeping state allowed men to see and hear things that are always in existence.[1] If the latter statements are true, it would mean that Egypt had already taken a first step away from a primitive animistic attitude towards a more realistic one consistent with her different religious ideology.

As to Greek literature, suffice it to mention that it reveals a belief in the divine and prophetic character of dreams. In Homer, Zeus is described as the sender of dreams. Prophetic dreams were dependent on the sacredness of certain spots such as Delphi, and the Oracle of Delphi was controlled by Apollo, the great sender of veridical dreams. At incubation at the temple of Æsculapius at Epidaurus, the God would appear in person in a dream. The Orphic religion believed in the divine nature of dreams as did its descendant, the Pythagorean philosophy.

The Jewish and Christian religious scriptures are full of well-known examples of dreams which are believed to show God's will.

[1] George Foucart, Hastings' *Encyclopedia of Religion and Ethics*, Vol. V, p. 37.

One particular type of supernatural and prophetic vision which seems to be common to many religions and nations should be especially mentioned, namely, that which announces the birth of a great hero or prophet. Whether in each instance these were actual visions or were merely part of a tradition that was widely diffused, or were the later projections into the past of an elaborated and usual fantasy common to many peoples, is impossible to distinguish. Probably all three processes took place at various times and places.

Of this class is the tale of the dream of Satui, father of the great Egyptian magician Senosiris.

" Now Satui went to sleep and dreamed a dream. Someone spoke to him saying, ' Thy wife has conceived, and the child she will bear, will be called Senosiris, and many are the miracles that will be done by him in the land of Egypt.' " [1]

Very similar is the dream in which the hawk is sent from Egypt to Philip to announce the miraculous birth of Alexander.[2]

A poetic rendering from the " Life of Zoroaster " gives the traditional dream of Daghdú, the mother of the great prophet, in which his birth is announced [3] :

> " To Daghdú then the heavenly stripling said—
> ' Arise, nor let thy heart grow faint with dread ;
> Comfort thee, for from thee a child shall spring
> On whom shall rest the favour of heaven's King :
> The world beholds the glad event with joy
> And future ages hail the promised boy.' "

Of precisely the same pattern are the visions of the annunciation of the birth of Christ to Joseph and to Mary :

" But when he thought on these things, behold, an angel of the Lord appeared unto him in a dream, saying, Joseph, thou

---

[1] Foucart, op. cit., p. 33.   [2] Ibid., p. 37.

[3] F. Seafield, Literature and Curiosities of Dreams, Vol. II, p. 45. London, 1865.

son of David, fear not to take unto thee Mary thy wife ; for that which is conceived in her is of the Holy Ghost. And she shall call his name Jesus ; for it is he that shall save his people from their sins." [1]

And :

" And the angel said unto her, Fear not, Mary ; for thou hast found favour with God. And behold, thou shalt conceive in thy womb, and bring forth a son, and shalt call his name Jesus. He shall be great, and shall be called the Son of the Most High ; and the Lord God shall give unto him the throne of his father David : and he shall reign over the house of Jacob for ever ; and of his kingdom there shall be no end." [2]

It is amazing how this pattern persists throughout the ages and in many lands.

" The advent of the Muhammedan apostle and the consequent fall of the Pagan power were disclosed in a dream to Khusru, one of the last of the Sasanians. A plane of fire, spreading over heaven and earth foretold to the obscure father of the first of the Buwaihide princes the foundation of the glory of his family, and the radiant stars in the dream of the Moghul Kachúli Behádur predicted the birth of his descendant Tímúr and the devastating influence of the empire of Ghengís Khán and his successors. Similar announcements were made by dreams to Actia, the mother of Augustus, Arlotta the mother of William of Normandy ; of the birth of Cyrus, and in more modern history those of Scanderbeg and of St. Bernard." [3]

Among the Teutons, the significance of dreams was only prophetic and there were no revelations from the Gods. In Scandinavia dreams were not only divorced from religion

---

[1] *New Testament*, St. Matthew, ch. i, verses 20–1, Authorized Version, Revised 1881 (Oxford).

[2] *Ibid.*, St. Luke, ch. i, verses 30–3, Authorized Version, Revised 1881 (Oxford).

[3] N. Bland, " On the Muhammedan Science of Tabir or Interpretation of Dreams," *J. of Royal Asiatic Soc.*, Vol. XVI, p. 121, 1856.

but also from magic. Interpretation was not due to magical powers, but was " found in combination with a philosophy and a knowledge of the world." In the Heimskringla, King Haldan the Black consults his wisest counsellor about his dream. Gudrun, in the Lay of Atli, says dreaming of iron portends fire, and Hogni believes that a dream of the polar bear means a storm in the East. The dream is often used as a literary device to deepen the atmosphere of doom. The idea of the materialization of man's spirit in dreams, in animal form, is a usual motive and occurs frequently. In others the guardian spirit or a deceased member of the family appears and warns of danger or death, as in the Icelandic tale of the dream of Thorstein in which three female guardian spirits come weeping to Thorstein warning him he is to be murdered. The warning is in vain, since to the Teutonic conception dreams are seldom warnings to be profited by, but are foreshadowings of an inevitable doom or fate. Nightmares are not regarded as dreams, but as the actual presence of a " mara " or " alp." In Scandinavia, the interpretation of dreams was a secular art, and the Icelandic Bishop, Saint Thorlak, took great pleasure in reciting his dreams.[1]

During the Middle Ages, and after, ordinary dreams came to be regarded as instruments of the devil, although occasional dreams were regarded as divine, and in England the study of dreams was denounced by an early Archbishop together with magic.[2] Luther, however, believed that through dreams self-knowledge could be furthered " both concerning sin and Satan, our foes ; and the friends and fathers of filthy dreams." [3] In fact he urged the importance of studying dreams in order to repent of sin and prevent the consequences of what might follow. He says of man's

[1] B. S. Phillpotts, Hastings' *Encyclopedia of Religion and Ethics*, Vol. V, pp. 37–8.

[2] B. S. Phillpotts, *ibid.*, p. 38.

[3] Philip Goodwin, *The Mystery of Dreams Historically Considered* ; F. Seafield, *Literature and Curiosities of Dreams*, Vol. I, pp. 145–6.

" most delightful and beloved sin," his " most prevalent and predominant sin," that,

" In the night-time, and in the midst of man's sleep may this sin arise and run out in his dreams. That's a man's well beloved, which lieth all night betwixt his breasts, that's a man's Delilah-lust which leaneth upon his lap in sleep." [1]

" Again much of Satan, in his subtle designs, may hereby come to be discovered. Ignorance of the Devil's artifice is not fit for Christians." [2]

Although Luther admitted that some dreams could be divine he would pray that God would not speak anything to him in his dreams. He rather distrusted this type of dream as " full of fallacies and falsities," and preferred to rest on divine scripture for guidance, as being more reliable. [3]

It is easy to see here in part the development of that rational spirit which played an important rôle in the protestant reformation, and already " divine " dreams are mistrusted and the recognition of dreams as expressions of desires is tacitly admitted. Without attempting to trace in further detail the gradually changing attitude towards dreams throughout the ages, all the changes and variations of which are apparent in Seafield's [4] important record of dreams and dream interpretations from the earliest historical days down to the mid-nineteenth century, and without attempting to prove a universal evolution from animism to rationalism, it is nevertheless a general rule that wherever the spirit of reason appears it tends to drive out animism. The rational mind refuses to regard dreams as caused by the presence of spirits, or as a journey to the spirit world, or as a reliable contact with deity. Processes that do not conform to rational laws such as dreams, lose the respect of rational mind which at first glance revolts against what seems a mere absurdity, until gradually whatever valid

---

[1] Philip Goodwin, *ibid.*, p. 154.   [2] Philip Goodwin, *ibid.*, pp. 146–7.
[3] Philip Goodwin, *ibid.*, p. 164.
[4] F. Seafield, *Literature and Curiosities of Dreams*. London, 1865.

significance these processes may have had, vanishes entirely. This attitude, however, could not be successful with regard to dreams which are living processes that continue to express themselves regardless of whatever standpoint is taken up towards them, and in every age some of the leading minds have always found the problem of dreams to be worthy of serious investigation. Although rationalism tends to drive out animism, noteworthy instances of the return of animism in some form or other occur even in " ages of reason," as in the case of Swedenborg who claimed that he travelled to the spirit world in his dreams and received a complete divine revelation of things spiritual, all in terms of the prevailing Christian culture to which he belonged.[1]

How the rationalistic spirit of a period, or more especially of an individual, can not only lead to a complete destruction of the animistic or religious attitude, but also to the complete devaluation of dream processes is shown in the following poem of Swift's, a parody of Petronius[2] :

On Dreams

" Those dreams that on the silent night intrude,
And with false flitting shades our minds delude,
Jove never sends us downwards from the skies ;
Nor can they from infernal mansions rise ;
But are all mere productions of the brain,
And fools consult interpreters in vain.

" For when in bed we rest our weary limbs,
The mind unburden'd sports in various whims ;
The busy head with mimic art runs o'er
The scenes and actions of the day before."

(And so forth, about the dreams of the tyrant, soldier, statesman, lawyer, physician, the " grave divine " and the " hireling senator.")

Without presenting further material, quantities of which can be gleaned from Seafield, it is certain that a cursory

---

[1] Emanuel Swedenborg, *Heaven and Hell* (Everyman's Library).
[2] Seafield, *ibid.*, Vol. I, pp. 323-4.

review of some of the vast collection of dream material in pre-scientific ages uncovers two main trends in man's apprehension, and interpretation of dreams and visions :

1. An animistic attitude, meaning a belief in dreams as divine revelations of the spirit world, such an attitude being expressed in terms of the prevailing religious ideology of a culture ; and

2. A rationalistic attitude which tends to drive out the former and treats dreams according to the prevailing philosophic ideology of a culture or period.

These two approaches occur jointly and separately in various times and places, but on the whole the animistic approach can be said to belong definitely to pre-scientific ages, in spite of current spiritualistic belief and other regressive outcroppings. How much these two attitudes prevail in existing and recent primitive cultures is one of the main subjects to be treated in this work.

The foregoing tendencies apply to dream interpretation and analysis prior to Freud's *Interpretation of Dreams*, the first genuine scientific treatment of the subject, and the one reliable authority which makes it possible to treat dreams with an understanding of their true nature and significance as expressions of unconscious processes. In it the previous rationalistic literature of any importance on the subject is reviewed and analysed before his own discoveries are presented. Throughout the approaches of the different writers, it is easily discernible how specific philosophic or rationalistic points of view colour the thought on the subject and hence detract from their value as studies in pure science.

Since all dream interpretation among Western nations in historical ages, as well as among primitive peoples, is largely determined by the prevailing religious, philosophic, or cultural ideology, pertaining to each group, it is necessary to find out how far the same situation can be said to apply in the case of Freud's psychology of dreams. Since the present work is based in large part on Freud's method of interpretation, and his conclusion that dreams represent the disguised or undisguised expression of unconscious repressed wishes,[1] it becomes especially important to find out how far the method and conclusion are free from ideology irrelevant to the discovery of fact. It has often been stated that it is impossible to make psychology into an objective science, inasmuch as it is alleged that there is no control established for verifying observations of mental processes, and it is impossible to keep out preconceived philosophic conceptions. Freud's work has also been criticized in just this way by two of his former colleagues.

Jung broke away from him because he believed that Freud's interpretations were projections of prevailing scientific ideology, and hence were one-sided. Jung accordingly proceeded to propound his doctrine of " sacrificing the rational function " whose overvaluation by scientists he considers a mere prejudice of Western civilization, in order to give validity to the functions of feeling, intuition, and sensation, all of which, he maintains, are equally efficacious for the perception of the inner world of mind as well as the external world of nature and human culture. What Jung's sacrifice of reason, the main prop of science, has led to, seems to be a return to a form of animism, since to him the dream must be treated as a reality co-equal to that of the external world, but it is sufficient to point out that Jung's attempt to escape from the ruthlessness of reason has not led to a freedom from ideological colouring ; it has led rather to an eclectic and animistic ideology formed by an attempt to synthesize Oriental, Germanic, and primitive elements, a point of view which is not merely alien to the scientific spirit, but definitely depreciates its value.

Rank also severed relations with Freud's school of thought, partially on the grounds that no psychology could be a pure science because it was always socially conditioned, not excluding Freud's which was conditioned by nineteenth-

---

[1] Freud has slightly revised his original theory of dreams and now adds that the dream is " an attempted wish—fulfilment." Freud, *New Introductory Lectures on Psychoanalysis*, Lecture XXIX, p. 43.

century " bourgeois ideology." [1] His criticism is directed largely to " practical " or therapeutic rather than to theoretic psychology which he says, " should remain a method of investigation, a pure science." [2]

In the case of the criticism of these two former adherents of Freud's, and of culturally conditioned dream interpretation, is it still possible to show that Freud's method and conclusion with regard to dreams are free to be treated as pure science ? Do they differ from all that has gone before and much that has come afterward ? These questions can be positively answered by pointing out that Freud's method of observation of a wide number of cases which lead to similar conclusions, many of which can be tested by anthropological research, and controlled (as in the case of symbolism), [3] is the method of any science, and its validity stands or falls with any sound scientific method. As to the scientific spirit which forms hypotheses on the above basis, it undoubtedly is an historical product of Western culture and ideology, and as such colours Freud's work and dream interpretation. Although this method for approximating the truth, which is common to all the sciences, may not be perfect, as yet nothing superior to it has been discovered and until such a method has been brought forth by Freud's critics or others, his work on dreams should receive the same attention as accorded to any body of data to which a scientific method is applied.

Still, critics claim that Freud's psychology is coloured by bourgeois conceptions, a criticism generally directed against his discovery, in large part through dreams, of the unconscious conflicts which centre in the family relationship and

[1] O. Rank, " Modern Psychology and Social Change," pp. 96–9, *Action et Pensée*, May–July 1934, 10 *Année*, Nos. 5–6.

[2] O. Rank, *ibid.*, p. 107.

[3] Part II, Chap. III—chapter on Symbols. S. Freud, *New Introductory Lectures on Psychoanalysis*, p. 35 : " When one orders a deeply hypnotized person to dream of sexual activities, the sexual material in the dream that is thus provoked is represented by the symbols which are familiar to us."

the alleged momentous consequences for the individual and society of these conflicts. Such criticism is based on the assumption that the family is an institution confined exclusively to the nineteenth-century European bourgeoisie, an assumption which is obviously absurd in the face of anthropological research which has demonstrated the universal existence of the bilateral family in one form or another, within differing social and cultural structures. The critics can be answered by producing more evidence [1] to show that the identical conflicts of wishes arising from the family relationship, as discovered by Freud, exist also among many peoples and cultures, primitive and civilized, other than the European bourgeoisie, and a large part of the present work will be given over to producing more of such evidence from widespread primitive cultures.

Another fact of great importance which exonerates Freud from the accusation of over indulging in socially conditioned dream interpretation has not hitherto been sufficiently emphasized. He has amply demonstrated that the dream itself is the most important instrument for disclosing the cultural ideology which conditions the dreamer. If a bourgeois conscience is disclosed in the dreams of certain Europeans analysed by Freud, this does not mean that Freud is projecting anything into the dreams, but that the content of the dreams themselves, with associations, happen to disclose just such a cultural compulsive. Hence, on this basis, in the third part of the present work a large body of data from five different American Indian cultures is presented to show especially how the particular religious and cultural viewpoint of each group is disclosed through their respective dreams. If these are the true facts, they show that the dream is an instrument peculiarly fitted for accurately determining the facts of human nature in their relation to human culture and as such cannot be ignored by anthropologists.

To summarize, therefore, since Freud has applied a

[1] J. C. Flügel, *The Psychoanalytic Study of the Family*, 1931.

scientific method of observation to a large number of cases that can be controlled by anthropological research, and has discovered thereby that the dream is an important instrument for disclosing many fundamental facts about human nature and culture, he has freed the dream for all time from the fantasy overvaluations of mysticism and animism, on the one hand, and unscientific rationalizations on the other, that is, at least until such time as reason and the scientific method are discarded for a new cultural process which may be more efficacious in the testing of truth. The facts about dreams, therefore, as uncovered by Freud by the application of a scientific method are as free from projected pre-conceptions as those uncovered through the method of any science, and anthropological research can show that these same facts in varying forms and combinations exist under countless different cultural conditions. It has not hitherto been the function of science to form ideologies but to disclose them as formed by society. Freud has constantly kept this in mind, and even when his study of dreams disclosed the unconscious primitive impulses whose direction were of such importance for society, he still refrained from suggesting any new philosophy of life, " bourgeois " or otherwise. It is now being realized that each culture attempts its own social solution of its anti-social tendencies according to its own lights, hence Freud's great wisdom in refusing to suggest paths of " sublimation " through education or any other way. His task, that of the scientist, has been to uncover, and the function of society is to redirect in accordance with its collective aim, whatever this may be in different cultures. A study of primitive dreams, therefore, may also throw some light on how specific, more or less integrated cultures, direct their unconscious tendencies in accordance with their collective aims.

PART II

INTRODUCTION

THE following study starts with the premise that the dreams of modern man submitted to the process of analysis have been shown to be the disguised or undisguised expressions of wish-fulfilments or conflicts of desire which exist in the unconscious minds of individuals. These wish-conflicts and fulfilments are represented either directly in the dream or indirectly by symbols formed by the mental processes of condensation, displacement, dramatization and secondary elaboration. When symbolically represented, the wishes and conflicts themselves form the latent content of the dream, and are discovered by analysing the manifest content in conjunction with the associations of the dreamer, such associations leading not only to the latent meaning of the dream, but also to the causes of the latent wishes, which so often have been traced to an infantile origin.[1]

The latent wishes and conflicts have been found to express themselves in dreams in certain stereotyped forms, with more or less constant meaning, although the meaning does vary to some extent according to the associations and experience of the individual dreamer. The same forms and symbols, however, do arise not only in the dreams of persons undergoing analysis, but in dreams independently reported from all quarters of the earth. Although the meanings may vary for different individuals, the same meanings for particular symbols and forms appear repeatedly in all parts. Those who deal with scientific dream analysis call attention to the universal resistance to the discovery of the true

[1] S. Freud, *The Interpretation of Dreams*, 3rd ed.

17

meanings of the wishes and thoughts symbolized in dreams, and this factor must always be kept in mind in any study of the dream. Whatever may be the forms and symbols of the dreams and their constant or varying meanings, the conclusion of the psychoanalytic school is that the total number of ideas to be expressed in symbolic form is definitely limited to the repressed primary ideas of life, namely, those concerning the bodily self, the relation to the family, birth, love and death, which remain as the motive forces of human life and culture in the unconscious mind.[1]

This conclusion has been reached through the application of the analytic method to the mental processes of normal and abnormal individuals, and the dream with associative paths leading from it have been the gate and royal road to the discovery of numerous truths about human nature. The method is one that is not generally accepted by the world of science, and its validity and accuracy is questioned and doubted by many scientists largely because of the personal factor of the analyst whose supposedly influential part in the analytic process gives rise to the scientific need of an impartial control to check the material arising and to determine its true latent meaning. As is generally known, the analysts deny the possibility of discovering the deep motive forces of human nature and culture without the process of " psychoanalysis," because they maintain that it is the only method which can overcome the usual resistance to uncovering the repressed, unconscious, archaic and hitherto culturally unacceptable impulses of mankind. Be this as it may, the need for some sort of a control is admitted by all, and anthropology with its independent observations of primitive mentality and culture is the one science which can verify the psychoanalytic conclusions, and establish the connections between primitive mentality with its cultural expressions and the unconscious mind of " civilized " man.

One means of attempting this control is to report the

[1] E. Jones, " Theory of Symbolism," *Papers on Psychoanalysis*, p. 183, 3rd ed.

dreams and associations (wherever possible) of individuals of existing primitive societies, and observe their forms and contents. Since it is customary in anthropology to study the phenomena of primitive life in relation to the specific culture patterns of respective groups, it would seem that more light would be cast on the dream and its ultimate meaning if the form and content were studied in relation to the cultural environment of the dreamer. By doing this, possibly we can find out not only more of the psychology of the primitive individual but also more about the relation of the individual to his culture or group, as well as the influence of the culture on the individual. The primitive group is usually a more integrated social phenomenon than a so-called civilized group, and the primitive individual is much more an integral part of his culture, hence a study of his dreams in the light of his culture would be especially worth while.

Since few dreams of primitives have been analysed, and so far the records of associations to dreams are either very sketchy or entirely absent, it will be necessary in most cases to observe the content of the dream, associated only with the cultural environment of the dreamer. Where individual associations are given, individual psychology is disclosed, and where cultural environment is reflected in a dream, individual association being unknown, this may show the individual's degree of relation to his environment.

An anthropological, and descriptive and wherever possible analytic study, therefore, of dreams from primitive cultures will have as its goal the elucidation of the following :

(a) The nature of the form and content of the two classes of primitive dreams, the important sought vision of cultural significance, and the ordinary individual dream ;

(b) The function of the dream in primitive society, and the beliefs and theories about it ;

(c) The relation of the manifest content to the immediate culture ;

(d) The influence of dreams on primitive cultures, and

the extent to which culture items have originated in dreams ;

(e) The forms and symbols of primitive dreams together with their distribution and their constant or varying meanings ; and

(f) Whether analyses of primitive dreams and symbols with associations lead to the same latent motives and meanings as similarly analysed dreams and symbols of non-primitives.

Such a study of dreams taken from all sections of the earth will not only shed more light on primitive psychology but may also do so on the nature, formation and development of culture in its more primitive phases. Possibly it may be able to control psychoanalytic conclusions with regard to the limited number of ideas symbolized in dreams, namely, those about birth, love, death, the body and the immediate family, and with regard to the latent anti-social family conflict alleged to exist in the unconscious minds of all individuals, which is believed by one school of thought to be the most important force in the formation of culture.

Because of the widespread primitive valuation of fantasy as a form of reality, it would seem that much of primitive culture and customs would resemble dream structures. Such a resemblance has been pointed out in a particular group by W. H. R. Rivers.[1] Possibly this resemblance may be extended to all primitive culture taken in its anthropological sense as the sum total of the customs, beliefs, traditions and material transformations peculiar to more or less socially co-ordinated groups of peoples. These phenomena, in whatever stage they are studied, may have arisen secondarily, through historical development, diffusion, or independent social origin, or initially from expressions of multiple psychological elaborations of the primordial and universal father-mother-child-relationship. Whatever theory is held as to the origin and development of culture, sufficient material on dreams would make it possible to

[1] Rivers, cit. in Chap. I, p. 26.

show the exact influence, if any, in the formation of culture, of the " nuclear " family or " Œdipus " complex, which arises from the universal bilateral family group. In accordance with the evidence from all scientifically analysed dreams, and associations, all aspects of the psychological derivatives of this family relationship should appear in the dream contents, manifest or latent.

CHAPTER I

STRUCTURE, THEORY AND FUNCTION OF DREAMS IN PRIMITIVE CULTURES

THE dreams and visions of so-called primitive peoples always fall into two distinct classes, the unsought, or spontaneous dreams occurring in sleep, here called " individual " dreams, and the sought or induced " culture pattern " dreams of special tribal significance. The latter are sometimes called traditional dreams. In my study of American Indian dreams, I have shown how the culture pattern dreams and individual dreams occur in many culture areas with either type or both regarded by the natives as an important event of individual and cultural significance.[1] This division into the unsought and sought dreams and visions occurs in Australia,[2] in Melanesia,[3] in Polynesia,[4] and in Africa,[5] as well as in North America, but all groups do not have the induced culture pattern dreams or visions whose highest development occurs among the North American Indians. The process of producing the latter is often similar to the ancient temple incubation previously mentioned,[6] and is described in the North Ameri-

[1] I have pointed out that all " Culture Pattern " dreams are sought or induced and rarely occur spontaneously, and only occur as " individual dreams " in areas where the induced dream is highly developed. See Part III.

[2] W. E. Roth, *Superstition, Magic, and Medicine*, N. Queensland Ethnography, Bul. 5, No. 106.

[3] W. G. Ivens, *Melanesians of the S.E. Solomon Islands*, p. 14.

[4] Frazer, cit. on p. 46, Ref. 1.

[5] Rev. J. MacDonald, *Africana*, II, p. 101.

[6] Part I, pp. 3-5.

can part of the study.[1] Many groups of natives pay great attention to their regular night dreams and treat the events occurring in these as a form of reality,[2] although in a group such as the Crow Indians where the vision quest is the most important social event in tribal life, no especial attention is paid to ordinary night dreams,[3] and the Navajo who have no induced dreams, apart from the star-gazing visions of the professional diagnosticians,[4] treat the individual dreams that are emotionally upsetting to the dreamer as of such importance that it arouses the religious and ceremonial activities of the tribe to deal with the situation. Here the bad dream of the individual is regarded as an anti-social event.[5]

Elsewhere I give numerous examples of both types of dreams and show how the manifest content of the individual dreams reflect the culture, and how the culture pattern dreams in each tribe conform to a definite stereotyped pattern laid down by the culture.[6] The latter type exists only while a native culture is in full force, but disappears when the culture breaks down because of white or other influence. When such a breakdown occurs, the dream symbols of the old culture tend to disappear and individual dreams with little or no cultural symbolism take their place. This situation would seem to be at variance with Jung's conception of the " collective unconscious " which is alleged to comprise " archetypal " images pertaining to all mankind and inherited through a racial memory. Jung calls attention to the two types of dreams among primitives, the ordinary individual dreams, and those of collective importance, but he errs in saying that the ordinary dream has no importance for the primitive when much of the evidence is to the contrary, and he fails to point out that the images of the great cultural visions are collective only for a given

[1] Part III, p. 326.
[2] See discussion this chapter, pp. 27–30.
[3] Part III, p. 250.   [4] See Part III, pp. 216–17.
[5] Part III, pp. 207–48.   [6] Part III.

culture and not for all mankind.[1] Since these images disappear when a culture breaks down, it shows that their existence is dependent on cultural tradition and not on a " racial memory." The cultural images are therefore symbols which vary with different cultures and stand or fall with these.[2]

To illustrate further the structure of the two types of dreams, the following are added to show the difference in form and manifest content. The first is a typical sought vision experience full of cultural symbolism, from the old Menomini culture ; the second is an individual dream from the same area where the old culture has almost disappeared, with no cultural symbolism ; and the third is a Navajo " individual " dream which resulted in a religious curing ceremony. The last has cultural symbolism but not in stereotyped form as in the sought visions of other groups :

1. *Menomini Culture Pattern Vision.*

The power mentioned is recognizable as the morning star, one of the " great Powers above."

" After I had fasted eight days a tall man with a big red mouth appeared from the east. The solid earth bent under his steps as though it was a marsh. He said, ' I have pity on you. You shall never live to see your own grey hairs, and those of your children. You shall never be in danger if you make yourself a war club such as I have and always carry it with you wherever you go. When you are in trouble, pray to me and

---

[1] C. G. Jung, Zurich Seminar Notes, Nov. 1928 (unpub.).

[2] See chapter on symbols (pp. 99–131), where primitive symbols are regarded as of two kinds, those which pertain only to specific cultures and those which are the same everywhere. Primary ideas, that is, those concerning birth, love, death, the body and the parents, are regarded as the foundation or " archetypes " of all symbolism. These ideas are regarded as having their origin in the infancy of individuals and as arising from the universal bilateral family relationship. Symbols, therefore, are means of representing these ideas in varying forms.

offer me tobacco. Tobacco is what pleases me.' When he had said this he vanished." [1]

2. Modern Individual Ottawa Dream. Old Culture Non-existent. [2]

" I dreamt that I saw my mother coming. I knew that she was dead. I was very glad to see her coming. As she passed she didn't look at me at all, but she spoke and said to me, ' So you are going to leave to-day. Be careful, take good care of yourself and don't be foolish. I don't want you to get hurt or to get into jail.' Then I went away towards the woods where I found some camps. I entered one hut and saw a lot of groceries piled on the table. I also saw the tablecloth and the dishes. Then I went away and I saw a woman there who asked me, ' Are you looking for work ? ' ' Yes,' I answered. ' Well, I think you can get a job right here,' she said. I didn't see anybody else and I started to walk away from the camp. I hadn't gone very far when I woke up."

Comment. " Every time I dream of my mother I have a quarrel with my wife. All the groceries meant that I was going away. Indeed I did go away. I went to Indianapolis and I left my wife for a long time."

3. A Navajo Individual Dream which resulted in a Curing Ceremony. [3]

" I dreamed about a Chindi [4] chasing me and jumping on me. He was sitting on my waist and grabbed me where I was cut. I yelled for help to throw him off. I didn't know I was talking. That's the end of the dream."

Comment. " Someone spoke to me and asked me why I yelled. I told about the Chindi. After this dream my cut started to pain again and so they decided to have a sing over me. They got a medicine man who sung over me just a few songs from the Hozhonje. I got well again."

[1] See Part III, Eastern Woodlands Area, p. 266, Ref. 1.

[2] Collected by Dr. Paul Radin. See other Woodland dreams in Part III, pp. 266–96.

[3] J. S. Lincoln, Field Notes ; see also Part III, pp. 207–48.

[4] " Spirit."

The psychological structure of primitive dreams appears to be identical with that of non-primitive ones, as Professor Seligman has pointed out in his studies of type dreams.[1] Wish-fulfilment and conflict [2] are as evident in primitive dreams as elsewhere and the manifest content shows dramatization, symbolization, condensation, displacement, and secondary elaboration, or rationalization, of the latent wishes and conflicts.[3] The same structure has also been found to hold for myths,[4] and Rivers in studying these same processes among the Melanesians came to the conclusion that not only dreams and myths were of the same structure, but that primitive culture itself was also a manifestation or transformation of the latent wishes of the human mind, in which the processes of dramatization, symbolization, condensation, and secondary elaboration took place. He cites instances of each of these processes in rites, in art, in customs in which displacement of meaning occurs, and in the rationalized explanations of customs. He found that disguise and censorship which occur in the dream were also paralleled in primitive culture in the acts of priests and sorcerers who possess knowledge which is only allowed to reach people in a distorted form disguising its real nature. Referring to the dream and savage custom, he states that in both we view " the final and highly condensed product of a process leading back to times widely remote from our present standpoint, going back it may be in the one case to the infancy of the individual, in the other to the infancy of the race." [5]

The structure of dreams and myths and parallel structures in primitive culture can be regarded, therefore, as similar manifestations of the unconscious mind. This fact has often been emphasized by Freud.

[1] Cit., Chap. III, p. 104, Ref. 1.
[2] See ref. to Culture conflict dreams, Part III, p. 295.
[3] See my analyses in chapter on Symbolism.
[4] O. Rank, cit. on p. 121. Also Ref. 3, p. 109.
[5] W. H. R. Rivers, *Dreams and Primitive Culture*—Bulletin of John Rylands Library, Vol. 4, Nos. 3–4, Feb.–July 1918.

The often mentioned and widespread general theory of dreams among primitives is that the soul wanders while the body sleeps, and undergoes experiences in a supposedly real world.[1] This primitive explanation is " theory " only to the rational mind of modern man, and such an application of the conception has the defect of being a projection of an alien conception on to the primitive mind. To the primitives with this belief, such an explanation of the dream is not a theory in the sense of a logical deduction from the facts, but is merely a statement of his observations as to what occurs in his dreams. In other words, what he perceives in the dream is not recognized as images created by his own mind, but is regarded as having a reality of its own and an existence which is independent of the dreamer. The tendency of early anthropologists and missionaries was to treat this attitude towards the dream as worthy only of contempt, and to judge it from the heights of " scientific " reason as utterly senseless. By looking down in this manner on the primitive dream consciousness, they missed the opportunity of getting closer to primitive psychology, and they failed to understand the importance of treating native dreams and native attitudes towards " fantasy " in general, with sympathy if not with respect. Now modern psychology has come around to the acceptance of the dream as an indispensable phenomenon in the study of the mind, and realizes that through it the motives and character of human nature are discoverable, and that the primitive belief in the importance of the dream, wherever it may occur, and the frequent treating of it as a form of objective reality, acquires a new and understandable significance.

Lévy-Bruhl has presented data taken from literature which illustrate the attitude of many primitives towards the dream, which is regarded as a form of reality.[2] Some of his examples are taken from well-known sources and illustrate many cases of a widespread primitive attitude towards

---

[1] See Chap. II, pp. 44–9.
[2] LévyBruhl, *La Mentalité Primitive*, Chap. III, " Les Rêves."

fantasy. It is not necessary to accept his theory of a pre-logical mentality as an inclusive term for a description of the primitive mind, yet his emphasis of the primitive valuation of fantasy processes is an important contribution to the understanding of what differences there may be between primitive and civilized mentality. The differences are not in the functioning of the mind—as shown especially by Rivers [1] for unconscious processes ; and by Boas [2] who emphasizes that emotion, intellect and will are the same everywhere, and repeats Bastian's statement of " the appalling monotony of the fundamental ideas of mankind all over the globe." The distinctions between primitive and civilized mentality undoubtedly lie in the difference in valuation of those processes occurring in dream, myth, legend, folk-lore and supernatural beliefs which can be included in the term fantasy.

Tylor and early anthropologists used to speak of the primitive's inability to distinguish dream and reality. Although cases of such confusion do occur, the description is not altogether accurate as a universal generalization. An instance where such confusion does occur is recorded by Lévy-Bruhl in equatorial Africa where a chief, having dreamed that he had travelled to Portugal and England, donned European clothes in the morning and acted as if he had actually travelled to these countries. All his friends assembled around him and congratulated him.[3]

This case, if accurately reported, shows that there is no distinction between dream and reality, and the dream experience was taken as actual experience in the real world. Nevertheless, most cases show that in spite of regarding the experiences of the dream as real, primitives do distinguish between dreams and the perceptions of waking experience,[4] yet often the dream experience is regarded as having a greater reality value than an actual experience. To illus-

[1] W. H. R. Rivers, see p. 26, Ref. 5.
[2] F. Boas, *The Mind of Primitive Man*, p. 155.
[3] Lévy-Bruhl, *op. cit.*, p. 101.   [4] Lévy-Bruhl, *op. cit.*, p. 96.

trate, an Indian accused W. B. Grubb of stealing, and demanded an indemnity for thefts from his garden. He had dreamed that Grubb had stolen from him. Argument with the Indian showed that he realized that Grubb had not been in person in his garden, but he said, " If you had been there you would have taken them." He regarded the dream act as having been really wished by Grubb. Here the dream is given reality value at the expense of actual experience, yet there is no confusion between the two kinds of experience.

To the Tikopia, a Polynesian people inhabiting an island south-east of the Solomon Islands,

" a dream experience is a reality—not identical with the reality of waking life, contrary to some anthropological opinion, there is no confusion between them—but an adventure of the spirit. It may be deemed true or false as a portrayal of events, the figures of the dream may be considered to be masquerading for purposes of deception, but their spiritual character is never doubted."

The experiences of people in dreams are regarded as proof of the existence of spirits.[1]

Cases are recorded where an action in a dream entails responsibility for the act as if committed in reality, as in the Ashanti dreams of adultery which lead to an adultery fine,[2] and in Borneo where a man escaped for protection to a European because another man had dreamed that the former stuck the latter's father-in-law with a spear,[3] and also among the Kai of New Guinea where adultery dreams are actually punishable in reality.[4]

The Maori place great importance on dreams and believe that the spirit lives an independent existence in a dream world, which is regarded as real.[5]

[1] Raymond Firth, " Meaning of Dreams in Tikopia," *Essays Presented to C. G. Seligman*, p. 66.
[2] R. S. Rattray, *Religion and Art in Ashanti*, Chap. XXI, pp. 192–204.
[3] Lévy-Bruhl, *op. cit.*, p. 102.   [4] *Ibid.*
[5] Elsden Best, " Omens and Superstitious Beliefs of the Maori," *J. of the Polynesian Society*, Vol. VII, No. 27, Sept. 1898, p. 124 *seq.*

The Jesuit fathers in North America noticed that the animals seen in the dreams of the Indians were not confused by the latter with the identical animals which they met with in hunting.[1]

Fantasy and perceptions of the external world, therefore, are not necessarily and always indistinguishable among primitives, although cases of such confusion do occasionally occur, but both are in many cases of equivalent value and both are often regarded as forms of objective reality.

Psychoanalysis has shown that an overvaluation of fantasy processes is one of the characteristics of neurotics, and of the child mind, as well as of primitives, but it would be a mistake to regard this situation, as often seems to be implied, as the exclusive attribute of the primitive mind, because much evidence exists to show that a fine sense of reality is not absent even among primitives.[2] The tendency to overvalue fantasy, however, is certainly more prevalent among primitives than among other groups of peoples.

The explanation of the overvaluation of fantasy or " omnipotence of thought " among neurotics, as given by the Freudian school, is that fantasy represents the expression of deep anti-social wishes of the unconscious mind, which are unacceptable to the conscious mind and culturally incapable of being lived out in reality. Since these wishes which comprise, among others, tendencies such as incest and parricide are culturally unacceptable, they are expressed in symbols or disguised forms of fantasy. The retention of the deep wishes, which are consciously not known as such, is the chief motive for treating as real the fantasies which express the wishes. Since the deep wish is not recognized as real, the fantasy or dream representing it takes its place as the reality, and manifest content of the dream is taken at its face value. In other words, the wish gives the life to the fantasy. This seems to be the situation with many primitive cases as well as with the neurotic. A case where a primitive

---

[1] *Relations des Jésuites*, LVXI, pp. 236–8.
[2] See Chap. III, p. 100.

medicine man treats the manifest content of the dream at its face value is clearly illustrated in the following experience among the Navajo Indians [1] :

" The following experience of the writer's in having a dream of his interpreted by a Navajo medicine man, apart from whatever value it may have as ethnological data, is presented as a background for the comparison of a primitive method of dream interpretation with modern psychoanalytic methods. The comparison, which is left to those who may be interested, can reasonably be made without being in any way far-fetched, because of the similar emphasis on the importance of the dream in diagnosing and treating illness, stressed by both the primitive man and the modern psychoanalyst. Especially is the significance of the dream important to the Navajo Indians in Arizona, where, ' Diagnosticians are called upon to cure sickness caused by dreams or to prevent sickness predicted by dreams. Indian informants did not hesitate to distinguish good dreams from bad dreams nor were they reticent about telling their dreams. P. said that if the dream is not serious, the individual may pray at dawn in his doorway with or without some special stone before him which has been chanted over for this purpose by some diagnostician. He may pray to the Sun-God (whom C. considers the " highest god ") or he may pray to a particular god or spirit of some animal made manifest by the dream. If the dream be more serious, he must go to a diagnostician who will use his chants and minor rituals, and more powerful objects and prayers. If the dream be still more serious, the diagnostician will advise a ceremony by a shaman. The writer wishes to stress the importance which his informants gave to their dreams as factors in their everyday life.' [2]

" Emphasis is given to the native quality of the experience to be related, because it is considered of value as showing in the medicine man an unusually pure example of Navajo mentality relatively uninfluenced by white culture. This statement is supported by the facts that the medicine man was very old,

[1] J. S. Lincoln, " A Dream Interpretation and Curing Ceremony of a Navajo Medicine Man," *Action et Pensée*, Nov.-Dec. 1932. Geneva.

[2] William Morgan, " Navajo Diagnosticians," *American Anthropologist*, Vol. 33, No. 4, July–Sept. 1931, pp. 400–1.

spoke no English, and had a deformity from birth (no lower legs) which kept him from mixing in active life with its contacts with white civilization, in the same manner as many of his tribesmen. Through the interpreter (L.H.) who was brought up with the Navajos and has spoken their language since a small child, Nanai (i.e. the Crawler), informed us of the special medicine tradition pertaining to his clan, giving the names of his four predecessors in this profession. How he began his study of the medicine art under his uncle's tutelage, who trained him because of his deformity, was related as follows : ' Ever since I was a little child, I was with my uncle, and as early as I remember my uncle said : " This is for you, my nephew, you will need it. I sympathize with you." '

" The dreamer went to the medicine man's *hogan*[1] in the heart of the Navajo reservation in Arizona and seated on a sheepskin before the central fire which was surrounded by the old man's family, he told him his dream :

" *The Dream :* ' I dreamed of a very large egg made out of a hard rocky substance. I cracked open the egg and out flew a young but full grown eagle. It was indoors and the eagle flew all around trying to fly out, but it could not get out because the window was shut.'

" *The Interpretation :* ' The eagle belongs to the bird group of higher spirits which is one of a group of three allied spirits, namely, the wind, the lightning, and the birds, all of which live on the top of San Francisco mountain. These spirits can wreak great havoc and destruction if offended. They can also be friendly. The eagle cannot fly out because you must have offended the bird spirit, possibly by walking on its nest, or perhaps your father had committed the offence.'

" The dreamer then offered the old man a polished abalone shell as a gift. The latter turned it over and over murmuring something about the wide water from which it came, and said, ' That is what I need, thank you ! ' After this simple expression of appreciation he requested to have sent him for his medicine collection a certain fleshy growth to be secured from the groin of a beaver dried in the sun. Following a long pause he mentioned that sometimes white doctors had cured Indians where medicine men had failed, and Indian medicine men

[1] Hut.

had cured white men where the white doctors had failed, and suggested that the dreamer return on the following day and he would hold a medicine ' sing ' to appease the offended spirit, and give the dreamer as a cure for bad dreams a medicine drink to be drunk out of the abalone shell.

" Returning on the next day, the dreamer seated himself on the left of the old man in the hogan. There ensued a period of silence before the latter announced his opinion that there was no reverence any more for the great spirits and because of that the great destructive forces like the whirlwind were let loose. After a simple meal the dreamer was told that the bad dream would be cured before nightfall and that he would be given full rights as a Navajo which would be necessary in order that the medicine be effective. The Eagle ' sing ' was chosen to be sung in order to ' blow away the wings ' and release the eagle spirit of the dream.

" *The Ceremony or Chant of Restoration (Hozhonji)*.[1] From out of his medicine bag Nanai, ' the Crawler,' took an open gourd with a long spout, and an abalone shell, and filling both with water, placed them on a little mound of sand on the floor. He took out a bundle of eagle feathers and a little whistle, and with the latter made a screeching noise like a bird to attract the attention of the eagle spirit. Powdered herbs were sprinkled on the waters of the shell and the gourd. He then began to sing in a low voice a slow rhythmic song to invoke the bird. With gradually increasing crescendo he sang, repeating over and over what sounded like the same song, each time ending with a low but emphasized, expulsive, long-sustained note. During the singing which grew in emotional intensity as he proceeded, he took an eagle feather, wrapped a string of shells and claws around it, and dipped the end first in the gourd, then in the shell, stirring each dramatically and with vigour. At the same time the faith and fervour of feeling revealed in his expression and singing almost seemed to bring the spirit into presence. One could see that Nanai knew he was talking directly to the bird.

" Communion with the Eagle spirit having once been established, the song went on at the same high pitch of intensity,

---

[1] Part III, p. 210, No. 11. In *Action et Pensée*, the ceremony is called the Eagle Chant, but this is a mistake.

and he turned towards the dreamer with the bundle of eagle feathers and struck him with them on the head, the hands, the abdomen, the knees, and the feet. Some of the herb-sprinkled water from the gourd was offered to the dreamer to drink, followed by a similar drink from the abalone shell. From the shell some of the aromatic smelling liquid was poured on his hands and rubbed on his face and hair, and he was instructed to look up towards the smoke hole and blow hard, to ' blow away the wings of the Eagle spirit on the wind.' Four times he was struck with the feathers, and four times he took the curing drinks, and four times he blew up toward the smoke hole. At this point in the ceremony the nature and tone of the singing changed and took on a lighter, airy, more released quality, and seemed to have the joyous sound of a bird soaring, flying to freedom.

" ' It is gone,' said Nanai, when he stopped singing. From out of his medicine bundle he took a few grains of pollen mixed with honey and gave them to the dreamer to eat. Afterwards he took a sharp pointed object which he called a petrified eagle's claw and inserted it and extracted it four times from the latter's mouth. As a final act of the treatment, a chain of shells, wild-cat claws, and eagle claws were pressed to his head, to his hands, his knees, his chest, and his feet. There followed a short prayer and the dreamer was told he would have no more bad dreams.

" *Comment :* Throughout this experience what chiefly impressed the dreamer was the medicine man's direct approach to the dream and his acceptance of the manifest content of the dream as revealing the whole purport of the dream. The following were the outstanding impressions derived :

" 1. Offence to a spirit was the cause of the dream-fantasy.

" 2. The medicine man's approach was a dealing directly with the dream-fantasy taken as a reality, with no apparent distinction between the fantasy bird in the mind of the dreamer, and the supposedly independent Eagle spirit. By him they were treated as identical and were regarded as belonging to a world of real beings.

" 3. The cure of dreams and the appeasing of the spirit were both achieved by one process of establishing direct relations with the fantasy-reality.

" 4. There was a complete absence of any attempt to explain the dream in terms of symbols with disguised meanings, or to give an explanation in other terms than the language of the dream. The whole interpretation and treatment remained in the fantasy realm.

" 5. The emotional tone of the medicine man indicated faith and belief in the spirit as a reality, and the emotional effect of the ceremony on a suggestive patient with no intellectual resistances would undoubtedly have reacted strongly on the imagination."

Jung, who broke away from the psychoanalytic school, denies that fantasy is just the disguised expression of repressed unconscious wishes, and he has undergone a kind of animistic regression towards a primitive attitude with regard to fantasy. He maintains, with some justice, that we have no right to look down on the primitive attitude from rationalistic heights, and judge it as inferior to our own attitude, which is not necessarily immune in preventing a return of the power of fantasy over reason, in neurosis and insanity. He treats the dream in a manner very similar to the interpretation of the medicine man just recorded. He believes that the surface or manifest content of the dream means just what it says without the necessity of looking for disguises or latent meanings. A perusal of some of his dream analyses,[1] however, show that he is not always consistent in his method, because often sexual dreams he will interpret not at their face value, in accordance with his theory, but he will regard these as " symbolic " of some lack of social adjustment on the part of the dreamer.[2] A realization that some primitive attitudes towards fantasy have certain true intuitions with regard to unconscious processes (a subject to which I shall refer farther on) does not mean

[1] C. G. Jung, Seminar Notes, Zurich, 1928 (unpub.).
[2] See Discussion of Freudian and Jungian theories of symbolism, Part II, Chap. III, pp. 101–3.

that we should " sacrifice our rational function " to which we owe all the achievements of science and " civilization " in order to return to a primitive animistic point of view. Jung believes also that the fantasies of the unconscious should be assigned a reality value equivalent to that of the perceptions of the external world, an attitude which he believes the primitive showed great wisdom in maintaining.[1]

Although scientific psychology will never accept Jung's method of dream interpretation as a means of reaching the latent motives of the unconscious mind, Jung's work will probably have the surface value of giving a closer understanding of primitive animistic attitudes towards fantasy, which he has approached through unconscious regression, and conscious effort to correlate unconscious thinking with primitive animism, both of which have many points of resemblance.[2]

To return to those primitive cases of true intuitions of unconscious processes : Baudouin has called attention to the fact that modern psychology has returned by a long detour to corroborate in detail what many primitives have always dimly realized.[3] The function of dreams in primitive life varies with different cultures, but the true intuitions realized by occasional groups and now corroborated by modern psychology are that the dream represents a wish, and is a phenomenon whose importance is recognized for guidance in daily life and for the diagnosis of illness. Some groups such as the Navajo [4] are even dimly aware that anti-social tendencies are lurking in the dream, hence the efforts of the group to cure the individual of his bad dreams and restore him as a healthy member of society.

That the dream is regarded as a wish, though not of the dreamers, and not as the genuine latent wish, is shown in

---

[1] Jung, op. cit.   [2] See Ref. 1, p. 100.
[3] Baudouin, " La Mentalité Primitive," Action et Pensée, Nov. 1931. Geneva.
[4] Part III, pp. 207-48.

the case mentioned where the Indian demanded an indemnity from the man whom he saw in a dream stealing from his garden. He admitted that the man had not actually been there, but that if he had been there he would have stolen. The dream was believed to show a desire to steal on the part of the person appearing in the dream.[1]

Among the ancient Hurons where dreams were a universal oracle and revealed to the Indian, " his guardian spirit, taught him the cure of his diseases, warned him of the devices of sorcerers, guided him to the lurking places of his enemies or the haunts of game and unfolded the secrets of good and evil destiny," [2] there prevailed a belief that dreams revealed the secret and hidden wishes of the soul, a primitive intuition coming very close to the modern discovery that dreams represent unconscious wishes. The primitive, to be sure, never consciously realizes the exact nature of the wish in the dream but often he comes very close to it. I shall quote in detail the Huron dream theory as recorded by the Jesuit father, Lalemant [3] :

" Outre les desirs que nous avons communément, qui nous sont libres, ou au moins volontaires, qui proviennent d'une connoissance precedente de quelque bonté qu'on ait conceu estre dans la chose desirée, les Hurons croyent que nos ames ont d'autres desirs, comme naturels et cachez ; lesquels ils disent prouenir du fond de l'ame a de certains objets :

" Or ils croyent que nostre ame donne a connoistre ces desirs naturels, par les songes, comme par sa parole, en sorte que ces desirs estant effectuez, elle est contente ; mais au contraire si on ne luy accorde ce qu'elle desire, elle s'indigne, non seulement ne procurant pas a son corps le bien et le bon-heur qu'elle vouloit luy procurer, mais souuent mesme se reuoltant contre luy, luy causant diuerses maladies et la mort mesme.

[1] p. 29, this chapter.
[2] F. Parkman, *Pioneers of France in the New World*, p. 347, note.
[3] *Relations des Jésuites dans la Nouvelle France*, Quebec, 1858 ; Relation, 1648 ; Vol. 2, Chap. XII, pp. 70-1 : " Des Principales superstitions qu'ayent les Hurons dans leur infidelité, et premierement leur sentiment touchant les songes."

" Or de scauoir d'ou vient ce pouvoir a l'ame, tant pour le bien que pour le mal, c'est ce dont les Hurons ne s'enquestent pas ; car n'estans ny Physiciens, ny Philosophes, ils n'examinent pas ces choses dans leur fond, et s'arrestent aux premieres notions qu'ils en ont sans en rechercher les causes plus cachées— " En suite de ces opinions erronnées, la pluspart des Hurons sont fort attentifs a remarquer leurs songes et a fournir a leur ame ce qu'elle leur a representé durant le temps de leur sommeil. Si par exemple ils ont veu une espée, en songe, ils taschent de l'avoir ; s'ils ont songé qu'ils faisoient un festin, ils en font un a leur reseuil, s'ils ont dequoy ; et ainsi des autres choses. Et ils appellent cela Ondinnonk, un desir secret de l'ame declaré par le songe."

Similarly, " selon les Iroquois toute maladie est un desir de l'ame et on ne meurt que parce que leur desir n'est pas accomplie." [1]

Another example of an intuitive primitive belief that approaches modern discovery is the belief among the Navajo that incest with a forbidden relative is the cause of all mental derangement.[2] It is well known that the Freudian school discovers incestuous tendencies at the bases of neuroses and psychoses.

My example of dream interpretation by a Navajo medicine man recorded above [3] is a case similar to many primitive dream interpretations in different groups, where no attempt is made to look behind the manifest content of the dream for deeper meanings. It is important, however, to point out that all primitive groups do not interpret dreams in this " Jungian " manner. For instance, among the African Ashanti dreams are interpreted by attributing a meaning directly opposite to that given in the manifest content, or by an elementary analytic process, the manifest content being rejected and the symbolic nature of the dream image recognized and its true meaning or latent content sought

---

[1] P. F. X. de Charlevoix, *Journal d'un voyage dans l'Amerique septentrionale*, III, pp. 369–70, 1744.
[2] Part III, p. 240, Ref. 1.   [3] pp. 31–5.

by association. For instance, to dream that a hunter has killed an elephant means that some chief is going to die. In Africa the elephant is commonly a symbol of the king, or of great power and strength and the Ashanti occasionally refer to a chief as " Elephant." To dream of a house without a roof means that someone will die in the house, because a usual association is the belief that in the spirit world houses have no roofs.[1]

Among the Mongolian Naga also the widespread primitive attitude of treating fantasy at its face value does not pertain. Here symbols have certain definite collective or individual meanings ; thus red in a dream means blood, while dreams of fire mean children, a large family, or death (going out). The individual may interpret his own dream when the effect is strong, but will consult friends when in doubt as to its meaning. Interpretation is by a well-developed method of free association,[2] as shown in the following examples [3] :

Dream of Ekyimo of Pangti. " I had another dream the night before last : I was alone standing in my house. Then I went to Yimlamo's house. Yimlamo married a woman of my clan so I call him brother-in-law. I found him and his wife there. We sat and did not talk. Then Yezanlo came. My paternal uncle married a woman of his clan so I call him ' father-in-law.' Yezanlo said to me, ' The villagers are dragging three " genna " stones (i.e. monoliths) for you to-day. Two they have brought up and left outside Yimpuntheng's house. For the other one we searched for wood to make a sledge. While we were looking for wood the stone disappeared.' I did not say anything but I felt very ashamed because I had nothing ready for the ceremony—I had prepared no rice, been and bought no pigs or cattle for meat.

---

[1] C. G. Seligman, Appendix to Chap. XXI of R. S. Rattray's *Religion and Art in Ashanti*. Other examples and analyses given.

[2] C. G. Seligman, " Anthropology and Psychology," *J. of Roy. Anth. Inst.*, Vol. LIV, p. 38, 1924.

[3] Unpublished letter of J. H. Mills to C. G. Seligman, 1923.

" The meaning is as follows : Either one of the men of Yezanlo's division will die or one of my clan will die. If one dreams of genna stones or posts being dragged it means someone is going to die. Because the stones were left in front of Yimpuntheng's house which is in Yezanlo's division of the village someone is likely to die in that division. Or it may be one of my clan because I had the dream. If the stones had been dragged to my house it would have meant that either my wife or I were going to die. Yimlano is not affected, it does not matter that the conversation took place in his house." [1]

It seems, therefore, that two definite types of primitive dream interpretation occur in different parts of the world, one which treats the manifest content directly without seeking latent meanings as among the extinct Huron, and the Navajo, and one which rejects the manifest content and seeks latent meanings and meanings of symbols through association, as among the Ashanti and the Naga. It is curious that these two methods roughly correspond to Jungian and Freudian methods respectively, and it would be interesting to see if further research would discover that all primitive methods of dream interpretation fell into these two classes.

Among the Trobrianders,[2] however, a situation exists which may seem at first glance to differ from that among other groups. They apparently dream little, and have little interest in their dreams ; they seldom relate them spontaneously ; they do not regard the ordinary dream as having prophetic or other importance and they have no code of symbolic explanation at all. On the other hand there is a class of traditional dreams which Malinowski calls " official dreams " in contradistinction to the ordinary or " free dreams." These traditional dreams have to do with the success of expeditions, with the success of ceremonial trading,

---

[1] Another example of a Naga dream and interpretation is given in Part II, Chap. III, on p. 119, Ref. 4.

[2] Malinowski, *Sex and Repression in Savage Society*, pp. 92–7.

and magicians have dreams associated with the performance of magic. Special induced dreams associated with magic and resulting from a spell or rite also occur. Love magic is supposed to produce a dream which awakens the amorous wish. To these people, therefore, the dream is regarded as the cause of the wish, in opposition to Freudian theory. The two types of dreams called " free " and " official " correspond to the division of " individual " and " culture pattern " dreams used in my classification of American Indian dreams,[1] examples of which I have given above.[2] Here as among the Crow Indians the culture pattern dream is regarded as of importance to the exclusion of ordinary dreams.

One other group that should be mentioned in connection with dream theories is the coastal Solomon Islanders, where the opinion of a field worker is that on the whole dreaming is less frequent than in our society.[3] One native theory is that dead men return and talk to people in their dreams, which is a corollary to the widespread belief in the dream as a real world in which dead and living meet. It is recognized among these people that some individuals are able to interpret dreams, but no cases of individual interpretations are recorded, yet there is a definite conventional system of symbolic interpretations, and the usual " type " dreams occur with meanings identical to those occurring in all parts of the world as studied by Professor Seligman.[4] For instance, dreams of flying mean success, fire means reproductive energy or creative energy, loss of a tooth means death of a near relative, and dreams of raw meat mean disaster or death.

A classification of 86 verbatim reports of dreams and 21

---

[1] See tables in which the emphasis of different groups differs with the two types of dreams. Part III, pp. 325-7.

[2] pp. 24-5.

[3] Blackwood, B., *Both Sides of Buka Passage*, chapter on " Dreams of Solomon Islanders " (unpub.).

[4] C. G. Seligman, cit. in Chap. III, p. 104, Refs. 1-5.

recollected dreams according to the manifest content deal
with the following outstanding incidents [1] :

Death and spirits of the dead . . .	38
Incidents of everyday life	20
Incidents with sexual implications . .	18
Food and eating	14
Fighting, beating, or being beaten . .	12
Incidents involving animals . . .	12
Going a journey	10
Falling from a height	9
Climbing a hill	7
Sleep	6
Trying to move and being fixed to the spot	5
Physical disabilities	5
Urination and defaecation	4
Childbirth and suckling	3
Going into water to wash	3
Flying through the air	3
Ceremonies and dances	3

Miss Blackwood concludes that the great majority of the
dreams deal with the everyday life of the natives as reflected
in the manifest contents, a situation which I also found in
my study of American Indians' dreams, which all reflect the
culture of the dreamers. Death dreams are more numerous
in the above group and are very usual among other groups
of primitives, notably the Kwakiutl Indians of British
Columbia,[2] and the Navajo.[3] The symbolism in Miss
Blackwood's collection of dreams is believed to be less than
that of any similar collection of our own, and she suggests
that the material supports Professor Seligman's conclusion
that symbolism in primitive people is simpler and more
directly connected with the symbolized than among ourselves.

In conclusion, however primitive theories of the dream
may vary, and its function in the life of a group may differ

[1] Blackwood, B., *op. cit.* (unpub.).   [2] Part III, p. 323.
[3] Part III, p. 245.

with different cultures, or whatever methods of interpretation may prevail, enough has been presented to emphasize what an immensely important part is played by dreams in the individual and cultural life of primitive societies the world over, even among those groups where the amount of dreaming does not appear to be great.

CHAPTER II

CULTURE ITEMS ORIGINATING IN DREAMS OR VISIONS, AND THE INFLUENCE OF DREAMS ON PRIMITIVE CULTURE

I. IN his great pioneer and classical work, Sir Edward Tylor first presented the evidence showing how the early religious beliefs of primitive man arose from images seen in dreams. He was the first to point out that dreams were often regarded by the primitive mind as having a reality equal to that of the external world, and from such a valuation they gave rise to a host of religious beliefs. This attitude towards dream imagery, regarded by the primitive as evidence of a real world inhabited by spirits, forms the foundation-stone to the whole theory of animism or belief in spiritual beings which Tylor considers the nucleus of all later religious beliefs. Many field anthropologists have recorded numerous instances of dreams affecting religious beliefs, and have corroborated Tylor in this respect. Starting from the images seen by the primitive dreamer of himself and others, wandering, visiting, dancing, fishing, and engaging in many kinds of activities, there arose the belief in an independent soul or shadow which wanders and lives independently in a dream world. The dream was the reality experience of the soul or shadow while the body slept. Belief in ghosts, apparitions, spectres and spirits also arose from the same course. In like manner, there grew up the belief in the continued, permanent or temporary, existence of the soul after death, since the evidence of their dreams showed it alive and confronting them. Moreover, in their dreams many primitives visited the abode of the dead and returned to tell about it. How this belief in the immortality of souls arose at least in part from the influence of dreams is best stated by Tylor himself :

" Moreover visits from or to the dead are matters of personal experience and personal testimony. When in dream or vision the seer beholds the spirits of the departed, they give him tidings from the other world or he may even rise and travel thither himself, and return to tell the living what he has seen among the dead. . . . Now such visions are naturally apt to reproduce the thoughts with which the seer's mind was already furnished. Every idea once lodged in the mind of a savage, a barbarian, or an enthusiast is ready thus to be brought back to him from without. It is a vicious circle ; what he believes he therefore sees, and what he sees he therefore believes."

Thus the Red Indian visits his Happy Hunting Grounds, the Tongan, his shadowy island of Bolotu, the Greek enters Hades and looks on the Elysian Fields, and the Christian beholds the heights of Heaven and the depths of Hell.[1]

Specifically, a review of some of the evidence shows conclusively that from dreams the beliefs in the existence of the soul or double, in the continued existence of the spirits of the dead, and in the immortality of the soul, and in an abode of the dead, either originated or were in part derived. They occur in widely separated parts of the earth. For instance :

The Karens of Burmah believe that dreams are what his *la* or soul sees and experiences in its journeys when the body is asleep.[2]

The belief that human souls come from without to visit the sleeper who sees them as dreams, is found among the Ojibway, and the British Columbia Indians of North America, and among tribes in West Africa. Among the latter all their dreams are regarded as visits from the spirits of the dead.[3]

To the Greek, the dream soul was what to the modern savage it still is.[4]

[1] Tylor, *Primitive Culture*, Vol. II, p. 49.
[2] *Ibid.*, Vol. I, p. 440.   [3] *Ibid.*, pp. 442–3.   [4] *Ibid.*, p. 444.

Dreams influencing the belief in immortality and in which deceased ancestors appear, also the belief that the soul wanders in dreams, all occur throughout N. America, Polynesia, Micronesia, and Melanesia, as well as Australia.[1]

In N. America, among the Navajos are reported collections of dreams influencing the conception of life after death (W. Morgan).[2]

Among the Dakota Indians, dreams are regarded as revelations from the spirit world.[3]

The following dream is a good example of the sort which is a source of the belief in the survival of the soul after death ; and is taken from the Tongans : When Finnow the king died, a noble lady who mourned his death and slept on his grave, told to his widow a dream which she had dreamt several nights over at the graveyard. " She said that in her dream the late king appeared to her, and, with a countenance full of sorrow asked why there yet remained so many evil-designing persons in the islands ; for he declared that since he had been at Bolotoo, he had been disturbed by the plots of wicked men conspiring against his son, therefore, was he come to warn her of the danger. Finally he bade her set in order the pebbles on his grave and pay every attention to his burial ground. With that he vanished." [4]

Visits to the other world in dreams are reported from the N. and S. Massim of New Guinea [5] as well as from the Kiwai Papuans.[6]

Here is a typical example of a visit to Adíri the abode of the dead of the Kiwai Papuans : " There was a Mawáta woman called Amára who had been to Adíri and subsequently returned to life. Her husband Báua had died before her. When she came to Adíri she saw two heavy posts like iron, one on each side of the way, and they were constantly clashing together thus preventing anybody from going in. But when Amára came

---

[1] Frazer, *Belief in Immortality*, Vols. I, II, III.
[2] Part III, p. 247, note 1.　　　　[3] *Ibid.*, p. 253 (*d*).
[4] Frazer, *Belief in Immortality*, Vol. II, p. 92.
[5] C. G. Seligman, *Melanesians of Br. New Guinea*, pp. 190, 653, 654, 734–5.
[6] G. Landtman, *Folk Tales of the Kiwai Papuans*, Helsingfors, 1917, No. 64. See No. 63. For dead appearing in dreams, see Nos. 94–101.

near the posts lifted themselves up, enabling her to pass, and when she was through, they began banging together again. She saw a great crowd of spirits at Adíri, and her husband Báua was there among others. Some boys playing on the beach called out to the leaders, ' You fellow come, one woman here, you come make out who belong that woman.' The leaders came, ' Oh, that Amára.' Báua said, ' Oh that my wife he come,' and he bade her, ' You no come close to where devil (spirits) he stop, you stand up long way, I go ask big man belong this place.' (I think Sido that, the narrator interpolated.) Amára waited, and Báua went to ask the leader, ' What you say ? I take him woman belong me ? I send him back ? ' The leader came to see her and said, ' One day you keep him night-time he go back.'

" Báua said to the people, ' I think more better you dress up, make dance belong that woman.' The people decked themselves with ornaments and held a dance, and the row of dancers, two and two together, was long enough to reach from Mawáta to the Gésovamúba point (about a mile). Báua stood beside his wife while the people were dancing. Just before sunset he said to her, ' I make you go back. You no time (your time is not) finish yet, you life yet. You look out (after) place belong dead man (the buying ground) good. You tell him all Mawáta man he look out good too.'

" At Adíri there were all kinds of wonderful food, some red, some blue, and some white, there were coconuts, sugar cane, bababas, taro, and other garden produce, like those of ordinary people. Báua said, ' I no give you kaikai, suppose I give, you dead right up, you no go back. More better I no give you kaikai.' When her time was up he told her, ' You turn that way,' making her face her home. He hit her on the back and at the same moment the two bars separated, and she flew right between them to her own place. Her spirit entered her body, and the woman woke up." [1]

The North American Indian Ghost Dance, a kind of Messianic cult showing traces of Christian influence, arose at the end of the last century from the spontaneous vision

[1] G. Landtman, *Folk Tales of the Kiwai Papuans*, Helsingfors, 1917, No. 64. See No. 63. For dead appearing in dreams, see Nos. 94–101.

of its founder or "prophet." The vision is similar in form to the usual Indian dream of the next world but definitely shows its Christian influence [1] :

One day after an eclipse of the Sun, Wovoka said that the Sun died and he fell unconscious. He was taken up to the other world and saw God and all the people who had died long ago engaged in their old sports and pastimes and all happy and forever young. It was a pleasant land full of game. God told him to go back and tell people to love one another, to have no quarrelling, and to live in peace with the whites, to work, and not to lie or steal, and to put away all war practices. If they obeyed they would be united with their old friends in the other world where there would be no death or sickness or old age. He was then given the dance and instructions. God gave him control over the elements, to make it rain or snow, and God made him deputy of Indian affairs in the West, and Governor Harrison deputy in the East, while God himself took charge of the world above. He then returned to earth to preach.

It may not be amiss to call attention here to an important modern religious sect of the Christian faith which arose as the result of the visions of the founder. I refer to Swedenborg whose detailed descriptions of his repeated visits to Heaven and to Hell in his dreams and visions are of exactly the same nature as those of various primitives who visited in dreams the abodes of their dead ! [2]

Among the Andaman Islanders the fact that the words for dream, double, and shadow are from the same root in the Northern Tribes gives added corroboration to the contention that the belief in the soul originated in dreams. [3]

Thus even from the scattered evidence [4] so far recorded,

[1] J. Mooney, " The Ghost Dance," 14th Ann. Rep. B.A.E., 1892–3, pp. 771–2 (Smithsonian).

[2] Swedenborg, Heaven and Hell, Everyman's Library, 1931.

[3] A. R. Radcliffe-Brown, The Andaman Islands, p. 167.

[4] Among the Thonga dreams do not seem to play the part attributed to them by animistic theory in the formation of primitive beliefs, yet ancestor Gods communicate in dreams and the dreamer makes offerings on awaking.—Junod, Life of a S. African Tribe, Vol. II, pp. 341, 359.

it can be taken as established that numerous religious beliefs have been fashioned on dreams,[1] and largely on dreams of the dead. Besides the beliefs in immortality, in spirits, and in the soul so arising, it has been suggested that the dream is also the source of ancestor worship and of the idea of transmigration of souls, since in dreams transformation or interchangeability takes place so easily whereby a person can change into another or even into an animal. This identity of men and animals with neither distinguished, seems to be associated with the worship of ancestors and with totemism, since the totem animal and the ancestor are often identified by primitives.[2] Such pregnant suggestions lead one to investigate the possibility that elements of totemism itself may have originated in dreams and here again the evidence appears to be very striking.[3]

II. Before pursuing this subject, however, it is important to review certain facts which show the influence of dreams on human behaviour and culture in general. Such an influence has often been mentioned, but much scientific study is still needed to illuminate the thorny problems of the interrelations of psychological processes and culture. Much more clarity is needed to establish which processes, if any, are inherent in the individual and which are culturally determined. The influence of the culture on the form and manifest content of the dream is one that has been already studied (Part III), but the reverse process will now be considered. This is naturally a problem for the psychologist as well as the anthropologist. Of course it is impossible to do more here than to allow some of the facts to speak for themselves in regard to the influence of the dream on the culture. It is known that dreams influence the mood of

[1] For the influence of dreams on religious cults and beliefs, see review referring to the Bible, Mohammedanism, Joan of Arc, Dance of St. John, Flagellants, Quakers, French Prophets, Dervishes, etc., in J. Mooney, " The Ghost Dance," 14th *Ann. Rep. B.A.E.*, 1892-3, pp. 928-52.

[2] E. Jones, *On the Nightmare*, pp. 62-71.

[3] See pp. 54-66, this chapter.

the next day [1] and give rise to behaviour appropriate to the dream situation. Among many primitives the dream is an element upon which a man is prepared to act and to suffer. [2] Professor Berthold Laufer even goes so far as to say that,

" it is quite safe to assert now that dreams have exerted an enormous influence on the formation of human behaviour and culture. Many motives of legends and fairy tales have justly been traced to dreams ; many mythical concepts and motives of art and even works of art have been inspired by them," [3]

but he also warns against those specialists or " pandreamists " who attempt to trace all events to dreams. [4] Without falling into this class it is still possible to present some facts which show that specific culture items have originated in dreams. Equally important are the beliefs about dreams which have exerted an enormous influence in cultural action. It is understood that " originating in dreams " does not mean that the dream is the ultimate origin [5] of a culture item, but, that it is merely the continuation of previous mental and cultural experiences which are given form in the dream. The dream is regarded as an intermediate stage between the initial mental process and the cultural result, where such a result is indicated. Nevertheless, the expression " originating in dreams " will be used to indicate that a specific culture item is traced to the dream, whatever the origin of the latter may be.

Attention is first called to certain primitive groups in which the dream plays an especially important rôle, and can be said to be the most influential phenomenon in the cultural life of the tribe. Such groups are the Yuma and Mohave Indians of the Lower Colorado Region in North America, where the belief in dreams is the basis of every-

[1] E. Jones, *Papers on Psychoanalysis*, 3rd ed., pp. 247–54.
[2] C. G. Seligman, Huxley Memorial Lecture, 1932 ; *J. of Royal Anth. Inst.*, Vol. LXII, p. 193.
[3] B. Laufer, " Inspirational Dreams in Eastern Asia," *J. of Am. Folk Lore*, Vol. 44, 1931, pp. 208–16.
[4] B. Laufer, *op. cit.*   [5] E. Jones, *op. cit.*

thing in life, and the foundation of all religion, tradition, ritual, song and shamanistic power.[1] Another group in the opposite quarter of the globe, where, according to Landtman, the dream is the leading guide in life, are the Kiwai of British New Guinea. Here it shapes beliefs and supernatural practices. It forms one of the sources from which the ideas of the spirit world are obtained, and it furnishes advice on the difficulties of everyday life.[2]

Among the Crow Indians, where success in life is the result of the vision quest, and where sacred ceremonies, songs, methods of painting and war parties are traced to its influence,[3] the dream or vision is the central focus of the culture. This life determining vision is found in varying forms throughout the Plains and Woodlands area in North America.[4]

Among the ancient Hurons also, the dream was their oracle, prophet, doctor, and master [5] ; and an early Jesuit father says, " Les Iroquois n'ont a proprement parler qu'une seule divinité qui est le songe."[6]

From groups throughout the world, where the culture is not necessarily built about the dream, are reported instances of the influence of dreams on everyday life and actions. For instance :

Among the Hervey Islanders some of the most important events in national history were determined by dreams, according to W. W. Gills' statement, although no examples are given.[7]

Among the Mantia of the Malay peninsular a man would not choose a locality for plantation unless he had a favourable dream about it giving supernatural sanction.[8]

[1] A. Kroeber. Part III, pp. 195, 196.
[2] G. Landtman, *The Kiwai Papuans of British New Guinea*, pp. 276-9.
[3] Lowie, Part III, p. 249 *seq.*   [4] Part III, pp. 249-96.
[5] *Relations des Jesuites dans la Nouvelle France*, Rel. X (1636), p. 170, Quebec, 1858.
[6] *Ibid.*, Rel. LIV (1669-70), p. 96.
[7] Gill, W. W., *Mangaia*, p. 347.
[8] Skeat and Blagden, *Malay Races*, Vol. I, p. 365.

A whole Australian tribe decamped because one man dreamt of a certain owl which the wise men interpreted as foreboding an attack from certain other tribes.[1]

A Cherokee dreamed of being bitten by a snake and was treated exactly as if he had in reality been bitten.[2]

A Huron Indian dreamed he was being burned alive by his enemies, and was given a long ceremony to avert the evil.[2]

The Macusi and Gran Chaco Indians of South America act in accord with their dreams which they are often incapable of distinguishing from reality.[3]

In Kamtchatka, " si quel' qu'un veut obtenir les faveurs d'une jeune fille, il lui suffit de raconter qu'il a rêvé qu'il les a eues, elle considere alors comme un grant peché de les lui refuser." [4]

To these examples should be added those that show the influence of dreams on ensuing action because of special beliefs about them. If you dream of such and such a thing you must do such and such a thing. These occur everywhere and many examples are given in the present work, but the following are typical :

Among the Jakun of Nigeria to dream of ancestors requires libations.[5]

In Morocco if you dream of a departed member of your family you should give alms at his grave. If you dream of bees you should offer food to the scribes at the Mosque.[6]

Among the Ashanti to dream of adultery leads to an adultery fine.[7]

Among the Kiwai Papuans if a harpooner dreams that he kills a man he spears a male dugong, if he dreams he kills a woman he kills a female dugong.[8]

[1] Tylor, *Primitive Culture*, 4th ed., p. 121.
[2] Frazer, *Golden Bough*, " The Magic Art," Vol. I, pp. 172–3.
[3] *Ibid.*, Vol. III, p. 36.
[4] Lévy-Bruhl, *La Mentalité Primitive*, Chap. III, " Les Rêves," p. 116.
[5] Letter to Professor Seligman.
[6] Letter to Professor Seligman from Westermarck.
[7] C. G. Seligman, Huxley Lecture, 1932.
[8] Landtman, " Kiwai-Papuans," *op. cit.*, pp. 276–9.

Among the Navajo Indians a man performed a sacrifice and said a prayer because he believed it would avert the consequence of his dream.[1]

Among the Didinga of S.E. Sudan if one dreams that one kills a certain man for witchcraft, one must call the next day on that man and perform various actions to avert the consequences.[2]

Hence no more need be said on the importance of the dream's influence in a general way on the conduct of the everyday life of primitives throughout the world. It will now be worth while to examine specifically different cultural items under separate headings, and to find out how many of them did originate in a dream and if possible how often. In many cases the specific dream of origin will be given, especially where it is thought that the dream in question is not just a fantasy elaboration projected back into the past to explain an origin, a situation which often occurs and makes it necessary to be constantly on guard to separate true dreams from invented ones.

Obvious examples of elaborated fantasies projected back into the past as a dream to explain origins are the following :

In the Epic of Gilgames of Ancient Babylon is stated that in the story of the Deluge, the impending destruction of mankind was said to have been revealed in a dream.[3]

Among the Kiwai the dreams purporting to be the origins of the first use of the bullroarer, the first use of fire, the gift of the first coconut, and of the first banana are recorded in detail. They are all of an exactly similar nature with those dreams in which some new object or gift is conferred.[4]

---

[1] J. S. Lincoln, Navajo Material, Part III, p. 234.
[2] Driberg, Man, Aug. 1920, pp. 141–3.
[3] A. H. Sayce, in Hastings' Encyclopedia of Religion and Ethics, Vol. 5, p. 33.
[4] G. Landtman, Folk Tales of the Kiwai Papuans, Helsingfors, 1917, Nos. 201, 275, 263, 268.

In Australia, the Wichita myth tells of the first man and woman and says, " After the man and the woman were made they dreamed that things were made for them, and when they woke they had the things of which they had dreamed." [1]

Among the Kiwai the origins of the Turtle, and the Taera Ceremonies are explained by dreams, but there is no record to show that these are actual dreams, hence it is safer to regard them as projections on the past to explain their origins.[2]

Among the Sabimba or Malayan Sea Gypsies, their avoidance of water is explained by saying that their ancestors were warned in dreams that if the race took to bathing, they would be visited by tempests.[3]

Among the Menomini Indians the Society of Dreamers and the Dream Dance originated in the vision of a little girl according to the myth. This of course could easily have happened since they are accustomed to dream dances and ceremonies.[4]

III. " TOTEMS " ACQUIRED IN DREAMS.

Whatever may be the social development and organization that has arisen around the phenomena formerly and erroneously grouped together as " totemism," whether they are a system of heraldry or a method of reckoning descent,[5] or the foundation of a clan organization,[6] or a religious and ceremonial cult,[7] or Guardian Spirit customs,[8] all the elements even if not appearing together in the same group of peoples often have in common the nuclear fact that a mythical or real species of animal or object regarded as guardian, protector, and/or ancestor, is the focus of many

---

[1] G. Roheim, *Social Anthropology*, p. 96.

[2] G. Landtman, *ibid.*, Nos. 284, 287.

[3] Skeat and Blagden, *Pagan Races of the Malay Peninsular*, Vol. II, p. 367.

[4] A. Skinner, " Social Life and Ceremonial Bundles of the Menomini Indians," *Amer. Museum of Nat. Hist. Anthro. Papers*, Vol. 13, 1915, pp. 532–9.

[5] N.W. Coast Indians of N. America. See example where crest, guardian and clan totem are identical, p. 57, this chapter.

[6] Africa.   [7] Australia.   [8] N. America.

of the varying beliefs and observances. This animal or object is the totem and has been acquired through inheritance or adoption, or by the individual in various ways, one of which is through the dream. Without discussing the forms, development, and diffusion of totemism, which is not regarded as an independent process,[1] it is proposed to re-emphasize those facts which show how many individuals have acquired the totem or the mythical or real animal or object as protector or guardian, through dreams. If what has developed later from such an acquisition of a protector, in the social organization of tribes is not regarded as totemism, it still does not alter the above facts of the initial acquisition of a spirit protector. The word totem, for convenience, will be used to include any protector or mystical guardian acquired in a dream, towards whom an emotionally significant attitude arises in the dreamer or members of his group, whether a later form of social organization or belief developed from it or not.

Frazer has suggested that it is possible that clan totems as well as guardian spirits may have originated in dreams.[2] Of guardian spirits acquired in dreams and visions, the North American material teems with instances.[3] Although the word " totem " is an Algonquian word applying originally only to the clan totem, it is often used by ethnologists to designate the guardian acquired in a vision. A. C. Fletcher calls the guardian spirit among the Omaha the " personal totem." Here the visionary had to kill the animal he saw in a trance and preserve part as a talisman. " Thus among the Omaha a man was supposed to partake of the nature of his guardian spirit, just as among some totemic peoples a man is thought to partake of the nature of his clan totem." [4]

Boas believes that the hereditary " manitou " which is identical with the guardian spirit acquired in a vision,

---

[1] Lowie, *Primitive Religion.*

[2] Frazer, *Totemism and Exogamy*, Vol. II, p. 455.   [3] Part III.

[4] A. C. Fletcher, *The Import of the Totem* (quoted by Frazer, *ibid.*, p. 400).

became the totem of the clan, among the Kwakiutl Indians.[1] He says that,

> " The close similarity between the clan legends and those of the acquisition of spirits presiding over secret societies as well as the ultimate relation between these and the social organizations of the tribes, allow us to apply the same argument to the consideration of the growth of the secret societies and lead us to the conclusion that the same psychical factor that moulded the clans into their present shape moulded the secret societies." [2]

Thus among these people, the individual totem or guardian spirit, the clan totem, and the secret societies are all ultimately derived from the dream.

Hill-Tout also believes that the clan totem developed out of the guardian spirit which was acquired in a dream among many North American tribes. He regards the individual guardian spirit, the tutelary animal of a secret society, and the clan totem as essentially alike. He states that the concept of a " ghostly helper or tutelary spirit " is the essential element in totemism. " This is totemism in its pure and naked state, i.e. shorn of its social accessories." [3] Goldenweiser believes that Hill-Tout may have proved his case for sections of British Columbia and for the Omaha, but that it is arbitrary when applied to other groups in North America and in Australia.[4] At all events, here are more instances of dream origins of clan and individual totems. Hill-Tout's conception, however, is very similar to that of Hose and McDougall with regard to the " Ngarong " or secret helper who appears in dreams among

[1] More accurately, the Kwakiutl can only obtain in a vision those guardians which are hereditary in his clan. Boas equates the guardians of the Kwakiutl with the Manitou of the Algonkins. Frazer, *ibid.*, p. 442. (See also Boas, p. 499, cit. on p. 88 of this chapter.)

[2] F. Boas, *The Social Organization and Secret Societies of the Kwakiutl Indians.*—Rep. of U.S. National Museum for 1895, p. 662.

[3] C. Hill-Tout, " Totemism : its Origin and Import," *Transactions of the Royal Society of Canada*, 2nd series, Vol. IX, 1903, p. 64.

[4] A. Goldenweiser, *History, Psychology and Culture*, pp. 310–35.

the Dyaks of Borneo, a situation which these authors regard as "incipient totemism." I shall return to this theory farther on.[1]

Hill-Tout mentions the oft quoted but significant case of the origin of the Bear Totem among the Tsimshians which he says is one of scores of similar ones that could be cited. Whether this case is myth or dream is psychologically irrelevant, since records of actual dreams of precisely the same nature occur in which similar guardians are acquired,[2] as is also the situation among the Kwakiutl.[3] It is safer, therefore, to regard this example (quoted below) as a myth of origin rather than a dream[4] :

"A man was out hunting and met a black bear who took him to his home and taught him many useful things. After a lengthy stay with the bear the man returned home. All the people became afraid of him, he looked and acted so like a bear. Someone took him in hand and rubbed him with magic herbs and he became a man again. Thereafter whenever he went hunting his friend the bear helped him. He built a house and painted the bear on the front of it and his sister made a dancing blanket, the design of which represented a bear. Thereafter the descendants of his sister used the bear for their crest and were known as the Bear clan."

What is especially significant here is the illustration of the psychological mechanism by which an object of the real world is transformed by the mind into a symbol which acquires emotional value individually and socially[5] ; the example also shows a case where a guardian spirit, a crest and a clan totem are identical.

Goldenweiser is of the opinion that no particular set of features can be taken as characteristic of totemism for not one of the features invariably occurs in conjunction with others. He says that there is no evidence of any one feature

---

[1] This chapter, pp. 60-4.
[2] Hill-Tout, *ibid.*, p. 77.   [3] Part III, p. 301, note 1.
[4] Hill-Tout, *ibid.*. p. 77.   [5] See next chapter on Symbols.

being primary psychologically.[1] Boas also holds that all totemic phenomena are not derived from the same historical or psychological sources.[2] The former says that the various beliefs and practices which become fused in totemism need not be psychological derivatives of the original totemic nucleus, nor need they be of local origin.[3] On the other hand he defines totemism as "the tendency of definite social units to become associated with objects and symbols of emotional value," or "Totemism is the specific socialization of emotional values."[4] He has previously admitted, however, that Hill-Tout had proved his case for certain tribes, namely, that the concept of a ghostly helper or tutelary spirit which often is acquired in dreams is the essential element in totemism. Goldenweiser's definition in itself admits that there is a psychological basis to totemism in the "emotional values," even if these are constantly changing in time and place.[5] The objects and symbols of emotional value are presumably the totems themselves, and I am dealing in this chapter only with those instances where the totems originate in dreams, without attempting to generalize or put forth a theory of totemism that embraces divergent or independent social processes.[6]

---

[1] Goldenweiser, *op. cit.*, p. 311.   [2] *Ibid.*, p. 344.
[3] *Ibid.*, p. 314.   [4] *Ibid.*, pp. 318–19.   [5] *Ibid.*, p. 318.
[6] In connection with my study of symbolism (see Bantu Fan Legend, pp. 154–67) in the following chapters, I cannot refrain from tentatively developing the above ideas. From the standpoint of the objects and symbols of emotional value (Goldenweiser, *ibid.*, p. 318) the existence of totemic phenomena of any sort means that there is a " totem " associated with these phenomena even if the latter are not psychologically or historically derived from the former within a given group of people. The totem, therefore, in whatever form, whether it is a symbol on a crest, a guardian spirit, a clan animal, or a name. is the object or symbol of emotional value. If this is true the totem itself as a symbol of emotional value has psychological significance, even if the different social processes of different groups associated with their respective totems are not always derived from the emotional attitude towards the totem.

Farther on (pp. 93–8) and in the next chapter (pp. 111–16) is

It is interesting to recall that in Australia, the Alcheringa or age of the mythical ancestors, means " dream

recorded how the totem, both individual and clan, is in many different parts of the earth consciously or unconsciously regarded as father by the natives. If it should turn out that this attitude is universal, the conflicting emotional values attached to the idea of father would, therefore, be the constant psychological factor of totemism, and the fact that " totemism flourishes only when carried by a sib system " (Goldenweiser, *ibid.*, p. 356) is the constant social factor. Moreover sibs are always exogamous (*ibid.*, p. 355). This means that wherever there is a sib, there is an incest taboo. (Brenda Z. Seligman, *The Incest Barrier*, cit. on p. 135). Hence constantly associated with totemism are conflicting emotional values with regard to the totem father and incest taboos preventing sexual relations with mother or sister or their conventional substitutes.

Within a given group, however, the sib system is not necessarily derived from the emotional values attached to the totem either historically or psychologically since the system may have been borrowed from other groups and the totem of the group may have been in existence prior to the borrowing of the sib. Hence the psychology of the incest taboo inherent in the sib system pertains to the group where the sib arose, and the psychology of the father conflict inherent in the emotional attitude towards the totem (name, guardian, crest, clan totem, etc.) also pertains primarily to the group in which this attitude arose. To repeat, the totem and the exogamous sib are not necessarily historically or psychologically derived from each other according to ethnologists, but are independent phenomena with independent psychology ; nevertheless, both are usual features of totemism wherever it occurs. What is the factor then that binds these independently originating phenomena together, the totem and the exogamous sib ?

In Chap. IV I have presented added proofs of the widespread antisocial, nuclear family, or " Œdipus " complex which primitive culture in varying forms attempts to socialize (pp. 132–87). This complex which pertains to individual psychology, comprises conflicting emotions of hate and love for the father, and incestuous tendencies for the mother, all of which must be socialized in order that a group may live together harmoniously.

Primitive groups are constantly seeking new solutions to this " complex " and this effort may turn out to be one of the important determinants in the assimilation by a culture of foreign elements. With regard to totemism, the attitude towards the totem attempts to socialize the father conflicts of individuals, and the adoption of an exogamous sib attempts to socialize the incestuous tendencies. If these turn out

times,"[1] and the totem is generally regarded as ancestor. Here also the Kurnai medicine men possessed a personal totem of their own which they obtained by dreaming about the animal, a lace-lizard or a kangaroo as the case might be.[2] Frazer believes that the Australian generally gets his individual totem by dreaming that he has been transformed into an animal of that species,[3] and dreaming of the personal totem and clan totem among the natives of Cape York is usual, although these totems are not now acquired in the dream.[4]

A most significant and plausible theory of how clan totemism may actually originate is put forward by Hose and McDougall, based on the convincing evidence of the belief in the *Ngarong* or Secret Helper found among the Sea Dyaks of Borneo.[5] This belief based on dream experience is regarded as a case of incipient totemism which failed to develop into

to be the true facts, totemism, together with other features of primitive society, represent in varying forms attempts to socialize the unconscious, anti-social, nuclear family complex of individuals even though the social features of totemism vary and are diffused from group to group. The co-ordinating factor is the anti-social family complex which is a constant and possibly universal tendency of individuals which cultural processes attempt to solve.

This modified Freudian theory of totemism is still subject to further research to establish that the " totem " invariably is a father symbol. Until that has been done the theory still applies to those numerous cases, many of which I have recorded, where the totem is definitely regarded as father by the native, as in some Australian tribes, the Lango of Sudan, the Bantu Fan, and many N. American Indian Tribes, and the Dyaks of Borneo, provided the word totem is applicable to the " *Ngarong* " or spirit protector of the latter. At all events, with regard to the latter, the natives often regard this " *Ngarong* " as father or ancestor. (See pp. 93–8, 111–16.)

[1] G. Roheim, *Social Anthropology*, p. 95.
[2] Frazer, *Totemism and Exogamy*, Vol. I, p. 497.
[3] Frazer, quoted in cit. 5, below (p. 111).
[4] Donald F. Thomson, " The Hero Cult Initiation and Totemism on Cape York," *J. of Roy. Anth. Inst.*, Vol. LXIII, 1933, July–Dec., pp. 497–8, 501 (see also Chap. III, p. 114).
[5] Hose and McDougall, *Pagan Tribes of Borneo*, pp. 91–112.

a system of clan totems, and is of such importance in the present context that it should be presented in detail. No reason is given, however, to explain why a system of clan totemism did not arise.

" The *Ngarong* seems to be usually the spirit of some ancestor or dead relative, but not always so, and it is not clear that it is always conceived as the spirit of a deceased human being. This spirit becomes the special protector of some individual Iban, to whom in a dream, he manifests himself, in the first place in human form, and announces that he will be his secret helper ; and he may or may not inform the dreamer in what form he will appear in future." On the day after the dream the man will wander through the jungle looking for signs by which he may recognize his secret helper. The actions of animals he meets or objects which seem unusual will be interpreted as the abode of the *Ngarong*. " Sometimes the *Ngarong* then assumes the form of an Iban and speaks with him, promising all kinds of help and good fortune. If this occurs the seer usually faints away, and when he comes to himself again the *Ngarong* will have disappeared. Or again, a man may be told in his dream that if he will go into the jungle he will meet his *Ngarong* in the form of a wild boar. He will then of course, go to seek it, and if by chance other men of his house should kill a wild boar that day, he will go to them and beg for its head or buy it at a good price if need be, carry it home to his bedplace, offer it cooked rice and kill fowl before it, smearing the blood on the head and on himself, and humbly begging for pardon. On the following night he hopes to dream of *Ngarong* again, and perhaps he is told in his dream to take the tusks from the dead boar and that they will bring him good luck. Unless he dreams something of this sort, he feels that he has been mistaken, and that the boar was not really his secret helper.

" Perhaps only one in a hundred men is fortunate enough to have a secret helper, though it is ardently desired by many of them. Many a young man goes to sleep on the grave of some distinguished person, or in some wild and lonely spot, and lives for some days on a very restricted diet, hoping that a secret helper will come to him in his dreams.

" When as is most commonly the case, the secret helper takes on the form of some animal, all individuals of that species become objects of especial regard to the fortunate Iban ; he will not kill or eat any such animal, and he will as far as possible restrain others from doing so. A *Ngarong* may after a time manifest itself in some new form, but even then the Iban will continue to respect the animal form in which it first appeared.

" In some cases the cult of a secret helper will spread through a whole family or household. The children and grandchildren will usually respect the species of animal to which a man's secret helper belongs, and will perhaps sacrifice fowls or pigs to it occasionally, although they expect no help from it ; but it is asserted that if the great-grandchildren of a man behave well to his secret helper, it will often befriend them just as much as its original protégé." [1]

The following are taken from among the examples of dreams in which this type of guardian appears :

" Payang, an old Katibas Iban, tells us that he has been helped by a python ever since he was a youth, when a man came to him in a dream and said, ' Sometimes I become a python and sometimes a cobra, and I will always help you.' It has certainly helped him very much, but he does not know whether it has helped his children ; nevertheless he has forbidden them to kill it. He does not like to speak of it. . . . Payang concluded by saying that he had no doubt that we white men have secret helpers, very much more powerful than the Iban's and that to them we owe our ability to do so many wonderful things." [2]

" Of similar cases among other tribes of guardian animals appearing to men in dreams and claiming their respect and gratitude, we must mention the case of Aban Jau, a powerful chief of the Sebops, a Klemantan subtribe. He had hunted and eaten the wild pig freely like all his fellow-tribesmen until once in a dream a wild boar appeared to him, and told him that he had always helped him in his fighting. Thereafter Aban Jau refused until the day of his death, to kill or eat either the wild or the domestic pig, although he would still consult for omens the livers of pigs killed by others." [3]

" A Kayan became blood-brother to a crocodile in a dream,

[1] Hose and McDougall, *ibid.*   [2] *Ibid.*   [3] *Ibid.*, pp. 110–11.

and from then on could be called Baya (crocodile). In the same way a Kayan chief had come to regard himself as both son and nephew to crocodiles, and believed they brought him success in hunting and carried him ashore (in a dream) when he fell into the river. The cousin of this chief, too, regarded himself as specially befriended by crocodiles because his great-grandfather had become blood-brother to one in a dream. It is clear that this family regard themselves as related by blood to the crocodile and bound to them by special ties of gratitude." [1]

From the above the authors go on to state that the *Ngarong* may assume the form of some curious natural object or of some animal which receives the attention of one man only. In some cases regard for the particular animal which is believed to be animated by the *Ngarong* is extended to the whole species, and the species approaches very closely the clan totem in some of its varieties. [2] They point out how easy it would be to imagine how from such beginnings a system of clan totems could arise, around which would grow up various myths of origin, various magical practices, and various religious rites. A comparison of this practice with similar ones from other parts of the world show that the dreams which convince individuals of these tribes of Borneo of the reality of their special relation to some animal, and lead them to respect all animals of some one species, are of the same nature and produce similar results. They call attention to the practice in Australia already referred to, [3] and to the tribes of North America where the individual totem is usually the first animal of which a youth dreams during the puberty fasts. [4]

" Such dream experiences are then the vera causa of the inception of faith in individual totems among the peoples in which totemism is most highly developed ; and among the tribes of the Sarawak we find cases which illustrate how a similar faith, strengthened by further dreams and by the good fortune of its possessor, may spread to all the members of his family

---

[1] *Op. cit.*, pp. 110–11. [2] *Op. cit.*, 109, 111.
[3] p. 60, Refs. 1, 2, 3 and 4. [4] See Part III.

or of his household and to his descendants, until in some cases the guardian animal becomes almost, though not quite, a clan-totem."[1]

It would be worth while to pursue the study of the dream origins of totems of individuals and clans throughout the world in much greater detail to corroborate the material already at hand. From the facts already quoted, however, the dream origins of totems among many peoples can no longer be regarded as mere theory but rather as established fact, and it would not be surprising to find that often a study of the origins of totemic phenomena would lead in the direction of the dream. Again, as previously cited, in North America leading anthropologists affirm that the totem of a clan is simply the guardian spirit or personal totem of an ancestor acquired in a dream at puberty. Among the Yuman Maricopa, on the other hand, where the basis of religion was dream experience with spirit birds and animals " the spirit dreamed of might well have been one of the totems of the dreamer, yet such was not the case."[2] Many examples of these guardian spirit dreams and visions are given in Part III from the Woodlands, Plains, and North-West Coast culture areas and show clearly how numerous cases of individual totems are acquired.[3] An especially good example of incipient totemism similar to that in Borneo is found among the North-East Maidus of California, where hereditary patrons are dreamed of in the same family from generation to generation. They are acquired by the Shamans whose office is an hereditary one, but anyone who has the necessary dreams can become a shaman. For instance, " Whatever animal a man dreams of during his first set of dreams when he is just beginning to be a shaman, that animal he may

---

[1] Hose and McDougall, *op. cit.*, p. 111.

[2] Leslie Spier, *Yuman Tribes of the Gila River*, p. 186.

[3] Boas, Fletcher, cit. pp. 55–6, Part III (Woodlands) (Plains) (N.W. Coast).

never eat or kill. Should he do so, he would die. ' If he kills his dream he kills himself.' " [1]

From the African Ashanti is recorded the following :

" The appearance of ancestors in animal or semi-animal form is another fact of great interest, especially as there is no clear evidence of totemism among the Ashanti. It may, however, be suggested that the appearance of an ancestor in animal form is psychologically equivalent to the conscious identification of the ancestor with the totem animal among other African peoples." [2]

There are recorded several examples of Ashanti dreams in which ancestors appear in animal or semi-animal form, such as :

" I saw an ancestor of mine who was half human and half an antelope—that was a bad ghost."

" I dreamed that a bongo was about to gore me with its horns. I awoke and was afraid, and next day I consulted the God Senaman at Tanosu, and the god spoke as follows : ' I came to you as a bongo to see if you were going to hang or wound yourself because of sorrow.' "

" I once dreamed I went to some far place and saw a very tall person with an enormous head. . . . The next morning I went with my mother to a priest at Tanosu ; the priest shook hands at once and said, ' What did you see in the night ? ' I told him and he said I was not to be afraid as it was a good dream and was only my father's god, Adare, who had come to visit me, and that I must give him a fowl." [3]

Hence, many cases of individual totems or their psychological equivalents, " incipient totemism ", and even clan totems all having precisely the same background in the dream or vision are found in Australia, North America, Africa, and Borneo.

---

[1] Frazer, *Totemism and Exogamy*, Vol. III, p. 497.

[2] C. G. Seligman, in R. S. Rattray, *Religion and Art in Ashanti*, appendix to Chap. XXI.

[3] R. S. Rattray, *Religion and Art in Ashanti*, Chap. XXI, pp. 192–204.

IV. Sacrifices demanded in and resulting from Dreams.

The demanding of a sacrifice by an ancestor or god in a dream or vision seems to be a very old type of pattern. It would be extremely interesting to find out how many sacrificial cults and practices developed from such a source.

"And it came to pass after these things, that God did tempt Abraham, and said unto him, Abraham ; and he said, Behold, here I am.

" And he said, Take now thy son, thine only son Isaac, whom thou lovest, and get thee into the land of Moriah ; and offer him there for a burnt offering upon one of the mountains which I will tell thee of.

"And Abraham rose up early in the morning, and saddled his ass, and took two of his young men with him, and Isaac his son, and clave the wood for the burnt offering, and rose up, and went unto the place of which God had told him.

" Then on the third day Abraham lifted up his eyes, and saw the place afar off.

"And Abraham said unto his young men, Abide ye here with the ass ; and I and the lad will go yonder and worship and come again to you.

"And Abraham took the wood of the burnt offering, and laid it upon Isaac his son ; and he took the fire in his hand, and a knife ; and they went both of them together.

"And Isaac spake unto Abraham his father, and said, My father ; and he said, Here am I, my son. And he said, Behold the fire and the wood ; but where is the lamb for a burnt offering ?

"And Abraham said, My son, God will provide himself a lamb for a burnt offering : so they went both of them together.

"And they came to the place which God had told him of ; and Abraham built an altar there, and laid the wood in order, and bound Isaac his son, and laid him on the altar upon the wood.

"And Abraham stretched forth his hand, and took the knife to slay his son." [1]

[1] Genesis, Chap. xxii, verses 1–10.

Instances are recorded where the sacrifice demanded by the dream leads to the act as it would have in the case of Abraham if it had not been for other countermanding influences. For instance, among the Shilluks of the White Nile where the practice of the slaughter of the Divine Ķing prevails,

" When a millet crop threatens to fail or a murrain breaks out among the beasts, one of the dead kings will appear to somebody in a dream and demand a sacrifice. The dream is reported to the king and he orders a bullock and a cow to be sent to the grave of the dead king who appeared in a vision of the night to the sleeper." [1]

The following is an example of a sacrifice demanded in a dream leading to a substitute act for the one demanded :

" Among the Mentras or aborigines of Malacca of Indo-China in the search for gaharu or aloes, if a man has found a promising tree, and on going home dreams that the guardian spirit of the tree demands a human victim as the price of his property, the dreamer will try next day to catch somebody asleep and to smear his forehead with lime. This causes the guardian spirit of the tree to carry away the soul of the sleeper to the land of the dead, whereas the original dreamer gets a good supply of aloes wood.[2] "

In Africa, among the Ashanti if one dreams of ancestors coming home followed by a sheep, then you know you are to sacrifice a sheep to them.[3] This is in accord with the general African custom that dreams are commonly taken to indicate that the dead man requires a sacrifice.[4] This attitude holds strongly among the Dagomba and Moshi tribes of the Gold Coast where a common form of dream is to dream of seeing the dead. The interpretation is invari-

---

[1] Frazer, *The Golden Bough*, Vol. VI, p. 162.
[2] *Ibid.*, Vol. III, p. 404.
[3] R. S. Rattray, *Religion and Art in Ashanti*, Chap. XXI.
[4] C. G. Seligman in appendix to Chap. XXI of *ibid.*

ably the same ; that a sacrifice is required by the dead soul from the dreamer.[1]

This custom is not quite similar to those instances in which the sacrifice is directly demanded by the dream itself, but the cultural result is the same, namely, a sacrificial act takes place because of a dream.

Among the Menomini Indians of North America of the Eastern Woodlands culture area in those puberty fasting dreams in which the powers of evil appeared, sacrifices were often demanded. For instance, in those dreams in which snakes or horned snakes appeared, which were almost always regarded as evil, sacrifices of dogs or tobacco were required. Occasionally the evil power in a dream would demand a human sacrifice. " The power might demand the first living thing the dreamer met when he started home, or perhaps the life of the father's first born. Death would follow a refusal to comply." [2]

Dreams of dead relatives in which the father appears and demands a sacrifice are common to the Sudanese Arabs and Nile Negroids as well as among the Veddas and the Papuo-Melanesians.[3]

V. Cures, Charms, Medicine, Shamanistic Powers, Magic and Witchcraft Received in Dreams.

Examples of cures, charms, special medicine, and the powers of a shaman arising for the first time in dreams are found all over the world. Usually the new cure or medicine given in the dream is apt to be a variation of some existing method pertaining to the culture, but there are deviations probably dependent on the degree of individual variability from the cultural norm.[4]

[1] A. W. Cardinall, " Dreams Among the Dagomba and Moshi," *Man*, May 1927, pp. 87–8, No. 59.

[2] See Part III, p. 266, Ref. 1, and p. 268.

[3] C. G. Seligman, " Anthropology and Psychology," *J. of R. Anth. Inst.*, Vol. LIV, p. 35.

[4] See R. Lowie, *Primitive Society*.

In Australia cases are reported of cures and charms received in dreams. Among the Mukjarawauit one man says that his dead uncle appeared to him in sleep and taught him charms against sickness and other evils. The Chepara tribe believe that male ancestors visit sleepers and impart charms to avert evil magic.[1]

In the Andaman Islands the powers of the medicine man, who is known as a " dreamer," and the cure of the sick are dependent on dreams :

" All unpleasant dreams are regarded as bad, all pleasant ones good. The natives believe that sickness is often caused by dreams. A man in the early stages of an attack of fever, may have a bad dream. When the fever develops he explains it as due to the dream. If a man has a painful dream he will not venture out of the camp the following day, but will stay at home until the effect has worn off. The natives believe that they can communicate in dreams with the spirits, but the power to do this regularly is the privilege of certain special individuals, known as *oku-jumu* or ' dreamers.' However, an ordinary individual may occasionally have dreams of this kind.

" The powers of a ' dreamer ' are obtained by direct contact with the spirits and in a less degree through ordinary dreams. If the dreams of a man or boy are extraordinary, that is, if he sees spirits either of the dead known to him when alive or spirits of the forest or the sea, he may acquire the reputation of a medicine man. A ' dreamer ' is privileged to dream in a way that less favoured persons do not. In his dreams he can communicate with spirits, and can cause the illness of an enemy or cure that of a friend. In dreams he acquires magical knowledge for curing illness and preventing bad weather. When a person is ill he is often consulted as to the best means of treating the patient. Sometimes the medicine man will promise to cure the patient by means of dreams. It is believed that in his dreams he can communicate with spirits and persuade them to cure the sick person." [2]

[1] Frazer, *Belief in Immortality*, Vol. I, p. 139.
[2] A. R. Radcliffe-Brown, *The Andaman Islanders*, pp. 167, 177-8.

Among the Sea Dyaks of Borneo a man chooses certain objects as charms or amulets because of a dream.

" A man dreams that something of value is to be given him, and then if on waking his eye falls upon a crystal of quartz, or any other slightly peculiar object, he takes it and hangs it above his sleeping-place ; when going to bed he addresses it, saying that he wants a dream favourable to any business he may have in hand. If such a dream comes to him, the thing becomes ' siap ' ; but if his dreams are inauspicious, the object is rejected." [1]

In Africa, among the Ashanti is recorded this dream :

" The last dream I had about my uncle was that he came to me and gave me some leaves. I related my dream to others. At that time a child was very ill in the house, and they told me to make medicine with the leaves, and I did so and the child recovered." [2]

In North America throughout many different Indian culture areas are recorded innumerable instances of cures and shamanistic powers received in dreams and visions. A great many examples are given in detail in Part III. There are presented, dreams in which shamanistic powers are conferred, among the Paviotso [3] ; dreams which lead a young man to train to become a medicine man, and dreams which lead to seeking cures and ritual ceremonies from their bad effects on the dreamer, among the Navajo [4] ; the dreams and visions of medicine men which confer power over disease and weather and offer magic protection, among the Blackfoot Indians, where, " A Doctor is one who treats disease by virtue of powers obtained through dreams or visions" [5] ; visions in which medicine and ceremonial instruc-

---

[1] Hose and McDougall, *Pagan Tribes of Borneo*, Vol. II, p. 125.
[2] R. S. Rattray, *Religion and Art in Ashanti*, Chap. XXI, pp. 192–204.
[3] See this chapter, pp. 71–3.
[4] Part III, pp. 233–7, 218–48.
[5] *Ibid.*, pp. 253, 258–63, A, b, c, e ;   B, b ;   C, c ; D, a ;   – E, a, b ;   – G, a, c, d, e.

tions are presented among the Crow Indians [1] ; puberty fast dreams in which immunity from disease is offered among the Ojibway,[2] and mention of how medicine is secured among the Menomini [3] ; also dreams and descriptions of how shamans receive their power among the Ojibway [4] and the Yavapai.[5] The power to cure disease is also given to the would-be shamans in a dream by a supernatural being, who is usually the same one who appeared to his ancestor, among the Bella Coola of British Columbia.[6]

Among the very primitive Paviotso of Nevada, shamanistic powers are also most commonly acquired in dreams. These powers come to adult men and women and not at puberty, usually in unsought dreams, but they are also inherited or sought through visionary experience in caves. Shamans interpret dreams causing illness, and death is believed to follow a refusal to comply with the dictates of dreams.[7]

The *unsought dreams* are of eagles, owls, deer, antelope, bears, mountain sheep, or snakes who come to a person a number of times in a dream. The animal tells the dreamer he is to be a doctor and teaches him the necessary songs.[7]

Sometimes shamans *inherit their power* from a deceased father, mother, aunt, uncle, or grandparent. The dead relative visits them in dreams and tells the dreamer that he or she is to take the power and become a shaman. After a few such visits and instructions from the deceased, the power itself appears in the dreams, and the relative no longer comes. The power then belongs to the dreamer.[8]

[1] Part III, pp. 253-5, Nos. 1, 4, 6 ; p. 256, Nos. 3, 4.
[2] pp. 275-6, No. 5.   [3] pp. 266-70.
[4] pp. 271-6.
[5] Barbara Aitken, " Temperament in Native American Religion." Reprint from *J. of Roy. Anth. Inst.*, Vol. IX, July–Dec. 1930, pp. 370-1.
[6] McIlwraith, Letter to Prof. Seligman (unpub.).
[7] Willard Z. Park, " Paviotso Shamanism," *American Anthropologist*, Vol. 36, No. 1, Jan.–March 1934, p. 99.
[8] *Ibid.*, p. 101.

The following dream is an example of one in which shamanistic power is acquired by a woman who dreamed of her dead father :

" When Rosie's father had been dead about eighteen years she started to dream about him. She dreamed that he came to her and told her to be a shaman. Then a rattlesnake came to her in dreams and told her to get eagle feathers, white paint, wild tobacco. The snake gave her the songs that she sings when she is curing. The snake appeared three or four times before she believed that she would be a shaman. Now she dreams about the rattlesnake quite frequently and she learns new songs and is told how to cure sick people in this way." [1]

Shamanistic powers are also acquired in *sought visions* :

" Sometimes a man will get his power from his father. A father will tell his son to be a shaman. The son will start to dream and go into trances. His father tells him that he will be a shaman some day. The son dreams for a long time and then the father teaches him to cure sick people. He never learns this when he is a boy. He must be a man. Both father and son may be shamans at the same time." [2]

A typical vision quest and experience is as follows :

(Told by Dick Mahwee) : " There is a mountain below Dayton. Men go to the cave on this mountain to get power. Women never go into this cave. They get their power in dreams. I went there when I was about twenty-five. I stayed in the cave all night. When I got inside I said what I wanted. I said I wanted to be a shaman and cure sick people. I lay down on the floor and then I heard lots of different animals going through the cave. They would say, ' Somebody is here.' The animals do that to see if a man is brave. They try to make him run out of the cave. Then I heard lots of noises. After a while I heard people singing and dancing. Then the chief talked to the people who were singing and dancing. I listened to this for a long time and then I felt as if I were in a daze. I

---

[1] Willard Z. Park, "Paviotso Shamanism," *American Anthropologist*, Vol. 36, No. 1, Jan.–March 1934, p. 101.
[2] *Ibid.*, p. 102.

could hear two chiefs at the dance talking back and forth. Then down at the bottom of a cliff I could see a man. He was very sick. A shaman was singing for him and doctoring him. I heard the songs of the shaman. A woman with a wet sage brush branch in her hand was dancing. She went around the fire jumping. Every time she jumped she said ' Hu ! ' The sick man was getting worse. I could hear him groan. The shaman didn't sing any more and all the people were crying. It was past midnight now. The people mourned until daylight and then they stopped. I was lying on a rock and it started to crack like breaking ice. Then a tall slender man stood in front of me. He said, ' You want to be a shaman. You must do as I tell you. First get your eagle feathers and do what I tell you with them. You have chosen this and it may be hard for you. The feather is to guide you. You can bring the souls of dead people back with it. Do that, otherwise you will have a hard time. At the bottom of this cliff there is some water. Bathe in it and paint yourself with white paint. Don't be impatient but wait for my instructions.' I did what he told me and I learned my songs and how to cure the sick when this tall man came to me in dreams. He helps me doctor people and tells me what to do." [1, 2]

It is needless to seek any more evidence for the dream origins of numerous cures and medicine powers among many primitives. What is needed, however, is a special study of the influence, and diffusion of the items so arising as well as psychological analyses of the dreams before one can

[1] *Ibid.*, p. 103.

[2] What is especially interesting with regard to the Paviotso dreams is that both the unsought spontaneous or " individual " dreams and the induced " culture pattern " dreams appear to be identical in form and content, with both types of equal importance to the native. This situation differs again from the attitude towards dreams in other areas where the culture pattern dreams and individual dreams assume different rôles of varying importance in tribal life. See table illustrating these differences, in Part III, pp. 325–7. Among the Omaha also, individuals will dream stereotyped pattern dreams without any apparent previous knowledge of them.—See Part II, Chap. IV, p. 172 and Ref._4.

estimate the true importance of the dream as a cultural initiator.

Other powers of a similar nature, those of magic and of witchcraft, or sorcery, are in some cases known to be derived in the same manner. Among the Kiwai mythical beings were accustomed to appear in dreams and give instructions in the magic of making gardens, of finding pigs, and of making pigs destroy an enemy's garden, as well as the power to be transformed into a snake.[1]

A certain well-known mythical being named Wáwa often used to appear to a man named Sáibu. He showed him a certain object which would kill men and a human bone that would protect the garden against pigs.[2]

" Some wild pigs had destroyed Samári's garden. The next night he dreamt that a man came to him from the bush. The stranger carried his bows and arrows, he was painted with mud and held the tail of a pig in his mouth. Samári did not know who the man was. The newcomer handed him the pig's tail and a piece of earth, and told him to chew a little of the latter together with a small piece of a young taro root and spit the juice on the digging stick which he used when planting taro. This would give him a rich crop. If he wanted to destroy somebody's garden he was to chew a fragment of the pig's tail and spit it into the garden, telling the pigs to come. *Samári still kept these ' medicines,' which he had found on awakening.*" [3]

Here is a dream from the same people in which, not only magical instruction is given but also in which stringent food taboos are laid down :

" A Mawáta man named Gibúma dreamt that he was hunting in the bush and saw there a large iguana with two wings and four legs. Having flown up into a tree, the iguana closed its wings and walked on its legs. It was an etenga who in the night assumed the shape of a man. This being taught Gibúma many things. He was forbidden to eat the meat of tame pigs but not that of wild pigs. The etenga also forbade him to taste

[1] G. Landtman, *Folk Tales of the Kiwai Papuans*, p. 196 and No. 125.
[2] *Ibid.*, No. 104.   [3] *Ibid.*, No. 128.

dugong meat without first eating a piece of a starfish, but as that fish is considered a ' Poison,' Gibúma never dared to eat either the one or the other. Some men have died from neglecting the food directions given them by an etenga, and therefore Gibúma was careful that the same fate should not befall him. He was also taught how to find pigs when hunting in the bush and how to cause pigs to destroy an enemy's garden.

" In order to prevent pigs from ruining a garden he was to put a star-fish under the fence, for these fish have a mouth like a man and frighten pigs away by calling out to them, although nobody else can hear their voice." [1]

Magic gifts such as the quartz crystal, the water of life, were given in visions to the young initiates among the Kwakiutl Indians of the north-west coast of North America.[2]

Mention of witchcraft and sorcery derived from dreams occur among the Ekoi of Africa where a large proportion of the witchcraft occurrences take place in the " astral world " of dreams [3] ; and among the Menomini Indians where the acceptance of a vision from one of the " powers below " makes one a sorcerer.[4] Among the Paviotso of Nevada the witch doctor also gets his power from dreams.[5] I have no doubt that examples could be multiplied with further research.[6]

VI. Ceremonies, Dances and Songs from Dreams and Visions.

From scattered parts of the world are also found instances of ceremonies, dances and songs which appear to originate in the sought or unsought dreams and visions of primitive peoples. It is necessary to be especially careful in this field to distinguish the numerous examples of elaborations of

[1] *Op. cit.*, No. 126. Reported by Gibúma.
[2] Part III, p. 302.
[3] P. A. Talbot, *The Peoples of S. Nigeria*, Vol. II, p. 205.
[4] Part III, p. 268.
[5] Willard Z. Park, " Paviotso Shamanism," *American Anthropologist*, Vol. 36, No. 1, Jan.–March 1934, p. 110. See also pp. 71 and 73 of present chapter. [6] See p. 312, No. 41.

fantasy given as a dream and projected back into the past to explain the origin of a given ceremony. Since such examples are of exactly the same pattern as those authentic dreams recorded directly from the actual dreamer, may they not merely show that real dream origins are the prototypes of these elaborations and form part of the cultural experience. Several examples of these projected explanations in the form of dreams have already been given.[1]

Again the Kiwai Papuans in the same way received ceremonies, songs, and other instructions from various mythical spirits one of whom was Wáwa already referred to. Here is one in which the text and tune of a new song, and a dance by the spirits was revealed. It does not say if in this case they were taken up by other members of the tribe but it is stated that this often takes place.[2]

" (By Sáibu, Mawáta :) He saw some spirits of dead people who were clearing the burying ground. Among the rest there was the spirit of his dead father, who on seeing Sáibu thought that he too was dead. And he asked Sáibu, ' What thing kill you that time you come dead? ' ' No, no, father,' Sáibu answered, ' I no dead.' But the father insisted that Sáibu was dead. The spirits held a dance and sang, ' Oh, mére, wére, mére, méreaia, meréaia.' Sáibu understood that they were calling upon him, for mére in the Mawáta language means son. Again they sang. ' Oh, bába, kúnuidáni ngonu kadji wuidani (this is said to be Sáibai language) Who belong that pickanniny (Sáibu), who go cook kaikai for him? ' ' A búru, burúia búru rúbi búri rubía (Mawáta-language). Outside people (somebody who is not dead) he been come.' The narrator said that he had never heard any of these texts or tunes except in that dream. Certain other men too when dreaming have heard songs of the spirits." [3]

Among the Melanesians of the South-East Solomon Islands the ceremonial use of lime and an incantation are

[1] See pp. 53–4.
[2] G. Landtman, *Folk Tales of the Kiwai Papuans*, p. 196.
[3] *Op. cit.*, No. 96.

stated to have originated similarly. Sea spirits also are credited with visiting men in sleep and revealing new dances to them[1].

In Australia, many initiation ceremonies are supposed to have been adopted directly from what is seen in visions or in sleep by special individuals. Here each totem has its own ceremonies, and each of the latter are the property of an individual who has either inherited it from someone who has previously acquired it in dream or vision, or else he has received it directly himself in a dream.[2]

In North America again, are the most numerous examples recorded of ceremonies and songs having a widespread cultural usage which can be traced definitely to their origins in the dreams of specific individuals. Many of these are recorded in Part III. Among the Crow Indians are some unusually good examples of sacred ceremonies and songs traced to visions.[3] New chapters of the ceremonial Tobacco Society have been founded from time to time on individual visions, which are presented in detail.[4] In like manner songs and ritualistic instructions of the Blackfoot[5]; dances of initiates to the Winter Ceremonial and songs of the Kwakiutl,[6] songs and magic given by totemic guardian spirits of the Thompson Indians,[7] and specific songs of the Yuma,[8] are all first beheld in the dreams and visions of vision seekers and initiates.[9]

---

[1] W. G. Ivens, *Melanesians of S.E. Solomon Isles*, p. 14.
[2] Spencer and Gillen, *Native Tribes of Central Australia*, p. 278.
[3] Part III, p. 255, No. 7.   [4] *Ibid.*, p. 257, Nos. 5, 1, 2, 3.
[5] *Ibid.*, p. 259, Exp. *d, f.*   [6] *Ibid.*, p. 298 and p. 311, No. 37.
[7] J. Teit. " The Thompson Indians of Brit. Columbia," *American Museum of Nat. Hist. Memoirs*, 2–4, 1900, pp. 320, 354, 356, 365, 368, 372.
[8] Part III, Yuma, Dream 1, p. 198.
[9] Mention should be made of the songs with words and music which came to the Chippewa after fasting or physical suffering—in dreams and visions or under the influence of dreams and visions. All the dream experiences are stereotyped culture pattern phenomena. See Chippewa Music-Bul. 45, *B.A.E.*, pp. 118–37, by F. Densmore.

VII. MATERIAL CULTURE FROM DREAMS.

In this field there are also instances of objects and methods which first seem to take form in the images seen in sleep, or in the induced vision. Here is such a dream from the Kiwai Papuans, which not only includes another dance given by the spirits, but also teaches a new method of spearing dugong :

" (By Gaméa, Mawáta :) He found himself at Gánalai, on the beach near Mawáta, where there were many spirits of dead people, men and women. Two men with very large heads were beating their drums, and the rest were dancing, two women in front of the others and two behind, with the men in the centre. Gaméa described the dance in detail.

" After a while Gaméa saw two old-fashioned canoes nearing the shore, and one provided with three and the other with four mat sails and the people on board wearing the dress and ornaments of old times. The canoes were beached and attached to poles in the ground, and the new-comers were kindly received by the Mawáta people, who prepared a meal for them. Gaméa recognized the visitors as some Tudu people who had died before. They said, ' We fellow come learn (teach) you fellow spear dugong turtle,' and they taught the Mawáta men various methods of doing this. The Tudu men built harpooning platforms off the Gésovamúba point, although that is no place for spearing dugong and turtle, and from all the platforms the Mawáta men speared many of the animals. After that the Tudu people sailed away ; the dugong were cut up, and the meat was put on hot stones and covered with earth to get cooked. Two Mawáta men named Garíbu and Paí dressed up to represent spirits and danced before the people. They held long sticks in their hands, and to find out when the meat was done they thrust the sticks into it and then removed and smelt them. When the meat was ready, all the people began to eat. On awakening Gaméa was delighted at this happy dream, and he taught his boy this new method of spearing dugong." [1]

From the Melanesians of the South-East Solomon Islands

[1] G. Landtman, *op. cit.*, No. 94.

the designs of two clubs were revealed in dreams to their maker.[1]

Specific methods of painting and war parties are traced to the vision among the Crow Indians,[2] and sacred bundles for war, hunting and witchcraft are derived from the Gods through dreams among the Menomini Indians.[3]

From the Ashanti an informant states : " I often dream of my brother who was a hunter and he shows me where to go. Any antelope I kill I give him a piece with some water." [4]

Professor Laufer has also investigated this subject, and states that in Eastern Asia besides mythical concepts, that motives of art and even works of art have been inspired by dreams. He believes that the majority of fabulous monsters and chimæras which so abundantly pervade the oriental arts owe their origins to dreams and visions.[5] He says :

" Many hundreds, more probably even thousands, of dreams are recorded in the Chinese annals and in the biographies of individuals, and have had a sometimes far-reaching effect on the course of historical events ; but despite this abundance of material no one has ever made a special study of Indian or Chinese dreams. Of all categories of dreams the inspirational dream is the most interesting, because it has proved a creative force in literature, science, and art, or stimulated ambition of one sort or another." [6]

He gives many examples of inspirational dreams from the earliest days and several which resulted in specific paintings which are well-known. He tells of Wu Ting (1324–1266 B.C.), a ruler of the Shang dynasty who after the loss of his aged teacher sought a new counsellor. This Emperor

[1] W. G. Ivens, *op. cit.*, p. 14. Designs are reproduced.
[2] Part III, p. 249.   [3] *Ibid.*, p. 270, No. 13.
[4] R. S. Rattray, *Religion and Art in Ashanti*, pp. 192–204.
[5] B. Laufer, " The Inspirational Dream in E. Asia," *J. of Am. Folk-Lore*, Vol. 44, 1931, pp. 200–9.
[6] *Ibid.*

addressed a prayer to Shang-ti the supreme God asking to have revealed to him in a dream the man for whom he sought. In his dream he saw the man but he searched in vain for him throughout the land. " A portrait was then made of the man, as he had appeared to the emperor in his dream, and this was circulated throughout the empire." This led to the discovery of the man who turned out to be a common workman, who was then raised to the post of prime minister.[1, 2]

Another instance of the same sort of painting was done by the Buddhist monk Kwan Hiu who lived from A.D. 832 to 912. He specialized in the painting of the Arhats, the most advanced disciples of the Buddha. In his biography is stated,

" Every time he desired to paint one of the venerable saints, he first recited a prayer, and then in his dreams obtained the respective figure of the Arhat. Awakening, he fixed this dream picture in his mind and painted it accordingly, so that his portraits did not conform to the customary standard."

This is corroborated from another source which says,

" Kwan Hiu painted the pictures of the sixteen Arhats with long bushy eyebrows, with drooping cheeks and high noses,

---

[1] *Op. cit.*, p. 212.

[2] More recent examples of inspirational dreams are those of Pau Chin Hau, who founded a new religious monotheistic cult of the same name in the Chin Hills of Burma, under the inspiration of a series of his dreams extending from 1900 to 1931. In one dream a new script was " revealed," which afterwards he taught to his followers. It has spread and is the most recent addition to the numerous Indian scripts. Pau Chin Hau describes the origin of this script as follows : " In 1902 I had another dream. In this dream I saw an Englishman who appeared to me to be divine. He wanted me to learn lessons taught by means of stones in the shape of letters which put together formed a book. I tried to learn the same and eventually succeeded and my eyes then opened." Pau Chin Hau's complete signed declaration of his visions is given on pp. 217, 218, of the *Census of India*, 1931, Vol. XI, Part I, Burma, and the dream script is reproduced on p. 195. The script appears to have several letters of the English Alphabet.

leaning against a pine-tree or a rock, or seated in a landscape, men of a strangely foreign appearance or a Hindu face. When people marvelled at his pictures and interrogated him, he replied, ' I paint what I see in my dreams.' "

In his honour a temple was erected at She, called the " Hall of the Arhats Corresponding to Dreams." [1] Reproductions of Kwan Hiu's dream paintings [2] are found in Laufer's ' T'ang, Sung, and Yuan Paintings,' Plates VII–VIII.

The same author elaborates on the facts which show how the beliefs in the immortality of the soul, and of a supernatural world have been inspired and influenced by visions and dreams, and he points to the numerous examples of paintings of the world beyond, inspired by dreams, in China. [3] He warns again, to discriminate between those dreams which are the real or subjectively true ones, and those that are purely literary motives or patterns, the latter being a later development which must have grown out of the former. Referring also to the dream designs of the Plains Indians he disagrees with Wissler's opinion that these designs are not newly derived in dreams, and that the dream is only a philosophy accounting for the origin of the present styles of decorative designs, and gives his own opinion that these designs must have been inspired in the past by dreams and were then handed down from generation to generation. " The decorative motives may have changed in the course of time, while the original dream story persisted or evolved into a mere pattern." [4] Since there are numerous authentic cases of new items appearing in the dreams of American Indians and elsewhere, it seems probable that the designs in question did so originate at some time.

A contemporary design dreamed by a person well known to the writer, and related to him the morning after the dream, is reproduced to illustrate the fact that a completely

[1] *Op. cit.*, pp. 212–13.   [2] See frontispiece.
[3] *Op. cit.*, p. 214.   [4] *Op. cit.*, p. 215.

new design can be presented in a dream. The design has been made into a bookplate :

VIII. CAREER VISIONS AND DREAMS.

Mention should be made again of the guardian spirit and puberty visions among the American Indians, as determiners of specific individual careers. Primitive careers are not numerous, but their choice by the individual is often rigorously determined by the induced vision at puberty or later, under the supervision of parents, medicine men, or tribal authorities.[1] That success in life is entirely due to the vision among the Crow Indians is well known.[1] Attention has also been called to the careers of shaman, and of sorcerer, practically being forced on the individual by the compulsion of the vision, often regardless of conscious volition.[1] This type of vision in varying forms is found among the Indians of the Plains, Woodlands and Colorado Region. The careers of warrior, and hunter are also in many cases similarly determined. Some of the determining visions for a hunting career are recorded for the Menomini,[1] and the Ojibway,[1] and several which lead to the choice of a warrior's career, for the Crow,[1] and Ojibway.[1] In every case it is always the guardian or protector, that is, the " totem " or ancestor who appears in the vision and authorizes the seer

[1] See Part III.

what career he shall pursue or what favours shall be conferred on him.

Among the Paviotso of Nevada careers are undertaken because of an unsought dream thrice repeated, or after an individual's conscious choice of a career is endorsed by a vision sought in caves. The careers of hunter, gambler and shaman are undertaken after a vision confers the necessary power and confirms a choice openly declared in a cave.[1]

In the same connection is the widespread custom of the sexual transformation of men into women, whereby a man renounces his manhood, dresses like a woman, marries another man, and undertakes a woman's work, in fact he takes up the career of being a woman. He becomes a berdache according to the North American terminology. How such a transformation takes place, often only after a terrific and tragic conflict, compelled by the vision at puberty, among the Ogallala Sioux Indians is described again, because of its interest in illustrating psychological conflict and inner compulsion ; as well as because of its symbolism :

" Among some tribes in this family of Indians, to dream of the moon is regarded as a grave calamity. The man sees the moon having two hands, one holds a bow and arrows, the other the burden strap of a woman. The moon bids the dreamer take his choice, when the man reaches to take the bow, the hands suddenly cross and try to force the strap upon the man who struggles to waken before he takes it, and he also tries to succeed in capturing the bow. In either event he escapes the penalty of the dream. Should he fail and become possessed of the strap he is doomed to be like a woman." He then becomes a berdache or in some cases commits suicide to avoid the dictates of his dream.[2]

Besides being found among the American Indians, these transformations of sex carried out in obedience to intimations received in dreams, are found in the Aleutians, among the

[1] Cit. on p. 75, Ref. 5.
[2] A. C. Fletcher, " Ogallala Sioux," *Reports of Peabody Museum*, Vol. 3, p. 281, note 4.

Patagonians of South America, among the Bugis of the Southern Celibes, in the Pelew Islands where priests dress as women, and among the Sea Dyaks of Borneo. Among the latter, " The call to transform himself into a woman is said to come as a supernatural command thrice repeated in dreams ; to disregard the command would mean death." The same type of compulsive vision is also found among the Chukchi.[1]

What is of particular interest in these dream or vision determined careers is the compulsive nature of the phenomena. The command in the vision cannot be refused, and although the recipient may struggle against the consequences and even seek a better vision (Woodlands), his fate is determined, and he can do nothing but comply or kill himself. The vision rules his life with an iron hand, not only because of the social and religious sanction given to it, but psychologically speaking because it is determined by the inner compulsions and identifications of his own nature.

IX. Miscellaneous Culture Items and Primitive Acts determined by Dreams.

There are isolated examples of various phases of primitive culture, which arose because of dreams. It is not known if there is any other corroborative material or parallels among other peoples, but they are put forward on their own worth and as fields for further research.

(a) *Murder and Cannibalism.*—Among the Ojibway Indians formerly acts of murder and of cannibalism were instigated by dreams.

" It is a universal tradition among the Indians that in the primitive ages there were anthropophagous giants called *Windigos*. The people's fancy is so busy with them as well as with the isolated cases of real cannibalism, that they began to dream of them, and these dreams, here and there, degenerate to such a point that a man is gained over to the idea that he is fated to be a *windigo*.

[1] Frazer, *The Golden Bough*, Vol. VI, p. 255. See pp. 213, Ref. 4 ; 214, Ref. 1.

" Such dreams vary greatly. At times a man will merely dream that he must kill so many persons during his life ; another dream adds that he must also devour them ; and as these strange beings believe in their dreams as they do in the stars, they act in accordance with their gloomy suggestions.

" Some few years back a man lived here who dreamed that he must kill seven men during his life, and would not be suffered to stop till he had completed that number. He was naturally not at all bloodthirsty or of murderous propensities ; merely the dark destiny in which he believed drove him to such deeds of horror. He had dreamed of it perhaps, several times ; the dream made him melancholy and brooding, but he must obey it, and so soon as an opportunity offered, he killed a fellow being. Thrice had he already thrust his knife into the heart of his innocent brethren when punishment or destiny overtook him. He had also friends cognizant of his dreams, for such poor tortured dreamers can rarely keep their secret entirely to themselves. . . . A few of his victims' friends had joined together to put him out of the way. They did so, and the whole community applauded them for freeing them from such a monster.

". . . If a man live much apart and out of the world, if he appear to be melancholy and is tortured by evil dreams, then people begin to fear he may end by becoming a *windigo*, and he is himself attacked by the fatalistic apprehension, and is driven towards a gloomy fate. At times, when a man is quarrelling with his wife, he will say, ' Squaw, take care. Thou wilt drive me so far that I shall turn *windigo* ' (que je me mettrai *windigo*)." [1]

Among the Kwakiutl Indians a cannibalistic cult and definite cannibalistic acts are centred in the visions of the initiates prior to the Winter Ceremonial. One cannot say here that the cult is a result of the vision because it is known that this particular cult has been borrowed from neighbouring tribes within the last century.[2] It would be more accurate to state that the borrowed cannibalistic cult

[1] J. G. Kohl, *Kitchi-Gami, Wanderings Round Lake Superior*, pp. 358–60. London, Chapman & Hall, 1860.
[2] Chap. III, p. 105, Ref. 4 ; Boas, Part III, p. 297 *seq.*

induced the visions which in turn produced cannibalistic acts.

Among the extinct Hurons, a man dreaming that he had killed his wife made it an excuse for killing her in fact.[1]

(b) *War.*—Among the Menomini it is recorded that the Sauk War began because of the dream of a young man.

" A young man had just received his sacred dream. In it he had been told by the powers above that he must go and visit a white man and this man would give him a rifle and plenty of ammunition." [2]

Amongst the Blackfoot, dreams were formerly regarded as sent by the Sun to enable them to look ahead and tell what is going to happen.

" A dream, especially if it is a strong one,—that is, if the dream is very clear and vivid,—is almost always obeyed. As dreams start them on the war path, so, if a dream threatening bad luck comes to a member of a war party even if in the enemy's country and just about to make an attack on a camp, the party is likely to turn about and go home without making any hostile demonstrations." [3]

(c) *Secret Societies.*—The Secret Societies of the Kwakiutl Indians formed for the Winter Ceremonial are made up of groups who have received the same secret or powers from their protectors in their visions.[4]

Similarly the secret doctoring societies of the Omaha were comprised of members who were supposed to have had the same vision, each society having its own specific admission vision.[5]

(d) *Names.*—Among the Lapps, when a woman was with child and near the time of her delivery, a deceased ancestor or relation used to appear to her in a dream and inform

---

[1] F. Parkman, *Pioneers of France in the New World*, p. 347, note 1.
[2] Part III, Woodlands Area, p. 270.
[3] G. B. Grinell, *Blackfoot Lodge Tales*, p. 263.
[4] Part III, North-west Coast Area, p. 299. See p. 56.
[5] See p. 170, Fletcher and La Flèche, cit. 2.

her what dead person was to be born again in her infant, and whose name the child was, therefore, to bear. If the woman had no such dream, it fell to the father or the relatives to determine the name by divination or by consulting a wizard.[1]

Among the Sakai, and Jakun of the Malay Peninsular, the new-born infant receives its name according to the dream.[2]

Special names are given in visions for use at the Winter Ceremonial, among the Kwakiutl.[3]

Among the early Pottawatomies, names were given to a child, sometimes according to some dream of the child's,[4] and among the Delaware, a boy's name was given to him in the same way as his initiation vision in which he received his guardian spirit.[5]

(e) *Myths.*—Among the Yuma all myths are dreamed by the individual. Examples of myth dreams are presented in Part III and are the only ones known to the writer. Laufer states that many mythical concepts are dreamed,[6] and it has been amply demonstrated that the psychological pattern of the myth is identical with that of the dream.[7] Whether the myth preceded the dream or the dream preceded the myth is still too early to decide conclusively.[8] Since, however, the dream has been shown to influence so many aspects of culture, it seems logical to infer that it may also be the background from which myths are elaborated.

(f) *Drama.*—Among the Nootka Indians of the northwest, the sacred dramas, the incidents of which are con-

---

[1] Frazer, *The Golden Bough*, Vol. III, p. 368.
[2] Skeat and Blagden, *Pagan Races of the Malay Peninsular*, Vol. II, p. 201.
[3] Part III, p. 299.
[4] Frazer, *Totemism and Exogamy*, Vol. III, p. 380,—from Father de Smet.
[5] *Ibid.*, p. 395,—from Father de Smet.
[6] This chapter, p. 79, cit. 5.
[7] Abraham, *Dreams and Myths*, Ref. 3 on p. 109.
[8] Jones, *On the Nightmare*, p. 66.

nected with mythological legends, originated in guardian spirit visions.[1]

(g) Religious Conversions from Dreams.

It may not be amiss in the present context to mention a people in Africa where conversions to Christianity often took place only through the dictates of dreams. Among a fairly civilized group of Basuto where dreams still play a great part in their lives, many converts were easily made because of their ability to accept readily a belief in the resurrection. A large number, however, refused to be converted, and investigation showed that they consciously wished to be, but would not until they had received a dream telling them to join the new faith. One man, although his wife was a Christian, waited for years for a supernatural occurrence but he always refused to be baptized, saying that he had no dream. He died dreamless and unbaptized.[2]

The natives frequently dream of the dead, and of visits to heaven, but the dead visit the dreamer, rather than the dreamer the abode of the dead.

Examples of dreams which led to baptism and conversion are the following as recorded by a missionary [2] :

" Up among the mountains, behind one of my remoter stations, is a steep valley ; and up this valley, at the end of everything, is a village. I had never been there, and am still not aware that anyone from there had ever been to see me. Late one afternoon, then, a man came from this village to call me to a ' sick ' woman of whom, as we went, he related these facts. A month previously (or thereabouts) the woman's heathen husband died. A week later (or thereabouts) she awoke one night screaming, and had said that as she lay asleep she had felt a hand on her shoulder. Awakening—such was her language, but of course she spoke of her dream—she saw her

---

[1] Boas, *Social Org. and Secret Societies of the Kwakiutl*, Rep. of U.S. Nat. Museum, 1895, p. 506.

[2] Robert Keable, " A People of Dreams," *The Hibbert Journal*, April, 1921, pp. 522–31.

dead husband, in his ordinary clothes and so ' real ' that she forgot for the moment that he was dead. She gave a cry of joy, and demanded where he had been to return to the hut so late. On that he had said : ' Send at once for the priest at —— and be washed from your sins.' ' But why do you come now to tell me that ? ' she asked. ' Lest you die as I have done, unwashed,' he replied awfully. And at that she remembered his death, was convulsed with terror, and found herself awake.

" Her folk had temporized with her, and had not sent for me, none of them being Christian there ; but ten days or so later she had dreamed again. This time her husband was angry, had said nothing, had not indeed needed to say anything, for she had known instinctively his anger and the reason for it. From that time she had eaten next to nothing, and had been in a kind of fit all day long, merely reiterating that I must be sent for. But the night before she had dreamed that a white priest came in, in a white vestment, and laying hands on her had healed her.

" The sequel is soon told. I heard her moaning, like that of an animal in pain, some distance from the hut, and she took no notice of my entrance. When I could see no sign of ordinary sickness, I knelt and prayed, and in my prayer commanded her to be at peace, and laid my hand on her. Her moanings died down at once. They concluded soon after I had finished the prayer. She sat awhile not speaking, but then arose and gave me food. From that day she entered on her instruction, and was baptized last year : and she has brought with her a dozen or more from that village."

The following is a similar experience :

" The heathen wife of a Christian husband, who had steadily resisted baptism, dreamed for four nights running as follows : (1) that she was lost on the veldt, in terror, and running over rough ground on which she finally stumbled and woke ; (2) that she was again on the veldt ; (3) that she was again running, but that the light was clearer and in the shape of a cross ; (4) that she reached a deep kloof and saw on the other side, beneath a luminous cross, the figure of a woman clothed in white, holding up and out a child. The kloof was full of worshipping people on their knees, through whom she could not make her way, and in the course of a frenzied attempt she awoke. The moment I entered the hut the next morning, an arresting thing took place. She literally threw herself out of bed and upon her knees, but at my side rather than before me, her hands clasped as if holding the feet of someone next but needless to say unseen by me. She exclaimed again and again : ' Ahe, Mofumahali ! ' (' Oh, Queen ! Oh, Queen ! '), and, when lifted up by her husband, said repeatedly : ' The woman has come in with the Priest ! ' She was apparently very ill, with a temperature of 105, and I baptized her at once. She has made a resolute convert." [1]

X. NON-PRIMITIVE CASES OF THE INFLUENCE OF DREAMS.

Although the belief in the importance of the dream and its influence grows less as people become less animistically minded, still there are many cases where the dream gives form to the solution of problems, and to literary and artistic creations on which the mind is previously concentrated among individuals of " civilized " nations.

For instance, Otanes the Persian general, in consequence of a vision in a dream, repeopled Samos, which contrary to the orders of Darius, his master, he had laid waste and left without inhabitants.[2]

Saint Cyprian was instructed in a dream to mix water with wine in the Eucharist.[3]

The Divina Commedia was inspired by a dream ; Tartini's " Sonata du Diable " is a plagiarism from a violin played by a dream devil, Hermas wrote his " Pastor " to the dictation of a voice heard in sleep ; Condorcet saw in a dream the final stages of a difficult calculation, and Condillac frequently developed and finished a subject in his dreams.[4] Robert Louis Stevenson for years used to put himself to sleep by reciting tales to himself, as his father did before him ; later on he dreamt complete stories, including large

[1] *Op. cit.* Other similar experiences are given.
[2] Seafield, *Literature and Classification of Dreams*, Vol. II, p. 52.
[3] *Ibid.*, Vol. I, p. 142.
[4] *Ibid.*, pp. 255, 262 ; Vol. II, p. 19.

parts of Dr. Jekyll and Mr. Hyde, which he wrote and published verbatim.[1]

The Siamese author Luong-Vichivathlen had no intention of becoming a writer until his spiritual teacher, dead for five years, appeared to him in a dream and gave him a pair of spectacles, telling him to take them and use them to write books.[2]

This dream seems to be of a nature very similar to those primitive ones in which the guardian or deceased ancestor or father appears and gives instructions.

There is the case of Professor Hilprecht, stated to be well authenticated, who was able in a dream to solve a difficulty connected with two Babylonian inscriptions, which had not previously been recognized as complementary. The information came in dramatic form when an old Babylonian priest appeared in his dream and gave him the clue to the problem.[3]

Of course the story of how Coleridge wrote Kubla Khan directly from his dream is well known. A scholarly study which traces through Coleridge's note-book the associations which lead to the production of Kubla Khan has been done by Professor John Livingston Lowes in his *Road to Xanadu*. Without touching the latent content of this dream it is nevertheless an interesting historical study of the working of the imagination in artistic creation. In connection with the dream palace constructed by Kubla Khan in the poem, is brought forward this extraordinary tale or coincidence :

" There is a singular coincidence to which Henri Cordier has called attention in his edition of Yule's *Cathay and the Way Thither*. In a thirteenth-century Arabic account of Xanadu (Shang-tu), which was not translated into any occidental language until years after Coleridge had dreamed his dream, occurs this state-

[1] R. L. Stevenson, *Across the Plains* (Ox. Univ. Press, 1931), Chap. VIII, pp. 333–48.
[2] R. Dangel, *Imago*, Vol. 17, Heft 1, 1931, pp. 126–9.
[3] *Encyclop. Brit.*, p. 560. 11th Ed., Vol. 8.

ment : ' *On the eastern side of that city a karsi or palace was built called Langtiu, after a plan which the Kaan had seen in a dream and retained in his memory.*' In ancient tradition the stately pleasure-dome of Kubla Khan itself came into being, like the poem as the embodiment of a remembered vision in a dream." [1]

XI. CONCLUSION.

Thus the dream continues to exert its influence on the life and actions of peoples long after they have renounced all belief in its importance and its divine origin. How man's attitude has changed towards these phenomena as he gradually learned, at least in part, to distinguish reality from fantasy, is best stated by Tylor :

" But along the course of these myriad narratives of human phantoms appearing in dreams to cheer or torment, to warn or inform, or to demand fulfilment of their own desires, the problem of dream apparitions may be traced in progress of gradual determination from the earlier conviction that a disembodied soul really comes into the presence of the sleeper, toward the later opinion that such a phantasm is produced in the dreamer's mind without the perception of any external objective figure.

" The evidence of visions corresponds with the evidence of dreams in their bearing on primitive theories of the soul, and the two classes of phenomena substantiate and supplement one another. Even in healthy waking life, the savage or barbarian has never learnt to make that rigid distinction between subjective and objective, between imagination and reality, to enforce which is one of the main results of scientific education." [2]

Probably it is because of this equal valuation given to both fantasy and the external world that so much of primitive culture is a direct result of the dream.[3] So far we have

---

[1] John Livingston Lowes, *The Road to Xanadu* (Constable & Co.), p. 358, and Note.

[2] E. B. Tylor, *Primitive Culture*, p. 445.

[3] For discussion and examples of how primitives distinguish dreams and reality see previous chapter, pp. 27–30.

found that cases of almost all aspects of primitive culture throughout the world have been derived from the dream. A review will show that even from the scattered evidence presented, besides the religious beliefs in the immortality of the soul, in spirits, and in an abode of the dead ; and besides the influence of the dream in a general way on the emotions and activities of primitive men, numerous specific items of primitive culture owe their origin at least in part to a preceding dream. To enumerate : so originating are many types of " totems," many sacrificial acts ; numerous cures, charms, medicine and Shamanistic powers ; as well as magic, taboos and witchcraft ; many instances of ceremonies, songs and dances ; specific objects and methods of material culture, especially works of art ; individual careers both normal and abnormal ; acts of murder and cannibalism, war, secret societies, names, myths and drama. Since these are drawn from all parts of the earth, one can but conclude that a large part of primitive culture is a result of the dream, or more accurately a result of the psychological and cultural processes behind the dream. These processes are given form in the dream, and influence the culture directly from the latter.

If this conclusion is correct, one should attempt to find out its significance, and whether it throws any more light on the nature of culture itself or on the individual's relation to his cultural group.

The most striking fact that occurs in the dream contents of cases mentioned throughout this work is that practically all of the culture items that originate from them are presented by a being or spirit, in human or animal form, who is generally regarded by the native as a dead relative, ancestor, father, or God. The being called the guardian spirit, protector, or " totem," by anthropologists, is associated and interpreted by the primitive as dead relative, and very often as the dead father. The spirit may come as a late king (Tonga), a deceased ancestor in the form of python, crocodile regarded as father or wild boar (Borneo), as a dead ancestor or relative in animal form (Ashanti), as a dead king (Shilluk), as an evil power in the form of a snake (Menomini), as a God (Menomini), as totem or ancestor (Australia), as guardian, totem, dead father (Kwakiutl), and as dead father (Kiwai Papuans),[1] and as deceased father or relative among the Paviotso of Nevada.[2] Another outstanding situation is that the majority of culture items that arise from the dream do so from what I have called the culture pattern dream in my study of the dreams of American Indian cultures. These comprise those dreams or visions that are induced by the culture either by a definite vision quest, the instruction of medicine men, or the directions of parents, or in any way whereby the culture requires a vision or dream for guidance. Such dreams occur among the Kiwai of New Guinea, the Australians, the Sea Dyaks of Borneo, and the Andaman Islanders. Culture items do not seem to originate so often in individual night dreams, or if they do so it is because these are influenced by pattern dreams. For instance among the Navajo where the individual dream predominates and there is no induced culture pattern dream,[3] with the exception of the visions of the professional diagnosticians or stargazers, there seem to be no instances of culture items arising in dreams apart from those which influence the conception of life after death.[4] Among the Kwakiutl I have examples of individual spontaneous dreams which do confer supernatural powers, but this is in a culture where the induced vision is very highly developed. Among the Paviotso, however, career visions arise spontaneously and are identical in form and content with sought pattern visions.

In other words much of primitive culture is derived from the dead

---

[1] "Among the Thonga of S. Africa, in cases of possession, the possessing spirit is sometimes revealed in a dream as a chief long since dead."—Junod, *Life of a S. African Tribe*, Vol. II, p. 438.

[2] pp. 71–3. This chapter, p. 73, Ref. 2.

[3] See Part III, pp. 207–48.

[4] W. Morgan, Part III, p. 247.

father or ancestor spirit, who communicates through the culture pattern dream or vision, the dream image being accepted by the primitive as the real father or ancestor. It is important to realize that this makes the totem or father the carrier of culture.[1] What

[1] It might plausibly be thought that only among those tribes with patrilineal descent, that is, who reckon descent from the father as head of the family, would one find the totem or father spirit as culture carrier through the vision. A mere recording of the type of descent among the tribes whose visions are here presented show conclusively that there is absolutely no correlation between the culture-initiating vision in which the totem-father appears, and the kinship classification or method of reckoning descent. Among the groups recorded are patrilineal, matrilineal, and patrilineal-matrilineal peoples, yet amongst all of them it is the father-ancestor totem who is sought in the vision for individual and cultural guidance.

With regard to the mother's brother as father substitute, over which there has been controversy (Malinowski, *Sex and Repression in Savage Society*, controversy with Jones, pp. 135–41, 143, 142–7), Hill-Tout has pointed out some time ago, that, " Under mother-right the head of the clan is invariably a man, the elder male relative on the maternal side, and the clan name is not so much the property of the woman as of her elder brother or her conventional ' father,' that is her maternal uncle. The ' fathers ' of the group, that is the maternal uncles, are just as much heads and ' founders of houses ' and clans in the matriarchal state as under the more advanced state of patriarchal rule. And they do found family and group totems, the evidence from our northern coast tribes makes clear beyond the shadow of a doubt." " The founders of families and totem crests are as invariably men under matriarchy as under patriarchy, the essential difference only between the states in this regard being that, under one the descent is through ' the conventional father,' under the other through the ' real or ostensible father.' " (Hill-Tout, " Totemism : Its Origin and Import," *Transactions of the R.S. of Canada*, 2nd Series, Vol. IX, 1903, p. 77).

Farther on I have analysed a Crow Indian vision in which the mother's brother is psychologically equivalent to the father (p. 146).

Hence, the instinctive turning to the father as leader for guidance, a childhood attitude, would in the individual be psychologically and historically prior to regarding the maternal uncle as head of the family. The maternal uncle inherits the child's attitude toward the father, and becomes a substitute father. Malinowski (*The Father in Primitive Psychology*) has shown in a matrilineal society, that the father assumes first place as authority and guide for the child for a considerable

does this mean in the light of wish-fulfilment and conflict which make up the dynamics of the dream? What the dream appears to express from the point of view of the individual dreamer, is the wish to receive the power or potency to live from the father or ancestor. With his authority one can carry on and become part of society. He confers the gifts and abilities necessary to face life, or so the nature wishes, according to the content of his dream. The emotional attitude to the guardian ancestor or father who appears in the dream is on one hand that of fear and hostility, and on the other of veneration and love, in other words a widespread attitude towards deity. Possibly this attitude may be the same as early stages of the belief in God the Father, an idea suggested by Freud's analysis of the father image projection, which forms the basis of the conventional idea of God.

At least this much of the latent wishes of the dream can be surmised without the use of any other psychological method, that is, with regard to the induced culture pattern dream, because the associations given by the culture are

period prior to the assumption of authority by the maternal uncle. The real father, therefore, remains the prototype of paternity.

The lack of correlation between the vision pattern in which the father-totem appears, and the kinship-descent pattern, may also be explainable on the grounds that both are independently diffused.

Recent information shows that ignorance of physiological paternity is not a universal attribute of primitives in their native state even in Australia, for among the natives of Cape York of the Kolso Yu'o, Ompela and Kanfu tribes the belief is that the seminal fluid of the male produces the child, and the mother is of no consequence. This receives added corroboration from their use of contraceptives. (D. F. Thompson, " The Hero Cult, Initiation and Totemism in Cape York," *J. of R.A.I.*, Vol. LXIII, 1933, July–Dec., p. 505 *seq.*).

In Africa also, among the Central Bantu, Babemba, generally classed as a matrilineal tribe, they " are perfectly aware of the physiological function of the father in the conception of the child, and this very rôle is made the basis of important paternal rights." In Bemba culture " it seems to be the actual fact of physiological fatherhood which is recognized as the basis of the father's rights over his child " (A. I. Richards in *Essays Presented to C. G. Seligman*, p. 276, 1934).

known in many cases, especially in respect to the ancestral totem or guardian, and these are sufficient to explain the latent meanings. This would not apply to those individual dreams where individual associations are unknown.

Practically all the dreams referred to in this chapter are culture pattern dreams which represent the culture's demand that the individual shall conform to its way, that is, the way of life laid down by the ancestors, who appear in the dream and authorize the individual specifically what he shall do or be. Hence we find a twofold purpose expressed in the culture pattern vision ; in the first place the determination of the culture, or the group, that the individual shall comply with the ancestral and traditional pattern ; and in the second place the wish of the individual to receive the blessings and favours from the " totem " father or ancestor, whom at the same time he regards, for some reason not apparent on the surface of the dream, with hostility and fear. Since in some areas these dreams occur at puberty, when the individual must renounce his infantile attitudes toward the parents and face his own cultural milieu as an adult, he instinctively turns to the ancestor or father for guidance, or is compelled to do so by the tribal custom to go out and seek a vision. The vision, that is, the successful career vision, means then a normal renouncing of the parental ties and an identification with the ancestor or father for the purpose of meeting life in harmony with his surrounding. The vision causing a man to become a berdache, therefore, indicates that an abnormal choice of identification is made, viz. the young man identifies himself with the mother and becomes a woman. The moon in this case is obviously a female or mother symbol (Ogallala Sioux),[1] and he receives his abnormal fate from her hands.

To conclude, the importance of the dream as an initiator of primitive culture must, therefore, be given its due emphasis in any study which attempts to reach a closer understanding of the nature of primitive culture itself. Its significance has

[1] p. 83.

hitherto not been sufficiently grasped. It is because the primitive mind often assigns a reality value to the fantasy world equal to that of the external world, and even has difficulty at times in distinguishing the two,[1] that the dream is allowed to dictate in large measure the course of life. Because of this valuation of fantasy, with its cultural results, we are enabled to approach directly the specific mental motives which result in specific aspects of culture. So far I have shown how even the manifest content of many dreams reveals a conflict of wish with regard to the father or ancestor. This conflict appears to be one of the important psychological motives behind the culture initiating dreams, hence behind culture itself. To reach the full dynamics of motive and wish expressed in the dream would, therefore, be equivalent to reaching the foundation in human motive on which culture rests. In other words the psychology of primitive culture would stand revealed as the foundation on which history and diffusion weave their varied patterns. To reach the totality of motive expressed in the culture-initiating dream, a study of the latent content through the medium of symbols and association is essential. I would go so far as to say that only by getting at the latent meaning of the dream can we understand anything of the nature of primitive culture.

[1] See Chap. I, pp. 27–30.

CHAPTER III

SYMBOLS, TYPES AND FORMS OF PRIMITIVE DREAMS

IN the previous chapter the recorded native dreams and associations of many widespread peoples indicate clearly that the " totem " spirit appearing in dreams is often a father image, expressed either directly as father or ancestor or in symbolic form as an animal. A further investigation of native associations to culture pattern visions will be attempted, and an effort will also be made to study the forms and symbols of the individual dreams of various groups, but very little can be done with the latter series of dreams in reaching the latent meanings, because of the lack of individual native associations recorded. Several collections of individual dreams have been made by field workers, but the failure to record associations makes them almost valueless from a psychological standpoint.

The consensus of opinion, however, is that the symbolism among primitives is more directly connected with the symbolized than among ourselves, on account of the low threshold between the conscious and unconscious,[1] and that secondary elaboration is not intensive because repression is only skin deep.[2] Some of my material on individual dreams corroborates this point,[3] that the conscious and unconscious of primitives seems to be not nearly so differentiated as among ourselves. Although Lévy-Bruhl's " pre-logic " mentality as a blanket description applied to the primitive mind

---

[1] C. G. Seligman, Huxley Memorial Lecture, 1932, *J. of R.A.I.*, Vol. LXII, p. 193 *seq.*

[2] G. Roheim, quoted in Ref. 1.   [3] Part III.

is rightly not accepted by field workers, his work has the merit of being at least a lucid description of the " secondary functioning " of the unconscious mind,[1] with which the primitive is often in closer contact than ourselves. It is possible to see the value of Lévy-Bruhl's work from this standpoint, without falling into the error of regarding " primitive " man as exclusively pre-logical in all his thinking and actions. That instances of advanced logical thinking and shrewd judgment based on a fine perception of external reality do occur has been brought out by Dr. Paul Radin in *Primitive Man as Philosopher*.

The task of interpreting individual dreams even without associations will, therefore, be possible in those cases where there is absence of symbolism and the latent and manifest contents are identical, in other words where the latent wish is clearly stated without symbolic representation, and in those cases where the symbolism is so thin that the meaning is clearly seen behind it. For instance, the obvious unconscious desire to kill is the only possible meaning of the following dream of a man of the East Solomon Islands, a member of a former war-like tribe whose fighting activities are now suppressed :

" I dreamed about a man named Kariko, who wanted to kill people. He said to me, ' Come on, let us go and kill all the people here.' "[2]

In the following it is hardly necessary to have associations to discover the overwhelming fixation on the mother so obviously expressed in the dream of a Jukun man of Nigeria :

" A Jukun said that he had been pestered for months with the dream that he was going up the Benue in a steamer with

[1] I refer to a-logical fantasy thinking, participation, co-existence of logically contradictory ideas, the regarding of fantasy as an objective reality, all of which are attributes of the unconscious mind as found through the analyses of modern individuals as well. " Secondary " is the usual psychoanalytic term for all unconscious processes other than the primary ideas treated in this chapter.

[2] Miss Blackwood, Chap. XVII, p. 36, No. 12 (unpub.).

his mother. He enjoyed the sensation at first, but soon grew tired and finally horror-stricken as the boat steamed on and on to Eternity." [1]

The Freudian theory of symbolism is regarded as the most useful and accurate means of approaching the latent dream meanings. Only a perusal of the dream material will show whether the acceptance of the theory is justifiable, and whether most cases of primitive dreams are amenable to a Freudian interpretation, as believed by Professor Seligman.[2] Symbolism is regarded as the expression of a transformed unconscious, repressed wish, so transformed by the mind, in order to relieve the affect and disguise the true meaning of the wish, which is generally felt as painful or regarded as culturally unacceptable. That this is the purpose of symbolism in dreams and other unconscious processes, can be taken as established among contemporary cases analysed. It is intended to give sufficient examples of primitive dreams to show that in spite of the closeness of the conscious to the unconscious (i.e. of the symbol to the symbolized) symbolism in the sense mentioned also occurs. It is known that, among other tendencies, parricide and incest, types of the painful ideas arising in dreams, are culturally tabooed amongst most peoples,[3] even among primitives who are probably more conscious of them than ourselves. These ideas must, therefore, be a greater temptation to them than to ourselves, whose dreams reveal the same motives. Hence it remains to be seen whether examination of the primitive dream material shows these negative and culturally tabooed aspects of the family complex symbolized, or otherwise expressed. This subject will be pursued farther on.

[1] C. K. Meek, note to Professor Seligman (unpub.).

[2] C. G. Seligman, Huxley Memorial Lecture, 1932, *J. of R.A.I.*, Vol. LXII.

[3] There are cases where incest was formerly culturally acceptable, such as the brother-sister royal marriages of ancient Egypt. The widespread custom of the slaughter of the Divine King in Africa and India, can plausibly be regarded as substitute parricide, especially since king or ruler is generally a symbol for father.

The Freudian interpretation of symbols is considerably simplified by Jones, who states that only a very limited number of primary ideas can be symbolized, namely, those concerning the bodily self, the relation to the family, birth, love, and death. Thus to him (in contradistinction to the Jungian school, which treats symbols as inter-representations of ideas regardless of whether they are primary or secondary)[1] symbolism is a process of representation, whereby all symbols, which may amount to thousands in number, are limited to being representations of only the above repressed primary ideas and no others. Thus,

" All psychoanalytic experience goes to show that the primary ideas of life, the only ones that can be symbolized—those, namely, concerning the bodily self, the relations to the family, birth, love, and death—retain in the unconscious throughout life their original importance, and that from them is derived a very large part of the more secondary interests of the conscious mind. As energy flows from them, and never to them, and as they constitute the most repressed part of the mind, it is comprehensible that symbolism should take place in one direction only. Only what is repressed is symbolized ; only what is repressed needs to be symbolized. This conclusion is the touchstone of the psychoanalytic theory of symbolism." [2]

The dreams of primitives should be able to corroborate this theory and wherever possible such corroboration will be attempted. Thus symbolism in the sense of mere representation of one idea by another is to be excluded. Jung, for instance, will make statements such as the ball symbolizes the sun, and the killing of the bull means the killing of the old man in ourselves.[3] Symbols and primary ideas are thus confused or regarded as identical. In other words, he places the secondary ideas or symbols of primary ideas on the same level of meaning with the primary ideas, and

[1] See table on following page.

[2] E. Jones, " The Theory of Symbolism," *Papers in Psychoanalysis*, 3rd ed., p. 183.

[3] C. G. Jung, Seminar Notes, Nov. 1928 (unpub.). Jung also speaks of the mother and father imagos as symbols.

all are regarded as inter-representations of each other. The following diagrams show Jung's conception (if properly understood, and it is impossible to be certain) of the symbol, together with the undoubtedly more accurate and sensible Freudian one :

Jung. Sun—Ball—Father—Lion—King
Pole—Steeple—Phallus—Sword—Snake
Cave—Mother—Church—Sea—Queen

Any one of these ideas on a single line would be regarded as a symbol of any of the others.

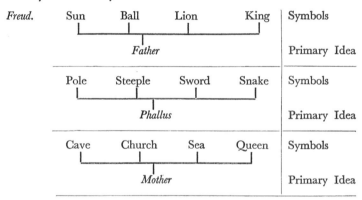

In this conception of symbolism, energy flows only in the direction of the secondary ideas from the repressed primary ideas of life, and never in the reverse direction from the symbol to the primary idea. All the symbols of a given primary idea may be fused with each other as is often the case in the condensation work of the dream, but all " symbolize " only their primary ideas. Hence Mother, Father, Phallus, can never be symbols since they are primary. An attempt to make them into such leads to absurdity. Often primary ideas are condensed with each other in dreams, such as phallus and father.

Some of the important problems that arise in connection with the symbols and types of primitive dreams have been dealt with in detail by Professor Seligman. He has shown that the essential dream mechanisms of non-Europeans are the same as those of ourselves,[1] and that dreams with the same manifest content to which identical latent meanings are attached occur in cognate groups and among peoples of diverse race and every stage of culture.[2] Such dreams are of the dead, anxiety and conflict dreams and some of the so-called type dreams, those which deal with flying, falling, climbing, raw meat and tooth losing. These occur throughout Europe, Asia and Africa, and I can add instances of their occurring among many North American Indians.[3] He shows what an important bearing the type dreams have on the problems of diffusion and independent origin, since it is not likely that a diffusion of dreams occurs. Wherever the same dream occurs in different peoples it means that the unconscious is similar.[4] If the latter is true, type dreams as identical products of the unconscious mind, occurring among different peoples of unrelated races, and in various stages of culture, as well as among peoples of similar or identical beliefs, customs and techniques, indicate the probability of an independent origin in each instance.[5] The importance of this conclusion cannot be overestimated, especially since it might conceivably be extended to those dreams which act as originators of culture items, dealt with in the previous chapter. If it can be established that a diffusion of dreams does not take place, yet customs in widespread parts of the world arise from dreams, it would prove the independent origin of culture items so originating. As a matter of fact it is necessary to be especially cautious at this point, and to find out if diffusion of dreams does or does not take place. I think that with individual dreams, no one could prove an instance of one being transmitted to another person, cer-

[1] C. G. Seligman, " Anthropology and Psychology," *J. of R. Anth. Inst.*, Vol. LIV, p. 46, 1924.
[2] *Ibid.*   [3] *Ibid.*, and Part III, Navajo and Yuma sections.
[4] C. G. Seligman, " The Unconscious in Relation to Anthropology." *Br. J. of Psychology*, Vol. XVIII, Part 4, 1928, pp. 314–87.
[5] Huxley Memorial Lecture, 1932, *J. of R. Anth. Inst.*

tainly not by the mere telling of it. Yet this does not seem to hold with culture pattern dreams and visions within a given group, and in those curious instances of apparent thought-transference in dreams which seem to occur in some primitive groups,[1] it is impossible to say whether they prove diffusion or independent origin. As to the culture pattern visions in North America, many of which are induced, the vision seeker is instructed to seek a vision and with his mind concentrated on a culturally determined field of imagery he keeps on dreaming until he dreams right,[2] or else keeps seeking the appropriate vision until he obtains it.[3] The visions within a given group are all of the same pattern, with individual variations. Hence the tribal consciousness of what is seen in the vision, and the individual familiarity with this pattern, before going out to seek the vision, means that the specific vision form is diffused to individuals within the tribe from the traditional experience. Such a tribal vision pattern can also be transmitted to another group which previously did not have it, as in the case of the Kwakiutl cannibalistic vision cult, parts of which were borrowed within the last century from other tribes.[4] It would be interesting to compare the exact details of visions in two groups to see how much of the visions were identical, but unfortunately I have only the records from the Kwakiutl.

Instances of thought transference and telepathy in dreams have been reported among the coastal Solomon Islands,[5] in the West Solomons,[6] and among the Melanesians of

---

[1] See notes, pp. 105-7, and Appendix, pp. 329-33.
[2] Woodlands, Part III.　　　　　　　[3] Crow, Part III.
[4] F. Boas, *Social Organization and Secret Societies of the Kwakiutl Indians*, Report of American National Museum, 1895, p. 664.
The ceremonial of cannibalism was introduced among various northern tribes recently, although its foundation, the idea of a spirit who is killing people, is present among all tribes. The custom of devouring men was introduced among the Kwakiutl about 60 years ago (written 1895) and was derived from the Heiltsug.
[5] Blackwood, B. (unpub.). Cit. on p. 41.
[6] Rivers, *Instinct and the Unconscious*, 1922, pp. 94-6.

British New Guinea.[1] It often takes the form of the same dreams, being dreamed simultaneously by different people. Of a similar nature is the curious coincidence that occurred during one of Jung's seminars in Zurich which I attended. I quote it below for what it may be worth without expressing any opinion of my own.[2]

If some control can be established to prove the authenticity of thought transference [3] in dreams,[4] one would still

[1] C. G. Seligman, *The Melanesians of British New Guinea*, p. 654.

[2] "The mood of our second meeting, on November 14th, was somewhat upset. We talked of bull scenes and bull dreams, and of how in ancient Athens the important men, and at one time the daughter of a senator and even Sophocles told their dreams. All this has brought interesting coincidences to light. It was on the 21st that we discussed the meaning of the bull-fight. The man whose dreams we have been discussing is still alive. From the 20th to the 24th he spent four days making a picture which he brought to me because he was so astonished at it. He drew the head of the sacred bull, holding the disc of the sun between his horns. The source of this bull drawing is a synchronistic event, because we had been discussing the man's dream in our lecture. Also, two days after the last seminar, I received a letter from a patient and friend in Mexico, who had been to a bull-fight and must have written just about the day we first spoke of the bull. She described the supreme moment when the bull, confused, faces the matador, and the matador standing before him makes the supreme gesture of scorn. He represents perfect conscious control, perfect style and consummate grace as well as daring. This is needed in order to live in a world of weltering unconsciousness, in the bosom of barbarism. If you weaken anywhere you are done for. The toreador is the hero, the only shining light in all the darkness, rage and lack of control. He is the perfect discipline.

"This is what we call coincidence. This shows how a dream lives, is a living thing, a living situation, not the rustling of dry paper. It is an animal, with feelers and many umbilical cords. It produces while we are talking about it " (C. G. Jung, Seminar Notes, Zurich, 1928, unpub.).

[3] For thought transference in dreams, see also R. Keable, " A People of Dreams," *The Hibbert Journal*, April, 1921, pp. 530, 531 (Basuto Bantu).

[4] Freud, *New Introductory Lectures on Psychoanalysis*, 1933, Lecture XXX. (See Appendix for quotations from the references in footnotes 1–4 this page, and 5–6 of preceding page.)

have to find out whether a person's dreams influence or are diffused to another person's, or whether those of both arose independently, but simultaneously, as a mere coincidence. Hence, diffusion of dreams may exist among those of the induced culture pattern variety, but they are of a quite different process from the ordinary spontaneous individual dreams, which probably are not diffused. The evidence, therefore, for the independent origin of culture items arising in dreams is not proved, because they arise in diffusable visions, and only seldom from the individual dreams. What still holds, however, is the independent origin of type dreams, and of any cultural results which may arise from them.

Professor Seligman has also shown how in dream symbolism certain substances and objects have the same value to the unconscious of savages as to that of Europeans.[1] He gives the examples of a psychotic Papua-Melanesian who " When remonstrated with for defæcating on the verandah, replied, ' It is not faeces but money ' " ; and one from among the Ashanti, who interpret the dream of falling into a latrine as it " means you are going to get money." These examples are similar to the unconscious symbols found among Europeans undergoing analysis. The ideas of money, wealth, property, mud, filth, destruction, death and going away are often found associated with, or as symbols of excrement by analysts. To add other examples from scattered parts : in Siam to dream of excrement signifies fortune and riches [2]; an Arabic Muhammedan dream interpretation says gold means to depart from, " Gold a thing which easily departs or is soon lost or spent," [3] and in Tangier if you dream that your clothes are full of excrements it means wealth [4] ; among

---

[1] Huxley Memorial Lecture, p. 215, 1932.

[2] R. Dängel, *Siamesische Traumdeutungskunst*, Leipzig, Vol. VII, part 3, 1931.

[3] " Muhammedan Dream Interp.," *J. of Royal Asiatic Society*, Vol. XVI, 1856, No. 35.

[4] E. Westermarck, *Dream Interp. among the Moors* (unpub. note to C. G. S.).

the Kiwai of New Guinea, " a dream in which a man finds himself in a place full of excrement forbodes the death of somebody " [1]; among the Naga, to go through mud in a dream means wealth [2]; in China to dream of the W.C. is lucky and signifies fortune [3]; among the Sinhalese to dream of cow dung on the floor means fear from thieves [4]; and in England a similar " culture pattern " occurs when thieves defaecate on the floor after robbing a house [5]; and even in Ancient Egypt to dream of eating dung means " eating his possessions in his house." [6]

There are also those examples where the unconscious of savages produces sexual fantasies similar to those produced by Caucasians. For instance, the vulva regarded as wound [7] is found among the folk tales of the Kiwai [8] as well as in individual dreams, for, " If a man dreams before a fight that he is carrying a baby girl with a large vulva, it portends death to him ; the vulva represents the arrow wound he will receive." [9]

The widespread myth of the Vagina Dentata is distributed throughout North America,[10] and is found also in Samoa, and occurs as a legend among the Ainu,[11] and as an individual dream among the Kiwai in the following form ; quite similar to the myth and legend forms occurring elsewhere :

[1] G. Landtman, *Folk Tales of Kiwai Papuans*, No. 385, p. 441.
[2] A. G. O. Hodgson, Letter to Prof. Seligman (unpub.).
[3] Translation of *Chow Kung's Book of Dreams*, No. 33 (note to Prof. Seligman).
[4] P. de Zoyes, note to Prof. Seligman.
[5] Statement of C. G. Seligman.
[6] Alan H. Gardiner, *Hieratic Papyri in the British Museum*, 3rd series, Chester Beatty Gift, Papyrus No. III. " The Dream Book," p. 14 (5, 15) (Revises).
[7] See O. Pfister, *Die Frommigkeit des Graften Ludwig von Zinzendorf* (Leipzig and Wien).
[8] G. Landtman, *op. cit.*, No. 386.
[9] G. Landtman, *The Kiwai Papuans of Br. New Guinea*, pp. 276–9.
[10] Letter from Margaret Meade to Prof. Seligman (unpub.).
[11] Unpub. notes of Prof. Seligman.

" By Gibúma, Mawáta. He was asked by a woman to have connection with her, but did not venture to do so, for her vulva was provided with sharp teeth and opened and closed continuously like a mouth. Again and again he tried to muster up courage but shrank back every time. At last the woman got up and attacked him with a piece of wood, and he fled into the water. But he found that he could not swim, and to add to his horror a crocodile came towards him and was about to catch him when he opened his eyes." [1]

To state, as some anthropologists do,[2] that this widespread pattern appearing in myth, legend and dream has no psychological significance but is merely a result of diffusion, is tantamount to saying that the human mind plays no part in the formation and spread of culture. Since this sexual anxiety fantasy occurs in diffusable myths and legends, as well as in non-diffusable individual dreams, it would be more logical either to regard them all as products of the same unconscious way of thinking, or to find out whether the myths and legends may not have originated in dreams, the former being secondary elaborations and the latter the initial expression of universally similar psychic material. Some anthropologists write as if myths, legends and folklore existed in a sort of vacuum totally without relation to the human mind in spite of the fact that they are in large part of identical psychological structure.[3] This attitude may be sufficient in a study of the processes of diffusion, but certainly throws no light on the meaning of culture itself.

There are other obvious examples where the unconscious of primitives produces dreams with meanings (either disguised or symbolized) similar to our own. It is realized that the symbol is not confined to the dream, but is a product of the unconscious mind in any of its expressions, hence

---

[1] G. Landtman, *Folk Tales of the Kiwai Papuans*, No. 398.

[2] M. Meade, letter to Professor Seligman (unpub.).

[3] Rivers, *Dreams and Primitive Culture*, Ref. 5, p. 26, Chap. I ; K. Abraham, " Dreams and Myths," *Nervous and Mental Disease, Monograph Series*, No. 15, New York, 1913.

some of the symbols to be referred to occur not only in the dream, but also in myth, legend and folklore.[1] The usual dream among non-primitives of finding oneself naked in public and feeling ashamed does not seem to occur among primitives until white influence causes them to wear clothes and feel conscious of their bodies. From two modern Ottawa Indians whose culture is rapidly disappearing, are recorded from one a dream of being naked in an empty house in the city where he had hid,[2] and from another a dream in which he feels ashamed of his nakedness.[3] The dream of being naked seems, however, to occur among the Moshi of Central Africa because there is recorded the belief that, " to dream of being naked and fat is a sign of one's death."[4]

So far examples show the human mind in its primary levels expressing itself in similar fashion on certain subjects in many parts of the world among people of varied cultural development. Further research must determine whether the unconscious mind is universally similar and comprises the same archaic patterns of idea and wish structures everywhere. A study of comparative symbols occurring in dreams, or elsewhere, with individual and cultural associations would determine this all-important point. Following Professor Seligman, a few more leads in this direction are here attempted. Common symbols occurring in dreams of Europeans and their meanings constant or varied were first presented by Freud in his great classic on dreams.[5] This work remains the only authority on the meaning of the latent contents of dreams, and as Havelock Ellis says, if this work does not contain the whole truth it will at least lead to its discovery.

[1] See Chap. IV with conclusion for justification for interpreting ontogeny and phylogeny in the same manner.
[2] Part III, p. 281, No. 20.   [3] p. 287, No. 8, Part III.
[4] A. W. Cardinall, " Dreams among the Dagomba and Moshi," *Man*, May 1927, pp. 87–8, 59.
[5] S. Freud, *The Interpretation of Dreams*, p. 230 *seq.*

Freud calls attention to the two classes of dreams, those that have the same meaning every time, and those which must be subjected to the most widely different interpretations in spite of identical or similar content.[1] Of the first type is the examination dream regarded as denoting anxiety, which is a result of punishments suffered for childish misdeeds. Professor Seligman has found that this dream occurs in similar form in old China, where a similar cultural condition existed.[2] Freud shows that there is no fixed unambiguous interpretation to a dream,[3] and emphasizes that symbolism is not peculiar to the dream but to unconscious thinking.[4] He also states that a symbol may often have to be interpreted not symbolically but according to its real meaning.[5] The occurrence of the following symbols and latent meanings are from Freud's list, and I shall compare them in each case with instances of identical or similar symbols and meanings, occurring amongst primitives or other peoples for whom I have any data. Freud's symbols and meanings are put first in each case.[6]

1. *Father* is often symbolized by King or Emperor. In America President and Governor are also the symbols. In dreams analysed Pope, chief or any authority or head person are usual for father. In the last chapter I have shown how among primitives the guardian or protector, or " individual totem " or ancestor (i.e. the authority for the dreamer), in a dream is often regarded as father. God as supreme father is of course widespread. Among primitives the symbol for father is often a real or mythical animal, possibly the clan totem animal as well. In America animals such as the bear (Navajo),[7] (Kwakiutl),[8] (Crow)[9] ; the eagle (Wood-

[1] S. Freud, *op. cit.*, p. 230.
[2] C. G. Seligman, " Anthropology and Psychology," *J. of Roy. Anth. Inst.*, Vol. LIV, 1924, p. 40.
[3] S. Freud, *ibid.*, p. 246.   [4] *Ibid.*, p. 245.
[5] *Ibid.*, p. 246.   [6] *Ibid.*, pp. 230–59.
[7] Part III, p. 218, No. 4. Also Part II, Chap. IV, p. 175 *seq.*
[8] Part III, p. 316, No. 55. Also p. 323.
[9] Chap. IV, pp. 145–7.

lands [1] and Navajo) [2] ; the bear, and rattlesnake (Paviotso) [3] ; as well as the Thunder Bird (Woodlands),[4] (Blackfoot),[5] (Cheyenne, Arapahoe) [6] are father symbols. Among the latter two " Father and grandfather are terms of affection applied to anything held sacred or awful." [6] In Africa, elephant and king are associated, the king being addressed as Great Elephant among the Zulus.[7] Among the Ashanti the chief may sometimes be referred to as elephant.[8] Ancestors in animal or semi-animal form can be considered as having the same symbolic significance, such as the Pharaoh as a human-headed bull.[9] In Central Africa, chief is commonly represented by a lion and in second-century Rome a lion in a dream meant emperor or king.[10] An eighth-century Persian dream interpretation says, " If you see a white elephant, it means hope from the kings." [11]

Lowie calls attention to the historic unity of Eurasiatic and American bear ceremonial and ideology. Among some of the features common to both areas are the use of kinship terms to describe the bear, such as among the Penobscot, as well as among the Yukaghir, and Yakut, all of whom refer to it as " Grandfather." Conciliatory speeches made to the animal before killing it, and post-mortem rites such as the disposal of the skull are traced from the Atlantic coast of America to Western Siberia. Lowie regards this situation as justifying the inference of diffusion.[12] The kinship

[1] Part III.   [2] Part III.
[3] Part II, Chap. II, pp. 71–2. [4] Part III.
[5] Part III, p. 260, C, *b*.
[6] Mooney's Ghost Dance Religion, *B.A.E.*—14th *Ann. Rep.*, Part 2, p. 970.
[7] C. G. Seligman, Appendix to Chap. XXI of Rattray's *Religion and Art in Ashanti*.
[8] *Ibid.*   [9] *Ibid.*
[10] H. J. Rose, ref. on p. 127 this chap. See discussion, pp. 128–31.
[11] Translation of eighth-century Persian Dream Book, *Islamic Culture*, Vol. VI, 1932, pp. 569–85.
[12] R. H. Lowie, " Religious Ideas and Practices," *Essays presented to C. G. Seligman*, p. 185.

term and personification applied to the animal, however, show it to be a father symbol, even if these usages arose as a result of diffusion. The diffusion of a custom over a wide area might easily be because of its appropriateness as a means of expressing an unconscious primary idea common to the peoples of the whole area. Although the " psychic unity of mankind," which anthropologists now realize underlies all manifestations of diffusion and independent invention, may not explain any specific cultural resemblance,[1] there is no justification for regarding the surface facts of diffusion in themselves as explaining the nature of culture, especially since diffusion is possible only on the basis of this " psychic unity." Any added evidence, however slight, as to the nature of this unity which is not necessarily universally known even by anthropologists, is, therefore, of equal importance as the facts of history and diffusion themselves.

A man of the Lotuko speaking Lango in the south of the Sudan on the east bank of the Nile dreamed of a lion and recognized that this represented his father. He and his father both belonged to the lion totem, since they are patrilineal people.[2] Another Lango looked on the crocodile as his clan animal. He would sacrifice to what he claimed were real crocodiles, " yet as he stated that he saw his father in crocodile form in dreams there is some suggestion that they were ancestors in animal form." [3] The latter is identical with the example among the Dyak of Borneo where a chief regards himself as son or nephew of a crocodile spirit who appeared in a dream.[4] The crocodile totem among the Bantu Fan is also invariably regarded as father.[5]

In Australia among the Wakilbura tribe the totem animal is spoken of as father.

---

[1] *Ibid.*, p. 183. [2] Related to me by Prof. Seligman.
[3] C. G. Seligman and Z. Brenda, *Pagan Tribes of the Nilotic Sudan,* p. 358.
[4] See p. 63, previous chapter.
[5] See p. 154 *seq.*

" A man of the Frilled Lizard totem holds that reptile sacred and he not only refrains from killing it, but would prevent others doing so in his presence. He goes so far as to seek revenge for the killing of his own totem by killing the man's ' father ' who did it." [1]

The following totem animals are called " the fathers " and vary according to locality, Wood-chuck, Black Duck, Porcupine and Yellow Beaked Eagle Hawk.[2]

Among the natives of Cape York in Australia, the personal totem of the individual comes from the mother's moiety and sometimes from the clan, and its name "*yartjima*" means mother's father, whereas the word "*pola*" for clan totem, which is handed down from generation to generation in the patrilineal line means father's father.[3]

Supernatural ogres and mythical monsters and spirits are often father symbols. The following is a folk tale from the Melanesians of British New Guinea (abbreviated) :

A mother feeds her son some berries from a certain plant. He wants more and she promises him that he may accompany her the next day, but early in the morning she goes out before he is up. She does the same on the following day. Finally he gets up in time to accompany her. They go to the berry bush and the son eats the whole plant including the roots. He becomes very sick and his mother has to leave him behind in the bush. " After dusk had set in, an ogre *Wavineruatonu* by name, came to see how the cucumber he had planted was getting on, and he saw it had disappeared. As he was looking about to see what had become of it, he muttered to himself, ' I'd like to know who has eaten up my plant.' The boy thought it was his father, and called out ' Father, Father,' etc." [4]

Among the Maori of New Zealand, " If you see an

---

[1] G. Roheim, *Social Anthropology*, p. 77.   [2] *Ibid.*, p. 83.

[3] Donald F. Thomson, " The Hero Cult Initiation and Totemism on Cape York," *J. of Roy. Anth. Inst.*, Vol. LXIII, July–Dec. 1933, pp. 493, 499.

[4] C. G. Seligman, *The Melanesians of British New Guinea*, Story 15, pp. 392–5.

atua [1] hovering in a dream, then it is probably the spirit of a dead relative, your father maybe. . . ."

Among the Kwakiutl Indians, where numerous individual dreams are recorded about the dead father and cannibalistic spirits,[2] the mythical cannibal spirit who appears in the visions of initiates is obviously a father symbol. He is the great and terrible *Baxbakualanuxai'wae* or " the first one to eat man at the mouth of the river in the north." He is a cannibal living on the mountains who is always in pursuit of man.[3] Psychologically he appears to be identical to the pursuing robbers, ghosts and others occurring in those dreams mentioned by Freud as signifying the father.[4] In individual dreams among the Kwakiutl the dead father often appears openly as the Grizzly Bear, or Master of the Salmon.[5]

The Sun as king and father is a very widespread symbol especially in sun-worshipping religions.[6] It occurs often in North America in the Woodlands, Plains, South-east, and South-west. A Navajo Medicine Man said to me, " The Sun is our god and that is our father. The Changing Woman or the White Shell Woman (moon?) is our mother. We pray to them and they prevent us from telling you the full story at this time of the year." [7]

Among the Naga to see the Sun in a dream foretold the death of a parent.[8] The Sun does not only appear as father symbol since, " in dreams, myths, and similar material, we find the image of the sun used to symbolize the eye, the father, or the phallus."[9] In the Andaman Islands among

[1] Elsdon Best, " Omens and Superstitious Beliefs of the Maori— Omens derived from Dreams," *J. of Polynesian Society*, Vol. VII, No. 27, Sept. 1898, p. 124 *seq.*
[2] Part III, p. 323.   [3] Part III, pp. 298, 301–3.
[4] S. Freud, *previous cit.*, p. 245.   [5] Part III, p. 323.
[6] C. F. Oldham, *The Sun and the Serpent*, pp. 203–5.
[7] Part III, p. 213.
[8] J. H. Hutton, unpublished note to Prof. Seligman.
[9] E. Jones, " The Theory of Symbolism," *Papers on Psychoanalysis*, p. 199.

some groups, the Sun is regarded as female and the Moon as male which is probably a reversal of the general tendency.[1] Among the Omaha sky is a father symbol.[2] In the Navajo myth of Sontso, or the Big Star, the personified " Black Star " is called father.[3] Likewise in China, " Sickness and death to the parents of those who dream of the setting of Sun and Moon." [4]

All of the above appear also in the dreams of whites undergoing analysis as father symbols, namely, kings, chiefs, authorities, animals, monsters, spirits and constellations. The symbols seem to vary according to environment and the reality experience in the external world, but only sufficiently for the mind to use an available object most appropriate to the primary idea,[5] which the symbols represent. Such available objects are supplied by nature and existing culture, or were handed down by cultural tradition which forms part of the individual's experience. No evidence exists to show that the symbols are in any way mentally inherited or formed other than through the individual's reactions to his environment and cultural heritage. Since father symbols are images representing the father, individuals could not have been born with them or have acquired them without experience of a real or " substitute " father. If this is the true situation, cultural tradition sufficiently cancels all need of the racial memory postulate.

2. *Mother* is often symbolized by Queen and Empress in dreams. Sea, church, earth, cave and moon are also common. Among primitives, mother symbols seem much

[1] Radcliffe-Brown, *The Andaman Islands*, pp. 141–2.

[2] R. F. Fortune, " Omaha Secret Societies," *Columbia Univ. Contributions to Anthropology*, Vol. XIV, 1932, p. 48.

[3] Miss M. Wheelwright, *The Myth of Sontso* (unpub.).

[4] *Chow Kung's Book of Dreams*, No. 9.

[5] See preceding chap., p. 57, for myth-vision origin of the Tsimshian Bear Totem. It is a good example of how an external object becomes a symbol which acquires emotional significance individually and socially.

more difficult to detect than father symbols, possibly because of deeper repression with regard to incestuous tendencies which explains the lack of spontaneous associations among the material recorded. There are many cases where parents are dreamed of directly without symbolization.[1] Old woman seems to be quite common as a thinly disguised mother symbol. It occurs in Australian myth [2] and among the Crow and Blackfoot of North America.[3] The earth as mother symbol is of course widespread in myth and folk-lore,[4] the following being an especially good example from the founder of an American Indian messianic cult, " Smohalla, the Prophet of the Columbia River Basin " (1870) [5] :

" My young men shall never work. Men who work can not dream, and wisdom comes to us in dreams. You ask me to plow the ground. Shall I take a knife and tear my mother's bosom ? You ask me to dig for stone. Shall I dig under her skin for her bones ? You ask me to cut grass and make hay and sell it and be rich like white men. But how dare I cut off my mother's hair ? "

There do not seem to be the totemic parallels for mother as there is for father, although in some guardian spirit dreams the mother often appears and confers powers along with the father,[6] however, she is not usually symbolized by the same animals and monsters as the father. The difficulty in acquiring data on mother symbols at least in dreams may be caused by the same situation which led Mrs. Seligman to conclude that the mother-son relation in primitive society presents no social problem and as an incest prohibition is less important than that between

[1] Part III (Navajo, Woodlands). Although there may be less repression in general among primitives, incestuous tendencies are probably more deeply repressed than any others.
[2] Roheim, *op. cit.*, p. 135.   [3] Part III, pp. 249–65.
[4] Jones, *op. cit.*, p. 178.
[5] *14th Annual Rep. B.A.E.*, 1892–3, p. 716.
[6] Part III, Blackfoot, pp. 258–63.

brother and sister.[1] Malinowski also believes that mother-son incest tendencies are of no importance or non-existent among the Trobrianders.[2] My own opinion is that the incestuous relation to the mother is more deeply repressed and would be regarded as the greatest crime, hence the difficulty in detecting it without psychological analysis of primitive dreams. Mrs. Seligman's work was written, however, prior to Roheim's analysis of Australian dreams in which the parent child incestuous tie is shown to exist in the unconscious.[3]

Moon as mother symbol is very widespread, occurring often in North America also, among the Sioux, Navajo, Blackfoot and Omaha.[4]

One of the Navajo deities is a bisexual character who can be regarded as a composite parent symbol for " in the Hotchonji ceremony the prayer goes down to the lower world and evil spirits as well as up to *Begochiddy* whose name means the love of a mother for her child and her milk ; although he is a man." [5]

3. *Phallus* is symbolized in analysed dreams by elongated objects such as sticks, tree trunks, umbrellas, weapons, knives, daggers, pikes, etc. It would be an endless task to find out whether among primitives every elongated object in a dream means a phallus, but scattered examples corroborate the tendency, and there is no reason to suppose that everywhere it would not be the same. Snake, child and relatives are usual symbols for phallus according to Freud, and all complicated machines and apparatus often represent the genitals. Demons in cloaks are also phallic symbols.

[1] Brenda Z. Seligman, " The Incest Barrier ; Its Rôle in Social Organization," *Br. J. of Psychology*, Genl. Sect., Vol. XXII, Part 3, Jan. 1932.

[2] Malinowski, *Sex and Repression in Savage Society*, pp. 95, 245 *seq*., 52, 271, 277.

[3] Roheim, " Women and their Life in Central Australia," *J. of Royal Anth. Inst.*, Vol. LXIII, 1933, Jan.–June.

[4] Part III and p. 170, Ref. 5.

[5] Miss Mary Wheelwright, unpublished material, Part III, p. 214.

Among primitives a few of the elongated objects which are definitely phallic symbols, either from association or by the use of the object in an unmistakably sexual manner, are arrow, gun barrel, tree, snake, among the American Indians [1]; spear, stone knife (used in ceremonial defloration), among the Australians [2]; snake and spear among the Kiwai and Melanesians of New Guinea [3]; carved door-post amongst the Naga.[4] A portion of a Naga dream and association illustrates the latter :

" Then I found myself in my house with my family. We all sat around the fire. There was a sudden gale of wind. I held the post fearing my house would be blown over. The gale stopped. I looked at all my posts and especially at the carved one in front of the door, and said ' If it had not been for this post my house would have fallen and I should have had a lot of trouble.' "

To " post " he associates, " No post fell so no important member of my clan will die. The excellence and strength of my carved post means I shall have fine sons and daughters."

Of a similar nature is this example from the class of dreams peculiar to women among the Menomini Indians, those of social preferment, or of brave sons, or of many children. " One may dream of a tall pole with a flag at the top. This is a sign that she will marry a chief's son." [5]

Among the Bantu Fan, the name of a fetish stone, which means, " the girl is no longer a virgin," shows it to be a phallic symbol.[6]

Façades of houses, complicated apparatus,[7] demons in cloaks, cravats, women's hats, all phallic symbols according

---

[1] Part III. [2] Roheim, *op. cit.*, pp. 234, 247.
[3] G. Landtman, *Folk Tales of the Kiwai Papuans*, Nos. 366, 390 ; C. G. Seligman, *Melanesians of Br. New Guinea*, p. 382, Story 4.
[4] Naga Hills, Dream of Lhuzekhu, a Sema of Bamhio, Prof. Seligman, unpub. material.
[5] Part III, p. 269. [6] See p. 161 and p. 166, Note 4.
[7] The Kwakiutl belief recorded on p. 301, paragraph 403, shows that a hunter's trap is a phallic symbol. If he dreams that a woman accepts his love, his trap will kill game.

to Freud, undoubtedly would occur in primitive dreams where white civilization adds its own items to the manifest content. It is impossible to say, without further analytic research, if these would signify male organs to primitives. The American Indians dream of automobiles,[1] aeroplanes, civilized clothing, and items of white culture. Since the unconscious mind sees only similarities and never differences, these objects are probably assimilated and condensed with previous images, which are similar in form and meaning to the unconscious mind. Examples of child as a phallic representation are given in the Australian dreams analysed by Roheim, where the condensation of father, child and phallus seems to occur,[2] and probably in some of the tooth dreams mentioned farther on.[3]

4. The *female genitals* and *womb* are symbolized by little cases, boxes, caskets, stoves, rooms, tables, boards, landscapes, wooded mountains and caves, as well as by all narrow alleys, spaces and entrances, and by locked doors. Again, all these must occur in the dreams of primitives everywhere, but lack of individual associations makes it impossible in most cases to do more than make arbitrary interpretations based on the assumption that the mind is the same everywhere. Freud has warned especially against doing this because of the impossibility of giving unambiguous interpretations. A good example of box as a womb symbol occurs in a Kwakiutl legend. The wooden box has many uses among these people including cooking, and " burying " their dead in wooden boxes hung up in trees. In the legend, the Sun is shut up in a box by " Day-Receptacle—Woman " who later gives birth to him along with the masks of daybreak and the cedar bark which have been shut up in the box with the Sun. The legend is to explain the origin of the daybreak mask.[4]

[1] See Chap. IV, pp. 177–8.   [2] Roheim, *op. cit.*, p. 241 *seq.*
[3] This chapter, pp. 129–31 ; pp. 140–1.
[4] F. Boas, *Social Organization and Secret Societies of the Kwakiutl Indians*, Report of the U.S. National Museum for 1895, p. 324.

There are many ancient Greek myths as well as tales from New Zealand and from India in which box symbolizes the womb, and in some the box is also represented by cave.[1]

5. *Birth.* Water dreams often mean pregnancy. In mythology as well as dreams the delivery of a child from the uterine waters is often represented by the entry of the child into water, as in the births of Adonis, Osiris, Moses and Bacchus.[2] Examples of water dreams meaning birth are given by Freud,[3] and Rank has given examples from mythology.[4] The latter calls attention to the fact that the Chaldeans " correctly interpreted these water dreams as birth dreams," and he also places food myths in the same category.

One primitive parallel is from the Dagomba of Africa, among whom there exists the belief that to dream of one's wife carrying water on the head means she will soon have a child.[5]

In Nyasaland tribes to dream of water or flood might mean that the dreamer's wife was commencing her period,[6] and in North America there is often a close parallelism between the observances of menstruation and of childbirth, as also seems to be the case among the Lapps.[7]

Among the Kwakiutl Indians, a dream of the late mother who advises a ceremonial purification after which the dreamer goes immediately into the water might be regarded as a birth dream or an incest dream. Mother and water are associated.[8]

[1] O. Rank, " The Myth of the Birth of the Hero," *Nervous and Mental Disease Monograph Series*, No. 18, 1914, p. 70, and Note 66.

[2] S. Freud, *The Interpretation of Dreams*, p. 244.

[3] *Ibid.*, p. 243.   [4] Rank, *op. cit.*, p. 71.

[5] A. W. Cardinall, " Dreams among the Dagomba and Moshi," *Man*, May 1927, pp. 87–8.

[6] A. G. O. Hodgson, " Dreams in Central Africa," *Man*, April 1926, pp. 66–8.

[7] R. H. Lowie, " Religious Ideas and Practices," *Essays Presented to C. G. Seligman*, p. 186.

[8] Part III, p. 313, No. 43.

Among the Polynesian Tikopia, " A woman dreams that she goes to the stream, fills her water-bottles and puts them in a kit on her back. It is believed that this indicates she will conceive and bear a girl-child." Dreams of sea fishing also portend conception of children.[1]

6. *Death.* As one of the type of dreams that have the same meaning every time, Freud mentions those of departure. Departure, he says, is the most frequent symbol of death.

Among the Navajo, one of my informants said he often dreamed of rattlesnakes biting him. " When Navajos dream that, it means they are going far away." [2] Obviously, the interpretation holds here also. An Ottawa Indian believed that a dream of his wife leaving him meant death.[3]

In Ancient Egypt to dream of seeing people afar off is bad, the dreamer's death is at hand.[4]

7. *Nightmares* or severe anxiety dreams are very common among primitives. Analysed dreams of this sort of non-primitives show the latent cause to be strongly repressed incest or other culturally unacceptable forms of sexuality.[5] Whether this holds among primitives is impossible to say without individual analysis and associations of such dreams. The following are some examples of this type of dream ; classed as nightmares by their recorders. Most of them show violent conflicts with spirits or dead relatives who chase and pursue the dreamer :

From the Kiwai of New Guinea.[6] (By Sáibu, Mawáta :) " One night a dead man named Kogéa came to Sáibu and said, ' You me (we) go coconut-place,' and they went together. When they arrived there Kogéa asked Sáibu to climb up a tree and fetch

[1] R. Firth, "Meaning of Dreams in Tikopia," *Essays Presented to C. G. Seligman,* p. 68.

[2] Part III, p. 229, R.T., No. 3.   [3] Part III, p. 280, No. 14.

[4] A. Gardiner, Translation of Egyptian Dream Papyrus. See p. 108, Ref. 6 (18-9, 1).

[5] E. Jones, *On the Nightmare.*

[6] G. Landtman, *Folk-tales of the Kiwai Papuans,* Nos. 101, 391, 392, 393, 394, 395, 398.

down some nuts. Sáibu did not want to but yielded at last. When he came down Kogéa wanted him to husk the coconuts, but as Sáibu was not willing, he did it himself. He sent Sáibu to a certain tree near by, where he found Kogéa's father Obéra, who was also dead. The two spirits met, and the old man said, 'You me (we) kill that man.' Obéra attacked Sáibu with a firebrand which he thrust against Sáibu's chest, while Kogéa tried to stab him with a sharp bone, and the terrified Sáibu fell on his back striking out with his hands and feet and whining in his dream, ' E-e-e ! ' Suddenly he woke up shrieking loudly, ' Ey-ey-ey ! ' and everybody in the house called out to him, ' What's the matter you, Sáibu ? ' "

(By Bíri, Ipisía :) " On relating the dream he was shuddering at the unpleasant experience he had had while dreaming. A large snake had been killed in the village on the previous day, and Bíri dreamed that it was still alive and chased him away to a dark place where he had never been before. He met some strange people there whom he could not see, only hear. Very much frightened he wanted them to light a fire, but they would not do so. They brought him a great quantity of some kind of food with an abominable smell and taste like excrements, and commanded him to eat it. Bíri did not dare refuse, and vomited again and again. At first he did so at ' that place ' (where he believed himself to have been in the dream), and he continued to be sick in his house after awakening."

(By Káku, Ipisía :) " He saw people without heads coming up from the water, and the first of them was an Auti man who had died when Káku was a boy. The man wanted to tell Káku something, but the latter was so frightened that he woke up, and although it was a long while till morning he sat up all the rest of the night for fear of dreaming the same thing again."

(By Gaméa, Mawáta :) " A man named Káiri dreamt that another man named Kesáve was attacked by a wild pig which gored him in the body so that the intestines ran out. Kesáve came crawling to the place where the people were. The intestines were put back into the belly, and the wound was closed up. Kesáve got up, but after a while his stomach began to swell out more and more, till Káiri became so frightened that he woke up."

(By Menégi, Mawáta :) " He was attacked by a ' bushman '

and tried to defend himself, but neither arrow, spear nor axe did the man any harm. Menégi got away into the water. After a while the ' bushman ' came for him again in the shape of a pig. Just as he was about to catch Menégi in the water, the latter woke up."

(By Gágu, Mawáta :) " He was caught by some ' bushmen ' who wanted to take out his intestines and put in those of kangaroo instead, as is their method of performing mauamo (sorcery), a kind of sorcery. They were already placing the point of a knife against his stomach, when he woke up screaming." [1]

(By Gibúma, Mawáta :) The " vagina dentata " dream previously recorded. [2]

From the African Moshi. The following are three nightmares of a small boy who slept near the recorder :

(1) He was being chased by a man with a head like a frog who smelled horribly and who shouted at him.

(2) He was asleep with a dead man alongside him.

(3) He was chased by a lion. He had never seen one, but a few days before he had seen a new skin.

Older boys said the dreams meant nothing, but were inspired by the *Chichirigi* who are responsible for all forms of night pollutions. [3]

Since lion and animal headed man have been shown often to be father symbols in Africa, these dreams are obviously the same as those father pursuing dreams mentioned by Freud. [4]

Among the Navajo. I have recorded sixteen anxiety dreams of pursuit or trying to escape from chasing spirits. They follow the same patterns as the above. [5]

From the *Solomon Islands.* The following are another group of the same type of anxiety dreams in which spirits chase and frighten the dreamer. [6]

[1] G. Landtman, *op. cit.*　　　[2] p. 109, this chapter.
[3] A. W. Cardinall, " Dreams Among the Dagomba and Moshi," *Man,* May 1927, pp. 87–8.
[4] S. Freud, *The Interpretation of Dreams,* p. 245.
[5] Part III, p. 245.　　　[6] Blackwood, B., cit. on p. 41 (unpub.).

Rus (*Adult female*).

" I dreamed an *urar* seized me by the leg, and I was very frightened. This is a bad dream."

Nawi. (*Adolescent girl, aged about* 12.)

" I dreamed about an *urar*, it ran after me, and I was frightened, and I cried, and I fell down from a tree, and I ran away. My mother cried because of the *urar*, she thought it would eat me, so she cried about me. Then I went to sleep in the dark. This is a bad dream. When I woke up I felt frightened."

Tsikul. (*Adolescent boy, aged about* 14–15.)

" I dreamed about *urar*, we saw a lot of them coming towards the village. Then Tchub saw Talok, and said to him : ' Who is there,' Talok said : ' It is I.' Then we went inside a house, a house belonging to the *urar*, and stayed there, and the *urar* came up, and we saw them coming along the road. Then I said : ' Here are the *urar* coming along the road.' We were all afraid of them, the boys said : ' The *urar* want to eat us, we are afraid of them.' Then we said to them : ' You go back to your own place, and we will stay in our own place.' Then we saw a lot of *urar* and we all ran away and went inside a house. Then a dog cried out and barked at the *urar* in the bush, and Maniu went out and said : ' What are the dogs barking at ? ' We said to him : ' You go and see.' Then he said : ' There are *urar* here.' He saw them, and ran away, and ran inside the house. Then we saw the *urar* standing in the bush, and we said : ' I think they are real man.' Then Tchub looked round the village, and all the *urar* came up, and he called out : ' A lot of *urar*.' Tchub called out to the *urar*, and they ran away and went back to the bush, and we all ran back to the village, and we talked about the *urar* : ' Presently they will come back and eat us.' Then we lay down inside the house, we were afraid, and we lay down in the house. Then some people called out to us : ' You come out on the other side of the house.' We were asleep, but we got up and went out on the other side. Then the *urar* very nearly caught us and ate us. Then we called out to them, and said : ' You go back to your own place, what are you doing in our village ? This place belongs to us, your place is a long way off. We can't go to your place, it is a bad place, our place is a good place, there is plenty to eat here.'

We said to the *urar* : ' You go back to your own place, and we
will stay in our place, our nice village, not a bad place like
yours.' Then we went to sleep, and the *urar* went away, but
one *urar* stayed behind, on the front verandah, our front verandah, and we asked him : ' Who is there ? ' He said : ' It
is I, an *urar*. You come here, you come out on the other side.'
Then one man wanted to relieve himself, and the *urar* caught
him and took him to his hole. This is a bad dream, I was
frightened."

So far many symbols are found to occur with the same
latent meaning among primitives and non-primitives, and
we have merely extended somewhat what Jones has said on
phylogenetic parallels namely, that,

" One of the most amazing features of true symbolism is the
remarkable ubiquity of the same symbols, which are to be found,
not only in different fields of thought, dreams, wit, insanity,
poetry, etc., among a given class and at a given level of civilization, but among different races and at different epochs of the
world's history. A symbol which to-day we find, for instance,
in an obscene joke is also to be found in a mythical cult of
Ancient Greece, and another that we come across only in dream
analysis was used thousands of years ago in the sacred books
of the East. The following examples may be quoted in illustration of this correspondence. The idea of teeth, in dreams,
is often symbolically related to that of child-birth, a connection
that is hardly ever found in consciousness ; in the Song of Songs
we read : ' Thy teeth are as a flock of sheep which go up from
the washing, whereof everyone beareth twins, and there is not
one barren among them.' The idea of snake, which is never
consciously associated with that of the phallus, is regularly so
in dreams, being one of the most constant and invariable symbols
in primitive religions ; the two ideas are quite obviously inter-
changeable, so that it is often hard to distinguish phallic from
ophitic worship ; many traces of this are to be found even in
the Old Testament." [1] [2]

[1] E. Jones, " The Theory of Symbolism," *op. cit.*, p. 168.
[2] *Note.*—For a bibliography of works on symbolism, primitive and
otherwise, see Jones, *ibid.*, p. 169.

Further proof of the ubiquity of the same symbols occurs in a most interesting study of dream interpretations from Central Africa (information from ten headmen of Nyasaland) compared with the interpretations of the same subjects by Artemidorus of Ephesos of the second century A.D., a professional dream interpreter. These comparisons reveal some remarkable parallels in many cases.[1]

(1) *In Central Africa, flying dreams* mean *long life and good health*. In *Artemidorus*, the interpretations of such dreams is that it is unlucky to wish to be able to fly but not to be able to do so. Other such dreams are *lucky* but do not signify long life.

(2) *In Central Africa*, to *dream of fire* burning means *misfortune*. A great bush fire means *war*. In *Artemidorus, fire* in the sky meant *war* or *famine*.

(3) *In Central Africa*, to dream of *climbing a tree or a hill* means *promotion* to chieftainship or higher rank. In *Artemidorus*, to dream of going *downstairs* meant *demotion*.

(4) In *Central Africa, loss of a tooth* means the dreamer will *lose* a wife, a *child* or a near *relation*. In *Artemidorus*, to dream of the *loss of a tooth* meant to *lose a member of one's household*. *Teeth* were also connected *with children* ; to dream of holding *teeth fallen* from one's mouth meant the *loss of children* by *death* or otherwise.

(5) " Œdipus " dreams in *Central Africa*, that is connection with the mother or sister in a dream, means the dreamer is being bewitched by an unknown person. He (the dreamer) may procure medicine to put in his house to catch his enemy. Usually he is too ashamed to take any action or to mention the matter.

" Such dreams occur in *Artemidorus* but their significance is quite different."

(6) A *flood or river* dream in *Central Africa* means *misfortune* or a *law suit*, one informant (same as for 4) said it might

---

[1] A. G. O. Hodgson, " Dreams in Central Africa," *Man*, April 1926, pp. 66–8 ; H. J. Rose, " Central Africa and Artemidorus," *Man*, 1926, p. 211.

also mean the dreamer's wife was commencing her period.

In *Artemidorus* such dreams meant an *unfriendly jury*, or ill-tempered masters, etc.

(7) In *Central Africa*, a dream of illness or death means recovery; in *Artemidorus* "if a rich person dreams he is dead he will be rid of his illness."

(8) In *Central Africa*, a dream of frequent occurrence is that of being *chased downhill by a lion*, the common " symbol " for *chieftainship*. If the dreamer escapes he will become a chief or rise to importance ; if seized by a *lion* it means a *chief* is plotting against him.

In *Artemidorus*, a *lion* dream might mean the *emperor or king*, and to be chased by a *bull* meant great danger and threats by *men of high estate*.

(13) In *Central Africa*, to dream of *a snake round one's leg* means the dreamer will be *bound in prison* or in former times was a *slave*.

In *Artemidorus*, if a *dragon wraps itself around* one it signifies *bondage*.

(16) To dream of a *hearth stone in Central Africa* means one will see a *chief*.

In *Artemidorus*, if the *Hearth Goddess*, Hestia, is seen in a dream by a *king*, it signifies *his power*.

(18) In *Central Africa* to dream of *catching fish* means *money*.

In *Artemidorus*, if *fish* are slippery the dreamer will not be able to keep the *money* which will be lost or stolen.

As pointed out by Rose in these parallels, Artemidorus obviously had not studied the customs of Central Africa, and the people from the latter had not read the former's book. These instances, therefore, show how the human mind tends always and everywhere to think alike. Hence extreme caution must be used in accepting diffusionist views.

Besides showing that the mind everywhere tends to think alike, the above shows just how it thinks alike. The same applies to Professor Seligman's study of universal type dreams,[1] which are interpreted similarly in many widespread places. What is especially interesting is how, in different places, the same interpretations of the same symbols are made, not by revealing the unconscious primary idea represented by the symbol, but by giving another symbol nearer associatively to the primary idea than the one in the manifest content of the dream.

For instance, I have already given examples in Africa in which lion and chief are both father symbols. Thus, father is the primary idea behind both symbols. Yet in Central Africa and in Artemidorus dream interpretations, lion is interpreted as chief and as emperor respectively, the latter two being father symbols and nearer associatively, because of greater similarity to the primary idea of father, than is lion. I have regarded all symbols as " secondary " for the sake of convenience, whether they are associatively close to or distant from the idea or object symbolized. In this way it is easier to avoid confusing symbols and primary ideas, all of which are often condensed in dreams. The above parallels in interpretation and the " type " interpretations, therefore, show the same associative paths with the same symbols of the same primary ideas, arranged in the same order of association or similarity, with each interpretation approaching more closely to the primary meaning, without quite disclosing the primary idea itself.

To illustrate further, the tooth-losing dream was found by Professor Seligman to be practically universal and interpreted almost everywhere as meaning loss of a close relative or friend. Relative is thus a representation of tooth, and if the present theory of symbolism is correct, the former must be closer to the primary idea symbolized than is tooth. In the Central Africa—Artemidorus parallels, tooth, child

[1] C. G. Seligman, " Anthropology and Psychology," *J. of Roy. Anth. Inst.*, Vol. LIV, 1924, p. 37 *seq.* ; " The Unconscious in Relation to Anthropology," *Br. J. of Psychology*, Vol. XVIII, Part 4, 1928, pp. 374–87.

and relative are associated, as are tooth-losing and death. In European dreams analysed the ideas of tooth, child, relative, and male genital are often found to be unconsciously associated, male genital being the primary idea symbolized by the others and uncovered by analysis. Fear of losing a tooth in analysis has repeatedly been found to mean fear of castration.[1] Here also the ideas of tooth-losing, castration and death are all found associated in analysis, the latter two often being unconsciously regarded as identical. The secondary symbols occur in the Central Africa—Artemidorus parallels,[2] and in the universal type dreams in the order of,

tooth-losing—loss of a close relative or friend—death
and
tooth—relative—child

and occur also in the same sequence or in condensed imagery in analysis, which, however, carries the process one step further by uncovering also the primary ideas of " phallus " behind the symbols " tooth," " relative," " child " ; and " castration " behind the symbols " loss of a tooth," " loss of a close relative." It can, therefore, logically be assumed that wherever the same group of symbols occur associated together, analysis would uncover the same primary ideas behind them.[3] Added corrobora-

[1] According to Freud loss of a tooth in a woman's dream can also mean deliverance, because tooth and child are often associated, both being phallic symbols.

[2] Rose agrees with Prof. Seligman (unpublished letter) that the interpretations of Artemidorus apart from the dreams themselves do not necessarily represent any phenomena of the unconscious, but are the reflections of Artemidorus himself. It seems, however, that since the interpretations in many cases are exactly paralleled in Central Africa, they are more in the nature of spontaneous associations, and hence are expressions of the " secondary " aspects of the unconscious, i.e. symbolism.

[3] Precisely the same group of associated ideas occur among the Navajo where dreams of *death* of the self, neighbours, or *relatives*, and dreams of *loss of a tooth* require the curing Ceremony of Restoration (*Hozhonji*), (Part III, p. 208, IV).

tion is given to the discoveries of analysis with regard to primary ideas by those instances where the primary ideas are shown undisguised or directly stated in association or interpretation, such as I have shown for those examples among primitives where the primary ideas of father, mother, phallus, womb, birth and death are clearly revealed behind their various symbols. It would not, therefore, be surprising to find also the same primary ideas behind the tooth symbolism of primitives, as with non-primitives.[1]

[1] See ref. to Freud, Part I, p. 13, on verifying the meaning of symbols through hypnosis.

CHAPTER IV

"NUCLEAR COMPLEXES" IN PRIMITIVE CULTURES; THEIR DISCOVERY THROUGH ANALYSIS OF DREAM SYMBOLS

ANTHROPOLOGISTS still ask for the evidences of the "Œdipus" and "castration complexes" in primitive culture. Analysts have found that the primary ideas of the unconscious tend to occur typically as a nucleus of wishes centred in the universal bilateral family or (father-mother-child) relationship.[1] This nucleus comprising the "Œdipus and castration complexes" consists of incestuous desires for the mother, parricidal wishes towards the father, guilt feelings and consequent expectation of punishment in the form of castration. This complex is often reversed and occurs in many forms and combinations.[2] That these complexes or unconscious fantasies occur in every case analysed as vestiges from childhood unconscious thinking is amply proved and recorded in psychoanalytic literature, and any person seriously wanting proof has but to consult the literature or make an individual investigation of unconscious processes himself. All this applies to non-primitives.

In *Totem and Taboo*, Freud has made this nuclear family complex the motive force from which all human interest and culture is derived. Because many of his conclusions were based on the early investigators, Robertson Smith and Atkinson, who are no longer accepted as valid by

[1] Lowie, Malinowski.—Both believe in the universality of the bilateral family.

[2] For convenient list of forms and combinations of this complex, see Money-Kyrle, *The Meaning of Sacrifice*, pp. 213, 214 *seq.*

anthropologists, the tendency was to pass over this work as unimportant. What may turn out, however, is that his conclusions are correct with regard to the psychological basis of many elements of totemism, and the family relationship, and other cultural phenomena, in spite of Robertson Smith and Atkinson. The latter need not stand in the way of testing Freud's conclusions by searching for evidences of the nuclear complexes among the accepted facts of primitive culture instead of among unscientific authors.

Professor A. L. Kroeber has critically reviewed Freud's *Totem and Taboo*.[1] His criticism successfully destroys much of the hypothetical foundation on which Freud's main thesis is constructed ; the thesis itself, however, is left just where it was, namely, that the beginnings of religion, ethics, society and art meet in the Œdipus complex. Some of the hypothetical points which Kroeber successfully refutes are the Darwin-Atkinson theory of the Cyclopean family which is a pure guess without any proof whatsoever ; the idea that blood sacrifice is central for every ancient cult (according to Robertson Smith) since it only holds for Mediterranean cultures of the last 2000 years B.C., and the cultures influenced by the latter. He also shows that it is highly problematic that blood sacrifice is totemic ; that it is not established that exogamy and totem abstinence are the two fundamental prohibitions of totemism ; and that the statement that these two taboos are the oldest is pure assertion.

Kroeber, however, believes the work to be an important and valuable contribution, especially with regard to the correspondences between taboo customs and compulsion neurosis, and the parallels between the two aspects of totemism and the "ambivalence" of emotion in neurotics, and with regard to the "omnipotence of thought" in animism and magic. He had reluctantly to admit that ethnology can never free itself from the psychology that underlies it, and his remarks on how primitive societies have institution-

---

[1] A. L. Kroeber, "Totem and Taboo : An Ethnologic Psychoanalysis," *American Anthropologist*, Vol. 22 (1920), pp. 48–55.

alized such impulses as with us lead to neuroses are most apt.[1] Among primitives, he says :

" The individual of neurotic tendency finds an approved and therefore harmless outlet in taboo, magic, myth, and the like, whereas the non-neurotic, who at heart remains attached to reality, accepts these activities as forms which do not seriously disturb him." [2]

After stating that Freud brings " a point of view which henceforth can never be ignored without stultification," [3] and characterizing Frazer's efforts on which Freud relies considerably, as " prevailingly dilettantish playing," [4] he concludes with a plea for historical ethnology whose existence should be known by psychoanalysts.

All this review still leaves the way open, however, for testing whether the Œdipus complex does or does not pertain to the psychology which underlies ethnology.

This work of Freud's has also been criticized by Goldenweiser on the same points, and especially on Freud's assumption of a mass psyche or an inherited racial unconscious as the carrier of the Œdipus complex throughout the ages.[5] I agree that this also is pure assumption with no known proofs. What would seem more plausible, if the universality of the Œdipus complex is a fact, is that the individual recreation of this complex in relation to the family group, and cultural tradition, are the two factors which explain its continuity in ontogeny and in phylogeny.

It is certainly unfortunate that Freud's great discovery which has been so completely corroborated in the analysis of modern individuals should be applied in other domains

---

[1] Mrs. Seligman also recognizes how much of primitive ritual, " which gives full scope to the divided personality of its leaders, fulfils the function of releasing emotion into socially recognized channels, thus preventing individuals from discharging it erratically or anti-socially." (Brenda Z. Seligman, " The Unconscious in Social Heritage," *Essays Presented to C. G. Seligman*, pp. 313.)

[2] Kroeber, *op. cit.*, p. 54.   [3] *Ibid.*, p. 53.   [4] *Ibid.*

[5] A. Goldenweiser, *History, Psychology and Culture*, pp. 206-7.

of thought with so little regard to known facts, and on such shaky hypothetical foundations.

Mrs. Seligman, on the other hand, says of Freud's contributions,

" But the greatest gain of all was the discovery of the ever-present incest conflict within the family group of the civilized. As a nuclear complex—the legacy of a bygone drama enacted in the dim past—it has little interest, but as an ever-present problem for which some solution must be reached in every type of culture the idea of persistent incest conflict is most stimulating. We are thus directly indebted to the psychoanalysts for demonstrating that the behaviour towards near relatives is one that every individual has to learn during infancy and childhood, that it is compounded of conflicting emotions of love, hate, and revolt against power, and that successful solution makes the individual a normal member of society, failure an outcast either emotionally or morally. If this is so in Western European civilization, with its rich social heritage, its religious and legal sanctions, it is small wonder that savage man goes to great lengths in order to solve the problems that are involved." [1]

The only person who to any extent as a trained anthropologist, and a trained psychoanalyst, has given evidences of the nuclear complex in primitive life, is Roheim. He states that the universal fundamental psychic material of culture consists of the " Œdipus complex," and " castration anxiety." [2] This may be quite true, but it has never been proved to the satisfaction of other anthropologists. In view of the alleged momentous significance of these psychic forces in the formation of culture patterns, the anthropologist, however, must either establish their significance or disprove them entirely. For the sake of scientific honesty

[1] Brenda Z. Seligman, " The Incest Barrier : Its Rôle in Social Organization " (*Br. J. of Psychology*, Genl. Sect., Vol. XXII, Part 3, Jan. 1932, p. 253).
[2] Roheim, " Psycho-Analysis of Primitive Cultural Types " (*International J. of Psychoanalysis*, Vol. XIII, Parts 1 and 2, Jan.–April 1932, pp. 196–8).

alone he cannot ignore them, however unpleasant they may be to his cultural point of view, i.e. his "cultural compulsive," or however much they may upset his pre-existing ethnological theories. Roheim has shown that these nuclei exist among Australians in individual dreams, and form the basis of Australian totemism.[1] The facts are there, but lack of separation of data and interpretation makes his work lose the force that it might otherwise have.

Since a study of some of the symbols occurring in primitive life has shown them to represent the same primary ideas as elsewhere, a discovery of the nuclear complexes as constellations of these primary ideas should be facilitated. Repression among primitives may be less deep than among ourselves, nevertheless, a tendency such as incest is the most deeply repressed of all, hence it is the most difficult to detect in spite of symbols whose meaning is known or inferred from association or story. Also primitives are most reluctant and ashamed to refer to such subjects. This being the case, it will be necessary to go largely by the symbols whose meanings, individual or collective, are either known or clearly inferable from other known facts. It will not be possible to find in every case a complete " Œdipus " and " castration " nucleus expressed, but often only parts of these ; hence I shall split up the components as follows and treat them separately :

(1) *Incestuous desires*, for mother, sister, or any relatives who stand in the same kinship relations as these ; these primary ideas should be represented in dreams or elsewhere by any mother symbol.

(2) *Parricidal tendencies*, or death wishes towards the father, including conflicts with and escapes from the father, represented by chief, king, totem animal, spirit or ancestor, occurring in any known symbolic form in dreams, and indicated as well in all dreams and visions in which guilt feelings and attempts to appease or secure favours from supernatural beings who are regarded by the native as father or authority.

[1] Roheim, *Social Anthropology.*

(3) Anxiety or fear of punishment by the father and " *castration complexes* " may be expected to be represented by mutilation fantasies and customs and uncovered by analysis of symbols and associations similar to those known to represent this " complex," among non-primitives.

Thus, these tendencies may be discovered, wherever they exist in the individual or in cultural form by a reasonably secure knowledge of the true meaning of the symbols which represent the primary ideas of father, mother, phallus and death.

It can be stated that dread of incest is obviously the most widespread primitive fear on which is built up all the various incest prohibitions. As Mrs. Seligman has shown, " the family, the first human group, became consolidated by the acceptance of incest barriers, and the family group is the pattern on which all other groups are formed, namely, the clan and the classificatory system of relationship, and the seven methods of reckoning descent, all of which are extensions of the two primary incest prohibitions, that between parent and child and that between brother and sister." [1] Hence behind these barriers the incest tendency must still exist in the unconscious otherwise there would be no need for the barriers.[2]

The records are very meagre on these subjects, as far as dreams are concerned, nevertheless, a few cases among a people are sufficient proof to show the existence of a tendency.

In Africa, among the Ba-Kaonde, the word, " Chimalwamalwa " means, " the fear of death caused by committing

[1] Brenda Z. Seligman, *op. cit.*, p. 276.

[2] See also Mrs. Seligman's reply to Westermarck and others on incest aversion, which she regards as the negative expression of a corresponding desire for the forbidden thing. Little indication of mother-son incest is found in social behaviour of primitives, although it is not denied as a psychological tendency, whereas brother-sister, and father-daughter incest belong to both the domains of social behaviour as well as psychological tendency.—Brenda Z. Seligman, " The Incest Taboo," *The Sociological Review*, Jan. 1935, Vol. XXVII, No. 1.

incest." If a man commits incest he gets " *chimalwamalwa*," because he aroused the spirit of the first incest sinner. This example alone suggests that the whole nuclear Œdipus complex is a tribal fact expressed in one word in which practically the whole constellation of ideas exists.[1]

Among the Kaonde also are reported dreams of committing incest, but no explanation, association or interpretation is given.[2]

In Nyasaland connection with mother or sister in a dream means the dreamer is being bewitched by an unknown person ; usually he is too ashamed to take any action or to mention the matter.[3]

As mentioned before, " Œdipus " dreams are also recorded in Artemidorus.[4]

From Ancient Egypt come records of undisguised incest dreams with the mother. This is to be expected here because of absence of incest prohibitions,[5] at least among royalty.

In the Talmud, dreaming of having poured the oil of the olive-tree on the tree means the dreamer has had intercourse with his mother ; if he dreams that his eyes touch each other, it means that he has done the same with his sister.[6]

Purificatory ceremonies after dreams of intercourse with mother or sister are recorded from the Yagaddeva.[7]

An abnormal tie to the mother is recorded in a dream of a Jakun man of Nigeria already mentioned.[8]

[1] C. G. Seligman, " The Unconscious in Relation to Anthropology," *Br. J. of Psychology*, Vol. XVIII, Part 4, 1928, p. 386.

[2] F. H. Melland, *In Witchbound Africa*, p. 247.

[3] A. G. O. Hodgson, " Dreams in Central Africa " (*Man*, April 1926, pp. 66–8).

[4] p. 127.

[5] A. Gardiner, " Translation of Egyptian Dream Papyrus," see p. 108, Ref. 6, (pp. 123, 5).

[6] Sauer, " Das Wesen des Traumes in der talmudischen Literatur " (*Zt. f. Psychoanalyse*, I, 465, quoted by Roheim in letter to C. G. Seligman).

[7] Quoted by Roheim in letter to C. G. Seligman.

[8] Chap. III, pp. 100–1.

From Australia, Roheim has mentioned several incest dreams and myths.[1]

Among the Navajo of North America there exists the belief that all mental derangement is caused by incest with mother or sister, or even by dancing with someone of the kinship group with whom marriage is forbidden.[2]

From the Bush-Negroes of Suriname is reported the following :

" It was not in an investigation of Bush-Negro psychological processes, but during an attempt to obtain as much detail as possible regarding death-customs, that the answer came in forms of an Œdipus reaction, as ' correct ' psychoanalytically as though it had been stated by Freud himself. The question which had been asked was, ' When a man dies, do they destroy his house ? ' And the reply : ' Not unless he has done black magic. If it is an ordinary man, his widow lives there with his daughters.' ' What happens to his sons ? ' ' They are sent away for a long time.' ' Why ? ' ' Because the soul of a man loves his daughters but hates his sons, and if they remained in his house, his ghost would kill them.' ' And if a woman dies ? ' ' Then the husband continues to live there with his sons, for if it is a woman's ghost, she will destroy her daughters. But her sons, she loves them and watches over them.' [3] "

A group of dreams from the coastal Solomon Islands dealing with incest is recorded by Miss Blackwood [4] :

A few direct individual parricide dreams, which reveal undisguised death wishes towards the father and parents are recorded from the Navajo,[5] and the Kwakiutl [6] Indians of North America. The custom of killing the divine king in Africa and in India can be regarded, however, as substitute parricide where king is known to be a father symbol.

[1] Roheim, *Social Anthropology* and *J. of Royal Anthr. Inst.*
[2] Part III, p. 240.
[3] M. J. Herskovits, " Freudian Mechanisms in Negro Psychology " in *Essays Presented to C. G. Seligman*, p. 84. London, 1934.
[4] Blackwood, B., cit. on p. 41.
[5] Part III, p. 245, references. [6] *Ibid.*, p. 323, references.

The killing of kings among the Shilluk when they show signs of ill health or failing strength or in olden times at any time when a rival was able to make good his claim in single combat to the throne is amply described by Frazer based on Professor Seligman's material.[1]

All forms of sacrifice have been regarded in a psychoanalytic study, " less as the result of a primeval crime than as the symbolic expression of an unconscious desire for parricide which each individual has himself acquired." [2]

Further proof is of course needed to establish conclusively the " Œdipus " at the base of customs ; the places where deeper analysis is sure to find it, may, nevertheless, be indicated.

Many of the nightmare dreams from the Kiwai,[3] and from Africa,[4] show open and undisguised conflicts with, and attempts to escape from, the dead father who is in pursuit. Obviously these can be included as showing the conflict with the father or one aspect of the " Œdipus " conflict. As pointed out, anxiety and guilt feelings because of death wishes towards the father are clearly shown in the Moshi dreams, where lion is known to be a symbol of father.[4]

Undisguised death-wish dreams against the parents occur among the Navajo,[5] and I have mentioned a Navajo dream in which bears were chasing the dreamer, which was analysed by Dr. O. Pfister from a strictly psychoanalytic standpoint. The bear in this case turned out to be the father.[6]

As to castration symbols, I have already referred to the universal tooth-losing dream with its constant meaning of death of a close relative [7] or friend, and of the common symbols often associated with tooth—such as child. Analysis has found in dreams that tooth and child are phallic symbols,

[1] Frazer, *The Golden Bough*, Vol. 4, pp. 23, 14–58.
[2] Money-Kyrle, *The Meaning of Sacrifice*, pp. 259–60.
[3] pp. 122–6.　　　　[4] p. 124.
[5] Part III, p. 245.　　　　[6] This chapter, p. 175, and Ref. 1.
[7] pp. 129–31 of Chap. III.

and that loss of a tooth is a castration symbol. Since other analytic findings have been confirmed with regard to the leading primary ideas, one can assume that further research will establish the tooth-losing dream as often meaning castration anxiety.

The " vagina dentata " dreams and myths may also be regarded as springing from the unconscious anxiety or fear of losing the genitals. This is strictly true for the dreams, and true for the originators of the myths assuming that an individual originated them somewhere and at some time, possibly from dreams.[1] Phylogenetic parallels of this complex will probably be found to exist behind the various and widespread ceremonial mutilations occurring among primitives. Again, in analysis, the knocking out of a tooth, circumcision, the cutting off of hair, the cutting off of fingers, limbs and joints, and many other forms of mutilations occurring in dreams have been found to be the usual expressions of the castration " complex." One independent analyst has even altered the Freudian terminology to " mutilation complex," which he considers more correct, since he regards castration as only one form of the mutilation patterns occurring in dreams.[2] However, in accordance with Jones' theory of symbolism, mutilation would be the secondary idea or symbol employed to represent the more deeply repressed and archaic primary idea of castration, which is uncovered only by analysis. Limbs, finger joints, hair, along with teeth, child and relative are all found often to be phallic symbols.[3]

In a Persian dream book of the eighth century [4] are the following associations or secondary symbols which are often found together in analysis of individuals in the twentieth century : " If you dream that you are having your *hair cut* or see any doing the same, you will be *separated from your family*," and " If anyone sees, in a dream, that his body has

---

[1] See previous chapters.   [2] Baudouin.   [3] Flügel.
[4] Translation of eighth-century Persian Dream Book, *Islamic Culture*, Vol. VI, 1932, p. 569 *seq.*, Nos. 20, 42.

become *separated from his joints*, all his *relatives* and kinsmen *will die*."

Cutting off hair is often found associated with tooth-losing, and tooth-losing is found in universal type dreams to mean death of a relative. The latter is found to mean castration in many instances, and relative is found to mean phallus, and limbs and joints are also phallic symbols. Being separated from someone often means death. Hence the above symbols undoubtedly may cover the following latent meanings, castration for hair-cut, death for separation, phallus for relatives, limbs and joints.

Professor Seligman has reviewed the facts of the puberty rites of circumcision, and tooth extraction in Africa, from the Mediterranean to the Equator among Hamitic peoples, and from Khartoum to the Great Lakes among negroes, circumcision occurring in the former region and tooth extraction in the latter, with an area in between where both rites occur. Generally, however, one rite excludes the other.[1]

In Australia he shows how both rites overlap in places and he mentions the association of tooth and foreskin which are both regarded as agents of reincarnation (birth).[2] This obviously makes the tooth again a phallic symbol.

In his Huxley Memorial Lecture for 1932, Professor Seligman points out how initiation practices vary in different groups, especially with regard to the time at which they take place, which may be before or after puberty. In the same group of initiates there may be variation of two to four years. The severe operation and pain of these rites do not seem to impair the genital development or the sexual life which goes on regardless of whether initiation is or is not practised. He states that, " the initiation customs seem to be of little consequence with regard to the psychological aspect of family solidarity, i.e. the nuclear or Œdipus

---

[1] C. G. Seligman, " The Unconscious in Relation to Anthropology," *Br. J. of Psychology*, Vol. XVIII, Part 4, 1928, pp. 374–87.
[2] *Ibid.*

complex." [1] The rites, however, do symbolize and dramatize the castration and punishment of the youths for, and the freeing of them from, the " Œdipus." [2] Probably the reason why the severity of the rites have little influence on the initiates' psycho-sexual development is because of the fact stated earlier in the same lecture, that the primitive method of bringing up children and allowing them freedom in sexual matters from the earliest age allows them to develop quite free from the psychic trauma often caused by the educational methods of Western civilization. Psychologically, therefore, the initiates may have freed themselves from the " Œdipus " before the initiation rite takes place. The latter is the tribal and ceremonial enactment of the Œdipus drama, i.e. the giving of tribal sanction to the child now grown to manhood, who must be punished and released from his infantile anti-social tendencies, and made an adult and one of the social group. This tribal sanction does not necessarily coincide in time with individual sexual development.

The castration complex, therefore, must be sought in the individual and universal tooth-losing dream, and in tribal form in the initiation rites as a symbolic expression of the same tendency. If these are the true facts, mutilations such as the sacrifice of finger joints which occurs in India, Africa, the South Seas, Australia, and North America, [3] would equally be symbolic castration, since finger is often a phallic symbol in dreams.

Of the undisguised and classic examples of this unconscious fantasy occurring in myths, which apparently it is still necessary to quote, are the myth of Cronus who castrated his father and in turn was castrated by his son, that of Kali the phallic goddess who castrated and destroyed her consort Siva, the story of the mother of Attis conceived by putting in

---

[1] Huxley Lecture, 1932, pp. 214–15, *J. of R.A.I.*, Vol. LXIII, pp. 214–15.
[2] Th. Reik, *Ritual*.
[3] R. Frazer, *The Golden Bough*, Vol. 4, p. 219, and Lowie, *Crow Indians*.

her bosom a pomegranate sprung from the severed genitals of a man-monster named Agdestis, a sort of double of Attis.[1] The self-castration by priests of Cybele, and by the peasantry in Gaul should also be again mentioned.[2]

All the above is open to further proof with more detailed data on the latent meanings of primitive symbols, our only method of reaching deep psychological truths. Of course, any study of the psychology which underlies ethnologic data must take into consideration the facts of history and diffusion which occur on the surface of the psychological background. For instance an initiation rite which in itself may symbolize the castration complex may have been borrowed from another group. Hence the psychology of the rite belongs to the group of origin, nevertheless, the reason for its having been borrowed may be based on the psychology of the borrowing group. If, however, the same unconscious tendencies exist in the two groups the rite can be the vehicle for the expression of unconscious tendencies in both the borrowing group as well as in the group of origin.

THE NUCLEAR FAMILY AND MUTILATION COMPLEXES IN NORTH AMERICAN INDIAN CULTURE PATTERN VISIONS.

With a knowledge of the latent meanings of symbols acquired from individual or cultural associations, representing father, mother, and phallus, and by inference where symbolism appears to be only skin deep, it is possible to discover the Œdipus at least in some of its aspects. Thus conflicts of wishes towards, supplications to, and requests for protection and favours from the father or parents ; cravings for the mother, and self-punishments and mutilations in relation to any of these conflicts, would indicate the general patterns of the unconscious nuclear family complex as it is found in analysis, in dreams and myths, or elsewhere.

---

[1] Money-Kyrle, *The Meaning of Sacrifice*, pp. 101, 105, 119, 230.
[2] Money-Kyrle, *ibid.*, p. 230.

The Crow Indians. A rudimentary analysis of some of the Crow visions is here attempted [1] :

Painless Visions

" One-blue-head's vision.[2] He saw a person on a white-maned horse with his face painted red. He saw a chicken hawk feather tied to one of his shoulders. A voice said, ' Chief chicken-hawk is coming from there now.' "

Comment. " Other people have to torture themselves ; I never cut myself. Many people had no vision. . . . His medicine forbids him to bleed or cut off fingers or to eat blood, a taboo imposed by a vision." *Further comment.* " Some can tell before-hand when they are going to die. They say, ' My father is going to take me back,' then they die soon after. The only thing I prayed to specially was my feather, I might pray to the Sun any time."

Analysis : Associated to *Chief Chicken-Hawk* the supernatural being who is coming from *the other world,* is the comment about people who can tell beforehand when *they are going to die,* and the statement that they say, " ' *My father is going to take me back,'* then they die soon after." Also associated are, " I prayed to my *feather,* and I might pray to the *Sun.*" Hence Chief Chicken-Hawk, feather (phallic ?), and Sun are all associated with father, as father symbols. It is clear that his statement about others being able to foretell when they are going to die applies to himself, being a mere pro-jection on others. The vision and associations, therefore, show a fear of death, a fear and expectation of being taken away by the father, i.e. death wishes towards the father and himself. From the standpoint of unconscious wish-fulfil-ment, the taboo imposed by his dreams which forbids him to bleed or cut off fingers (in opposition to a usual Crow pattern) would show on the surface a wish not to comply with the painful custom, but more deeply a reaction from

[1] Lowie, see Part III, pp. 253–7.

[2] *Ibid.,* p. 253. Abbreviations are used since the records of visions are given in fuller version in Part III.

the self-punishing or castration tendency (cutting off fingers) arising from death wishes towards the father. In this vision we have clear proof, with definite individual associations, of the existence of strong father hostility and self-punishing tendencies from which, however, the dreamer wishes to escape, yet he still expects to be punished and killed by the father, as shown in the association, " My father is going to take me back."

Arm-around-the-neck's dream.[1] He failed when he sought a vision but he had dreams while sleeping.

Dream. " I saw a bear and a horse two different times ; also a bird. The bear I saw was singing to some people ; some of them fell down while he was singing, and he jumped on them, etc. . . ."

Comment. " My mother's brother had the bear for medicine, that may have been the reason for this dream." He would kill a bear if he wanted to although he likes bears.

Analysis : He associates *mother's brother* with bear. Mother's brother as head of the family (the Crows are matrilineal) is obviously a father substitute. Hence the bear or father undoubtedly was " the reason for this dream." He would kill a bear (father) if he wanted to although he likes them. What could be a more perfect illustration of his ambivalent hatred and death wishes towards, as well as his affection for, the father (or mother's brother) [2] with whom bear is directly associated.

Crow Sought Visions. " These were deliberate quests for a revelation. The more numerous attempts often failed. All ages sought visions, although the largest number were among males and adolescents. The would-be visionary retired to a lonely place, fasted four days and chopped off a finger joint as an offering to conciliate the spirits invoked. The Sun, or Old Man, or Coyote were the most frequently addressed. The Sun,

[1] Lowie, Part III, p. 254.
[2] See Malinowski-Jones controversy on mother's brother as father substitute ; also p. 95, Ref. 1.

the Bear, and Snakes are the chief protectors in visions. Besides, people who have seen a Snake do not kill snakes." [1]

It has just been found in the analysis of two visions that Bear, Sun and Chief Chicken-Hawk were father symbols in specific cultural form.[2] The first two are the chief protectors appearing in visions. Thus we have proof that the supernatural protectors whose aid and guidance are sought in visions represent the father. It is most significant that before seeking the latter's aid, the seeker inflicts punishment and torture on himself through fasting and chopping off a finger joint. In other words, he feels the need or rather is required by custom to punish and castrate himself (symbolically) probably in order to expiate his hostile wishes towards the father before demanding his protection.

The visions of Big Ox, a famous shaman.[3]

(a) He slept on a mountain and chopped off a little finger joint. He saw a bird who made him a chief. The bird had human heads, and five balls of different colour in front of him, etc.

(b) When old he became feeble-minded. He saw the No-drum dance in daytime. An old woman and a white man gave him a stick painted yellow and decorated with bells and feathers.

Analysis : Unfortunately there are no associations. However, the interpretation may be inferred from what has already been shown. He chops off a finger ; i.e. a symbolic castration, and he sees a bird who makes him a chief. Since the supernatural beings in the visions are often father symbols, the bird who makes him a chief may also be so

---

[1] Part III, p. 255, Ref. 1.

[2] Lowie makes it even more certain that all the supernatural patrons are father symbols when he says that, " It is understood a spirit appearing to a visionary adopts him as a child." The standard formula is, " You, my child I will make." " Hence the constant use of parent and child terms of relationship in the myths dealing with supernatural patrons." See p. 254, Note 1.

[3] Part III, p. 256.

regarded. He, therefore, sees the father who makes him father in turn. This would be the normal solution of renouncing the father hostility and becoming the leader in his place.

Arbitrarily, the vision when he is old, might mean the wish to receive again his sexual potency (yellow stick decorated with bells and feathers, as a phallic symbol) as a gift from the parents (old woman and white man).

If the above analyses are correct, they would apply to the whole group of culture-pattern visions which are all of stereotyped form,[1] and the " Œdipus " and " castration " complexes, at least in the father hostility and self-punishment aspects, are at the basis of Crow visions. The incestuous side of the " Œdipus " is not apparent in the visions, and only deep analysis can determine its existence. Since, however, the *raison d'être* for father hostility in the unconscious is always found to be because of the mother, further research would undoubtedly establish the incestuous tendencies also.

The self-torture pattern is culturally distinct from the vision quest among many of the American Indians, and the two were diffused as independent culture phenomena in many tribes.[2] Both self-torture and the vision quest, however, are Plains patterns and probably arose together and later were diffused independently. Wherever they were diffused they were accepted because of the psychological need of the borrowing groups which became endorsed by cultural sanction.

THE VISIONS OF BLACKFOOT MEDICINE MEN.[3]

Among the visions recorded there are no individual associations, but the symbolism is so thin that the family (father-mother-child) group is clearly seen in practically undisguised form, or else in stereotyped cultural form

---

[1] Lowie, Part III, p. 264. All culture pattern visions are of a stereotyped form peculiar to the specific culture.

[2] Benedict, Part III, p. 251. [3] Part III, pp. 258–63.

behind it. Since the majority of the dreams are of precisely the same cultural pattern, a correct analysis of a few would apply to all. In almost every one, the two parental beings, generally the Sun and Moon, appear and confer gifts and favours. It is usual for the Sun to appear as old man, and Moon as old woman, which are very thinly disguised parent symbols.

An old man and an old woman come into the tipi. The man has an iron whistle (gun barrel) [1] and the woman a wooden one. The dreamer chose the iron one. The old man gives his protection. He lives in the sky. He says, " In a fight do not fear guns." He was the morning star. The old woman was the moon. She was angry, threw the whistle into the fire and it became a snake and ran away. Later in another dream she returned and gave a wooden whistle. This conferred power to prevent childbearing. [2]

Analysis : Possibly this represents some bisexual solution of the family complex, in which both the father and mother contribute their favours. Both the whistles may be phallic symbols. Potency and manhood are the gifts conferred.

The following is a typical and obvious father-mother-child group, a symbolic family group [3] :

Sun man and Moon woman and their son the Morning Star appeared. The man gives him his body and says, " You will live as long as I." The woman gives power over rain. The son gives a hat, a plume of eagle feathers and tail feathers of a magpie.

Analysis : The Sun as father makes him like himself, which represents the normal father identification.

In one vision an undisguised family group, of a man and woman and six children confer gifts. [4]

---

[1] This is another example in which a new and foreign cultural element will appear in the manifest content of an old culture pattern dream.
[2] *Ibid.*, p. 258.
[3] Part III, p. 259, Exp. C, *a*.   [4] p. 261, Exp. D. *b*.

None of the visions varies from the pattern of a parental group who confer power to meet life. They represent a reconciliation with the parents and psychological identifications after renouncing the tie to the parents. These experiences are not necessarily individual visions since the Blackfoot have the custom of vision purchase,[1] therefore the visions do not necessarily express the immediate family complex of the individual but rather the solution of this complex as endorsed by tribal custom and tradition. In other words, the culture imposes upon all a fixed solution which arose on the foundations of the visions of a few. The stereotyped vision, therefore, is the tribal recognition of the need of a solution of the family or nuclear complex, by every individual. It lays down what this solution shall be.

The fact of a vision pattern having been borrowed from another group[2] merely strengthens the probability that an unconscious psychological need exists for which the borrowing took place. A new cult is taken up because it fulfills a psychological and social need better than an older one, as is illustrated in the rise and spread of the Ghost Dance religious cult throughout the different tribes.[3] A social solution of the Œdipus or family complex, being the most widespread necessity, new solutions are constantly being sought.

AMONG THE KWAKIUTL.

A very archaic and morbid form of Œdipus conflict together with a marked necrophily seems to exist at the base of Kwakiutl culture. The fear of death, and murderous cannibalistic wishes are most evident in dreams, myths and ceremonies in which even dead bodies are eaten. Out of 63 individual dreams recorded 28 are of the dead, and many of these of the dead father, grandfather or relatives and dead lovers. Two are undisguised dreams of sexual intercourse

[1] Benedict, Part III, p. 252 ; Ref. 1.
[2] *Ibid.* [3] Mooney, *14th Ann. Rep. B.A.E.*, Part II.

with a dead husband and a dead wife respectively.[1] Among their beliefs about dreams which deal so largely with death, are that nightmares indicate the death of a near relative, and that when a hunter dreams of cohabiting with a dead woman, it signifies bad luck.[2]

Analysts would accept the following individual dream and action as indicating an incestuous tendency with the symbolism of going into water as meaning entering the womb, birth and incest often being condensed in the unconscious.

" I dreamed of my late mother who asked me to rub my body always with branches of hemlock trees in the river behind our village in the morning and in the evening, ' and if you do this you will never be sick,' thus said my late mother to me. After that I went immediately into the water." (A usual ceremonial purification.) [3]

In the initiation legend recorded in full farther on,[4] which Boas says is identical with the visionary experiences of the youths of to-day,[5] the Œdipus pattern is easily discernible in the incidents. In it the youth who is in love with a girl must first live through his incestuous desires for the mother and hostility to the father, and secure their gifts and protection before he is accepted as an adult with full tribal standing. That he gets the protection and sanction of the parents but does not renounce his wishes towards them, the latter being institutionalized in the cannibalistic and necrophilic ceremonies, is portrayed in the incidents of the myth-vision and in the well-known resulting ceremonies. This is a good example of the criminal, archaic impulses being institutionalized in primitive life, that in civilization would lead to neurosis, insanity, or crime, as mentioned by Kroeber.[6]

[1] Part III, pp. 314, 319, Nos. 49, 63.
[2] Boas, J. of Am. Folklore, Vol. 45, April–June 1932, par. 393, 576, b. See Part III, pp. 300–1.
[3] p. 313, No. 43. [4] Ibid., p. 301 seq. [5] Ibid., p. 301, Ref. 1.
[6] Ref. this chapter, pp. 133–4.

In the vision the youth, on hearing cries in the woods (the unconscious), jumps in a pond (the mother womb) and rubs his body with hemlock. A mythical woman appears (mother) whom he seizes in a swooning embrace and holds her until he secures from her the gifts of property, the water of life and the apron which burns everything. After the mother goes away he plays with his sweetheart again. Soon he runs into the father, in the shape of Bax bakualanuXsi'wae, the " first-to-eat-man at-the-mouth-of the river in-the North," who lives by pursuing and eating men. The latter teaches him songs and ceremonies and gives him the magical harpoon which kills everything (phallic sadistic [1]), the red cedar bark, the fire which burns everything (sexual potency), the water of life, and the quartz crystal.

The records describe how the initiate returns in a frenzy after his vision, as a cannibal himself who must be exorcised from his mad ecstasy.[2] Here is seen the tribal sanction and outlet for his necrophilic father hostility.

The pattern in this tribe seems to be psychologically akin to Freud's " primal crime " in which the desire to kill and eat the father is alleged. It is not necessary, however, to seek its origins in the mythical past, there is plenty of evidence of it as a psychological pattern in history and in the realistic present.

This vision cult has been diffused from the Kwakiutl to other tribes.[3] Hence again this is a case where the psychology of the cult belongs to the group of origin, yet also

[1] The existence of sadistic tendencies is shown in the following belief in which the association of love and killing occurs. If the owner of a trap dreams of a woman who refused his love, his trap will fall without killing anything. If he dreams that the woman accepts him, his trap will have killed game.—Boas, *J. of Am. Folklore*, cit. Part III, p. 301, par. 403 ; see also p. 119 and Note 7 in the present chapter.

[2] Part III, pp. 299, 301 *seq.*

[3] The Haidas borrowed the Cannibal and other secret societies from the Tsimshian and Bella Bellas in 1700.—Boas, *Social Organization and Secret Societies of the Kwakiutl*, p. 545.

a case where the cult solves a psychological need in the borrowing groups. It may be possible for a cult to induce a psychological state in a group which previously did not have it, but only on the foundation of the same unconscious tendencies regarding the parent-child relationship in some of its unconscious forms.[1] As Goldenweiser has stated, the mechanism of the assimilation and receptivity of culture is psychological [2] ; this is a subject, however, about which we know very little and is practically a virgin field of research. A knowledge of the forms and solutions of the nuclear family complex in different groups will however clarify this hitherto obscure subject.

I have attempted above a few leads in this direction, and if the analyses and inferences are correct I have established that the unconscious nuclear family complex exists at the basis of the Crow vision quest, the culture pattern visions of Blackfoot medicine men, and the vision and ceremonial cult of the Kwakiutl. In each one of these groups the outlines of specific aspects of this complex are discernible, and each group has its own cultural solution which differs from the solutions of the others.

Thus among the Crow is found a strong father hostility expiated by the self-punishing customs of fasting, starvation and the chopping off of a finger joint, the latter symbolizing a self-castration which many vision seekers must undergo before they attempt reconciliation with the father symbolized in the vision. The favour and protection of the father, therefore, is a *sine qua non* which must be obtained before an individual can attain any social standing in the tribe at all.[3] The culture thus recognizes the social

---

[1] That the same unconscious tendencies exist among the different groups to which the cannibal societies cult was recently diffused is corroborated by the fact that the idea of a spirit who is killing people was present among all the tribes prior to the diffusion of the cult. See Note 4, p. 105, Chap. III.

[2] Goldenweiser, *History, Psychology and Culture*, p. 115.

[3] Lowie says that all success in life was due to the vision, and that those who secured none were social nobodies, Part III, p. 249 *seq.*

importance of solving the unconscious father hostility, and prescribes a means in the vision quest and self-torture customs.

Among the Blackfoot the solution seems to be a simple reconciliation with the parents symbolized in the visions, which reveal the mechanism of psychological identifications with the parents for the purpose of meeting life as an adult with the gifts and talents that result from these identifications. The information here is meagre, and the conclusion only tentative. What is certain, however, is the family group symbolized in the visions.

Among the Kwakiutl, there is evidence in the dreams, myths and ceremonies of incestuous necrophilic tendencies for the mother, and violent cannibalistic and sadistic death wishes towards the father, which are not renounced or punished or converted into higher forms of expression, but institutionalized and expressed directly in barely disguised symbolism in the Secret Society and Winter ceremonials.

An especially important subject of investigation would, therefore, be to find out the exact culture differences that correspond to the above distinctions, and it is not improbable that future research would discover that many cultural variations of different peoples were determined in large part by attempts at different collective and religious solutions of the anti-social " nuclear " family complex, even while allowing for the facts of history and diffusion.

An " Œdipus " Legend from the Bantu Fan.

From the African Fan is recorded a most significant legend with associated ceremonies and " totemic " practices in which parricide, incest, self-punishment and ceremonial and tribal socialization of these tendencies are directly stated with practically no symbolic disguise. Father Trille believes that the legend shows that the totemic phenomena of the tribe are indigenous to the tribe and not importations from elsewhere. He believes that this and other similar legends, as well as genealogies and survivals of totemic cults, make it possible to trace " totemism " to the origins of the tribe.[1] If these are the true facts, it means that the psychology of the culture is not complicated by processes of diffusion and can be regarded as a direct and native expression of the tribe.[2]

There are many kinds of totems among these people, namely, those of the nation, the tribe, the clan, the village, the phratry, the family and the individual, and all of them are characterized by the root word " *mvame* " which occurs in the names of each. This root word means, " Ancestor " and " father of the race." The whole name of the " individual totem " means " father protector." [3]

The Legend is of Ngurangurane, the son of the Crocodile, the national totem, and his name means " la vengeance est pleinement satisfaite." [4] All the individuals questioned were unanimous in regarding him as the father of all the Fan.[5] How this hero, who is the son of a chief's daughter and the Great Crocodile, kills his father and frees his people is the story of the legend, which I shall present with only few omissions because of its importance in the present context.

In the legend the hero regards his mother's father who was killed by the Crocodile as chief of the race, and it is shown how he (hero) is the illegitimate son of the Crocodile and this chief's daughter. The Crocodile or national totem

---

[1] R. P. H. Trilles, " Le Totemisme chez les Fan," pp. 176–247, *Collection Internationale de Monographies Ethnologiques*, Bibliothèque Anthropos, Tome I, Fasc. 4, 1912.

[2] Roheim has quoted this myth also, in a condensed form. He has treated it, however, as a " primal horde " myth. My detailed analysis shows it to be a double Œdipus myth, without any need to conjure up the " primal horde " theory. See Roheim, *The Riddle of the Sphinx*, p. 191.

[3] R. P. H. Trilles, *op. cit.*, pp. 84–6.

[4] *Ibid.*, p. 184, Note 3.　　　　[5] *Ibid.*, p. 185.

is regarded by all the Fan as the father of the father of the race. Thus is shown the pattern of the hero's mother's father (the human head of the race) being killed by the Crocodile (the mythical totemic father) before the latter is in turn killed by the hero, his son. The girl marries the mythical father (substitute for her own father) and the hero can be regarded as the son of an incestuous union of father and daughter. It is directly stated that the hero kills the Crocodile, his own father, in order to free his mother from the assaults of the father.[1] Here we find the complete " Œdipus " pattern, both male and female. The girl's wishes to be possessed by her father are realized completely, and the boy's wishes to kill his father and possess his mother are all realized in the legend.

If this legend is indigenous and arose in the early history of the tribe as believed by Father Trille,[2] it shows that the " Œdipus " pattern is a psychological tendency pertaining to the tribe and expressed in legendary form.

In connection with the marriage of the hero's mother, Father Trille mentions a custom which shows how an illegitimate child is regarded as belonging to the mother's father. Since the myth gives a certain tribal sanction to an incestuous union of father and daughter, the custom may show that any illegitimate child is unconsciously suspected as belonging to, i.e. as being child of, the mother's father and he brings honour to his mother, in the same manner as the hero in the legend. Father Trille says,

" Il arrive frequemment aujourd'hui encore que des jeunes filles ont un enfant. Loin d'étre un déshonneur, c'est au contraire un honneur qui augmente le prix de la jeune fille, en prouvant sa fécondité. Mais lorsqu'elle se marie, son enfant ne la suit pas ; il appartient toujours a la tribu du père de la jeune fille, qui est considéré alors comme le vrai père de l'enfant. A défaut d'un père connu, c'est l'oncle maternel qui possédera l'enfant, et tel est le cas pour Ngurangurane." [3]

[1] R. P. H. Trilles, *op. cit.*
[2] *Ibid.*, p. 204.   [3] *Ibid.*, p. 196, Note 1.

"NUCLEAR COMPLEXES" IN PRIMITIVE CULTURES

La Legende de Ngurangurane, le fils du Crocodile.[1]

"Donc, il y avait à cette époque, il y a de cela bien longtemps, bien longtemps, un très grand féticheur nommé Ngurangurane, le fils du Crocodile. Et voici comment il était né, c'est la première chose ; ce qu'il fit et comment il mourut, c'est la seconde. Dire toutes ses actions, c'est impossible, et d'ailleurs qui se les rappellerait ?

"I. *Comment il était né c'est la première chose.*

"A cette époque-la, les Fân demeuraient au bord d'un grand fleuve, grand, si grand, qu'on ne pouvait apercevoir l'autre rive ; ils pêchaient sur le bord, mais ils n'allaient pas sur le fleuve ; nul encore ne leur avait appris à creuser des canots : celui qui le leur apprit, ce fut Ngurangurane : Ngurangurane apprit cet art aux hommes de sa famille, et sa famille, c'étaient ' les hommes.' . . . C'étaient les Fân.

"Dans le fleuve vivait un énorme crocodile (ngan ese, un maître crocodile, ou le chef des crocodiles). Sa tête était plus longue que cette case, ses yeux plus gros qu'un cabri tout entier, ses dents coupaient un homme en deux comme je coupe une banane, cris ! Il était couvert d'énormes écailles ; un homme le frappait de ses javelots, to, to. Mais pfut, le javelot retombait, et celui qui faisait cela, ce pouvait être l'homme le plus robuste : pfut, le javelot retombait. C'était un animal terrible.

"Or, un jour, il vint dans le village de Ngurangurane, mais celui-ci n'était pas encore né. Et celui qui commandait les Fân était un grand chef, et il commandait a beaucoup d'hommes. Il commandait aux Fân et à d'autres encore. Ngan Esa vint donc un jour dans le village des Fân et il appelle le Chef :

" ' Chef, je t'appelle.'

"Le chef accourt aussitôt. Et le chef crocodile dit au Chef homme :

" ' Bège mélo (Ecoute attentivement).'

"Et le chef homme répondit : ' Mélo.' (Oreilles : C'est-à-dire, ' J'écoute bien.')

" ' Ce que tu feras à partir d'auhourd'hui, le voici. Chaque jour j'ai faim, et je pense que la chair de l'homme me vaut mieux que la chair du poisson. Chaque jour, tu attacheras un

[1] *Ibid.*, pp. 185–202, several pages omitted.

esclave et tu me l'apporteras sur les bords du fleuve, un homme un jour, une femme un jour, et le premier de chaque lune, une jeune fille bien peinte avec le ' baza' et bien luisante de graisse. Tu feras ainsi. Si tu oses ne pas obéir, je mangerai tout ton village. Voilà, c'est fini. Tais-toi.'
" Et le chef crocodile, sans ajouter un mot, retourna au fleuve. Et au village, on commença les lamentations funèbres. Et chacun dit : ' Je suis mort.' Chacun le dit, le chef, les hommes, les femmes. Le lendemain, au matin, quand le soleil se lève, le crocodile chef était sur le bord du fleuve. Wah ! Wah ! sa gueule était énorme, plus longue que cette case, ses yeux gros comme un cabri tout entier. Les crocodiles que l'on voit aujourd'hui, ne sont plus des crocodiles ! Ce crocodile chef était comme le ' ndzin.' (Legendary animal.) Et l'on se hâta d'apporter au crocodile chef ce qu'il avait demandé, un homme un jour, une femme un jour, et le premier de chaque lune, une jeune fille ornée de rouge et de d'huile, toute luisante de graisse. L'on fit ce que le crocodile chef avait ordonné, et nul n'osait désobéir, car il avait partout ses guerriers, les autres crocodiles.

" Et le nom de ce crocodile, c'était Ombure : les eaux obéissaient à Ombure, les forêts obéissaient a Ombure, ses ' hommes ' étaient partout, il était chef de la forêt, mais il était surtout chef de l'eau. Et chaque jour il mangeait soit un homme, soit une femme, et il était très content, et très ami avec les Fân. Mais ceux-ci avaient fini de donner tous leurs esclaves, et le chef avait livré tout ce qu'il avait comme richesses pour en acheter. Il n'avait plus un coffre, plus une dent d'éléphant ! Il lui fallait fournir un homme, un homme fân. Et le chef des Fân réunit tous ses hommes dans son ' abèñe ' : il leur parla longtemps, longtemps, et après lui, les autres guerriers parlèrent aussi long-temps. Quand la palabre fut terminée, tout le monde était d'accord et pensait avec un seul cœur : on devait partir. Le chef dit alors : ' Voilà cette question de départ reglée : nous irons loin, loin d'ici par dela les montagnes. Quand nous serons loin, bien loin du fleuve, par dela les montagnes, Ombure ne pourra plus nous atteindre, et nous serons heureux.' Et il fut décidé que l'on ne renouvellerait plus les plantations, et qu'à la fin de la saison, toute la tribu quitterait les bords du fleuve ; Et ainsi fut fait.

" Au commencement de la saison sèche, lorsque les eaux sont basses et qu'il fait bon voyager, la tribu se mit en marche. Le premier jour, on alla vite, vite, etc. . . .

" Le premier jour, beaucoup regardaient derrière eux, croyant entendre le crocodile : Wah ! Wah ! et le dernier avait froid dans son cœur ! Mais on n'entendit rien. Et le second jour la marche fut la même, et l'on entendit rien. Et le troisième jour, la marche fut la même, et l'on entendit rien.

" Le premier jour, cependant, le crocodile chef était sorti de l'eau suivant son habitude pour venir a l'endroit ou l'on avait coutume de mettre l'esclave qui lui était destiné. Il vient : Wah ! Wah ! Rien. Qu'est ce ceci ? Il prend aussitôt la route du village.

" ' Chef des hommes, je t'appelle.'

" Rien ! Il n'entend aucun bruit ; il entre, toutes les cases sont abandonnées ; il va aux plantations, les plantations sont abandonnées : Wah ! Wah ! Il parcourt tous les villages, tous les villages sont abandonnés ; il parcourt toutes les plantations, toutes les plantations sont abandonnées.

" Ombure entre alors dans une fureur épouvantable, et se replonge dans le fleuve pour consulter son fétiche, et il chante " :
(There follows his appeals to the spirits of the waters, the thunder, the tempest and the forest to tell him where the men had gone.

They finally tell him and he follows on the Fan's trail. The Fan continued their migrations for many years after crossing plains and mountains and finally settled on the border of a lake and built new villages.)   " Le chef réunit alors ses hommes pour donner un nom au village, et on l'appella : ' Akurengan (la délivrance du Crocodile).'

" Or, cette nuit-là même, vers minuit, un grand bruit se fait entendre et une voix crie : ' Venez, venez ici ! ' Et tous sortent, fort effrayés. Que voient-ils ? Car la lune éclairait bien ! Ombure était au milieu du village *!* Il était devant la case du grand chef. Que faire ! Où fuir ? Où se cacher ? Nul n'osait y songer ! *Et quand le grand chef sortit de sa case pour voir ce qui se passait, yu, ce fut le premier pris ! D'un coup de dent, Ombure le cassa en deux :* Krô, krô, kwas : ' *Voilà Akurengan,' dit-il seulement.*[1]

---

[1] Italics mine throughout this legend.

" Et il retourna vers le lac.

" Les guerriers, tremblants, élirent aussitôt un autre chef, le frère de l'ancien, suivant la loi, et le matin, *on prit la femme de l'ancien chef,* et on vint l'attacher sur les bords du lac, en offrande à Ombure. Et celui-ci vint ; la femme pleurait. Krô, krô, *il la mangea.* Mais le soir, il revint au village, et appela le chef :
" ' Chef, je t'appelle.'

(Here follows the same demands for sacrifices as in the former village. After many more years of wars, to secure captives for Ombure, the people became tired of his demands and had forgotten how he caught up to them when they escaped from him before. They all abandon the village again and depart, but Ombure forces them to return with the help of the forest and tempest spirits.)

. . . " Ombure les attend. Mais Ombure est vieux, au lieu de deux hommes, il exige maintenant : ' Vous me donnerez chaque jour deux jeunes filles en sacrifice.'

" Et les Fân durent obéir et chaque jour amener deux jeunes filles a Ombure, deux jeunes filles peintes en rouge, reluisantes et frottées d'huile. C'est leur fête de mariage.

" Elles pleurent et se lamentent, les filles des Fân ; elles pleurent et se lamentent : c'est la fête des tristes fiançailles.

" Elles pleurent et se lamentent le soir : le matin, elles ne pleurent ni se lamentent : elles n'entendent plus parler leurs mères : elles sont au fond du lac, dans la grotte où demeure Ombure : elles le servent et il en fait sa nourriture.

" Mais un jour, il arriva ceci. *La jeune fille qui devait être exposée le soir sur le bord du fleuve, la jeune fille dont le tour était venu, c'était l'enfant du chef,* elle était jeune et elle était belle. Et, le soir, elle fut attachée sur le bord du lac avec sa compagne : la compagne ne revint pas, mais le lendemain, lorsque reparut le jour, la fille du chef etait encore la. Ombure l'avait epargnée.

" *Aussi on l'appela : Aléna kiri (l'aurore a paru).*

" *Mais neuf mois après, la fille du chef eut un enfant, un enfant mâle.* En souvenir de sa naissance, *ce garçon fut appelé Ngurangurane, le fils du crocodile.*

" Ngurangurane (Nganéngame) était donc fils d'Ombure, le crocodile chef : ceci est la première histoire. Ngurangurane était né ainsi.

" II. *La Mort d'Ombure.*

" Ngurangurane, l'enfant du crocodile Ombure et de la fille du chef, grandit, grandit, grandit chaque jour : d'enfant, il devient adolescent, d'adolescent il devient jeune homme. C'est alors le chef de son peuple. C'était un chef puissant et un très savant féticheur. *Dans son cœur, il avait deux désirs : venger la mort du chef de sa race, du père de sa mère, et délivrer son peuple du tribut que levait sur lui le crocodile.*

" Ce qu'il fit dans ce but, le voici.

" Dans la forêt, on trouve un arbre sacré, cela, vous le savez et cet arbre, on l'appelle ' palmier.' Coupez un palmier : la sève coule, coule abondante, et si vous attendez deux ou trois jours après l'avoir enfermée dans les vases de terre, vous aurez le ' dzan,' la boisson qui rend le cœur joyeux. Cela, nous le savons maintenant mais nos pères ne le savaient pas. Celui qui le leur a appris, c'est Ngurangurane, et le premier qui a bu le ' dzan,' c'est Ombure, le crocodile chef. *Qui avait fait connaître le ' dzan ' a Ngurangurane ? C'etait Ngonémane la pierre fétiche que lui avait donnée sa mère.*

" *Or, d'après l'avis de Ngonémane* (= *la fille a cessé d'être vierge : ce devait être un surnom d'Aléna kiri après son aventure*), Ngurangurane fit ceci : ' Appretez tous les vases de terre que vous possédez, tous, apportez-les dans ma case.' Il dit cela aux femmes : elles apportèrent donc tous les vases de terre qu'elles possédaient, . . ." (Here the hero has many pots filled with the liquor and placed on the edge of the lake next to the sacrificial captives. The Crocodile Ombure came out of the water and drank the " dzan," became intoxicated and fell asleep after singing a song. He drank so much that he forgot the sacrifices.)

" Il chante, et sur le sable, sans plus songer aux captifs, il s'endort, le cœur joyeux.

" Ngurangurane s'approche aussitôt d'Ombure endormi ; avec une forte corde, aidé des captives, il l'attache au poteau, puis brandissant avec force son javelot, il frappe l'animal endormi : sur les écailles épaisses, le javelot rebondit en arrière sans entamer le crocodile, et celui-ci, sans se réveiller, se secoue en disant : ' Qu'est-ce ceci ? un moustique m'a piqué.'

" Ngurangurane prend sa hache, sa forte hache de pierre ; d'un coup formidable, il blesse l'animal endormi : la hache rebondit sans blesser l'animal ; celui-ci commence a s'agiter :

les deux captives s'enfuient épouvantées. Ngurangurane fait alors un puissant fétiche :

" ' Tonnerre, dit-il, Tonnerre, c'est toi que j'appelle, apporte moi tes flèches.'

" Et le tonnerre vient en éclatant. *Mais quand il apprend qu'il doit tuer Ombure : ' C'est ton père, s'écrie-t-il, et c'est mon maître,' et il s'enfuit épouvanté. Mais Aléna kiri vient au secours de son fils, et elle apporte Ngonémane, la pierre fée. Et au nom de Ngonémane,* Ngurangurane dit :

" ' Éclair, je t'ordonne de frapper.'

" Et l'éclair frappe, car désobéir, il ne le pouvait pas. A la tête, entre les yeux, il frappe Ombure, et Ombure demeure sur la place, foudroyé, mort. *Celui qui l'a tué, c'est Ngurangurane, mais Ngurangurane ne l'a tué que grace au secours de Ngonémane.*

" Et la fin de ce récit, la voilà. Ngurangurane retourne en hâte au village. ' Vous tous, hommes du village, dit-il, vous tous, venez.' Et ils viennent tous sur les bords du lac, Ombure est là gisant mort, immense. ' Celui qui a tué le Crocodile Ombure c'est moi, Ngurangurane, celui qui a vengé le chef de sa race, c'est moi ; celui qui vous a délivrés, c'est moi, Ngurangurane.'

" Tous se rejouirent, et autour du cadavre, on dansa le Fanki (On danse encore auhourd'hui le Fanki aux funerailles des chefs.) [1] la grande danse des funerailles : on dansa le Fanki pour apaiser l'esprit d'Ombure.

" Et ceci, c'est la fin.

" III. *Le Culte du Crocodile.*

" Sur le bord du lac, le crocodile Ombure est étendu, et le lendemain, au matin, ce que fait Ngurangurane, le voici.

" Il prend son grand couteau, (de pierre) qui ne sert qu'aux funerailles pour les sacrifices, et il ordonne a ses hommes de retourner le cadavre. Ils obéissant et retournent le cadavre. Ngurangurane fend alors la peau : il la fend depuis la gueule jusqu'a l'anus, il la fend en long, et par deux fois, il la fend en largeur ; il la rabat encore de chaque côté ; *la chair est enlevée, mise sur le feu, tous les hommes ont leur part, chacun son morceau. A Ngurangurane, le cœur et la cervelle ; aux chefs et aux viellards, les parties nobles, et la langue, et les yeux ; aux femmes et aux enfants les*

[1] R. P. H. Trilles, *op. cit.*, p. 200, Note 1.

entrailles ; chacun a son morceau, chacun a sa part. *Ainsi nul ne pourra craindre.*

" Dans la peau desséchée et soigneusement recousue là où il le faut, Ngurangurane dispose alors des morceaux de bois pour en maintenir la courbure, et quand tout est prêt, Ngurangurane ordonne de la mettre sur le lac : elle flotte à la surface. Ngurangurane y monte, les pattes lui servent de pagaies, la queue flexible de gouvernail. Çà et là, il marche : à droite, à gauche, en arrière, en avant. Jusque là, les Fân ne savaient pas ce que c'était qu'une pirogue. Comme Ngurangurane, le premier, avait fait avec la peau du crocodile, tel ils firent dans la suite en creusant des troncs d'arbre. . . .

" Mais ce n'est pas tout. Ngurangurane avait vengé sa race, et c'était son premier devoir. Mais il était aussi fils du crocodile, et pour cela, il ordonna les grandes fêtes des funerailles, le Fanki, les grandes fêtes qui apaisent les esprits des morts. Pendant trente fois trente jours, les femmes ont pleuré Ombure : etc. . . .

" Pendant trente lunaisons, l'esprit irrité d'Ombure a parcouru les villages, cherchant sa vengeance et poursuivant les vivants, mais partout il a trouvé sa propre chair. Il ne peut se venger.

" Tous les jours, le tamtam de mort retentit, les danseurs se succèdent, *Ngurangurane préside a la céremonie* . . . et lui-même, le grand chef, de ses propres mains, *il reproduit l'image de l'ancêtre* : *il façonne un énorme Ombure.* On l'orne de blanc et de noir, de jaune et de rouge, et quand il est entièrement préparé, dans la tête, Ngurangurane introduit les os d'Ombure : *autour de l'ancêtre, les danses ont recommencé,* les danses circulaires. Toute la nuit, elles durent : jusqu'au matin, le tamtam retentit. Alors Ngurangurane s'approche seul : près d'Ombure, il a placé deux hommes, et l'un après l'autre il les immole, et le sang arrose Ombure. Les chairs sont placées près d'Ombure : près de sa tête, les têtes, près de son corps, les corps, près de ses pieds, les pieds. Et chacun prend sa part et se retire.

" A tous, Ngurangurane offre le cadeau des funerailles.

" Quand tout est terminé, Ngurangurane ordonne ceci :

" ' Ainsi nous ferons chaque année, ainsi chaque année nous honorerons Ombure.'

" Et les Fân, depuis ce temps-là, ont ainsi fait.

" Et c'est pour cela que Ombure, sous la figure de Ngan (crocodile) est encore aujourd'hui le ' mvamayon ' " (meaning father of the tribe and the national and tribal totem [1]) " des fils de Ngurangurane.

" Ceci est la fin de cette histoire.

" IV. Dans une quatrième reprise, le conteur nous fait assister aux transformations, et à la mort de Ngurangurane mis à mort par un traître, mais cette partie ne se rapportant pas a notre cadre actuel, il serait inutile de la donner ici."

As an ethnological fact, this legend shows that the National Totem of these people is regarded as the ancestor of the tribe and is called father by all the people. In this case sacrifice is a " totemic " phenomenon,[2] since sacrifices are made directly to the national totem both in the legend and in the ceremonies. In the myth the totem is killed and eaten and around this legendary fact or rather wish is centred an actual religious and ceremonial cult in which is dramatized directly the appeasing of the totem father for having been killed and eaten.

Psychologically, the legend and the totemic cult teem with proofs that here again the latent wishes of the unconscious mind occur in the " Œdipus " pattern precisely similar to that first discovered by Freud. For instance the following analysis springs directly from the native statements and interpretation with regard to the beings and objects mentioned in the legend. In this instance it is in no way possible to allege arbitrariness or a reading of alien psychology into the native facts and interpretations :

(1) The Crocodile, who is the legendary father of the father of the race, persecutes men by demanding human sacrifices. He is another example of the often mentioned and widespread pursuing father occurring in primitive and civilized dream, myth and folklore. He represents the expectation of punishment because of individual death wishes of men towards their fathers.

(2) He is appeased by giving him his demanded sacrifices in order to alleviate the guilty feelings towards him.

[1] R. P. H. Trilles, *op. cit.*, pp. 84, 86.
[2] See p. 133, this chapter, for Kroeber's statement on totemic sacrifice.

(3) In the legend the people try to escape from him, but he is always in pursuit and catches up to them every time. In other words men cannot escape from their guilty death wishes by running away from them.

(4) In this legend the wish for deliverance from the pursuing father or guilty death wishes becomes progressively stronger as the story unfolds. The deliverance can only take place by killing the father, but how is such a killing to be carried out without arousing the guilt feelings or in such a way as to satisfy them?

(5) The sanction for killing the father is very subtly arranged in the legend. The Crocodile, a legendary being, is regarded as the great father by the natives, and this being kills the human chief of the tribe who is the human father. The way is thus opened for the revenge for the killing of the human father. Now the culture hero, soon to be born, will have the right to kill the Crocodile father, backed by the talion law of revenge which seems always to be inherent in the unconscious mind everywhere. The hero has a cultural justification because his father killed the chief of the tribe.

(6) The hero is now ready to be born, and I have already pointed out how in his birth the incestuous desires of his mother for her father are realized. She is the daughter of the human chief, and she has a liaison with the mythical chief, both fathers to her.

(7) The hero is thus descended from the Crocodile, the mythical chief as well as the human chief through his mother.

(8) The hero is animated by the two desires stated in the legend as " to avenge the death of the chief of his race," that is of the father of his mother, and to deliver his people from the tribute levied on them by the Crocodile father. He thus has the cultural sanction to kill his actual father, the Crocodile, at the same time being enabled to realize his own death wishes and free his mother. Here is realized the complete " Œdipus."

(9) In order to kill his father and free his mother (i.e. possess his mother) he must be a man. In barely disguised symbolism the legend shows how he acquires sexual potency from his mother. She is the one who has given him the magic power to kill his father in the form of the fetish stone called Ngonémane. It is especially significant that the name of this stone means, " the girl is no longer a virgin," [1] which is also said to be a surname of the hero's mother.[1] That which causes the girl to be no longer a virgin is obviously the phallus, hence the fetish stone is a phallic symbol. Thus the mother presents her son with a magic phallus which bears her own name, which is the chief weapon or means of his succeeding in the murder of his father.[2] The hero killed his father only, " grace au secours de Ngonémane," [3] the magic phallus [4] presented to him by his mother. Clearly the incestuous wish for the mother is the purpose of killing his father. Together mother and son bring about the father's death.

(10) In the cult of the Crocodile which arose after his murder are shown the efforts to allay the guilt because of the deed. The Crocodile father is cut up and eaten by the hero and all the members of the tribe. They thus incorporate the qualities of the father and the son makes his first step in becoming the father himself. His further identification with the Crocodile father is shown when he makes a boat of its skin and climbs on board and paddles and steers it with its legs and tail.[5] This would show a cultural result arising from a father identification [6] which resolves in part the old death wishes.

---

[1] p. 161.   [2] p. 161.   [3] p. 162, this chapter.

[4] Since this fetish stone also made Ngurangurane acquainted with the intoxicating drink of " dzan " " qui rend le cœur joyeux " (this stone which was given to him by his mother), it shows that it is also a symbol of his mother's nipple which taught him to drink the " dzan," a symbol of her milk. Here nipple and phallus are definitely equated as has often been discovered in modern analyses of the unconscious. See p. 161.   [5] See p. 163.

[6] See pp. 167–81 on cultural results of " Œdipus " solutions.

(11) The guilt feelings for this " primal crime " (which seems to be identical with Freud's) are never entirely allayed. The hero now makes an image of the Crocodile father and all dance and sing about him, and he is even offered more human sacrifices to appease him in the same old way. This Crocodile father must be appeased annually and he thus becomes the National Totem around whom a religious and totemic cult arose.

(12) There are strong hints that the talion law of revenge still goes on, and that the hero is later killed for having killed his father,[1] but at this point the text stops and we are told that the hero was " mis a mort par un traître."

The above analysis based on native associations and interpretations shows, therefore, how among these people " totemism " to which human sacrifice is associated is rooted in the " Œdipus complex," and the case of these people is an exception to the general experience of anthropologists that " totemic sacrifice is practically unknown " as stated by Goldenweiser in his criticism of Freud.[2] This case also shows that it is not always correct to regard cultural traits peculiar to a particular tribe as explicable only historically and not psychologically.

CULTURE ARISING FROM " ŒDIPUS " DREAMS.

In Chapter II it was shown that often different items of primitive culture arose from dreams, and it was also shown that they tended to arise in dreams in which the deceased father appeared in symbolic form as " totem " animal, ancestor, or guardian, and gave instructions for new ceremonies, songs, dances, medicine, secret societies, careers and shamanistic powers. In other words, in these dreams from which cultural results arise, there is found on the surface one aspect of the " Œdipus " pattern, namely, the

[1] p. 167.
[2] Goldenweiser, *History, Psychology and Culture*, p. 206.

seeking to appease and secure the protection and favours of the father. It has just been shown how among some of the Crow examples, this appeasing of the father is because of the guilty death wishes which must be resolved before the individual is allowed to become a respected member of the group. In all analysed Œdipus dreams anywhere, the appeasing of the father, i.e. the ambivalent attitude of hate and love, always occurs. A discovery of one aspect of the deep unconscious nuclear pattern usually means that the whole pattern exists in some form or other which analysis would disclose. If this is true all the dreams referred to are Œdipus dreams, *and we, therefore, find that specific culture items arise directly from Œdipus dreams.*

Another very good example of this process is in the founding of a new chapter of the ceremonial Tobacco Society of the Crow Indians which arose directly from this vision [1] :

" Medicine Crow prayed to the Sun, cutting off a finger-joint, and was visited by a young man and a woman who were identical with the tobacco plant. They gave instructions for the foundation of the Strawberry chapter."

Analysis : In the analyses of other Crow culture pattern visions it was found by association that the spirits appealed to and symbolized in cultural form were parents or parental substitutes. Here again we find the theme of wanting to appease the father (Sun) first by punishing himself (presumably for his incestuous and death wishes) by a symbolic castration (cutting off a finger-joint), and being visited in a vision by the parents (young man and woman) who give instruction for the foundation of the Strawberry chapter. Thus reward and social standing are given for the conciliatory and self-punishing attitude. The tobacco plant, the emblem of the Society, is identified with the parents, and the founding of the chapter as a result of the vision with the accompanying ceremony would be an excellent

[1] Part III, p. 257.

example of the " sublimation " of the anti-social attitude towards the parents.[1]

Obviously much detailed analytic research must be done with the visions and dreams from which a definite cultural result arises to determine how often they arise as expressions of the unconscious nuclear family complex, as well as the processes which cause such dreams to have such a result. The problem is complicated by the facts : (1) that the symbolism of a culture pattern dream is culturally determined in the first place, and ; (2) that the dream is not an ultimate origin but merely gives form to previously existing psychological processes. My study of the manifest content of primitive dreams in relation to the culture (Part III) shows that the manifest content of the dream is determined by the culture.[2] The latent content has just been found in many cases to be some aspect of the unconscious nuclear family complex. This would mean, therefore, that the latent content of these dreams is determined by the family group itself. The latter statement would apply to those individual Œdipus dreams (where the culture does not require a vision quest) which are determined by the individual's infantile experience in relation to his parents, and to those " culture pattern " Œdipus dreams, where actually dreamed, fantasied or induced (and not purchased or inherited). In the latter group the family experience would still be the determining factor, only the dreamer's specific Œdipus reaction is expressed in stereotyped cultural form.

In culture pattern dreams which are purchased or transferred from father to son, as among the Kwakiutl, other North-west tribes, and the Omaha, we find in evidence the same Œdipus theme occurring in symbolic cultural form

[1] The visions recorded for the founding of two other chapters of the Tobacco Society need further analysis with associations before they can be stated to be Œdipus visions. In Vision 3 the Sun is Patron, and is probably the usual father symbol. Part III, p. 257, Nos. 2 and 3.

[2] Freud's experience of the day before.

specific to each group. I have shown this in a Kwakiutl traditional vision, and in the following examples from the " visions " on which are founded the membership of the Omaha secret societies, the content reveals the same pattern of a supernatural Patron who confers benefits. There is no reason to suppose that analysis would not show the Patron (Grizzly Bear, Buffalo, Thunder Bird) to be again the father, as in the other culture pattern visions, and possibly more so among the Omaha where descent is patrilineal,[1] and where in the family the father was recognized as having the highest authority over all the members, although the mother's brother assumed control of the children on the parents' death.[2]

The Omaha belief is that membership in the Secret Societies is obtained by virtue of a dream or vision,[3] and the membership of the Societies was made up of groups who had had the same vision. For instance the entrance to the Bear Society was supposed to be given to " those to whom the bear has shown compassion," by appearing in a dream or vision and conferring supernatural powers.[4] Similarly the Buffalo Society was made up of " those to whom the buffalo has shown compassion," and thus each of the other Societies had its own standardized admission vision.

In a recent study Fortune has shown [5] how an individual vision as an admission requirement to the Societies has come to be strictly irrelevant,[6] since the privilege of membership is hereditarily transmitted in the family, generally from father to son. All non-members believe, however, that the individual quest of a supernatural Patron entitles one to

[1] This may be irrelevant since I have pointed out that there is no correlation between father visions and descent patterns. See p. 95, Ref. 1, Chap. II.

[2] Fletcher and La Flèche, " The Omaha Tribe," *27th Ann. Rep. of B.A.E.*, 1905–06, p. 325.

[3] *Ibid.*, p. 459.   [4] Previous cit., p. 486.

[5] R. F. Fortune, " Omaha Secret Societies," *Columbia University Contrib. to Anthropology*, Vol. XIV, 1932, pp. 35–47, 53–75.

[6] *Ibid.*, p. 2.

membership, and all earnestly seek it. Members also speak as if their individual vision gave them the required powers. What actually happens, however, is that everyone is encouraged in the belief that the individual search for a supernatural Patron will be rewarded by a vision, and children are sent out between the ages of seven and eight to seek some sort of a supernatural experience under the instructions of their parents, and at puberty or after came the important rite of definitely seeking a supernatural Patron. The youth going out in this search had not heard any account of a previous vision, since visions were only told secretly and on special occasions. If his father possessed a power from revelation he would only tell his son in return for a heavy payment, and the son believed " that such an action might precipitate his father's death," [1] hence he continued his own search for an individual experience, supported by his father's hopes that the son would have a true experience, even if the father himself had not had one. The father believed that his own purchased vision arose from a true vision experience in the past even if he had had no such experience himself.

The youths often did have an individual experience of the supernatural. For instance the following is part of an individual vision which is not a transferred one [2] :

" ' The four Grizzly Bears were there in line. Their paws all dripped blood.' The visionary's hand, ' they dripped blood too.' The Bears sang,

' So with this gift
With this gift
We bless you,
We bless you.' "

After four days this visionary told his experience to an old man of the Grizzly Bear Society and was invited to eat with them, but not to join because his vision had not given him the full powers needed, which consisted in certain

[1] *Ibid.*, p. 40.   [2] *Ibid.*, p. 41.

miraculous " tricks." These could only be acquired along with a purchased family vision.

The custom of claiming a derived vision as personal, however, was widespread and was emphasized to hide the belief that transfer of a vision caused the death of the owner (often the father) who transferred it, hence the transfer was unmentionable because of the painful associations.[1] A man who got no vision realized he still could gain admission to a society by purchase of the family vision provided they already had a membership. The man who had the Grizzly Bear vision above might have been given right of purchase if he had relatives in a Society.[2]

The transfer of a vision was called, " to cause to see the supernatural," and was performed as follows : the initiator and novice went away privately and the former taught the traditional vision of the Society or the form of it that descended in his family and the sacred song or songs of the vision, etc. He then handed over the medicine bundle that went with the vision.

It was understood by outsiders that a man had such control of his supernatural Patron that he could induce vision of it in the novice whom, " he caused to see the supernatural." Thus vision by transfer was made to be real vision, and transfer and real vision were reconciled.[3]

Examples occur, however, of Society pattern dreams being dreamed individually and spontaneously by outside non-members. In one, the vision *per se* did not make the visionary a member, but his father had been a member. He dreamed the standard Buffalo Society vision after killing a buffalo. A buffalo appeared to him with water spouting from his nostril making a spray with a rainbow in it. The spray was directed to cleanse the buffalo's wound. Thus, independent " pattern " visions that are not purchased do occur as individual experiences.[4]

[1] Fortune, *op. cit.*, p. 45.
[3] *Ibid.*, p. 47.
[2] *Ibid.*, pp. 46–47.
[4] *Ibid.*, p. 69.

One informant had a vision of his own of Buffalo spirits. He had faith in this until his father " caused him to see " a vision, and he then put away his own.[1] Others used the solitary visions and despised the transfer initiations and some had both the solitary vision and transfer visions, but in the Society used the former. The Grizzly Bear vision and song referred to above was given to another man who had inherited the right of admission to the Grizzly Bear Society. Hence individual visions still play their part in the Societies in an indirect way.[2]

Generally, the solitary vision was regarded as socially unimportant whereas the acquired vision made a man socially prominent, respected and powerful.[3]

The investigation of Omaha visions so far shows the following :

(1) Admission visions and " tricks " of the Omaha Secret Societies are transferred in the family generally from father to son, by a process called, " made to see the supernatural." This could be a real inducing of the family vision in the initiate or merely a telling of the standard vision.[4]

(2) The transfer is believed to cause the death of the father or original owner, who often actually does die when a transfer is made.[5]

(3) All of the stock inherited visions of the society are of the usual psychological and cultural pattern in which the appearance of a supernatural Patron (father symbol), who confers specific gifts, occurs. Hence they show one aspect of the unconscious nuclear family complex.

(4) Individual unpurchased vision experiences also occur without any knowledge of the hereditary family visions of the Societies, and these are of exactly the same cultural and psychological pattern as the transferred visions. These

---

[1] *Ibid.*, p. 73.   [2] *Ibid.*, p. 54.   [3] *Ibid.*, p. 54.
[4] Dreams can be induced. For experimental dreams induced under hypnosis see *Psyche and Eros*, Vol. II, Jan.–Feb. 1921, pp. 1–11, and March–April 1921, pp. 90–9, by O. Pfister.
[5] Fortune, *op. cit.*, p. 45.

individual visions are occasionally still used in the Societies in conjunction with purchased tricks, the latter being the real qualification for membership.

(5) The investigation shows that actual individual visions which still occur without knowledge of the inherited ones, are probably the prototype of the inherited ones, because both are Œdipus dreams and the Œdipus pertains to individual psychology.

(6) The individual visions are attempts to solve the anti-social wishes towards the father and get the reward of being accepted as socially important.

(7) The Secret Society, inherited, Œdipus visions would therefore represent a giving of cultural form and sanction to former individual vision solutions of the family complex.

(8) That an inherited knowledge of certain miraculous " tricks " became the qualifications for membership over and above the vision could be explained on the grounds of wanting jealously to maintain a closed Doctoring Society (most of the Societies are Doctoring Societies) which could be done only by impressing the outsider with supernatural powers supported by convincing tricks. The vision itself indicated the solving of anti-social individual tendencies in the interests of the group and was a cultural requirement, but if too many were granted this power there would be no need for a Doctoring profession. It is the old " esoteric complex " of those who have a real or assumed special knowledge, capitalizing on it for their own benefit.

(9) The fact that transfer of a vision to a son results in the death of his father, yet the content of the vision shows an attempt to appease the father because of death wishes, may be psychologically significant. The vision (even though purchased) in itself symbolizes the solution of father hostility acceptable to the culture. Its owner then is absolved by the culture from his own father hostility as long as he possesses it. If he sells it he no longer is under cultural sanction, and when the protection of the supernatural Patron is withdrawn, his death wishes towards his own father now

return in full force and his guilt and unconscious need for punishment result in his own death. This analysis conforms with the usual functioning of unconscious fantasy on this subject and is offered for what it may be worth. It receives added support from the strong primitive belief in fantasy as a form of reality, what Freud calls the omnipotence of thought.

Also the son who purchases a vision which symbolizes a resolving of father hostility, at the same time causes the death of his father. Here we find simultaneously the ambivalent situation of the culture providing a solution to death wishes towards the father, while the recipient of the solution realizes his own death wishes by the actual death of his father. He knows his father may die when he buys the vision from him (many allow an hereditary vision to die out because of this knowledge) and when later he sells it he would, therefore, expect to be punished by his own death.

The pattern visions and Secret Societies of the Omaha represent, therefore, another cultural attempt to socialize the unconscious nuclear family complex.

Besides many examples of new cultural items arising directly from Œdipus dreams, such as a new chapter to a ceremonial society, or a new song or dance or other items, there is the situation where an Œdipus dream sets in motion preexisting cultural institutions. This would be the case among the Navajo where a dream with an emotionally disturbing effect on the dreamer leads to the organization of a traditional curing ceremony. I have brought out how among the Navajo practically all dreams are individual spontaneous dreams and not culture pattern dreams as among the Plains tribes.

Dr. Pfister has analysed an individual dream of this sort (with the ensuing curing ceremony) in which a man dreamed of bears pursuing him and afterwards fell into a state of neurotic anxiety.[1] This dream, through the usual channels

[1] See Part III, p. 219 and notes, for reference to Pfister's article and complete description of this case.

of Navajo diagnosis, led to a curing ceremony in which the man said he was cured of the bad effects of his dream. I consulted this man myself (a year later) and asked him about this dream. He told me how he repeatedly had been bothered with dreams of Bears pursuing him, and he gave us the reason for his dream that his father had seen the Mountain Chant ceremony while his mother was pregnant with him.[1] Thus he associated father with bear, and this corroborated Dr. Pfister's analysis of the dream as an Œdipus father-hostility dream.[2]

This case proves how an Œdipus dream sets in motion the whole Navajo religious ceremonial institution, to cure an individual's anti-social tendencies and to restore him to society.

Of the Navajo dreams in my collection from field and literature many are Œdipus dreams (subject to further analysis) resulting in a curing ceremony. I here attempt analysis of these which are of varying conclusiveness because of the difficulty of acquiring associations[3]:

No. 1. Shaman's Dream.[4] Gods came after him and tried to drag him away to a mountain. He had this dream again and again.

Analysis : This is of exactly the same pattern as that of the pursuing father because of death wishes, as in the preceding dream. He was advised to have a Night Chant, and his family said he must have it, thus showing how aware

---

[1] The Mountain Chant is one of the great nine-day religious curing ceremonies of the Navajo. They are public and social events in which are centred the religious, ceremonial and social life of the tribe. Described in detail by Washington Matthews, 5th Annual Report, B.A.E., 1883-4, and analysed by Pfister in relation to this case. See Ref. 1 previous page.

[2] Ibid., Ref. 1.

[3] Full text is given on pp. 218-40, Part III. Here abbreviated. Nos. same as in Part III.

[4] p. 218.

the culture is of the need for a solution of this eternal problem.

No. 8. "Sometimes I dream that my parents are dead whereas they are still alive." [1]

Analysis : An obvious death-wish dream. He does not mention a curing ceremony.

No. 3. Dream of Hasteen Hal.[2] "A *family of bears, mother, father*, and *two cubs* pursue him while in a cañon with high walls around him. *His own family and children* were with him. The bears fell down and *a man appeared* near where they were. The scene changes and the man was standing on the running-board of his car. Suddenly they are sitting in the car with a tire blown out. The man fixes the tire. The car starts off and they go on to the paved road with the man still standing on the running-board. When they get to the main road he wakes up."

Associations. "He had a fight with some Indians about a sheep transaction with a trader. The Indians didn't like it. 'That's how I got my start.'

" *The bears* were the Indians who fought me.

" *The man who fixed the tire* was a medicine man who performed a 'sing' over me.

" Before the man gave me a sing I had many accidents with my children and sheep.

" Lightning struck my sheep.

" I got a medicine man to perform a sing over me, my children and sheep.

" *After the sing* I never had any trouble again. I never heard any derogatory thing said about myself by others.

" Since then I made a good start and increased my sheep, and my children were never sick again.

" According to the dream I believe all that."

Analysis : He interprets the pursuing bears as the Indians who fought him because he got ahead of them in a transaction with a trader. This looks like a rationalization, since in the dream the bears are a family group mentioned

[1] p. 220.   [2] pp. 227–8.

in connection with his own family. It would seem therefore that his escape from the bears symbolized his wanting to escape from his unconscious guilty wishes towards the parents (father and mother bear.) It is obvious that he feels guilty about his transaction which helped him get ahead of the other Indians. That the man who appears when the bears (family) fall down is the medicine man who gave him a " sing " after he had had many accidents with his children and sheep shows that the dreamer unconsciously regarded these accidents as punishments for his guilty wishes towards the parents and needed the curing services of the medicine man. He projected his anxiety and need for punishment on to nature and external events.

The collapsed tire mended by the medicine man would represent the curing of the unconscious negative wishes, but the fact that the medicine man stays with him when he is cured and his family life is going ahead smoothly (when his car is repaired and the family reaches the smooth paved road) shows that his " transference " to the medicine man is what is keeping him from falling back into his old wishes and anxieties with regard to the parents. In other words his old wishes and anxieties are still present but held in abeyance by displaced affection and gratitude for the medicine man as a symbolic father, who has forgiven him for his guilty wishes and restored prosperity to his family.

If this analysis is correct it shows again how the curing ceremonies exist to solve the anti-social family complex of individuals.

What is especially interesting in this dream is the combination of old cultural symbols with acquired " civilized " symbols. This, however, does not alter the latent meaning of the dream which is expressed in both cultural forms. The breakdown of the automobile as a symbol of the breakdown of the sexual apparatus because of the parental complex shows the primitive mind using the same symbol to express the same primary idea as the " civilized."

Automobile is on Freud's list as generally symbolizing the genitals.[1]

Hasteen Hon's series of dreams [2] show that he is suffering from severe guilt anxiety, and expectation of punishment, as shown in the dream of being struck by lightning (No. 4) and his emotional reaction to being actually struck by lightning. In another dream a voice told him that he was going to be punished by having his leg broken because he had forgotten to perform a sacrifice before he crossed a river, (No. 3). This might signify a castration anxiety (leg broken).

After being struck by lightning he was given as a curing ceremony the *Natoye bakaji*, or Male Shooting Chant in which reference is made to the male and female divinities of Lightning, Thunder, Snakes and the Bear. We have found the bear to be a father symbol in individual dreams and probably these divinities are also father or parent symbols. Thus punishment by lightning means that the father is seeking revenge for death wishes and must be appeased in the ceremony. Appeasing the father is to allay the guilt feelings towards him.

The dream in which the voice told him that he was to be punished by having his leg broken (castration) leads to his being given the *Hozhonji*, a rite of blessing or restoration which figures in the blessing invoked upon the family, house and property.

It is interesting to see how the symbolism occurring in the curing ceremonies harmonizes with the symbols of specific dreams. Each ceremony seems to be especially designed for the cure of some specific form of the anti-social family complex. The latter is only a suggestion and would require long and specialized research before it could be conclusively proved.[3] I put it forth nevertheless. A

---

[1] See Chap. III, pp. 119–20.

[2] Part III, pp. 233-7.

[3] Especially since the ceremonies are known to have been borrowed from other tribes. This would not necessarily alter the suggestion,

sure knowledge of the latent meaning of Navajo symbols would also be necessary. The following type of information if correctly interpreted would corroborate my suggestion :

If a dreamer is emotionally affected by his dream he decides what curing ceremony he shall have from the dream itself, unless he does not know the nature of his ailment, in which case a star-gazer or 'diagnostician' is consulted who prescribes the appropriate ceremony.[1]

Dreams of snakes, buzzards, hawks and bird spirits require the *Hozhonae Chant* (translated by Washington Mathews as Chant of Terrestrial Beauty). [2]

Suggestion. This ceremony might be provided for the cure of incestuous tendencies, the earth being a mother symbol.

Dreams of death, that is, of one's own death, or the death of neighbours and relatives, also dreams that your teeth have fallen out require the *Hozhonji* or Chant of Restoration of the Family.[2]

Suggestion. Death dreams are generally death wishes, and the symbol of losing a tooth as often meaning castration anxiety because of death wishes is widespread. (Here again occurs the association of loss of a tooth, death of a relative as in the universal type dreams.) The *Hozhonji* is to restore the family, that is to protect it from death wishes towards the parents.

Dreams of lightning, of being badly hurt, of snakes biting you, of dangerous things require the *Natoye bakaji* or Male Shooting Chant in which the male and female divinities of Lightning, Thunder, Snakes, and the Bear are invoked.[3]

Suggestion. The Male Shooting Chant might be especially designed to appease the father because of expectation of punishment and to restore maleness. The divinities invoked are father symbols, and the name of the chant suggests the symbolism of sexual potency.

however, because the unconscious and social need of a solution to the Œdipus could be the determining co-ordinator of the dreams and ceremonies.

[1] Part III, pp. 207–9. [2] *Ibid.*, Part III, p. 208.
[3] *Ibid.*, Part III, p. 209.

Thus all the ceremonies exist to solve the unconscious psychological, anti-social tendencies which seem to be inherent in the family relationship, and to restore the individual to society. The Navajo prayer belonging to one of these ceremonies says [1] :

> " My feet restore Thou for me
> My legs restore Thou for me
> My body restore Thou for me
> My mind restore Thou for me
> My voice restore Thou for me
> Restore all for me in beauty
> Make beautiful all that is before me
> Make beautiful all that is behind me
> Make beautiful my words
> It is finished in beauty
> It is finished in beauty
> It is finished in beauty
> It is finished in beauty."

If the facts and analyses with regard to symbolic Œdipus dreams and their influence in the formation of culture, as well as their influence in the functioning of primitive institutions are true, they go a long way towards proving that Freud is right in his belief that religion, ethics, society and art are rooted in the Œdipus complex. It seems that this complex is inherent in the primordial, and universal family group which comprises the father-mother-child relationship, and arises from the instinctive anti-social tendencies of the individual (child) in relation to this group. As has already been stated by Malinowski,[2] it is not necessary to postulate a " mass psyche " or a " collective unconscious " as the carrier of these tendencies, or as a means of explaining phylogenetic parallels of this complex with its symbolic expressions, which appear in many instances to

---

[1] Washington Mathews, " The Mountain Chant, a Navajo Ceremony," *5th Ann. Rep. of B.A.E.*, 1883–4, p. 420.

[2] Malinowski, *Sex and Repression in Savage Society*, p. 277.

be identical in both individual dreams and in cultural processes.[1,2]

In a critical review of Jung's works,[3] Kroeber has stated with regard to psychoanalysis,

"But certain of its findings as to the conversion rather than extinction of repressed desires, for instance, and the significance of dream material have surely become a part of general psychology, and therefore relate to that form of activity which underlies all social phenomena and which the anthropologist can never wholly afford to ignore.

"The other point of contact is the assumption apparently typical of the school, that symbols into which the libido converts itself are phylogenetically transmitted and appear socially. The machinery of this assumed process is not examined. Its reality is considered established by the adduction of examples which may be so interpreted. Now if the psychoanalysts are right nearly all ethnology and culture history are waste of effort, except in so far as they contribute new raw materials."

He then goes on to declare that Jung's phylogenetic interpretations are put forward without any examination of their foundations.

To the latter statement every scientifically minded person would agree. That no anthropologist can afford "wholly" and even in part to ignore the psychological significance

---

[1] Roheim now inclines towards this viewpoint also. He says, "Since, however, an unconscious inheritance of this 'primal drama' has never been demonstrated in any analysis we have no justification for assuming it." He is the first analyst to state the fallaciousness of the primal horde theory of culture origins and the need of its reconsideration or rejection, and to realize that tradition and family conditions are sufficient to explain the transmission of the Œdipus. See discussion, G. Roheim, "Primitive High Gods," *The Psychoanalytic Quarterly*, N.Y., Vol. III, No. 1, Part II, Jan. 1934, pp. 120–3.

[2] In a later work, however, he still holds on to the "primal horde" theory for the explanation of certain myths whose elements cannot easily be derived from the Œdipus complex.—Roheim, *The Riddle of the Sphinx*, p. 173.

[3] A. L. Kroeber, "Review of Jung's Collected Papers," *American Anthropologist*, Vol. XX, July–Sept. 1918, pp. 323–4.

of the conversion of the libido into symbolic expressions which appear in individual dreams as a form of activity which underlies all social phenomena is also evident. It is true that psychoanalysts have not indicated the mechanism whereby the symbols into which the libido converts itself are phylogenetically transmitted and appear socially. They have contented themselves with the interpretation of cultural processes by relying on the concept of the mass psyche to explain phylogenetic parallels of individual processes, and this concept still remains an unproved assumption.

As to Professor Kroeber's fears that culture history may become waste of effort if the psychoanalysts' interpretations are correct, it seems less panicky to suggest instead that its task will continue to be a necessary sorting of the facts of history and diffusion, wherever this is possible, in order to reach the deeper and more significant foundation in human motive of which culture, in the last analysis, is an expression.

I have shown that many facts of primitive culture have arisen from Œdipus·dreams. More accurately this means that the dream gives form, generally symbolic, to the unconscious anti-social tendencies that are·inherent in the family relationship, and in many instances leads the individual to socialize these tendencies in some specific cultural act, which is incorporated by his group as a new and significant cultural element or institution. The symbolism occurring in the dream is thus transmitted to the new cultural element, as happens for instance in new ceremonies, songs and " totemic " processes, which arise from these dreams.[1]

If this conclusion is true it would explain the mechanism whereby the " symbols into which the libido converts itself are phylogenetically transmitted and appear socially." The Œdipus dream, i.e. the symbolic expression of the unconscious and widespread individual reactions to the family group, is, therefore, a carrier of culture. This fact is of

[1] See Chap. II.

such importance for the significance of and formation of culture that no harm is done in constantly restating it, especially since if true, it means that there is less need than ever to indulge in fruitless speculations as to first origins, because *we have a source of culture origins constantly with us, continually at work in the formation of culture.*

The problem is of course unduly simplified, especially with regard to what has been said about the phylo-genetic use of symbols which arose because of individual dreams. This undoubtedly is a most important mechanism, but it is complicated by the fact that the reverse process also takes place, as in the culture pattern dream in which the culture determines the symbols occurring in the dreams, and in the manifest content of all individual dreams in which the reflection of existing external culture plays a large part. Symbols which are universal with the same latent meaning everywhere are also culture products, and indicate that a cultural situation must exist that is eternally the same. Such a similarity of symbols is probably a reflection of certain universally similar aspects of the family group. Both processes of the influence of dreams on culture, and of culture on dreams do, however, occur.

A summary of the main conclusions of the last two chapters cover a wide range, but they are a direct result of following the facts to wherever they might lead. Many of them are tentative and subject to further research for corroboration or rejection in the event of evidence to the contrary being produced. If they are true, however, the ethnologist can no longer hide his head in the sand with regard to the facts of the psychology which underly ethnology, which no anthropologist can " wholly afford to ignore."

The main conclusions are :

(1) Individual dreams are not diffusable, whereas culture pattern dreams are.[1]

[1] pp. 104–7.

(2) The same groups of secondary ideas or symbols occur associated together among primitives, that are found in the mind of non-primitives prior to analysis and the uncovering of the primary ideas behind them.[1]

(3) A further study of many primitive dream symbols with associations have shown that the same primary ideas are often expressed by the same symbols as found in the unconscious of non-primitives. Certain substances and objects, sexual fantasies, the primary ideas of father, mother, phallus, birth and death are all expressed in the most widespread parts of the world by symbols identical with those first mentioned by Freud.[2]

(4) Primary ideas are also expressed by culturally determined symbols peculiar to specific cultures.[3]

(5) As primitive culture breaks down and " civilization " intervenes, " civilized " symbols appear in the manifest content of the dream.[4]

(6) It is suggested that the mind assimilates new symbols to represent old primary ideas, through the associative principles of similarity, and identity, and the associative mechanism of condensation, since the unconscious tends to see similarities, and never differences.

(7) Phylogenetic parallels in symbols and psychological processes pertaining to the individual are found everywhere.

(8) Evidence has been presented by uncovering the latent meanings of symbols through individual and cultural associations, to indicate that the nuclear Œdipus and castration complexes exist at the base of many individual dreams as well as at the roots of many cultural processes.[5]

(9) These complexes are regarded as being inevitable results of the family or father-mother-child relationship, and as anti-social tendencies which arise in every individual.

(10) It has been shown that the nuclear complexes exist at the base of the Crow Indian vision quest and self-torture customs, at the base of Blackfoot shamanistic vision, and

---

[1] pp. 126–31.   [2] pp. 107–26.   [3] Part III, and pp. 111–21.
[4] Part III and Chap. III.   [5] pp. 132–81.

at the basis of the Kwakiutl vision and cannibal cult, and at the core of Bantu Fan " totemic " practices and legend.[1]

(11) The nuclear complexes occur in varying forms in each of these cultures which provides its own specific socializing solution of these unconscious anti-social tendencies.

(12) All sought or induced " culture pattern " dreams are probably symbolic Œdipus dreams, in specific cultural form pertaining to each culture.

(13) It has been shown that instances (in Chapter II as well)[2] of almost every element of primitive culture have arisen directly because of Œdipus dreams, and I have analysed specific items among the Crow and Omaha so arising.[3]

(14) The influence of " individual " Œdipus dreams in setting in motion pre-existing cultural institutions among the Navajo has been tentatively analysed.[4]

(15) Since much of primitive culture seems to arise from Œdipus dreams, it indicates a mechanism whereby phylogenetic parallels to individual processes occur.[5]

(16) Since the " Œdipus " which pertains to the individual is a result of the family relationship and its solution gives rise to culture, the assumption of a mass psyche, which is unprovable, is no longer needed to explain phylogenetic parallels.

(17) If culture is constantly arising from Œdipus dreams in primitive society, this signifies that we have a source of culture always with us.

(18) The problem is complicated because of the reverse process of symbolism being determined by cultural influence.

(19) The suggestion is made that a most important subject for further ethnologic research is the mechanism of the diffusion and assimilation of culture which in the last analysis is psychological, i.e. it is only because of the " psychic unity " of man that diffusion in the sense of incorporation of foreign elements by a culture is at all

[1] pp. 144–67. [2] pp. 44–98.
[3] pp. 167–75. [4] pp. 175–81. [5] Preceding chapter.

possible. It is suggested that much of borrowing and assimilation takes place because of the unconscious and constant need of new solutions to and transformations of the anti-social nuclear family complex.

(20) It is also suggested that cultural differences of different peoples should be studied in the light of their respective attempts at religious and social solutions of the " Œdipus complex." [1]

[1] See pp. 152–4.

PART III

AMERICAN INDIAN DREAMS—THEIR SIGNIFICANCE
TO THE NATIVE AND THEIR RELATION TO
THE CULTURE PATTERN.

ANALYSIS OF CONTENTS

1. Introduction, Thesis and Conclusions.
2. The Data.
    I. Ethnologists' reports of native classifications, beliefs, interpretations and customs relative to the dream patterns of different culture areas.
    II. Examples of Indian dreams or visions, and other dream data from the following culture areas and tribes :
        Lower Colorado Region. The Yuma.
        South-west Culture Area. The Navajo.
        The Plains Culture Area. The Crow. The Blackfoot.
        The Eastern Woodlands Culture Area. The Menomini. The Ottawa. The Ojibway.
        The North-west Pacific Coast Culture Area. The Kwakiutl.
3. Analysis and Correlation of the Data to the Specific Indian Cultures.
    I. The data fall into classes :
        (A) Culture Pattern Dreams and Visions. These reflect the dreamer's relation to the supernatural as sanctioned by the specific cultures. The forms and manifest contents are rigorously determined by the culture. These represent the culture's demand on the individual.

189

(B) Individual Dreams. These reflect in their manifest contents :

    (*a*) The religious, social, and material culture of the dreamer's tribe.

        or

    (*b*) An absence of culture traits hence largely personal psychology.

    The forms of these dreams are not determined primarily by the cultures but by individual psychology. The dreams of this type represent the individual's relation or non-relation to the culture.

II. The analysis shows a correlation between the manifest dream contents and the respective culture patterns of the different areas. The correlation is determined by how much the manifest contents reflect culture items such as supernatural beings, stereotyped quests, puberty fasting, medicine, ritual, kinship, social customs and objects of material culture, or by an absence of culture items in the manifest contents.

1. INTRODUCTION AND THESIS

ANTHROPOLOGISTS have recorded the dreams of American Indians, but there is much work to be done in an attempt to co-ordinate the material from the standpoint of the different Indian classifications and beliefs, and in a comparative study of the relation of the dream contents to the specific culture patterns. The purpose of the following study is to gather together from the literature and field-notes available, examples of Indian dreams taken from different culture areas, and to state wherever possible their significance to the Indian,[1] that is, what his beliefs are about the dream, how he interprets them, how he classifies them, and how he distinguishes different types of dreams. Wherever possible the specific reaction or comment of the dreamer will be given, but because of serious omissions in the data of the recorders it will be possible in many cases to give only some information regarding the general tribal belief or conception relative to the dream.[1]

The data can definitely be divided into two groups : the culture pattern dreams, and the ordinary individual dreams. The former comprises those stereotyped dreams conceptually (to the Indian) indistinguishable from visions, which reflect the Indian's relation to the supernatural, and both as to form and manifest content are determined by the culture pattern (The Crow vision, the Ottawa puberty fasting dreams, Yuma myth dreaming, etc.). Their contents reflect only the respective beliefs of the different areas in the supernatural, and they occur only where the

[1] Use is made of Wissler's culture area concept for the classification of the different tribes according to their cultures. Clark Wissler, *The American Indian*, Chap. XIV.

culture requires a prior period of fasting, isolation, or self-torture, or some form of training or instruction. The latter group of individual dreams, whose form is not determined by the culture pattern, but whose content, it is intended to show, reflects the religious, social or material culture of the specific area of the dreamer, are called individual for want of a better term to distinguish them from the former group. They are regular night dreams and are not deliberately induced by the culture or individual. These individual dreams are of two kinds, those which reflect cultural phenomena, and those which reflect no cultural phenomena at all. The former occur in those areas where emphasis is laid by the native on this type of dream, and the latter which reflect no cultural phenomena at all deal with subjective personal phenomena, and occur in areas where the old Indian culture has broken down together with the old culturally determined pattern dreams, and the individual dreams which formerly reflected the culture. The latter also occur in all areas where an individual has for some reason or other lost contact with the culture either temporarily or permanently.

The deeper psychology of the latent contents of the dream are not treated in this study, and the manifest content is treated as a kind of mirror which reflects items of the cultural surroundings of the dreamer. Inasmuch as these items which are well recorded by anthropologists, do appear in the manifest dream contents, such a use of the dream as a cultural index seems quite justifiable.

From the data of the different culture areas emphasis is laid on the varying importance of pattern dreaming and individual dreaming, with some cultures stressing one and some the other, and some stressing both types.

Hence, if it can also be shown that when a culture breaks down, the pattern dream disappears along with the religious culture it formerly reflected, and the individual dreams in different areas reflect all the transitional stages from a distinctive Indian culture through the different stages of decline, to either the absorption of white culture, or to a state in which dreams have no obvious reference to any particular stage of culture, it means that there is a definite correlation between the manifest dream content and the culture pattern.

GENERAL CONCLUSION.

A perusal of the following data will show that the meaning of the dream to the native varies with the different culture areas. Where pattern dreams or visions occur they are regarded as the determining factors in fitting the individual to take part in the life of the tribe. They all reflect the different supernatural or religious traditions of specific cultures, and are the essential requirements of the cultures for the individual's main undertakings in life. Whether they are the myth dreams of the Yuma, or " career " visions of the Crow, or guardian spirit dreams of the Woodlands or North-west Coast cultures, they are all regarded by the native as the most important experience in his life. They represent the culture's demand that the individual shall conform to its ways along certain limited lines which it lays down by its specific tradition defined in its myths.

The individual dream is regarded as having meaning for the individual and represents no formal demand made by the culture. This applies for all culture areas where this type of dream is taken seriously. It is regarded as good or bad, favourable or unfavourable, pure or impure (Ojibway), partially from its content and partially from its effect on the dreamer (Navajo). It is interpreted (Navajo, Kwakiutl, Woodlands) largely from the point of view of its influence on the life of the individual. Where violation of taboos seem to be indicated by the dream it leads to purifications and other ceremonial acts (Navajo, Kwakiutl) and where illness is indicated it leads to curing ritual. In areas where the culture has broken down the individual still interprets his dreams and regards them as important for his life. The Navajo treatment of the individual dream seems to be in a class by itself, inasmuch as it is so intimately bound up with the whole religious, social, medicine, and ceremonial culture, which with the exception of Star-gazing visions of diagnosticians excludes any formal pattern dreaming.[1] Here it is still of primary importance to the individual, but when the individual is emotionally affected by it, it arouses the culture to interpret it and see where the individual has erred against himself, his family, or his culture, and through ceremony and social communion to restore him to itself. In all tribes where this type of dream is treated seriously it plays an important rôle in the everyday life of the native (Kwakiutl, Woodlands, Navajo). These kinds of dreams, therefore, can be regarded as the index or gauge of the individual in his relationship with his culture.

Finally, to repeat and sum up, the pattern dream or vision represents the culture's demand on the individual, and its manifest content reflects the culture first, and secondarily individual psychology. The individual dream, however, represents the individual in his relation or non-relation to the culture, and its manifest content reflects his psychology first and secondarily his culture.[2]

[1] See cit., p. 217.

[2] See tables at end, showing regional variations of culture pattern and individual dreams, pp. 325–7.

2. THE LOWER COLORADO REGION

INDIAN BELIEFS AND ATTITUDES TOWARDS THE DREAM

The Yuma.[1]

1. Conceptually if not terminologically there is a clear distinction between the power bestowing dream or dream-vision, and the less significant dream of everyday life.

2. Myth dreaming. The individual dreams the myth. It conforms to a pattern.

3. Dreaming is the direct basis of all religion, tradition, ritual, song and shamanistic power, and conditions authority.

4. Belief that dreaming begins before birth.

5. Belief that the dream has meaning and can be interpreted.

6. Regarded as bad :

  (*a*) The appearance of dead relatives in dreams.

  (*b*) Dreams of intercourse with deceased wife which will bring on painful urination.

  (*c*) Dreams of eating with dead relatives, a cause of sickness and death.

7. Dreaming is believed to be more real than waking.

8. Whatever is dreamed is believed either to have happened or is about to happen.

The Mohave.[2]

1. Belief in dreams as the basis of everything in life.

2. Knowledge not a thing to be learned but to be acquired.

3. Good dreaming equals luck. Bad dreaming equals " ill starred ".

[1] Cf. Forde C. Daryll, " Ethnography of Yuma Indians," *University of California. Pub. in Amer. Arch. and Ethnol.*, Vol. 28, No. 4, pp. 201–3, 272 ; E. W. Gifford, " Yuma Dreams and Omens," *Journal of Am. Folklore*, Vol. 39, 1926, pp. 58–66 incl. ; A. Kroeber, " Handbook of Indians of California," Ch. 51, *B.A.E. Bulletin*, 78, p. 783.

[2] Cf. Kroeber, " The Mohave : Dream life " *ibid.*. pp. 754, 755, 784. Refers to Yuma and Mohave.

4. There is no form of fasting or training for seeking dreams.

5. Highest development of dreaming system in North America. Individual instead of traditional connection with the supernatural.

6. Medicine man acquires powers by dreaming.

7. Nearly all ceremonies performed because they have been dreamed.

8. All myths and historical legends are known by the raconteurs because they have seen the events themselves in their dreams.

9. Belief that whatever happens in dreams will come to pass.

10. " If these tribes could express themselves in our abstract terminology, they would probably say that the phenomena of dreams have an absolute reality, but that they exist in a dimension in which there is no time and in which there is no distinction between spiritual and material." [1]

The Kamia of Imperial Valley. [2]

1. Dreams are best for young persons, as an old dreamer might die in his dreams.

2. Charles Bean's own dreams dealt with the place in which he lived.

3. He was ignorant as to whether shamans dreamt much.

4. Knowledge of the destiny of human souls was derived through dreams. (Comments of Charles Bean.)

To the Yuman Maricopa the dream experience was also the heart of their culture. Dream experience was at the bottom of all success in life, and learning was displaced by dreaming. [3]

EXAMPLES OF YUMA DREAMS

Joe Homer, the " best dreamer among the Yuma." The following are his statements concerning his powers and training as a dreamer :

" Before I was born I would sometimes steal out of my mother's womb while she was sleeping, but it was dark and I did not go far. Every good Doctor begins to understand before he is born,

---

[1] Cf. A. Kroeber, " The Mohave Indians " (*American Anthropologist*, No. 4, 1902, pp. 279–85 incl.).

[2] E. W. Gifford, *B.A.E. Bulletin*, 97, p. 72.

[3] Leslie Spier, *Yuman Tribes of the Gila River* (Univ. of Chicago Press, 1933), pp. 202, 238–69, 323, 160, 164, 169, 170, 172, 177, 223, 186, 178, 280–99, 154–7, 160.

so that when he is big he knows it all." He related that when he was small he took a trip to the sacred mountain and met the God Kumastamxo. Since that time he has power to go to him any time in his dreams. " It takes four days to tell about Kwikumat and Kumastamxo. I am the only man who can tell it right. I was present at the very beginning and saw and heard it all. I dreamed a little of it at a time." There follows a long account of this origin dream. Homer was forty-five years old at the time he related the above. He was blind with syphilis.[1]

Joe Homer, a speaker, singer, funeral orator. " A self-appointed repository of true doctrine." Also a methodist. His dreams which are the sanctions of his power as an authority on ritual and as a religious teacher were " supernatural in two dimensions." The dreams in which he learned to perform religious ritual are different from the dreams which endowed him with power as a funeral orator.[2]

Joe Homer's Dreams.[3]

Homer was fifty-six years old in 1921, and had become a Methodist. The dreams have the same character as " those of ourselves," and there is no mention of the old Yuma deities as in the dreams of his youth. He told the author some of his early dreams including a portion of the origin dream (really

[1] See Harrington, J. Peabody, " A Yuma Account of Origins," *J. of Am. Folklore*, Vol. 21, 1908, pp. 326-7.
Note, ibid.—Approval and disapproval of old men tend to unify versions of the same myth originating in dreams of various dreamers, hence Yuma myths are less variable than those of peoples who do not dream their mythology.

[2] See C. Daryll Forde, " Ethnog. of Yuma Indians," *University of California. Pub. in Amer. Arch. and Ethnol.*, Vol. 28, No. 4, Dec. 1931, p. 203.
Note, ibid., p. 272.—The dream vision conditions the authority of everyone from chief doctor to funeral orator or singer. Concepts of wealth, hereditary rights and mere ability are subordinated to the acquisition of supernatural power. With this dream religion is associated a military tradition. One dreams to secure victory. One is victorious in order to acquire supernatural strength and spiritual power.

[3] Recorded by E. W. Gifford in " Yuma Dreams and Omens." *J. of Am. Folklore*, Vol. 39, 1926, pp. 58–66 incl. This same dream was told to three ethnologists at different times. (*Reprinted by permission of J. of Am. Folklore.*)

several dreams) related by Harrington. Referring to the sacred mountain he states that it is, " Too big a place to dream about more than once."

1. Dream of Homer when eight or nine years old (summarized), in which he visited Awikame mountain and encountered the God Kumastamxo. While at a fiesta he went to sleep. At noon he heard a voice from the air to the North. It called his name and said, " I will come back and get you." He awoke. At sundown he got sleepy again. A voice called his name again and said two or three times, " I am coming." Someone was holding his right hand. He dreamt that, " I walked out with this person who was holding my hand. It was dark and I could not see him. Now he spoke to me saying, ' Let go.' Then I walked three or four steps after I had let go. I was on the mountain Awikame." He learned four songs there. " I brought you to learn these songs to do you good," said Kumastamxo. Afterwards he showed him the place where the ceremony is held. It was a flat place. " I looked north and saw a steamboat and two watermelon patches. I looked south and saw a tree that became tobacco. In the east I saw flat land. In the west I saw nothing. I looked up and saw a cloud half dark and half light. Kumastamxo told me that the cloud that comes from the east will be white and that the cloud that comes from the west will be dark."

2. Dream when twenty years old, about 1885. " When I was about twenty years old, staying in school and working I slept one night in one room, and I heard other boys or somebody go outdoors. Then a voice called to me in English : ' God wants to see you.' Several other persons were called, five young boys and one old man, making seven in all. I walked on the road, but did not go far. On the left-hand side was a very blue pond and a little way from it there was another pond. Close to the second pond was a bench. They had about eight washpans on the bench. I looked up toward the east and saw a green parrot in a cage, also a large black dog. Now the parrot was calling my companions by name and saying, ' You had better stop and wash your face, wash your hands and come right this way. Then I will tell you the news. I am the one who can tell you the right thing.' I heard the dog barking the same words that the parrot was speaking. Then five young

men turned around, took washpans, dumped out the old water and got fresh water from the pond. I stood by and said, ' I don't believe that bird.' Then I walked away.

" I saw a house with all sorts of flowers growing around it. It looked pretty. It was built after the white man's style. A negro came out with a white bulldog. He said, ' You had better go right up the street and go into that house and talk to God.' So I started. A young man accompanied me. He was not one of the original five who started out with me. He entered the house ahead of me, but was frightened. I waited for him to come out before I went in. He had four or five books when he came out. The person inside (god) had given these to him. When he came out, he dropped all the books. He picked up some and left others lying on the ground. I laughed at him. Then I went inside. God turned around and looked at me. He had long whiskers reaching down to his navel. He shook his head and said, ' That is all right.' He handed books to me which I took in my hand. I had no chance to go out because all the doors were locked. Then God said : ' Just a minute.' Then the room turned dark, and he asked me : ' How do you like the darkness ? ' I did not reply. ' Look out for yourself,' he said. Then came lightning and during the flash of lightning I saw a mountain and marked down one. ' Does the light hurt you ? ' asked God. I replied, ' It hurts me pretty badly. I will hold my head.' I went out but was very much frightened. I stubbed my toe against a rock and fell down. Then I awoke."

Homer's Comment. He said that although God's white skin was not visible he was apparently a Caucasian. He said had he washed his face when ordered to do so by the parrot, he would have died as did the five boys who washed their faces. The negro was telling the truth. " When I was in the house and it turned dark God told me lightning was coming. It hurt my head. Perhaps that is why I am now blind."

He thinks his blindness is due to wrong medicine intentionally given him by Cherokee Doctor at Fort Mohave at the time he was married to a Mohave woman, in opposition to agency authorities at Fort Mohave.[1]

[1] Homer formerly had night blindness before his present blindness set in. According to Harrington the present blindness is syphilitic in origin (p. 60). Gifford—*op. cit.*

3. *Falling Dream.* In response to the question as to whether he ever had dreams of falling he related :

" I was on horseback on a new road. I was going up a mountain. There was a river on my right. The road was in bad condition. At the top of the mountain I thought I would leave my horse and descend on foot, because there was no road where I wished to descend. I made my horse jump over a fifty-foot precipice, alighting all right. Then I woke up. I was very much frightened."

4. *Falling Dream.* " On another night I dreamed that I was in a buggy and was driving along a road which brought me to a bridge which was without boards. The river was below. I thought I might as well swim the horses across, so I stopped. The river was rising. The horses swam but there was no place to land. I was nearly drowned, and was very frightened. There was no opportunity to turn back. The horses drowned. Then I woke up."

DREAMS OF DECEMBER 1921

5. *Night of Dec. 14.* " I went to a house to which I did not know I was going. Two Yuma women were there. Some men came in and I went out. One woman went out with me and we sat down together. The woman's husband came and started a fight in the room. I remonstrated but the fight went on. After a while Frank Tehana (Gifford's Cocopa informant) came and stopped the fight. Then he asked me what it was all about. I threatened to put them all in jail when they dispersed. There was a fire in the open fireplace in the house, and the house belonged to an Indian named Alexander. The woman's husband quarrelled with the people in the house because his property had been taken. I was unacquainted with the woman and her husband. The woman who remained inside the house is dead, but I knew her when she was alive. I could see in this dream. After I left the house and was on my way home I fell down. Then I awoke."

He interpreted this dream as meaning that people were talking about the ethnological work which Gifford was doing and that these people thought that he and his informant were causing trouble.

6. *Dec. 17 Dream.* " I do not remember the dream very

clearly, I was on foot. I could see better than anyone else. I do not know in which direction I was going. I kept thinking of the road all along the way. After a while I met an Indian. He threatened to strike me on the head to frighten me. After I passed him I met two white men. They passed me without speaking. I came to a house and entered. I had a wife there, a Yuma woman, but I did not know she was my wife. However she told somebody I was her husband. A friend came in and asked me, ' Is that your wife ? ' I replied, ' No.'

" My wife had a child about two years old. A Mexican came in and tried to buy him. Many Yuma men and women came in also. ' Don't you sell that boy,' they said to the woman. The Mexican wore high top-boots and was dressed like a cowboy. He had a burro and a large spoon in his hands, which he wished to trade for the baby. The woman was very anxious to dispose of the baby, so she came and asked me if it was all right to trade the baby for the boots, the spoon and the burro. I said, ' It is up to you. I have no business to say anything.' So she stood there and cried. I went away and left her. That was all."

7. *Dec.* 18 *Dream.* " I tried to go to California on the train. I did not feel very well. I had rheumatism in my legs and could not walk well. I could not turn my head around on account of pain. I was trying to go to Los Angeles to be cured. I was in the car already and could see. I got out again and the train left. Somebody said that I should go and boil water and wash my feet and that would do me good. The person who gave this advice was a Yuma named Lincoln Johnson. We walked together a distance. He stepped in a hole and broke his leg. He lay there and tried to get someone to put him into an automobile and take him to hospital. Everyone refused and said, ' Let him lie there.' I felt very sad. Then I became angry and said, ' I will get my buggy and take him myself.' I was on the Arizona side of the (Colorado) river. I started to walk across the bridge. Then I thought to myself, ' I used to be blind. I never used to come over here without someone with me. Why is it I see better now ? ' I could run. I went and got the horse and buggy and was about to start. Then I awoke."

8. *Dec.* 21 *Dream.* " I could see. Two or three Yuma men were with me. I had been interpreting on the California side of the river. Everybody wanted me to be an interpreter. I

was interpreter for you (Gifford) at that time and was ready to work for you, but someone else wanted me. Somebody else came after me again. Later on you came. You told me that you would not need me that day. I had another chance to work at hand.

" You told me you were going to run a store close to Sanguinetti's in Yuma. That was a wonderful new store that you were opening. I just looked at the store from the outside. Later you got all of the goods in. You had a paper for orders and asked me if I wanted to order something. I said that I would order what I wanted, but that I forgot what I wanted. ' Do you want any cinnamon rolls ? ' you asked. Then you gave me a piece of one to taste. I did not taste it but went out.

" When I went out I met my companions. I said, ' I will be ready to go to Somerton soon.' My companions were Mike Jepson, Sennell Russell and a third man whom I did not remember. I had not started for Somerton when I woke up."

9. *Dec.* 22 *Dream.* " I could see. There were several Yuma Indians with me. Some are now dead, some are living. Somebody said, ' We are going to have a fiesta. We want to select one man to be in charge of the fiesta.' They called everybody together and talked it over. Then I stopped right at my home. I did not go. Somebody sent word to me to come and enjoy myself at the fiesta. I went over and they appointed me to take charge. I did not want to have charge of the fiesta because I was too busy. They were all very sad because I would not take the job. I just stayed there a while.

" It was afternoon. I heard a noise like thunder or drums. The sound was approaching. Everybody at the fiesta became frightened and ran away. One man, now dead, said to me, ' You will have to go up to the high place.' Some of the people climbed on top of the shade. A flood was coming from the Gila river. So I ran towards my place and arrived there. . . . Other fellows come along. They stop. I thought they were living people but they were three people now dead." He talks with them. The flood had drowned them. He feared going to the fiesta because dead people might be lying there. The fiesta is called off. There is only a slight flood. " Well, I am going to have a happy day and enjoy myself with them."

10. *Dec.* 27 *Dream.* " I was at home alone and able to see.

I went out to see some people whom I knew, who were living on the reservation. On the way I met no one except Mr. Grouch, the Methodist minister. He said he was going down to the Cocopa reservation to see the people and he wanted me to go with him. I told him that I was so busy I could not go. He said nothing further to me. Some people in an automobile passed by me and Mr. Grouch disappeared or went on. I seemed to be following him towards my house but could not find him. Then I woke up."

11. *Dec. 28 Dream.* " I did not know where I was. I was in a place that I had never seen before. There was a sandhill there and I tried to climb up it. I finally succeeded in reaching the top and stood there. There was nothing but dead men down below me. I did not know that these people had died before. The dead people were walking around and when they saw me they all went to the north-west. Later I climbed down from the sandhill, and met someone who came along the road. He was an Indian, but I did not know his face. He told me there were many people going west to have a fiesta. I said nothing to him but just passed by. I was going north-east. After a time I found my place. I did not know that I had a place there, but somebody told me it was mine. I had a friend there, a young man who brought a watermelon. He cut it apart and I tried to eat it, but did not succeed. Some men came in and said that there was going to be an Indian war. Then I ran away and hid. Then I awoke. I could see throughout the dream."

The following is a dream (not Homer's) interpreted by one man as favourable, and as unfavourable by another :

12. *Dream of Algodones man.* " I dreamed that I had all kinds of animals and birds around me on the mountain. I laid hold of all these things and killed them." " I call upon you to ask you the meaning of this dream."

Yuma Man's interpretation : " That means that you will be a good warrior and kill many people."

Pasqual's (Yuma chief) interpretation : " That dream is nothing. I can tell you what your dream means in a minute. It means that you are going to die, and that all kinds of birds and animals are going to come and eat you. That is what the dream means."

THE DREAM IN PRIMITIVE CULTURES

CORRELATION OF THE DREAMS TO THE CULTURE PATTERN

Dream 1. *A Myth Dream.* Obviously a *culture pattern dream* both as to form and to content. Clearly reflects the old Yuman relation to the supernatural, in its method of approach through the dream to the gods and the sacred mountain. The complete dream (Harrington) gives an origin and creation account. Hence the dream falls into that class which reflects the religious or supernatural belief of the culture.

Dream 2. Content of this dream shows a new religious influence other than the native. It also reflects the transitional environment of the dreamer, away from a purely Indian culture. Items such as : an English voice, God, school, washpans, books, reflect the influence of white culture. The fact of the dreamer being blind and dreaming of seeing and light shows that there is also a personal psychological aspect to the dream besides the objective cultural aspect. Since the form of this dream in no way conforms to any cultural pattern similar to Dream 1 it falls in the class of individual dreams, in this case reflecting the breakdown of Indian culture and the acquisition of white culture.

Dream 3. With the exception of mention of a bridge and a buggy, items of white culture, the content of this dream reflects no marked cultural phenomena. *An individual dream.*

Dream 4. Same.

Dream 5. Reflects mixed Indian-white culture, and immediate situation of the dreamer in relation to the ethnological work going on. *An individual dream reflecting objective cultural phenomena.*

Dream 6. Reflects mixed Indian-white culture. *Individual dream.*

Dream 7. Content reflects mixed Indian-white culture, mostly white and deals with the personal problems of seeing, and being cured. *An individual dream.*

Dream 8. Reflects white culture, and immediate situation. *An individual dream,* reflecting objective cultural situation.

Dream 9. Content deals with Yuma Indians, fiesta, dead people speaking. Reflects some of Indian social culture. *An individual dream.*

Dream 10. Reflects mixed social culture. Items such as Methodist minister and automobile. Absence of Indian culture. *Individual dream reflecting objective culture,* or breakdown and absence of Indian culture.

Dream 11. Items such as Indian, fiesta, dead people, show a reflection of existing Indian culture. Ability to see in dreams reflects personal psychology.

Dream 12. Content deals with killing animals and birds on a mountain. Reflects absence of any culture phenomena. *An individual dream.* Personal.

SUMMARY.

Culture Pattern Dreams. Dream 1. Reflecting the old Indian cultural attitude towards the supernatural, that is the religious or non-material culture.

Individual Dreams :
  (*a*) Reflecting objective or social and material culture or group :
      Dreams 9, 11—Reflect some Indian Culture.
      Dreams 5, 6, 7—Reflect mixed Indian-white Culture.
      Dreams 3, 8, 2, 10—Reflect Acquired White Culture.
  (*b*) Dreams 2, 7, 11, 12—Reflect personal subjective phenomena.

It is fortunate to have in the data a series of dreams [1] of one individual taken from different periods in his life, beginning at the age of eight or nine and extending to his fifty-sixth year. Their contents reflect the whole transition from the time the Indian culture was completely in force, through the stages of breakdown of this culture to the stage of acquisition of white culture or absence of a distinctive culture of any sort. Although the data are inadequate it would seem logical, nevertheless, to infer from what is available that in this region where dreaming was regarded as of much importance, that when the old Indian culture was in force, most dreams both as to form and content conformed to a definite culturally determined pattern, with the individual dream playing a very minor rôle. When,

[1] For additional Yuman Culture Pattern dreams see also J. Roheim, " Psychoanalysis of Primitive Cultural Types," *Int. J. of Psychoanalysis*, Vol. XIII, 1 and 2, 1932, pp. 185, 192.

however, the culture broke down, and in proportion as white culture was absorbed, the old culture pattern dream tended to disappear and the individual dream to take its place. What can be stated with plausibility from the evidence of the data is that there is a definite correlation between the manifest dream contents of the individual dreams and the religious and social culture pattern, or between the manifest content and the absence of culture.

This conclusion is also corroborated among the Yuman, Maricopa of the Gila River, where the songs and shamanism of the old culture have disappeared together with the pattern dreams. No living person among this group, with possibly one exception, has had dreams of the ancient type ! [1]

[1] Leslie Spier, *Yuman Tribes of the Gila River* (Univ. of Chicago Press, 1933), p. xi.

3. THE SOUTH-WEST CULTURE AREA

Some Navajo Beliefs, Attitudes and Customs Relative to
the Dream

It is impossible in the present study to present a comprehensive report of the Navajo dream philosophy and psychology, owing to the complexity of the subject which is
inextricably bound up with their religion, medicine, ceremonialism, and social life. Besides much unpublished work
has been assembled by Sapir and by the Franciscan Fathers,
which has not yet been co-ordinated and is awaiting the
completion of exhaustive research in the field. All that is
here attempted is to present an incomplete but significant
summary of the Navajo dream pattern in relation to the
cultural environment, and to record some examples of
Navajo dreams with the comments of the dreamers as
collected in the field by the writer and others.—Before
presenting the actual dream data, the following summary
of the salient Navajo attitudes and customs relative to the
dream reveals the importance of this phenomenon to these
Indians.

1. Belief in dreams as the cause of illness. Such dreams
are referred to diagnosticians who reveal the cause and
prescribe the cure.

" Diagnosticians are called upon to cure sickness caused by
dreams or to prevent sickness predicted by dreams. Indian
informants did not hesitate to distinguish good dreams from bad
dreams, nor were they reticent about telling their dreams. P.
said that if the dream is not serious, the individual may pray
at dawn in his doorway with or without some special stone
before him which has been chanted over for this purpose by

some diagnostician. He may pray to the sun-God (whom C. considers the highest God) or he may pray to a particular god or spirit of some animal made manifest by the dream. If the dream be more serious, he must go to a diagnostician who will use his chants and minor rituals and more powerful objects and prayers. If the dream be still more serious, the diagnostician will advise a ceremony by a shaman." [1]

2. Curing rituals. "Rituals and words, spoken or sung, to cure sickness caused by dreams, witches, and the spirits of animals, gods, and dead men have been tenaciously preserved by the Navajo." [2]

3. Determination of choice of appropriate ritual or "sing." [3]

(I) The dreamer himself decides what sing he shall have from the dream.

(II) A star-gazer is consulted only when the nature of the illness is not known.

(III) Dreams of snakes, buzzards, hawks and bird spirits require the *Hozhonae* Chant, or Chant of Terrestrial Beauty.[4]

(IV) Dreams of death, that is, that you are dead, that neighbours and relatives are dead, also dreams that your teeth have fallen out, require the *Hozhonji* Chant.[5]

[1] William Morgan, "Navajo Diagnosticians," *Amer. Anthropologist*, Vol. 33, No. 3, July–Sept. 1931, pp. 400–1.

[2] *Ibid.*, p. 402. *Note.*—For examples of these rituals and their origins in myths reference is made to Washington Mathews' "The Mountain Chant," in *B.A.E. Report, No.* 5, 1883–4, p. 379 ; *idem.*, "The Night Chant," *Memoirs of Amer. Museum of Nat. Hist.*, Vol. VI, 1902.

Note.—See also Franciscan Fathers, *An Ethnologic Dictionary of the Navajo Language*, pp. 380, 501.

[3] Information from Navajo informants Honarani and Taylor ; J. S. Lincoln, Navajo Field notes.

[4] See *Vocabulary of the Navajo Language*, The Franciscan Fathers, 1912, Vol. 2, p. 96.

[5] Chant of Restoration. A rite of blessing or restoration. It figures in the blessing invoked upon the family, house and property.—*Ibid.*, p. 96.

(V) Dreams of being badly hurt, of lightning, of snakes biting you, of dangerous things, require the *Natoye bakaji* or Male Shooting Chant.[1]

(VI) Dreams of Coyote, of being stranded on a rock, of going through a small hole in the rock, of flying, of waves falling over you, of being in an arroyo with waves rushing over you, of defending yourself against an enemy, of bees or wasps, flying rocks, of a whirlwind coming, of thunder, bears, snakes or prickly things, show you are under the sickness that will be helped by the *Sontsoji Hatral* or Star Chant.[2]

4. Dreams are regarded as good or bad according to the after effect of the dream. If it is bad, he assumes that something must be done about it—that he must do something to forestall the undesirable consequences.[3]

5. Belief that Gods, dreams, and sickness are causally related.[4]

6. Certain dreams have standardized interpretations, namely dreams about bears, snakes and owls.[5]

7. Death dreams have well-known interpretations.

" If a shaman during a ceremony dreams that his patient is going to die he must leave and another shaman must be called. A dream interpretation may sometimes either arise or be confirmed by observations of events in the external world. For example when a Navajo dreams that he is dead, he means that in his dream, he was in the next world with the spirits of the dead (four informants). To be there and to come back is not necessarily a bad dream ; but if the dead beckon to the dreamer or he shakes hands with the dead, it means that he is going to die." [6]

[1] Branches of this chant : 1. *Natoye bakaji*, Male Shooting ; 2. *Natoye baaji*, Female Shooting Chant ; 3. *Natoye Dzilkiji*, Mountain Chant of Shooting. Reference is made in these to the M. and F. divinities of Lightning, Thunder, Snakes, and the Bear.—*Ibid.*, p. 135.

[2] See pp. 213–14, information from Miss Wheelwright.

[3] William Morgan, " Navajo Dreams," *Amer. Anthrop.*, Vol. 34, No. 3, July–Sept. 1932, pp. 391.

[4] *Ibid.*, p. 391.   [5] *Ibid.*, p. 398.   [6] *Ibid.*, p. 402.

8. It is generally believed that Gods and spirits of deceased men and animals as well as witches may put dreams into one's head.[1]

9. Dreams form the basis of the belief that spirits retain their earthly appearance, and that in accordance with this belief parts of their burial customs come into being.[2]

10. " A pregnant woman especially must exercise the greatest care lest she observe anything in the shape of violence. The influence of bad dreams must be removed during the time of her pregnancy, both by herself and her husband. If this has been neglected the duty devolves upon the child, even at an advanced age."[3]

11. The medicine man, " White Hair's," dissertation on the dream and other matters [4] :

AT BLACK MOUNTAIN TRADING POST—NEAR CHIN LEE, ARIZONA

May 26. " White Hair "—Big Medicine Man. Specialized on the *Hozhonji* sing.

" Every dream that takes place is certain to happen. Whenever the evil spirits influence it, it really happens. Whenever we dream a bad dream we get a medicine man to perform a sing and say prayers which will banish the spirit."

I ask how can you tell a bad dream ?

Answer. " All bad dreams are from things that are dangerous. Sometimes the dream shows you are suffering from dangerous things. That shows the evil thing has an influence on you. Dreams which we think unsatisfactory to us are bad dreams. We dream and you dream too. Of course our dreams are different. We do a little something about our dreams, things like having a sing, to avoid our dreams, and what will happen from them in the future. Each Indian or human being and we all know that every nation dreams.

" When you are young you don't know anything about dreams, and as you get older you catch on to the meaning of your dreams

---

[1] William Morgan, *op. cit.*, p. 402.   [2] *Ibid.*, p. 404.
[3] The Franciscan Fathers, *An Ethnologic Dictionary of the Navajo Language*, p. 379.
[4] J. S. Lincoln, Navajo Field Notes, 1932.

and you will want to remember. Then whatever you dream will occur in the future. Sometimes you will dream about corn, squash and pumpkins and you will find you will raise the things you dream of. Sometimes you will dream of some place on the land in the country, and that means that you will take a trip in the country and see different places and good land and will have a good home.

"Anything I dreamed of really happened. It really does come true if you remember it correctly. According to what you dream it might come in a year or two years or maybe more. I never had a bad dream, only good ones.

"As a boy I dreamed I had white hair. I am glad of that and of the dreams of my boyhood.

"Lots of others told their dreams to me. Things hurt them or happened to them or they dreamed they were dead."

I ask what it means if you dream you are dead?

Answer. "When a person dreams they are dead it is bad. It means something will happen to yourself or your family. A person (with such a dream) will get a medicine man to give him a blessing to avoid his dream. After the blessing or a sing they won't dream again about anything like that. That might be the end of one's bad dreams. Good dreams would come after that and they mean good spirits are with you.

"When things were created every nation was created to dream. Some say that if they have good spirits they hear things in the air. I think there is something in that. Like the white people hear the radio. In the old days the Indians used to hear voices in the air.

"We're Navajos and I don't know what created us, but white people know what created them. Whatever created the white people has more ability and knowledge. We don't know much about what created us. Maybe because what created the Navajos hasn't much ability or mind. My grandfather used to tell me that when the world was created certain things were given to the Navajos, but the Navajos have no idea of what was given them. So what was given us was guessed by the white people and they took everything that was given to the Navajos. That is why white people are wise, because the first white man made a quick guess at those things. Wise white men use all they have taken from the Navajos. By working their minds and through their minds they make things, assemble everything, invent things. They are a high-standing people. In the first place if we had taken what was given to them or guessed what they were, we would have been as wise as the white people.

" My grandfather used to say that white people are on a higher plane than Indians. They have souls that are stronger than Navajos. They have more strength than the Indians. When the gods were creating this world, putting the mountains and water on this earth, they put the first people on this earth and made every one of them with souls, but according to my grandfather the Indians were created as the high standard of all nations ; but it was taken away from them and given to white people. To-day they are the highest standing in this world.

" I know a few things about the *Hozhonji* chant.

" When a person is old enough to go to the toilet and still wets his bed, the *Hozhonji* chant must be held over him. He must pay the medicine man in advance. . . . We pray and we sing in order to gain better knowledge and to prevent the evil spirits from getting at the family and ourselves. By this performance all these are banished.

" We pray to the Changing Woman with special prayers and songs. If we want to take a trip to the island where she lived, we would pray and offer a sacrifice to her before starting. We would also sing songs to her. Then on reaching the island before entering the cave we would repeat the prayers and songs. The reason why white people don't see her is because they don't know how to say the prayers and sing the songs even if they do go to the island." (I had told him of the cave on Santa Cruz Island and the trip of a Navajo to this cave.)

" The *Hozhonji* chant is for all the bad dreams or for hearing echoes or maybe for seeing the fire at night. The fire is a bad spirit. All these are bad signs. They are evil spirits fallen on someone in the family. It does not mean you yourself will get hurt but that someone in the family. Maybe your *hogan* will burn down or something else will happen. All you hear or see might mean that.

" The *Hozhonji* is more important to the Navajo than any other chant. There is no one alive who knows the full story of the *Hozhonji*. He can tell the full story only after the ground freezes and the snakes have gone home and the lightning has stopped. He doesn't know anyone besides himself who knows the full story of the *Hozhonji*.

" The *Hozhonji* is used when a woman is going to have a baby. It is the only thing which is holding up the earth with us. The White Shell woman is the one who keeps it up. She knows right now what I am saying. She can hear through the air and the sunlight. The *Hozhonji* ceremony is our father and our mother.

" The sun is our god and that is our father. The changing woman or the White Shell Woman is our mother. We pray to them and they prevent us from telling you the full story at this time of the year. We like to go by the rules of the old story."

12. Belief that " good " dreams only come true once in a while, whereas " bad " dreams always come true.[1]

13. " Now Navajo dreams are all different. Some dream good dreams, some bad. Some Navajos say they dream a lot, some not at all.

" I believe the soul wanders when I dream and comes back again afterward. If you dream of death, it means someone will die." [2]

14. Information from Hasteen Klah, medicine man, Newcombe, New Mexico, 17 November 1933.[3, 4]

[1] J. S. Lincoln, Navajo Notes, 1932 statement of Honarani.
[2] *Ibid.* (Charley Natani's remarks).
[3] Miss Mary Wheelwright, Field Notes (unpub.).
[4] See Chap. III, p. 118. *Note.*—This Klah is probably the same as kla referred to in a recent article as a transvestitite or hermaphrodite. Kla also came from Newcombe, N.M. He is described as a chanter who " has rationalized the status of the hermaphrodite deity of the Navaho into the position of a supreme god, a concept denied by all other informants." This agrees with Miss Wheelwright's statement to me with regard to " Klah's " conception of a supreme deity, hence it is more than likely that " Klah " and " kla " are the same. A study of his dreams in the light of his abnormality would be important. Another hermaphrodite refused to tell his dreams or discuss the subject.

See W. W. Hill, " The Status of the Hermaphrodite and Transvestitite in Navaho Culture," *American Anthropologist*, Vol. 37, April-June 1935, No. 2 (Part I), pp. 273, 278, 279.

" When his grandmother was at Bosco Redondo in exile she dreamed that she was standing on a rock near Crown Point (N.E. of Gallup), then she found herself near the Sun rock on top of the Chuskai Mountains, then she was on top *Tse des kai* near to the Sun rock and looking over the desert where Newcombe is, then came down to Teadlena below the mountains, then found herself on top of two Grey Hills towards Newcombe, and then at *Cheldehniche* (cottonwood trees up the wash), and then she was at the place where Klah lives and she woke up then and there she died. It had been her home before exile.

" His mother dreamed when she was a girl that she was a very old woman and she is still alive.

" You know whether you're dreaming true by your ears ringing, or a pricking in your nose or a twitching of your skin. If they dream about something they are doubtful about, they eat some pollen and pray to the *Yehs*. If it is a bad dream of anything sick or dead or of Coyote, they stay awake all night and pray, which usually clears it up, but if it returns they have a small *Hotchonji* ceremony belonging to some Chant. There seems to be few definite connections between dream and chant though Star dreams might need the Star ceremony, etc., but this is not certain.

" In the *Hotchonji* ceremony the prayer goes down to the lower world and evil spirits, as well as up to Begochiddy (whose name means the love of a mother for her child and her milk ; although he is a man).[1]

" The *Hozhonae* Chant only goes upward.

" Klah's particular dream when he was 10 was of *Tohntyel*, the great sea which he knew nothing about. Now he dreams of spirits and often that he is going to die. Last night he dreamed that he saw lots of sheep and goats but didn't want any of the meat.

" He says that the ' shaking hand ' and star-gazing are not Navajo but he thinks came from the Mescalero Apaches when they were fighting with them in ——. He had no use for either of these divining stunts, but had direct approach through prayer." [2]

---

[1] See Chap. III, p. 118 ; p. 213, Ref. 4. [2] *op. cit.*, Ref. 4.

15. The following beliefs about dreams are from the myth of *Sontso*. (Big Star.)

A story told by *Yuinth-naizi* (tall man) who comes from near the saw mill by Fort Defiance. He is of the *Tachini* Clan and also mentions his own beliefs about dreams. The story of the myth comes from a medicine man called *Dinneh-kloth* and later *Hasteen-baazhon* who lived up the Canyon de Chelly and died 26 years ago.[1] (According to Klah)—

The myth says,

" for when we dream, that is the spirit inside of us speaking, and when we hear sounds in our ears, or feel a pricking in our throats, or a twitching of our nerves, or a popping in our noses ; that is *Niltche B'yazh* (the Wind Spirit) telling us either to do or not to do something, in other words, a warning to pay attention. When we sleep the Spirit comes out and travels among other Spirits and brings back messages to us, and when our ears ring he is telling us what to do, for he has been out travelling and he is trying to give us a message, but our minds get in the way."

" The medicine man says that for him to dream of deer that are well and strong is fortunate for the patient whom he is treating. If he dreams this just before he is summoned to a patient he always knows that the ceremony will be successful. He always had that dream until a Navajo years ago asked him to go hunting and he killed some deer, and since he did that he cannot depend upon this dream. It doesn't matter what creature you dream about as long as it is healthy, but if it is weak or sick or deformed it is a bad dream. If you dream of success, even of a fight, it means success in whatever you undertake. If you dream of the Coyote, or of being on a rock that you cannot get down from, or of going through a small hole in the rock, or that you are flying, or of the waves falling over you, or of being in an arroyo with a river rushing on you, or to be defending yourself against an enemy ; also to dream of Bees or Wasps, or flying rocks, a Whirlwind coming, or of the Thunder, Bears, Snakes or of prickly things, then you are under the sickness that will be helped by *Sontsoji Hatral* (Star Chant). If you dream of *Sontso* (Big Star) or any of the Stars which are

[1] Miss Mary Wheelwright, Field Notes (unpub.).

frightening you four or five times, then you are suffering from the sickness which belongs to *Sontso*, and the painting of the body is to protect you against this trouble." [1]

In this myth is given the origin of " Star Gazing," the method of divination by dreams used by " Stargazers " or diagnosticians in prescribing appropriate curing ceremonies for illness caused by dreams or other factors.[2] Younger Brother, the hero of the myth, learns the Star Ceremony and Chant, one of the important curing ceremonies of the Navajos, from the Star spirits :

" Now he had finished learning the *Sontsoji Hatral* (Star Chant) of the Black, Blue, Yellow and White Stars, and the White Star told him to go back to his father, *Sontso Dithklith* (Black Star), and he also told Younger Brother that he should go back to the earth, but that before he went all the different Stars would come to see him and say good-bye. Younger Brother asked them all to come to the home of Black Star, and when they came they discussed how to send Younger Brother back to earth without harm. Black Star asked the others to give some gifts to take with him, and Black Star gave him a bolt of lightning, and the Black Cloud and a small star to use for star gazing, and Black Star told him again that in future *Niltche B'yazh* the Wind Spirit would be inside of him, and that he would speak to him in dreams. Then the other Stars asked Blue Star what he would give, and he gave Younger Brother a bolt of lightning called *Hatsol-rah*, sheet lightning, a blue cloud and *Akha* or fat used for ceremonials and known as *Klah Nascheen*, and he also told him that he would be helped in the future by his dreams. Then the Yellow Star offered *Hajih-gish* (Heat Lightning), a yellow cloud and a big star, and spoke about the Wind giving him help in dreams, and that he could use the big star for star gazing. The White Star gave him *Nahtseelit*, the rainbow, a white cloud and some fat for his ceremonials, and spoke again about his dreams, and they gave him the rainbow as a road back to earth." [3]

---

[1] Miss M. Wheelwright, *The Myth of Sontso*, pp. 56–7, 1933 (unpub.).
[2] See p. 208 and Notes 1 and 2.
[3] Miss Wheelwright, *ibid.*, pp. 61–2 (unpub.).

16. *Star-Gazing Visions.*

When a person is ailing or ill, he consults a diviner, who gazes at the sun or stars. After such gazing, he is able to tell which chant the patient should have sung for him.

For example, a prophet gazes at the sun, meanwhile singing, and after a time sees something characteristic of a particular sing, the Night Chant bundle or the *anadji* drum, for instance. He then tells the patient what he saw. The latter pays him a lamb or a dollar and a half to two dollars and engages a chanter.

A young girl was very ill with tuberculosis and her parents consulted a diviner. He gazed steadily at a star and sang. Suddenly, he saw the star open with a blazing *hogan* in the midst of it and around it. There was no overcoming such an omen and without a vestige of hope the man decreed that the girl would die. In less than a month his prophecy was fulfilled.

If it had been possible for the girl to get well, he would have seen a " white sign come around the *hogan* like frost." Another sign indicating death would be a " black sign around the *hogan* in the star."

" In 1914 a man who was gazing saw a black streak around a lung over a star and the woman whose fate he was reading died in about eight days." [1]

17. *Other Beliefs.* [2]

" To dream that horses, sheep or cattle die predicts sickness.

" The worst dream is that a member of the family died, or that teeth were pulled. Cure : a one-night sing (*xojoji*). [2]

" Little Mexican's wife dreamed she was very ill. She had *hatali* sing *xojoji* to counteract the effect.

" Dreams of snakes are not bad unless the snakes bite.

" Dreams have bad effects only when the dreamer does not overcome the evil powers he dreams of.

" If you wish a good dream to come true, you may hire a medicine man to sing. But it is not necessary, the dreamer himself may sprinkle meal and wish on it."

[1] Gladys A. Reichard, *Social Life of The Navajo Indians*, Columbia University Contrib. to Anthrop., Vol. VII, 1928, p. 149.

[2] *Ibid.*, p. 145. (Xojoji, hozhonji, hotchonji and hozho'ji are the same chant as spelled by different recorders.)

NAVAJO DREAMS WITH COMMENTS OF THE DREAMERS

1. *Shaman's Dream.*

" Last month he dreamed that many Gods came after him. They tried to drag him away to a mountain. Many Yei were among these Gods. Since then he has this dream again and again."

Comment. " He asked what he must do about this dream. O. said that the medicines and masks which he handled were too strong ; that the gods were trying to kill him. He must have a Night Chant.

" He was not sick but the ceremony would mean good health for the next few years. He did not want the ceremony but his family and others said he must have it." [1]

2. *Death Dream.*

" P. dreamed that he was in the next world and a black horse came by with a feather upon his back. The feather changed to P's brother who had long ago died, but the brother did not beckon to him, ' so the dream did not mean that he would die.'

3. " Once P. dreamed he was in the spirit-world where he was driving his sheep and goats. A great crowd of dead people were present. His goats got separated and he lost them, but he got back to earth though he does not remember how."

Comment. " Getting back to earth is important and an otherwise bad dream which would predict death, may thus be turned into a good one.[2]

4. The dream of a " Patient " who had bad dreams, and had been in a melancholy state of mind, who said he was cured by the Mountain Chant ceremony. Recorded by Mrs. Laura Adams Armer and a year later by myself. The ceremony was filmed by Mrs. Armer.

Dream. " Bears appeared and pursued me." " I would wake up in great fear and trembling."

---

[1] Cf. W. Morgan, *Amer. Anthropologist*, Vol. 34, No. 3, p. 390.
[2] *Ibid.*, p. 402. Morgan mentions that Dr. Paul Radin has previously noted that the Winnebago make this same distinction in their dreams about death (unpub.).

Comment. " We believe these things, and we must continue until the right ceremony is given to cure us. I think that now after the ceremony the bear will leave me and go away and not bother me any more. I haven't lived with my father since I was a little boy. My father married again. The reason for my illness was because my father saw the Mountain Chant while my mother was pregnant with me. My father should not have seen the chant at this time." [1, 2]

5. *Dec.* 1930. I ask a Navajo if he had any dreams. He says that he did not remember his dreams. Another man says some dreams are good, those about corn and rain ; others are bad, those about the dead.

6. *Dec.* 1930. A woman says she had dreams.

" I dreamt of the masked dancers, the Yays of the Night Chant coming into the *hogan*. I could see the medicine man and the patient, but did not know who they were. They were all dancing and singing and came in three times. The fourth time I woke up."

Comment. " I dreamt all the details of the chant and the ceremony. It was a good dream."

7. *Dec.* 1930. Hasteen Mellicano. When asked if he dreamt he replied with loud laughter, " I dream of father and grandfather just the way you do."

[1] J. S. Lincoln, Navajo Field Notes, Dec. 1930.

[2] *Note.*—The medicine man who performed this curing ceremony (*Nanai*) informed me that the myth on which the ceremony is based is about Red Bear's children and especially about a little neglected boy who is Red Bear's son. Although the ceremony is known as the Mountain Chant, the myth of its origin as reported by Washington Mathews (*B.A.E. Report No. V*, p. 387) does not correspond to the same myth which Nanai claims to be the origin of the Mountain Chant (*Dsilkidji Bakadji*) in which he is a specialist. He says there are four branches. Mrs. Armer and I assumed (probably erroneously) from the name of Red Bear's son, he might be the younger brother of Dsilyi Neyani, the hero of the myth reported by Mathews. The study of this case has been pursued in the psychoanalytic field by Dr. Oskar Pfister of Zurich based partly on the above information (O. Pfister, " Instinktive Psychoanalyse unter den. Navajo Indianern," *Imago*, Vol. XVIII, No. 1, 1932, pp. 108–9.

8. *Dec.* 1930. A Navajo at the Black Mountain said : " I dream of dead people, of mother and father and ancestors. Sometimes I dream that my parents are dead whereas they are still alive."[1]

The following collection of dreams and comments of the dreamers were assembled by myself in May and June of 1932 while staying at Black Mountain Trading Post near Chin Lee, Arizona. Of the nine individuals [2] who told me their dreams only one could speak English (R. T.). They all were still deeply imbued with much of the old Navajo culture which is shown in their dream contents and comments. I tried to get a consecutive series of dreams from the same individuals and succeeded in doing so for a brief period, but even this short time was sufficient to show the correlation of the manifest dream content to their culture. Several of the dreams are those of their grandparents, and these very clearly reflect the old Navajo life.

AT BLACK MOUNTAIN, MAY 1932

INFORMANT C. N. B.

1. *Dream when Fourteen Years Old and Events leading up to it.*

May 19. " When a little boy I went with my grandfather to Piñon. I stayed there three days. Afterwards I came back. The grandfather told us how to make arrows so we could kill people who steal. Grandfather told me to watch out when tending sheep so people wouldn't kill me. All then went to bed. Four of us went to bed, my grandfather, my uncle, myself and my grandmother. It was a *hogan* like this. There was a little river on the sand. My grandfather slept on the right of the door, then my grandmother, next my uncle and then myself. There was a corral for sheep outside. I went out once in a while to watch the sheep at night. I heard someone shoot when I went to sleep. Maybe I dreamed it. When asleep, I

---

[1] J. S. Lincoln, Navajo Field Notes, 1930, Nos. 5, 6, 7, 8 ; Lorenzo Hubbell interpreter.

[2] I have not given the names of informants except by initials.—The deeper analyses of some of their dreams in Part II makes it essential to preserve their anonymity.

heard somebody say, ' A Hopi is coming, shoot him.' In the dream all the family got up and began to eat. Everyone was scared. They didn't know which way to turn. My grandfather said maybe they have killed an eagle. After the shot the Hopi came in the *hogan*. He had a gun in his hand. The Hopi shot and a lot of dust came down. We thought the Hopi had killed my uncle, but the uncle didn't look as if he was shot."

Comment. " I thought the dream was reality. That is all. It is true. I would not tell you a lie. I had a dream last night, but don't remember. I couldn't forget this one. That is all. Maybe you think I wouldn't remember."

INFORMANT C. N. B. (*Armijo interpreter.*)

2. *May* 21 *Dream.* (*This one probably invented.*)

" I dreamt a bad dream about a dog. I went to a *hogan* but I do not know who the *hogan* belonged to. Then this grey dog chased me. I think it was this dog (Terry). So he got hold of my pants and tore 'em off. Then Mrs. Armijo got hold of the dog and pulled him away. The dog tore Mrs. Armijo's dress to pieces. We were then both fighting the dog. I was talking in my dream and my wife woke me up. I told my wife nothing was the matter. That is all."

3. *May* 28 *Dream.* (*Taylor interpreter.*)

" The time the woman had the baby in the *hogan*. We went to bed before the others came around. Three were sleeping together. Two women were in there and one woman had a baby in the night. I dreamed I was out some place with a man. There was a high rock and the edge of the rock on top was white. I and the man were up high near the top of the rock. It was very difficult to climb up or get over the rock. I thought my feet were slipping. I was ahead. We kept climbing and my feet slipped but I didn't fall. I had a hard time climbing. The other man behind was also slipping but coming along. He was the first to get up. I looked back at him and he shouted, ' you're going to fall.' He stood there with his hand up calling for help. There was wheat on the edge of the rock. I got hold of the wheat and reached for the other man but couldn't get hold of his hand, only his middle finger. I started pulling him up on top. When we got up on top, there was a sort of meadow. It was early in the morning and we walked East. There was dew on the grass. While we were walking along, the woman in the *hogan* screamed (reality) and I woke up."

Comment. " If I had dreamed that I had fallen, I think we wouldn't have lived long. The successful climb means we are going to live longer.—A good dream."

4. *Dream.* (*Taylor interpreter.*)

" Last night I dreamed of horses. I thought I had six horses, two of them sorrel, two bay and two black. All of them were American horses and were harnessed with chain, plough harness and I was ready to go out working with those horses, but I couldn't find the ploughs. The ploughs were gone. I started looking for them, but I couldn't find any. I started to look in another place and woke up."

C. N. B.'s WIFE.

1. *May* 27 *Dream.*

" This is an old dream. I thought I was weak and helpless. I don't know who spoke to me, but someone said, ' You are going to be very old.' I thought I was a very old woman in the dream. I don't know who spoke to me. That's the end."

2. — *A Recent Dream.*

" At the time you people (Lincolns) were first here, I dreamed of a dog which seemed to be a mad dog. That's all."

3. — " Four nights ago I dreamed of corn."

4. — *Another Dream.*

" I thought we were out on the farm working in the garden. There were some big weeds growing there and we were picking the tops off the weeds and putting them in rows in a sort of a circle. Toward evening after the day's work was done, I started fixing up our beds. We were putting them in the wagon box. We went to bed in the wagon. While we were asleep two cows came around, one was black and one was grey. They began to turn the wagon over. She told the old man to jump out and chase away the cows. He got up and chased them away. They ran away. One stumbled over the wagon tongue and fell on its back and spun around and fell dead. I was frightened. That's the end."

INFORMANT HASTEEN S.[1]

Dream. Told me in December 1930. A poor man.
" I dreamed of lots of food and good things to eat, but when I get to the food,—it vanishes."

No comment.

Hasteen S., Catholic, old man. Speaks no English. His father and mother formerly had lots of sheep. Now he is poor. Married. Has a *hogan*.

1. *May 19, 1932 Dream.*
Dreamt last night but couldn't remember.

Recent Dream. " I dreamed of lots of corn on this side and that side, five or six feet high. My corn was just a little bit of a thing. My corn was wormy. I planted twice and gave it up. Later on I thought I would plant some more. Mice came and ate all my corn. That is all."

Yesterday his wife, who he says hasn't much sense, dreamt of water.

2. *May 21 Dream.*
" There was a little narrow trail on the top of Tlojali Mountain. I was walking on this trail. It was so narrow that I could see down on both sides. Then it got so foggy that it started to sprinkle a little and I could see water running from both sides of the bank. I was surprised to see so little rain and water running. On top of the narrow trail was a lot of piñon trees and I could see lots of pinto horses. I was wondering who they belonged to and I thought they belonged to me. Where they were grazing there was lots of ' gramma grass ' just like a big patch of alfalfa. Then as I was walking where the horses were eating, there was lots of water raining but it wasn't raining hard —just a little sprinkle. So I left the horses to my right and since it was raining I got wet. I didn't have any blanket. I started to come back, but couldn't find my *hogan*. As I started to look for my *hogan*, it began to rain pretty hard. I started out walking, but afterwards I was riding a horse. I don't know where he came from. I finally went in a *hogan* which I found. Lightning came in the smoke hole. I was very much afraid of the lightning and thundering. I was so afraid that I got on

---

[1] Armijo interpreter. Except where otherwise indicated, my interpreter was Taylor, a Navajo. He had interpreted for the Franciscan Fathers, and the U.S. Government.

my horse and started going. My heart was beating fast from fear. When I got home to my *hogan* there was lots of water all around and it was still raining hard. I was looking for my wife who was a little way from the *hogan* because it was full of water. I looked into my hogan and the stove pipe was down and I saw lots of *Nashondichizi* (Molineras in Spanish). I looked again in the *hogan* and the water was rolling and roaring. All my blankets and sheepskins were whirling and roaring around the *hogan* on the water. So I set out towards the windmill and there was lots of water around the flat like last winter's snow. I came back to my *hogan* and I took my shoes off to try and save my blankets and my felts. When I wanted to get up I couldn't move. I finally got up and I felt very tired. That is all."

Comment. " A good dream. I prayed with ' djadite ' (little medicine bag) : good ; it is raining, everything will be all right now."

3. *May 25 Dream.*

The day after the Government Superintendent's speech to the Black Mountain chapter of the Navajos in which he promised to distribute farm implements and materials to the Indians.

" I dreamed last night of an old wagon standing in front of my hogan. I thought I was taking a trip to Fort Defiance to get some lumber. I went to Chin Lee and from there to this side of Floated Rock Mountain. This wagon I was using wasn't mine, because mine had a wide track and this had a narrow track. The lumber he was going after was given him at Fort Defiance. While going over the mountain, it started raining. They crossed Floated Rock while it was raining. The road was muddy all the way to Blue Canyon. They stopped there, boiled coffee and took some coffee and fed the horses. After lunch they started out again and set out through the valley. I met a man I knew who lived at the saw mill near Fort Defiance. The man asked me where I was going. I say, ' to Fort Defiance.' I get there and stop and unhook my team. Fort Defiance seems to be growing rapidly and has gotten to be a big town. There are tents at the mouth of the canyon used by working Navajos. When we stopped again, I met one of my relatives (Norcross). We greeted each other. I cooked some more supper and we had a meal together. He asked me if I came to Fort Defiance to work. I say ' No, I came here for some lumber that I asked for some time ago. I came after forty pieces of lumber.' The man was from Black Mountain. He questioned me again about how old I was when the Navajos came back from Fort Summer. I answer that I don't know very well in those days. I was just a little child. All I remember is that there was a general taking care of the Indians issuing rations. The applications were made out for each Indian and were of brass and tin and some of zinc. Whenever we need rations we show our brass or tin to the general. Whenever the Indians come for food they assemble near the adobe wall. I told the man where this wall used to be, but it isn't there any more. After talking about these things, the man left and I went to bed and slept. The next morning I went to the office and met the Superintendent there. I had a note to him about the lumber. While in the office a chief of the Navajos from Lucachuca named Charlatso came in. I greeted him. Charlatso asked me when I came. I replied, ' yesterday ' and told him I was after lumber which was promised to me. The Superintendent looked at the note and told me where to get the lumber. I went to the lumber yard and a man there showed me what lumber I could get. I bring the wagon around and start loading, piling the lumber flat. Another man came around and told me to pile edgeways. He showed me how to pile my load. Then I left and the Superintendent gave me a half sack of flour, some coffee, and a piece of bacon. I left after dinner and came out again near Floated Rock Mountain and towards morning I stopped near a well and unhooked the tent. Etc., etc. . . . trip back home to his *hogan* near Black Mountain. . . . His eyes popped open and he woke up."

Comment. " Don't know if it is good or not."

4. *May* 30 *Dream.*

" Night before last I dreamed about my field and I planted some beans, corn and pumpkins. I went out to see if they were growing and they were. They all began to sprout. I was wondering if the worms would eat them up. That's all."

5. — Last night. " I dreamed that I was at the Cañon de Chelly, somewhere below the White House. There was a place there that I know. I heard from others who were talking that

there was a way up there. I thought someone was telling me that the Navajos and Utes were fighting and the Navajos were trying to escape from the Utes by climbing this rock. While I was climbing the rock a Ute shot at me. Then I thought I would try to climb to the top. I started climbing, but it looked very difficult. When I got up it wasn't so bad. I looked around and saw timbers on both sides. I climbed to the top and I looked down and saw wagon tracks and I said to myself the Indians living there must get their wood from on top. I went and followed the wagon road and before I knew it I was at the bottom of the cañon. I looked around and saw my old home where I was raised as a boy. I went to it and saw a field of corn. The corn was ripe. There were all kinds, yellow, white and blue.

" I thought to myself I couldn't do anything with the corn and wondered how I could get it into my home. I didn't really know whether the corn belonged to me or not. I just started shocking the corn and putting it in piles anyway. I borrowed a wagon. I was piling it according to size to be sent away to white people, saving the best ones for myself. I wanted to send some to town to the fiesta. I put them to dry on the ground. That's all."

Comment. " The moon was just coming up when I went outside. I woke up early and scattered the corn pollen, made a blessing and prayed for good luck in the future to raise a good crop."

HASTEEN HAL, *President of Black Mountain Chapter.*

1. *May* 25. " I remember some of my old dreams. I believe in them. I used to live on the other side of Piñon and some time ago, during the last thirty years, I dreamed that, I thought I stepped outside of my *hogan* and saw a ' white aeroplane.' Then the Indians didn't know about planes. It came down and landed near my *hogan*. A man told me to get in the plane. I got in and we started off. When we got up in the air, we flew South. From the plane we could hardly see the horses below. We flew over Oraibi, and Hubbells store. It was hard to see things from there. Then I woke up. That is the end."

Comment. " I didn't believe in aeroplanes in those days and hadn't even seen an automobile. I hadn't even heard of aeroplanes at the time. When I woke up I told the Indians of my dream, but they wouldn't believe me. I said if it is true we shall hear about planes. Since then I have been to Gallup and have seen lots of white planes in the dream. I think my dream came true."

2. — " I had another dream about eighteen years ago. I was in the mountains in a sort of cañon. On the top of the mountain there was a plane. I found an old arrow sticking in a bush. While looking at the arrow I saw something flying towards me from the South. It landed ten yards from me. I thought it was an eagle, but the eagle changed into a white lady who started walking up to me. She was wearing a white gown. In her left arm she was carrying something that looked like veils. She walked up close to me and every time she came close to me, I tried to protect the arrow. Then the lady spoke to me. When I was a boy, I used to have an eagle pet and the lady said to me, ' I am the eagle you used to have.' She said she wanted one turquoise bead with a hole in it. When I looked for my beads, they weren't there. I started for home to get it, but I woke up before I got there."

Comment. Both these are good dreams. I thought I might get sick but nothing happened to me. I don't know what that means. Maybe sickness may come later on.

3. — " Some time ago I dreamed about bears while I was some place on a mountain. While I was there on the mountain, there was a cañon with walls all around. I was walking towards the East with my family. There were four bears walking in the cañon, mother and father and two cubs. While we were walking along the bears started running after me. About two or three yards from me the bears fell down and I saw a man coming on foot. The man came to where I was standing and stopped near me. My children were on my right. I looked down and the man seemed to be standing on the running-board of a car. Suddenly we were sitting in a car with tire trouble. The tire on the left front wheel had blown out. The man ran out and told me he wanted to fix my tire and then he said it was all right. We started out again. We were still going East. A little farther on we got on the paved road and were going right along. While we were going along the man who fixed

the tire was standing on the running-board. When we got to the paved road, that was the end of my dream."

Comment. " I had a fight with some Indians about some sheep I bought from a trader. The Indians kicked about it. That's how I got my start. I think the bears were the Indians who fought me. The man who fixed the tire was a medicine man, who performed a sing over me.[1] Before the man gave me a sing, I had many accidents with my children and my sheep. Lightning struck my sheep. I decided to get a medicine man to perform a sing over me, my children and my sheep. After the sing, I never had any trouble again. I never heard any derogatory thing said about myself by other people. Since then I made a good start and increased my sheep and my children never were sick again. According to the dream, I believe all that.

" I never did expect to get a car, which I did get.

" I had other dreams which I let pass. I didn't know someone would want to know about them."

" About forty years ago I started realizing about my dreams. I tried to remember my good dreams, but I forgot most of them. There are all kinds of people in this world of different nationalities and they all dream too. There are no people in this world who don't dream."

4. — *Dream of Two Weeks Ago.*

" Some time ago they had a meeting of chapter officers at Fort Defiance. The nurses took them through the hospital. They saw one man who was operated on for appendicitis. There were stitches : I dreamed that I was in the hospital with this man and was operated on for the same thing. I didn't feel any pain. I wondered why, and I put my hand on the cut and it didn't hurt at all. I woke up as he put his hand on the cut. That's the end."

[1] *Note.*—The " sing " given him was the " *hozho'ji*," a rite of blessing or restoration. " It figures in the blessing invoked upon the family, house, and property."—*Vocab. of the Navajo Language*, 1912, The Franciscan Fathers, Vol. II, p. 96. Not to be confused with the *hozhonae*, the Chant of " terrestrial beauty." *Ibid.*, p. 96. Corroborated by Taylor, White Hair and others.

INFORMANT R. T. (*Armijo interpreter*).

1. *May* 20 *Dream.*

" Fourteen or fifteen years ago, about four days before the Navajos started to die, before the epidemic of the flu, I dreamt that in four days Navajos would start to die. It was as if somebody in the dream came and said ' you will know that it will rain in four days.' That caused the flu. This dream caused the Navajos to die."

2. — " When a little child, I had a dream. Then I didn't have any sheep. I dreamed that some day I would have lots of sheep. I dreamed that little by little I would get more and more sheep."

3. — " I had lots of dreams about rattlesnakes who had bitten me. When Navajos dream that, it means that they are going far away."

4. *May* 17 " *Night when we were at Oraibi.*"

" I dreamt of a lot of sheep. They were cutting into bunches and were going away. I build bonfires to bring them back. I took the sheep on top of a big rock. I was climbing the rock, named Straight Rock which was very high looking back with a man called Straight Rock (*Se-dol Jai*). Then the man fell down. I was holding to a little piece of rock and didn't fall. I climbed up. Straight Rock fell, but didn't hurt himself. I got all the sheep together and brought them home. When we got home, I found lots of watermelons. I began to break the melons. Some were red inside and some were yellow. So I ate. That is all I remember."

No comment.

5. *May* 25 *Dream.*

" Last time I took a trip to Chin Lee, I heard there was a sick woman. I dreamed that I was at my farm at Chin Lee. While I was there a man called Grey-Singer (*Hta*) came along. He told me that the sick woman had recovered and was getting along fine. I said last time I was here she was in a serious condition. I left and went over to my mother's place. I thought my mother told me that my nephew was in school and was coming home in two days. I thought that was fine. I wanted him to come home and look after my sheep. Then I was over here (Black Mountain) riding a black horse. I heard there was a man by the name of *Tanesanitso* whose wife was sick. I wanted to go over there and see the patient. I dreamed I took a ride over there to see the patient and saw the man walking around the *hogan*. I thought *Tanesanitso* went over to the Utes country. He waved at me and told me to come faster. When I got there, he told me that he wanted me to do a little Star gazing. His wife seemed to be sick and wanted to find out about her illness. I did it for this woman and found out there was nothing serious about her. A little singing was prescribed for this woman. A cat scratched at the door and woke me up."

Comment. "The woman is really sick. If the dream is true the woman will recover."

6. *May 26.* "I am going to tell an old dream of my uncle now dead. The dream really happened. My uncle was not a medicine man. He lived south of San Francisco peak and there was a mesa there called Grey Mountain. He used to live there when my uncle was about fifteen. He dreamed that ' the Navajos were at war with the Utes ' and he thought someone said, ' the Utes are coming ' and all those living there went on the warpath. Then he thought the best way to get away from the Utes was to move down the cañon, because if he started moving west they would surely get to them (Navajos). They were all getting ready to move and his father went out to his neighbours to round them up and notify them about the Utes. He told them it was best to move down the cañon for safety. They had just a few head of goats and the neighbours had a few more. The same with the horses. They started to move all the stock down the cañon. While they were moving the stock they raised a lot of dust. They all started moving fast and his mother and family were at the bottom of the cañon. They crossed the creek at the bottom and started up. The neighbours had already crossed. His father ran back. His father saw dust in the distance. Then the Navajos were captured by the Utes. His father came back to where the others were and told them the Utes had captured their neighbours and had taken their stock and were moving away. They were very frightened. Then he woke up."

Comment. "This dream really happened. The Uncle told his mother and father about the dream the next morning. They were talking over whether it would really happen. It was a puzzle to them. In those days the Utes and Navajos were enemies. They discussed the dream and many came around and had a little ceremony. They did a little (*desti*) [1] Star-gazing and found the Utes were really coming. Star-gazing means the spirit gets into them and they can divine the truth. The spirit gets in their system. They must pray first and use medicine on their hands and arms. They must sing before the spirit hits their arm. They feel it. It runs down their arm to their hand. They get motion-in-the-hand. It makes marks on the ground.

" His uncle used to say that in a dream, ' a woman told him it would be the end of the world when you get white hair.'

Comment. " The uncle died in 1930 and his hair was just starting to get white. According to the dream, it was the end of the world for himself."

INFORMANT HASTEEN A. (*Armijo interpreter*).

1. *May* 20 *Dream. Medicine Man.*

" Last year I dreamed that there was a big fire coming from the earth, and the Navajos and their sheep were in front of it. Then all the Navajos who came and met us said it wasn't fire. Then the ' gods ' told me to go farther up and it would be all right. I do not know who told me that. They said to go up to a rock called *Tlojali* (where the fish are coming out) and all the Navajos went up to the rock. Some of the Navajos were on top and some on the bottom and I was the last one. I was trying to get ahead of the Navajos but my legs wouldn't carry me away from the fire. The fire in back was coming pretty close to me. Then I gave up."

Comment. " I have never been burned by fire. That is a fairly good dream. Nothing happened after I dreamed it."

2. *Ten Days Ago* (*Armijo interpreter*).

" I dreamed I was going on horseback. Somebody was standing in front, I don't know who. Then I said to the little girl on back of the horse with me, ' What is that over there my little mother ? ' My little mother didn't know what the thing was standing in front of us. So I left the horse and the little girl and went to see what the thing was. I walked towards

---

[1] *Note.*—" *Desti* " is star reading or divination by sight. *Vocab. of Navajo Language*, The Franciscan Fathers, Vol. II, p. 81.

the thing. As I got closer it was sinking. Finally I got to the spot where the thing was and it disappeared. There was a hole covered with a bunch of sticks and there was a Navajo sitting in the hole. His head was black and his body was grey. I think it was a ' *chindi.*' [1] So I turned back towards my horse and the little girl was crying, ' come back my uncle, come back my uncle.' So I got to the horse and tried to get on the horse but couldn't. I had one leg on top of the saddle and I said to my little mother, ' let's go, let's go ! ' The horse wouldn't go and I had my leg half way up the saddle. Then the ' *chindi* ' got hold of my leg and pulled me off the horse. The ' *chindi* ' got hold of my neck with his hand and his hand was very cold like ice. He got me by my throat. So I fought with the *chindi.*

I fought very hard and got loose from him. That's the end."

Comment. " After this dream nothing happened. It is a very bad dream for us Navajos."

3. *May* 21. *A bad dream of four years ago.*

" I was going with another Navajo looking for a pair of mocassins on horseback. He was sitting in back of me. We were going up a little hill. About the middle of the hill was a woman sitting there. We tied the horse to a bush and went to look for the pair of mocassins that the other man lost.

" I went to one direction, the other man to the other but we couldn't find the mocassins. Before he knew it the other man got into a mud hole and went down to his waist. The man was going down in the mud and I tried to reach him and help him out, but before I was aware of it he was down to his armpits in mud. I tried my best to help the man out, but he disappeared into the mud until I went back to where his horse was tied. I got on the horse and started to go, to keep on looking for the pair of mocassins. As I was riding along, I felt sorry for this man and turned back before I got to the place where the shoes were supposed to be."

Comment. " In reality the man that disappeared in the mud died two months later. That is all. The man was my cousin. This is a true dream."

---

[1] *Ch'indi*, corpse, ghost, spirit, an evil spirit.—*A Vocab. of The Navajo Language*, The Franciscan Fathers, Vol. II, p. 73.

4. *May 24. Dream of Night of 22nd.*

" I dreamed I was going some place and I saw a herd of cattle. One chased me. So I ran behind a rock. While I was sitting down the cow came after me and jumped on me very hard. Then the cow went away. I thought I would stay where I was but I changed my mind and started toward home." No good, a bad dream.

5. — " Last night (May 23) I dreamed I went to help another Navajo boy farm and it started to rain while we were planting. We went home because it was raining. Before we got to the *hogan*, it started to rain very hard. There was lots of water running in the valley. We stood there close together and the wash was running so we could not cross. That's all."

Comment. " A good dream."

6. *May 25 Dream (Armijo interpreter).*

" I dreamed I was at the *Yaybichay* dance. I was the leader of the dancers. We started to dance. I went into the cere-monial *hogan*. We undressed. I went into a crowd of lots of Navajos. Then a car went by and nearly hit me and I woke up."

7. *May 26 Dream.*

" Last night I dreamed about watering sheep. I took them to water and another band of sheep had come to water too. I thought the other band was going to get in my band. I tried to keep the two bands separate. One sheep started off from my band and ran into the other flock. I tried to grab a stick, but by the time I got up to get it, my eyes popped open and I woke up."

No comment.

INFORMANT HASTEEN HON.

1. *May 27.* " My father died when I was little. This is one of my grandmother's dreams. She died seventeen years ago. A year before they had a war with the Utes, she dreamed of some kind of Indians dressed in their costumes. They were fighting with Indians. At that time her husband was well-to-do. She had horses and sheep and other Indian wealth. She thought the Indians were capturing her sheep and horses. She told me that the year after the Utes captured these sheep and horses. In the morning the sheep and horses were taken out to graze. The Utes came and killed all the sheep save six and

the horses and all their possessions in the *hogan* were taken away and the Utes left them hardly anything."

Comment. " Any dreams like that I didn't use to believe. I usually thought they were false. After this dream, I realized that dreams were true."

2. — " Six years ago I had a brother at school in Sherman. He was strong and healthy and was well advanced in his education. I dreamed about this brother. I thought he came back, but he came back skinny and nothing but bone and as black as this stove pipe. Four months after my dream, we got news from Fort Defiance that my brother was sent back from Sherman to Fort Defiance very ill. I was notified by an Indian and I went over to Fort Defiance to see my brother. When I got to the hospital the nurses and Doctor told me where to go and see my brother. When I got to the bedside I saw my brother was in a serious condition. He was lying in bed just the way I dreamed of him and the Doctor said nothing could be done for the boy. I decided I wanted to take my brother home with me. The doctor said all right. I took him home, and after we had been home four days after that, the boy died. From then on I realized that what my grandmother had said was true. My dreams had come true, and I began to believe in the truth of my dreams."

3. — " I and another man were way down near the Colorado River. When we started to cross, I didn't pray but the other man did and also he made a sacrifice. Four days after we crossed, I dreamed about the crossing and the ceremony. I dreamed on the fourth night that we were on the other side of the river and someone told me I had made a mistake before crossing. This person said I should have prayed and done things in the right way before starting across the river.

" I thought this person told me I didn't believe in anything. He said, ' Some time ago you had a hard time with the sickness that I inflicted on you to punish you for not believing in anything. Now this will be the second time that I am going to give you a warning. This punishment will be worse and your leg will be broken.' That's what I dreamed.'

Comment. " I woke up early in the morning and I went out and did a little blessing for myself which might help me to avoid my dream. A month later I came home and hired a medicine man to sing over me. I thought that was a bad dream, that's why I got the medicine man to sing over me (*Hozhonji* Chant given) because I believed my first dream about my brother. If I didn't do this, my dream might happen again."

4. — " Two years ago, I had another dream. I was out some place, I don't know where. I thought it was raining. There was thunder and the clouds were going wrong all over. I thought I was standing outside watching the clouds coming this way and I thought someone spoke up and told me that I shouldn't look at the clouds that they are dangerous."

Comment. " After this dream, I didn't know it would happen. About August I and another man went out to Chin Lee. We didn't have any *hogan*. We unsaddled under a tree. While we were there it started to rain and it rained hard while we were sitting under the tree. Lightning was going here and there. In some way the lightning struck me and knocked me down senseless. I don't know how long I lay on the ground, but when I returned to consciousness I got up and recognized where I was and the man was with me. He told me what had happened. Lightning had struck me. When we came home we kept away from the family and hired a medicine man and had a sing over us.[1] When the singing was over I returned to my family and started going around. From then on I believed strongly in my dreams and wanted to become a medicine man. Now I am on the way training to be a medicine man. (Being trained by White Hair.) That is about all I can tell you. I don't like to tell my story with other Indians present because I really believe these things."

5. — " My wife had a dream last night. She dreamed a cyclone had come around. She thought it had passed south of her *hogan* near *Tsesetai* Rocks. She stepped out and saw the cyclone was going there and she thought water was running everywhere from the rock. She thought Hasteen Sani was there and called for bows and arrows. They gave him a bow and

---

[1] The *Natoye bakaji*, or Male Shooting Chant was given. *Natoye*, Shooting Chant (Branches) 1. Above ; 2. *Natoye ba'ah je*, Female Chant ; 3. *Natoye dzilkiji*, Mountain Chant. Reference is made to the male and female divinities of Lightning, Thunder, Snakes and the Bear. *A Vocab. of The Navajo Language*, The Franciscan Fathers, Vol. II, p. 135.

four arrows. Hasteen Sani stepped out and shot the arrows, one to the South, one to the North, one to the West, and one to the East. She thought Hasteen Sani said we should always do this whenever we hear a cyclone coming. Then again she thought her own father, who is now at Ship Rock, stepped out of the *hogan* towards the South and performed a blessing and a little sacrifice. The old man came back in the *hogan*. She was outside and thought somebody spoke to her and told her that every Navajo should have their bows and arrows, that these things shouldn't be forgotten or pass away. She was told to have an evening and a morning blessing from henceforth. That is the end."

Comment. " She didn't know which way the cyclone went, but it disappeared. Sixteen years ago a cyclone passed through just west of here. My wife was the first one to see it and she told the rest inside the *hogan*. They went out. Her father went out and told them all to come in. The old man took some medicine from the medicine bag and went out. They heard him praying outside. He prayed a long time, and came in and told them they could go out. They went out and a cyclone passed them and went way off to the other side of the mountains. In the dream last night she thought her father went out to do the same thing."

6. *May* 30. *Dream last March.*

" I was at my mother's place and White Hair was holding a sing. I dreamed the first night that Tom Armijo had a blacksmith shop and I wanted to have a hole bored in my hoe. When I gave him the hoe I walked up this hill and I saw rain going North near the top of the mountain and during the rain there was lightning. The lightning was fire and I could see fire coming out of the rain. The fire changed into smoke and smoke was coming out of the rain. I watched and a train came out of the rain up to the hill where Charley Natani lives. There was no track and the train was running on the ground all around. Finally, the train came up the hill and changed into two tractors pulling one another. That was the end of my dream."

Comment. " A good dream."

7. — *Night before Last.*

" I dreamed I was somewhere. There were a lot of Indians. I don't know if they were holding a sing or not. I don't think it was a sing. I was there and a man called Blue-Goat was singing a song called the ' corn song ' (*Natabigin*). I was listening to him and I don't know how many he sang but I listened to him from the beginning and thought he made a mistake. I stood and listened and when he got through I decided he didn't sing the song very well. I don't know what happened afterwards, but I woke up and that's the end of my dream."

Comment. " When we Navajos dream it only happens (comes true) once in a while. Bad dreams always happen."

INFORMANT FLAT FEET.

1. *May* 31. " When a boy I didn't believe my dreams but my father said that when you dream, something is really going to happen. He said that if you dream of falling from a cañon or a rock, or your horse has thrown you, that's a bad dream. It doesn't mean you will really fall, but that some of your relatives will die, probably your children. Since I married and had children, I dreamed my relatives and children had died. I should have gotten a medicine man to at least say some prayers for the family or myself. About eight years ago when I dreamed, I wasn't suffering from anything.

" I dreamed I had a big lump on my side and I thought someone told me the best way to get rid of it was to go to a Government doctor and he would fix it up for me."

Comment. " Two years later a little lump grew on my back. I didn't know it was going to develop but I have had it for five years."

2. — (" Last year I dreamed about it again and I thought I was sent to a hospital.) The Navajo medicine man (reality) couldn't cure it and I decided to go to the hospital. I went to Keams Cañon and to the doctor. The doctor said it was fat and he was going to cut it open. He did and took the bump out and I got well when I got back from the hospital."

3. — " I dreamed about a *Chindi* chasing me and jumping on me. He was sitting on my waist and grabbed me where I was cut. I yelled for help to throw him off. I didn't know I was talking. That's the end of the dream."

Comment. " Someone spoke to me and asked me why I yelled. I told about the *Chindi*. After this dream my cut started to pain again and so they decided to have a sing over me. They got a medicine man who sung over me just a few songs from the *Hozhonji*. I got well again."

4. — "I had another dream. I dreamed I was sick in a pretty bad condition and was suffering considerably."

Comment. "The next morning I told the family I had a bad dream, in which I was suffering and was dead. I wanted to hire a medicine man again, someone who could banish the *Chindi* and bad spirits. They hired a medicine man and he held the whole ceremony (*Hozhonji*) and fixed me up. After that I never had any bad dreams until last night."

5. — "I stayed down below here and went to bed. I didn't know I was sleeping flat. I thought the *Chindi* opened the door and started coming in. I was so scared of the *Chindi* that it almost knocked my breath out. I was saying, ' the *Chindi* is coming, the *Chindi* is coming.' When I woke up I found myself talking."

Comment. "I think I may have a ' sing ' for this dream."

INFORMANT HASTEEN N. "CRAZY" WOODCHOPPER AT BLACK MOUNTAIN TRADING POST (*Armijo interpreter*).

Regarded as crazy by the Navajos and whites. Unmarried. No property. Lives under a tree. Sold a large comfortable *hogan* for one little goat.

1. *May 19.* "Night before last I dreamed of a big heavy rainstorm. Last year I dreamed of a big snowstorm before the big snowstorm. It was true. I dreamed of snow and it came true and the dream I dreamed night before last about a rainstorm means it is going to happen this summer."

2. — "A while back I dreamed of a lady like Mrs. Lincoln coming. Her hair was snow white. That woman said to him to stay and take care of her at Keams Cañon. I dreamed the dream about the white-haired woman twice." (Probably refers to Mrs. Armer who lived in this same *hogan*.)

3. — "Last summer I dreamed that it was raining—yet not rain—something unknown."

4. — "Last night I dreamed of another big rainstorm and sheep were drowning. I couldn't see the hills, the water was so high."

5. — Same night. "I dreamed that all the Navajos of this country had died."

6. — Another dream, same night. "A rattlesnake had bitten him."

7. — Another time. "I dreamt that the *Hozhonae* was coming in. The medicine man for this ceremony came in and sat by me. That is all."

8. *May* 20. "Last night I dreamed something grabbed me by the back. It seems to me it was a bunch of children. The moon was coming out. It was like a flame of red fire. That's what I dreamed last night."

9. *May* 21. "The only thing I dreamed was that my pants were torn."

10. *May* 25. *Last week.*
"I dreamed I was on the other side of the mountain on foot. I met an Indian there. He wanted to take a trip to Tuba City but didn't know the way. I told him the way to Oraibi and from there to Tuba City. That is all."

11. — "Some time ago last winter, I dreamed about an owl and thought the owl spoke to me and told me there was a man to be taken to the East. The owl didn't say where. That's all."

12. *June* 9. (*Armijo interpreter.*)
"I dreamed there was a lot of water and a man was on the top swimming. My dream changed then and a flock of sheep were eating amiso brush and about eight died."

13. — Night before last. "I dreamed about a big windstorm and it blew all these houses away."

14. — "Night before last I dreamed too about a big Squaw dance. There were a lot of Indians in this Squaw dance."

15. — "I dreamed that a Navajo whom I don't know was praying over another Navajo whom I don't know."

16. — "I dreamed night before last that there was another big snowstorm."

17. — "And then I dreamed I starved to death."
Comment. "Why should I starve to death when there are so many stores around here. That is all."
Question. "Have you had any dreams about members of your family?"

18. — "I dreamed this about three nights ago. My mother and father were in the *hogan* where I live now. Also my sister who died here was here with them. That is all."

19. — (*L. Hubbell interpreter*). Told to me in December 1930 at Black Mountain. " I dreamed of corn and growing things. I also dreamed of dead people." I ask who ? He says, " Father and Mother and grandparents."

Taylor says that craziness is caused by having sexual relations with relatives, brother and sister, uncle and niece. The woodchopper is crazy because he had sexual relations with his sister. His sister and nephew are also crazy. They try to cure them by sweat baths and herbs. In a squaw dance you are not allowed to dance with your own relatives (i.e. parallel cousins). Craziness would not be caused by sexual relations with cross-cousins (not regarded as incestuous), but would be with parallel cousins. (Mother's brothers or sister's children.) [1]

[1] " Incest is pointed out as the cause of mental derangement." *An Ethnologic Dictionary of the Navajo Language.* The Franciscan Fathers, p. 350.

CORRELATION OF NAVAJO DREAMS TO THE CULTURE PATTERN

An area where *there are no dreaming requirements*

Dream 1. The manifest content of this dream reflects the Gods and *Yays*, which belong to the religious culture pattern of the Navajos. These beings are fully described in their myths. Not a culture pattern dream in the sense of the Yuma myth dream whose form is determined by the dreaming requirements of that area, but definitely an individual dream which reflects the Navajo religious pattern in the content while the form is dependent on individual psychology.

Dreams 2 *and* 3. These reflect the Navajo belief in a spirit world and in an after life for the dead.

Dream 4. This is definitely an individual dream dealing with a personal psychological problem, with a reflection in the content of an outstanding item of Navajo religious culture, namely the bear. The personal problem is shown by the emotional state of the dreamer afterwards, followed by his having a curing ceremony prescribed for him.

Dream 6. Reflects a Navajo curing ritual.

Dreams 7 *and* 8. Reflect personal psychology in relation to the family.

C. N. B.'s Dreams.

Dream 1. When fourteen years old. This dream contains a clear reflection of the older social culture pattern. Making arrows, tending sheep, the family in a *hogan*, the fear of the Hopi, all are typical of Navajo life. Its form conforms to no pattern, and like all Navajo dreams it is an individual dream.

Dream 2. *May* 21, 1932. Reflects the immediate external situation, the people at the post, the writer's dog, etc.

Dream 3. *May* 28. An individual dream probably reflecting an inner conflict or personal psychological problem. No culture items are reflected.

Dream 4. May 28. Reflects the occupational side of Navajo culture.

Summary. Dreams 1, 2 and 4 reflect phases of the Navajo social culture pattern, the older, the immediate, and the occupational respectively.

Dream 3 falls into the class of dreams which reflect an absence of culture and personal psychology.

C. N. B.'s WIFE'S DREAMS.

Four Dreams. One reflects personal psychology, the others the occupational phase of the social culture pattern.

HASTEEN DREAMS.

Dream (a). Dec. 1930. Reflects his personal desires.

Dreams 1, 2, 3, 4, 5, 1932. All reflect his care, concern and anxiety about his crops or other property.

Dream 3. Also reflects the Navajo dependency on white culture.

DREAMS TOLD BY R. T.

Dream 1. Fourteen or fifteen years ago. Reflects the Navajo belief in prophetic dreams. Also personal psychology.

Dream 2. Dreamt when a little child. Also prophetic. It reflects his wishes for property. A personal dream.

Dream 3. Often repeated. Reflects the Navajo awe of snakes, which belongs to their religious pattern.

Dream 4. May 17. Reflects sheep tending or occupational phase of social culture pattern.

Dream 5. May 25. Reflects the Navajo curing medicine technique for sick people.

Dream 6. Old dream of his uncle. Reflects the traditional enmity of the Navajos and the Utes, and the custom of divination or star-gazing, both typical of the older culture.

Dream 7. Prophetic dream of uncles. A personal dream.

Summary. Dreams 1 and 2 reflect personal psychology.

Dream 3 reflects the religious pattern.

Dreams 4 and 5 reflect the occupational, and the medicine phases of the social culture pattern.

Dream 6 reflects the older social culture.

Dream 7 reflects the personal psychology of an old timer.

DREAMS OF HASTEEN HAL.

Dream 1. An old dream (within thirty years). A prophetic dream. Reflects the Navajo belief in prophetic dreams and the advent of white culture.

Dream 2. About eighteen years ago. A fantasy based on infantile memories. Turquoise bead shows reflection of Navajo material culture.

Dream 3. Some time ago. Reflects Navajo mythical bears and acquisition of objects of white culture.

Dream 4. About May 11. Reflects contact with white culture.

Summary. Dream 1 is a personal dream.

Dream 2 reflects personal psychology and Navajo material culture.

Dream 3 reflects mixed Navajo and white influences.

Dream 4 reflects contact with white culture.

DREAMS TOLD BY HASTEEN HON.

Dream 1. His grandmother's dream (seventeen years ago). Reflects the struggle with Utes typical of the old culture.

Dream 2. Six years ago. A prophetic dream. It reflects the influence of white education.

Dream 3. Recently. This dream reflects Navajo ceremonialism, and belief in the supernatural.

Dream 4. Two years ago. This reflects nature and the elements and the belief that they are dangerous, as well as the supernatural. It is also prophetic.

Dream 5. His wife's dream. May 26. Reflects the Navajo belief in appeasing the elements by ceremony.

Dream 6. Last March. Reflects mixed Navajo-white culture influences, namely, Navajo fear of the elements and white mechanics.

Dream 7. *May* 25. Reflects Navajo ceremonialism.

Summary. Dream 1 reflects the activities of the older culture.

Dreams 3, 4, 5 reflect the religious pattern.

Dream 7 reflects ceremonialism.

Dreams 2 and 6 reflect white influence.

DREAMS OF HASTEEN A. (*Medicine Man*).

Dream 1. Last year. Reflects Navajo belief in Gods, and personal inner conflict.

Dream 2. Ten days ago. May 10. Reflects Navajo fear of the dead, and of spirits. Also reflects personal conflict.

Dream 3. Four years ago. Largely reflects personal struggle. Mocassins and the horse are the only culture items in the content.

Dream 4. *May* 22. A personal conflict.

Dream 5. *May* 23. Reflects concern with crops and the weather.

Dream 6. *May* 25. Reflects ceremonialism.

Dream 7. *May* 26. Reflects Navajo occupation of sheep tending.

Summary. Two dreams reflect the religious pattern and personal psychology.

Two reflect an absence of culture or personal psychology only.

Three reflect the social culture pattern, two of which reflect the occupational phase and one the ceremonial.

DREAMS OF " FLAT FEET "

Dream 1. About eight years ago. Repeated last year. A prophetic dream reflecting personal psychology.

Dream 3. This reflects the Navajo fear of the spirits of the dead and of ghosts.

Dream 4. Reflects his illness. A personal dream.

Dream 5. *May* 30. Reflects the Navajo fear of ghosts.

Summary. Two of these reflect no culture traits and two reflect the religious pattern.

DREAMS OF HASTEEN NAEZ, A " CRAZY MAN."

Of the nineteen short dreams of this man, who was obviously suffering from some sort of bad neurosis, fourteen contain no reflection of the culture pattern and are dreams revealing his psychology. Two dreams reflect the social culture pattern in their occupational and ceremonial phases respectively, and two reflect the religious pattern. Many of his personal dreams deal with nature and the elements, which are naturally not included as culture reflections.

SUMMARY FOR THIS AREA : *In which are found no culture pattern but exclusively individual dreams.*

Out of sixty-nine dreams of twelve individuals, there are found the following : Thirty dreams reflecting the social pattern out of which,

thirteen reflect the occupational pattern;
five reflect the ceremonial pattern;
four reflect a mixed Indian-white pattern;
four reflect the family;
one reflects the immediate situation;
three reflect the older culture of two generations ago;
fourteen dreams reflecting the religious culture pattern;
one dream reflecting the material culture pattern;
twenty-four dreams reflecting an absence of culture or
    personal psychology, twelve of which are of one individual
    who is regarded as crazy by the Navajos.

Amongst these same dreams are also the following types of dreams which viewed from the aspect here presented throw light on the form of the individual dreams of this tribe rather than on the content.

Nine prophetic dreams, or dreams which are believed to have foretold an event correctly.

Hal, Dream 1.
R., Dreams 1, 2, 6, 7.
Hon, Dreams 2, 4.
Flat Feet, Dream 1.
N., Dream 1.

Thirteen persecution dreams, or dreams of being pursued, chased, or attacked by some supernatural or real personality or animal.

Dreams 1 and 4.
C. N. B., Dreams 1, 2.
His wife, Dream 4.
Hal, Dream 3.
R., Dream 3.
A., Dreams 2, 4.
Flat Feet, Dreams 3, 5.
N., Dreams 6, 8.

Closely related to this type of dream are dreams of slipping or of being caught in some dangerous place.

C. N. B., Dream 3.
A., Dreams 1, 3.

Seven death dreams.

Dreams 2, 3, 8.
A., Dream 3.
N., Dreams 5, 19, 18.

Hence the above classifications show that in this tribe where there are no cultural requirements for dreaming, and no sought or induced culture pattern dreams,[1] all dreams recorded are individual dreams, falling into the two classes of those reflecting in their manifest contents some aspect of the culture, and those which are assumed to deal largely with personal psychology because of an absence of culture traits in their content. Both these types of individual dreams are regarded as of great importance by the Navajos and are inextricably bound up with their religion, ceremonialism, social life and medicine, in fact with the totality of their culture.

Both types are regarded by the Navajo as causing illness which may require curing rituals. The first type reflects different aspects of their culture from that of two generations ago down to the present day. Since there is as yet no real breakdown in their culture in spite of white influence, the majority of the dreams deal with this social situation. Those dreams of the second type, therefore, which show an absence of culture and are regarded as personal, are not personal because of a breakdown in the culture, but because the individual dreaming them has lost contact with the culture, either temporarily from some inner conflict or permanently because of mental illness, as is shown in the case of Hasteen N., who is regarded as mentally deranged by both the Navajos and the whites. A large majority of his dreams reveal no apparent culture reflections.

It is interesting to note that amongst the Yuma where the culture is in large part broken down, there is no way of restoring an individual to society which no longer exists,

---

[1] This applies to the great majority of Navajo dreams with the exception of the stargazing visions, obtained by the professional diagnosticians to prescribe curing ceremonies for the illnesses and bad dreams of individuals. These do conform to a definite pattern in form and content as in all sought visions. See examples of these pattern visions on p. 217.

but a Navajo who loses contact with his culture through illness is provided with a means of restoration in the curing rituals and ceremonies. His emotional state of mind and an interpretation of his dreams are the gauges for determining what is in general regarded or implied as his offence against the culture, which sets him outside the integrated social pattern. His culture provides, in the prescription of a curing ritual, for his re-entrance to society.

Of course the distinction here made between those dreams reflecting culture items and those which are purely personal is in many ways a convenience rather than an absolute category, because many of the dreams contain both cultural and personal aspects. I think, however, the facts justify such a general distinction, which may be of some use for those who care to pursue further a deeper research in the study of dreams. Especially worth while would be a research into the causes which produce the forms of many individual dreams, such as the prophetic dreams, persecution dreams and death dreams of the Navajos and other Indians.

To conclude, Morgan mentions that in his records of Navajo dreams he has examples of universal dreams, such as falling dreams, dreams of being lost, and dreams of losing a tooth, as well as dreams of animals and death dreams. He claims to have material showing the influence of dreams on the belief and conception of life after death. Repetitive dreams, he says, strengthen the traditional beliefs concerning dreams. All the dreams he has collected are considered " spontaneous " in contradistinction to those which coincide with some particular interval of initiation, fasting or burial. This distinction corresponds to the division made in this thesis between culture pattern and individual dreams, and the dreams here recorded also show the exclusiveness of the individual or " spontaneous " dream among the Navajo where there is no dreaming requirement determined by the culture. Morgan's article lays emphasis on the interdependence of dream interpretation with the Navajo religion and shows that dreams are factors influencing the everyday life of these Indians.[1]

[1] William Morgan, " Navajo Dreams," *Amer. Anthropologist*, Vol. 33, No. 3, July–Sept. 1932, pp. 390–404.

4. THE PLAINS CULTURE AREA

Customs, Requirements and Beliefs Relative to the Dream or Vision

(a) *The Crow Indians.*

1. Visions in Crow Life are very important. Sacred ceremonies, particular songs, specific methods of painting and war parties are traced to visions.

2. Success in life is conceived as the result of the vision. Probably all tried to secure one though many failed. Lack of success in life was attributed to lack of visions.

3. There is no verbal distinction in their language between dream and vision " though conceptually the distinction is rigidly maintained." [1]

4. Methods of inducing vision.

(I) Some went to the mountains and fasted. These generally dreamt of guns, coups and horses.

(II) Some dreamt in their lodges. These usually became rich and acquired many horses.

(III) Others, usually poor people, would fall asleep when tired and get a vision.

(IV) Some fasted at the tobacco garden.

(V) One man got a vision at the sun dance, also those participants who suspended themselves from poles.

(VI) A man might drag a buffalo or bear skull fastened to the pierced skin of his back, or a horse thus secured to his body, to secure a vision.

[1] Dreams and visions for the purpose of this thesis are regarded as identical phenomena.

(VII) According to Scratches-Face, some dreamt while out in a storm, others who have lost a sister or brother or close relative would chop off a finger and go to the mountains to have dreams.[1]

5. One man differentiates between dream experiences of two different types :

(1) The ordinary dreams without religious significance.
(2) The dreams that are reckoned the full equivalent of visions.[1]

The difference rests on a difference in subjective reaction, " one experience thrills and thereby convinces the beholder that he is in communication with the supernatural, the other does not." [1]

6. Dr. Lowie says he never succeeded in securing detailed narratives of ordinary dreams.[1]

7. One Crow assigns a specific character to visions of bears, badgers and rocks, to wit that of bestowing immunity to missiles.[1]

8. There are three ways of gaining supernatural power through a vision :

(1) The visionary may receive revelation without seeking or enduring hardship.
(2) He may be visited by supernatural beings in times of difficulty without courting them.
(3) He may go in quest of a vision, subjecting himself to suffering.

9. It is believed that a bug on the head makes people dream.

10. If a person dreams that a close relative is ill, he will cut off a lock of hair, take tobacco and meat and throw all three into the water. If the relative is far away the dreamer will build a sweatlodge and voice wishes on behalf of the kinsman.[2]

[1] R. H. Lowie, " The Religion of the Crow Indians," *Amer. Mus. of Nat. Hist. Anthro. Papers*, Vol. 25, pp. 317, 342, 323, 324.
[2] R. H. Lowie, *ibid.*, pp. 342, 323.

11. Through the transferability of medicine power it is possible for people without visions to participate in the benefits of others.

12. Visions may be bought and sold by those who failed to get one of their own.[1]

(b) *The Character of the Plains Vision Patterns.*[1]

According to R. F. Benedict the only blanket description of the plains vision pattern as a whole is that the vision is an affair of maturity and not of adolescence as it is in tribes east and west of the plains. What is sometimes taken to characterize the vision quest of the plains, namely the infliction of self-torture, the lack of laity-shamanistic distinction and the attaining of a guardian spirit, is shown by a close analysis of the different tribes of this area to be unevenly distributed and even lacking in some tribes. She maintains that local developments have overlaid the common pattern till it is hardly recognizable. For instance :

(1) Among the Arapahoe and Gros Ventre puberty fasting is unknown.

(2) Nor does puberty fasting occur in all the western plains north and south, according to myths and recorded experiences.

(3) In the east plains among the Assiniboine, Hidatsa and Omaha, the puberty fasting convention is practised in varying degrees, but in addition to the characteristic plains maturity fast.

(4) Self-torture is a plains pattern distinct from the vision quest and is combined with it in different proportions in each tribe.

(5) Among the Dakota and Pawnee, sharp distinctions existed between the laity and non-laity, but in general the guardian spirit idea carried with it (throughout the plains) the idea of a common exercise by all men of spiritual powers.

(6) The vision quest on the plains is a more general phenomenon than the acquisition of a guardian.

[1] R. F. Benedict, "The Vision in Plains Culture," *Amer. Anthropologist*, New Series, Vol. 24, p. 17.

(7) The concept of the purchase of a vision exists among the Blackfoot, Crow, Arapahoe, Hidatsa and Winnebago.

(8) Among the Hidatsa, a matriarchal line, the vision can be inherited in the father's line along with the medicine bundles.

(9) The transfer of a bundle or vision in the male line is found in varying intensity among the Crow, Arapahoe, Pawnee shamans, Omaha and Central Algonkins.

(10) Among the Omaha is found an absence of torture, a connection between acquiring a guardian and puberty fasting. Also the inheritance of visions and the requirement of dreaming the family dream. They attribute spiritual significance to the vision experience.

(11) The Omaha have a hierarchy of visions.
> (a) Animals in visions and dreams could bestow only the lowest degree of power.
> (b) Above these there ranged a cloud appearance and an eagle-winged human shape.
> (c) Above these came the sound of a human voice. They also used a fasting tent made by the mother and father of the dreamer.

(12) The Pawnee vision complex shows a different psychic attitude which is opposite to that of the Crow. To him the vision is a means of spiritual contact rather than a mechanistic means of controlling forces and events as with the Crow.[1]

(c) *The Mandan Indians.*

Dreams afford the motives of many of their actions even for the penances which they impose on themselves. They think that all which appears in their dreams must be true. Before they became acquainted with firearms, a Mandan dreamed of a weapon with which they could kill their enemies at a great distance and soon after the white men brought them the first gun. In like manner they dreamed of horses before they obtained any. In many cases the guardian spirit is revealed to the fasting youth in a dream. If he dreams of a piece of cherry wood or of an animal, it is a good omen. The young men who follow such a dreamer to the battle have great confidence in his guardian spirit or " medicine." [2]

[1] R. F. Benedict, *op. cit.*, pp. 1–19.

[2] James O. Dorsey, " A Study of Siouan Cults," 11*th Annual Report of the Bureau of Ethnology*, pp. 87–90.

(*d*) *The Dakota Indians.*

" Their dreams according to their own account are revelations made from the spirit-world, and their prophetic visions are what they saw and knew in a former state of existence. It is then, only natural that their dreams and visions should be clothed in words, many of which the multitude do not understand." [1]

(*e*) *The Blackfoot Indians.*

Amongst these Indians a medicine man is " one skilled in handling of bundles and conducting their ceremonies," whereas a doctor is " one who treats disease by virtue of powers obtained through dreams or visions." A medicine man may or may not be a doctor. By transfer or purchase a medicine man may acquire the visions of others. A doctor to be such must have experiences himself which confer on him the power to cure the sick. [2]

CROW DREAMS AND VISIONS

PAINLESS VISIONS. (*Relatively few in number.*)

1. *One-Blue-Head's vision.*

He saw a person on a white-maned horse with his face painted red. He saw a chicken hawk feather tied to one of his shoulders. A voice said, " Chief chicken-hawk is coming from there now."

Comment. " Other people have to torture themselves : I never cut myself. Many people had no vision. . . . Somehow, I don't know how they tell a vision from an ordinary dream. A common dream and medicine dream or vision are quite different." His medicine forbids him to bleed or cut off fingers or to eat blood, a taboo imposed by a vision. [3]

Further comment. " Some can tell beforehand when they are going to die. They say, ' My father is going to take me

---

[1] S. R. Riggs, " Dakota Grammar Texts and Ethnography," *U.S. Geog. and Geolog. Survey of Rocky Mt. Region*, Vol. 9, p. 166.

[2] Clark Wissler, " Ceremonial Bundles of the Blackfoot Indians," *Amer. Mus. of Nat. Hist. Anthro. Papers*, Vol. 7, Part II, p. 71.

[3] R. H. Lowie, " The Religion of the Crow Indians," *Amer. Mus. of Nat. Hist. Anthro. Papers*, 1918–22, Vol. 25, p. 325.

back,' then they die soon after. The only thing I prayed to specially was my feather. I might pray to the Sun any time." [1]

2. *Arm-around-the-neck.*

He failed when he sought a vision, but he had dreams while sleeping.

Dream (1). " I saw a bear and a horse two different times ; also a bird. The bear I saw was singing to some people ; some of them fell down while he was singing, and he jumped on them. He held his arm towards the people while singing and when he was done the trees and brush in front of him fell down, He said, ' Of everything I shall have plenty.' "

Comment. " My mother's brother had the bear for medicine, that may have been the reason for this dream." He would kill a bear if he wanted to although he likes them.

Dream (2). " I saw the horses singing ; they did not lie to me. I dreamt someone was kicking my foot and there were horses all around me with ropes to their necks and fastened to my body. I heard someone say, ' Wherever you go you shall have horses.' "

Comment. " Ever since he has had horses. He thinks the dream was given by dogs. He went to sleep with dogs about him. So I thought they took pity on me and gave me horses."

Dream (3). " I saw a bird singing. I saw a man driving a herd of horses with this bird tied to his head and singing. These were the words of his song : ' Wherever I go, horse a good one, I shall have.' The man was riding a pinto horse. I heard someone say to me, ' When he does that, he brings good horses.' "

Comment. " I don't know where the dream came from." Another way of getting visions is to go out hunting and have dreams, but those obtained from thirsting are the

---

[1] " Finally may be noted the expression ' my father ' as applied to the visitant. It is understood a spirit appearing to a visionary adopts him as a child. The standard formula is, ' You, my child I will Make.' Hence the constant use of parent and child terms of relationship in the myths dealing with supernat. patrons."—*Ibid.*, p. 326.

strongest. The men who fasted became chiefs and were lucky at everything.[1]

3. *Old-Dog.*

He had never gone out to fast but had dreamt while sleeping in his tent. He dreamt of the tobacco.

4. *His Brother.*

He had fasted and seen a little buzzard which appeared in human guise, painted his face and sang against the enemy.

Comment (Old-Dog's). The brother gave Old-Dog his medicine power with four feathers of this bird, and Old-Dog subsequently dreamt of taking a gun from the enemy and striking him. (The latter dream was indirectly derived from a vision.) [1]

5. *He-Calls-Fat.*

He was visited by the dipper while awake and sitting down.

6. *Bull-All-The-Time.*

He secured a martial vision through torture and fasting. He was blessed with another for doctoring while asleep in his tipi. He saw a horse fastened to a rope, and heard a person sing. The horse was a sign he would get horses as fees for cures. He was told to doctor people. He saw an old man in red paint holding a pipe. The man blew over the patient through the pipe stem.

7. *Vision of Grey-Bull's Grandfather.*

Two birds come in, change into people, give him songs and " medicine " and power in war. This medicine was transmitted to Grey-Bull and determined one of his fasting-visions.[2]

AN UNSOUGHT STRESS VISION.

1. *Lone-Tree's Vision.* This was obtained during his flight from the enemy. A thunder-bird with lightning in his eyes appeared and offered protection.

SOUGHT VISIONS.

These were deliberate quests for a revelation. The most numerous attempts often failed. All ages did it, although the largest number were among males and adolescents. The would-be visionary retired to a lonely place, fasted four days and

[1] R. H. Lowie, "The Religion of the Crow Indians," *Amer. Mus. of Nat. Hist. Anthro. Papers*, Vol. 25, pp. 327-8.

[2] *Ibid.*, pp. 328-9. (Quotations from pp. 317-42 of *idem*. Reprinted by permission of Amer. Mus. of Nat. Hist.)

chopped off a finger joint as an offering to conciliate the spirits invoked. The Sun, or Old Man, or Coyote were the most frequently addressed. The Sun, the Bear and Snakes are the chief protectors in visions. Besides, people who have seen a Snake do not kill snakes.

1. *White-Arms' Vision*. During sleep. He saw a person riding a brown horse singing. He was covered with feathers and ornaments. He sang a song, " My child to my song listen. The ground my ear is. My child we love you."

Comment. " I joined the church and now the one who gave me the song is teasing me at night, but I won't listen to him."

2. *Lone-Tree's Visions.*
   (a) He first cut off a strip of flesh. He saw the Dipper who gave him food and said. " What you are eating is human flesh." He vomited. He saw braided hair on the Dipper and on the long queue, the Seven Stars.
   (b) He slept in an eagle's nest and dreamt he saw a bald-headed eagle who told him he was to become a captain. *Note.*—The truth of a vision is tested by its subsequent success.

3. *Big Ox. A Famous Shaman.*
   (a) He slept on a mountain and chopped off a little finger joint. He saw a bird who made him a chief. The bird had human heads, and five balls of different colour in front of him, and one of them being pure white.
   (b) When old he became feeble-minded. He saw the No-drum dance in the daytime. An old woman and a white man gave him the vision and a Crow spoke to him in Crow. They gave him a stick painted yellow and decorated with bells and feathers.

4. *Muskrat's Visions.*
   (a) She was pregnant after her husband's death and was out mourning the death of her husband and fell asleep. She saw a person who said, "Take and chew that weed and you will give birth without suffering." It happened as told.
   (b) She went out mourning for her brother and saw better and more powerful weed for the same purpose.
   (c) She has a horse inside her and was compelled inwardly to go to the bear dance. The horse's tail came out of her mouth.

(*d*) She also was given a weasel medicine in a vision. She has a weasel inside her. She was also given a whistle.

(*e*) Tobacco medicine was given her from the vision of a hawk.

5. *Tobacco Society Revelations.*

(1) *Medicine Crow* prayed to the Sun, cutting off a finger joint, and was visited by a young man and a woman who were identical with the tobacco plant. They gave instructions for the foundation of the Strawberry chapter.

(2) *Big-Shoulder-Blade* saw buffalo as young men wearing buffalo capes, promising vengeance for the death of his brother. Hence he founded the Buffalo chapter and killed an enemy as old as his brother.

(3) *Sore-Tail.* He was poor and fasted. The Sun visited him and sent an Eagle who showed him a special kind of lodge, and taught him a song. He became the richest Crow after founding the Eagle chapter.

6. *Hillside.* He dragged a buffalo skull, fasted and mutilated his back. He dreamt of a man with a buffalo foot who said, " Wait, poor fellow, you will eat now." A buffalo with grey hair licked him.

Comment. " This showed I was to live to be an old man."

7. *Medicine Crow's Vision.* He fasted near some skulls for four nights. On the fourth morning he heard a shout and whistling like a train. A voice said, " There is something coming to meet you from over there." He saw a young handsome white man. " Had he spoken to me in English. I might be able to speak English, but he addressed me in Crow. Had I been a white man and seen the vision, I think I should be wealthy to-day." The man in the dream said that he (dreamer) would be known about and would be a chief. He yawned showing gold teeth. He had a strawberry pinned on him. He said pointing East, " a great many white are in that direction. You will be taken there four times. The last time you will be an old man."

Since then he has been East once and expects to go three more times.

ORDINARY DREAMS.

Informants usually spoke of seeing ripe berries and themselves eating them, or the country covered with snow, or the ice floating down the river, or for example, " I saw the hay crop being cut, may we all do the same."

1. *Grey-Bull.* He dreamed of martial experiences day and night.
2. *Crow Girl.* She dreamt she was riding a mouse loaded with lodge poles.
3. The usual dreams of flying and falling.
4. *Bear-Gets-Up.*
   (a) He frequently dreamt of deceased friends.
   (b) He dreamt of himself being feasted by an old woman of his clan.
   (c) He dreamt of himself engaged in conversation with Dr. Lowie.
5. *Young Crane.*
   (a) She dreamt of the next winter and of seeing ice and snow.
   (b) After her husband had been killed she dreamt of him lying down with her. This frightened her.

BLACKFOOT DREAMS AND VISIONS (*Condensed*). " *The Subjective experiences of seven medicine men.*" [1]

Medicine Man A.

Experience (a). *Vision.* Sun appeared as an old man and gave him a drum and a song, both to be used in making clear weather. Used to divert the flood from his own tipi and not from his rivals.

Dream. Next year. Sun appeared as an old white-haired man carrying a drum. He taught a new song and use of drum. Drum gives power over all living things, even the grass.

Experience (b). *Dreams.* An old man and an old woman came into the tipi. The man had an iron whistle (gun-barrel) and the woman a wooden one. The dreamer chose the iron one. The old man gives his protection. He lives in the sky. He says, " In a fight do not fear guns." He was the morning star. The old woman was the moon. She was angry, threw the whistle into the fire and it became a snake and ran away. Later in another dream she returned and gave a wooden whistle. This conferred power to prevent childbearing.

[1] Clark Wissler, " Ceremonial Bundles of the Blackfoot Indians," *Amer. Mus. of Nat. Hist. Anthro. Papers,* Vol. 12, Part II, pp. 71–85. (Reprinted by permission of Amer. Mus. of Nat. Hist.)

Experience (c). Dream. An old man with white hair appears. He gives a shell necklace. It confers power to make clear weather.

Experience (d). Dream. Saw an old woman facing the sun. At her side was an old man with a headdress like the dreamer's. He saw through her and her face was painted with a black circle and a dot on the nose. The old man sang four songs. In the sun dance he painted the face of the woman the same. This dream gives ritualistic directions.

Experience (e). Dream. A medicine woman gave some paint which gives immunity from smallpox.

Experience (f). Dream. The sun came and said, " Look at the old woman's face (moon)." He saw through her head and saw paint on her face. The Sun says to paint the face this way. The Sun says to wear a cap of running fisher skin with one feather. It gives power to turn away rain. Also sun dance ritual directions are given.

Medicine Man B.
Experience (a). Dream.
Experience (b). Dream. Saw a man with very long hair. The hair was painted red. Buffalo rocks were tied to his hair. " This is what made his hair grow long." Dreamer got powers to make hair grow long.

Experience (c). He was ill and expected to die. He had a sweat house built and people prayed. He went to sleep.

Dream. An old man with grey hair and beard came to him. He said, " Give me the letter." " I have no letter," I replied. " Yes, you have a letter." He pulled a letter from his (dreamer's) abdomen. " This is what made you sick," said he, " now you will get well." The letter resembled a piece of glass with writing on one side. He recovered.

Medicine Man C.
Experience (a). He went out and fasted. He dreamed nothing the first and second night. The third morning he had a little dream of no importance. The fourth morning. . . .

Dream. Sun man and moon woman and their son, the morning star, appeared. The man gives him his body and says, " You will live as long as I," The woman gives power over rain. The son gives for a hat, a plume of eagle feathers and tail feathers of a magpie. Given power over the rain at the sun dance.

Experience (b). Dream. Of thunder bird in the autumn who says, " My son, I am going away." Dream of thunder bird the following spring who says to give Indians a feather from the tail of a magpie, " for all those who do not receive one will be struck by lightning " (partial).

Experience (c). He saw where eagles had killed and carried a rabbit to nest. He says, " These birds seem to have some power. I will sleep here." In sleep he heard eagles fighting over their powers. The male turned into a person, took yellow paint and rubbed it on his arm and took a knife and cut his veins. The female bird turned into a woman and called to me. " Now watch me, I shall cure this man." She took some white paint, spat on it and rubbed it on her forehead. At once the man was cured. She directs him to do same with a person whose veins are cut. Conferred power to stop bleeding.

Experience (d). Gave power to handle red hot stones.

Experience (e). Dream. A hawk turned into a man and said he would give power to fly to a ridge. In reality he attempts it, gets hurt and becomes sick. He says, " This is the one time in which I was fooled in my dreams."

Medicine Man D.

Experience (a). He sought power. He goes to a medicine man who tells him he will be a great chief and he will have a dream and get some power. The medicine man sings and prepares him and paints him. He tells him, " Now when you go out to sleep you must stay with it. You must not run away. If you run away you will not get power to become a great man." He goes out. Stays seven days and nights and finally has a dream.

Dream. A Raven and a man appeared. The Raven made a smudge, sang and took red paint, prayed and said, " not to try to dodge bullets for they won't hit you." Not to let anyone throw a moccasin or hit him with it " or you will lose your power." The man (in the dream) made a smudge out of sage, sang a song, " I want to eat a person," and made the sound of a coyote. He put white paint on the dreamer's body and red on his nose and mouth, and yellow on his head, breast and back. He gave power to " doctor " men shot by bullets, and power to take out bullets and power to take out things sticking in the throat.

Experience (*b*). He slept in a dangerous place where others had been frightened away for five days and nights.

Dream. He was going in one direction and a man called from another to enter his *tipi*. There were six children in the family. Among them was a girl. The man said, " I give you all my children, my clothes and my *tipi*. Now, shut your eyes." The woman confided to him he was to get a puzzle. When his eyes were shut he found something in his throat. It felt like something slippery passing down. The man said : " Do you feel anything going into you ? " " Yes." " Well," said the man, " I gave you that." After this you will drink much water. You must never chew anything like gum or lake grass, the onion kind you must never put into your mouth."

Reality. Once he made a mistake and felt a movement in his stomach and up towards his throat as if something was trying to get out, " but I knocked it back." This thing requires him to drink much water. Every day he must take a swim, " as I do not feel right unless I do."

Medicine Man E.

Experience (*a*). Once he owned a running fisher *tipi*. Every evening and every morning he burned incense.

Dream. Four minks came in. They ran up and down his body. A man and his wife and a yellow dog came in. The man and wife were painted red.—" It was in this way that I got the medicine of the minks " (partial).

Experience (*b*). *Dream.* In the forest an owl was singing. He could see nothing. He got up four times. The fourth time he saw an owl. The owl sang a song four times. It seemed to be a man. The owl invited him into his *tipi*. He went in. The owl sang the same song again four times. The words were, " Where you sit is medicine." The owl gave him his power and " this power enabled me to cure people."

Medicine Man F.

Experience (*a*). No dream or vision. Medicine learned directly from the skunk.

Experience (*b*). Medicine learned directly from woodpecker and another bird.

Experience (c). Direct speech with owls who told him he would be fortunate and have property.

Experience (d). *Dream*. Buffalo Bulls. Two leaders in herd who wore war bonnets of eagle feathers, painted one-half red and one-half blue. Faces same. Bodies painted yellow. Gave war bonnet. Gave power to get food, etc.

Medicine Man G. (skilled in " Cree Medicine," has to do with diseases of women, but also applies to other kinds of sickness and love affairs).

Experience (a). " Whenever an Indian sleeps and especially when he has a dream, he appeals to the power of a moth or butterfly." As a boy he wanted to be somebody. He sought a vision.

Dream. He saw a boy, while making a hole in the ground to build a fire. The boy asked him to visit his father. The third time he accepts. He opened a door in the rock, and entered. A family of three were inside, a man, woman and the boy. The woman signals that he will be offered medicine by the husband but he must decline everything save the owl feathers. The man offers. He chooses the feathers (four times). The man gives them and says, " My son you will never be killed in battle. . . ." Predicts that balls will go through him. Gave power to let balls go through him (without harm ?).

Experience (b). *Dream*. A man appears and gives a weasel skin and a squirrel tail and gives power to cure disorders of the bowels.

Experience (c). *Dream*. A man appears and said : " I give you my body. You must carve its image in wood and carry it with you. Whenever anyone has a hemorrhage put the image on his body and the hemorrhage will stop." Gave power to cure wounds, disorders of the bowels and hemorrhage.

Experience (d). After his wife died he mourned and slept on the prairie. One night he slept on a ridge where Indians were buried. He fell ill. At noon he recovered when people were in the *tipi*. At the moment of recovery he could see through the *tipi*.

Vision. He saw the ridge where he had slept. He saw the dead sitting in grave boxes. He saw them get out and shake off their clothes. He took up his blankets and started towards the camp led by a woman and a baby. The people around didn't see and thought him crazy. The procession of dead came up to the *tipi*, painted. They came and stood before him. One of the dead took the baby and put it down on a small red neckcloth. One said, " We shall kill this young man with the baby." The dead danced around. He saw his own dead body. One of the dead took the baby, swung it three times and threw it at my body. " My body dodged." Each of the dead tried to hit my body with the baby, but none succeeded. Then one said, " Well, we shall have to let him go this time." One of the dead said, " My son, we will give you a neck-cloth which belonged to the baby." This will give power to cure cramps and rheumatism. It also has power to pick up red-hot stones and fire. Hence, the formula neck-cloth, red-hot stones and tea.

Experience (e). He saw a dog that had been shot through the neck and kidneys. He felt sorry for the dog and carried him home, fed him and took care of him. He slept beside him. He had a bad dream. Then the dog became a man and spoke and said, " Now I will give you some roots for medicine and show you how to use them. Whenever you see anyone who is ill, and feel sorry for him, use this medicine and he will be well." One of these medicines is good for sore throat.

CORRELATION OF THE DREAMS AND VISIONS TO THE CULTURE

(a) The Crow Indians.

Dr. Lowie has shown how all the dreams and visions with religious significance, whether they are painless visions, unsought stress visions, or deliberately sought visions preceded by fasting and self-torture, conform both in form and manifest content to a stereotyped pattern determined by the culture. They all reflect the Crow relation to the supernatural, the representatives of which confer some power or favour on the dreamer. These kinds of dreams are regarded as being of great importance and give the supernatural sanction for all important undertakings in life.

The ordinary dreams without religious significance are not regarded as of any special significance, and conform to no such pattern. The manifest contents of these, however, as in the other areas reflect aspects of the social culture as well as personal psychology.

Hence, to sum up, there is found in this tribe where dreaming is an essential requirement for most undertakings in life, highly significant culture pattern dreams and visions, as well as individual dreams which are not considered important and are not even told in detail.

(b) The Blackfoot Indians.

Among these Indians also, all the dreams and visions of the medicine men here recorded conform in their form to an absolute pattern. In every one of them some supernatural being appears and gives the dreamer something (which often becomes a new variation of their culture) [1]

[1] See Chap. II, p. 94.

which confers power or gives directions. They either confer power over objects, the elements, enemies, or disease, or they give ritualistic instructions. The manifest contents all reflect the religious pattern of this tribe. An exception might possibly be made for the content of one of these dreams (Medicine man D, dream *b*), whose form is in accord with the usual pattern of a supernatural or mysterious being presenting something. Only in this case what is presented is a " puzzle " or problem related to his personal health. This might be considered a culture pattern dream in form, yet whose content reflects mainly personal psychology.

Customs, Beliefs and Classifications Relative to the
Dream and a Few Examples of Dreams

MENOMINI DREAM FASTING OF YOUTHS AND MAIDENS [1]

1. The youths and maidens at fifteen retired and fasted eight to ten days, and prayed for a supernatural vision, " keeping his mind on things above the earth, in the heavens, the abode of all the powers of good."

(I) If the vision was of something on high, of the sun, moon, stars, thunderbirds, or heavenly birds it was an omen of good.

(a) A young man would be a great hunter if the spirit promised specific boons and agreed to watch over him.

(b) In extraordinary cases, guardians would give some living thing to be incorporated in the body of the dreamer. This was the guardian power in a small form.

(c) Sometimes objects were given him to keep in his medicine-bag.

(II) For a girl, " to dream of things on high meant long life, happiness, virtue and perhaps social elevation."

(a) In one instance a girl dreamt, " of a large fat man, who appeared and told her that she would have a long life, that she had power over the winds, and that she might hear of what people said of her no matter how far away they were when they spoke."

[1] Alanson Skinner, " Social Life and Ceremonial Bundles of the Menomini Indians," *Amer. Mus. of Nat. Hist. Anthro. Papers*, Vol. 13, 1915, pp. 42–51, 79, 80, 95, 173–82, 434, 532–9.

(b) She dreamt also, " of the sun, who said she would have a long life and promised protection." " Should she desire anything and pray to the sun for it, it would be granted her. The sun commanded her always to wear a red waist as a sign of the eight virgins who lived in the east. All these things were a reward for her suffering, for she had fasted ten days."

(III) Sometimes the faster dreamed of something below the skies, on or under the earth.

2. Animals, excepting supernatural monsters, rarely appeared as guardians.

3. Parents commanded the dreamer to break the fast : " Eat ! You have dreamed what is useless, if not evil," they cried. The faster rested and tried again. If the evil dream persisted, the third time it had to be accepted.

4. The fasting of girls and the repetition of their dreams to their parents, are found among the Menomini, Central Algonkin, and it is said the same holds true among the Woodland Potawatomi. Among the Eastern Cree the fasting dream must never be repeated lest it give offence to the spirits.

5. " A careful study leads us to believe that all Menomini puberty dreams conform to certain unformulated rules." The faster is bound to have a dream the subject of which will be confined to one of four sets of " strong Powers " :

(a) One of the Gods above.
(b) One of the Gods below.
(c) One of the Manitou animals.
(d) The sacred metal cylinder.

The form of the first three is more or less fixed, in which a being appears, offers aid and patronage, and exacts a pledge.

If it is about the powers above, it is a good vision. The Sun is the greatest power and grants war honours. The Morning Star is also important. " Most dreamers who see the Moon break their fast and try to dream again of something else, as a man with the moon for his patron will only be strong when it is full and will die a lingering death." The moon is less powerful than the sun. It is a poor thing to dream of though it is not evil. If the moon persists in appearing as it often does, it must be accepted. It brings long life but life that will end in misery. People having the moon for a patron are strong when it is full, and weak and sickly when it is on the wane.

When one of the " Powers below " appears, the dreamer ceases fasting and tries again later, " for all these powers are evil."

They include, horned hairy snakes, underground bears and panthers. The acceptance of such a dream makes one a sorcerer. If such a dream occurs three times it must be accepted. There is a story in which an evil power made a second rendezvous with the dreamer, who was seen and pitied by a good power, a thunderer, who intercepted the dreamer from going to keep tryst with the evil power, and bribed him not to go. The thunderer kept the appointment and slew the evil one.

A few informants declared that there were rare occasions on which a snake dream was not altogether evil, but the majority condemned all horned snake dreams. Such dreams are regarded as irksome and require sacrifices of dogs, and tobacco, etc.

Evil attributes are not conferred for a long time after acceptance, only during a period of long training and of offerings, sometimes requiring human sacrifice. " The power might demand the first living thing the dreamer met when he started home, or perhaps the life of the father's first born. Death would follow a refusal to comply."

Animal Dreams. These are rare among the Menomini but usual among the Eastern Cree and Saulteaux. Dreams of the bear and buffalo are the most common. The bear gave hunting and healing powers, the buffalo gave war and healing powers, the weasel gave courage and success in hunting and war. Among the Oshkosh the chief was a buffalo dreamer. Lice were sometimes appointed by the dream guardian to remain and care for the dreamer. Ants had protective power.

Small animals were sometimes incorporated in the body of the dreamer, placed there by the great powers. These remained for life, unless the possessor ate food out of a dish touched by a menstruating woman ; then the medicine was likely to be vomited forth and kill the owner.

Dreams concerned with the Sacred Metal Cylinder. This object is believed to stand in the centre of the heavens. " A dreamer sometimes had a vision in which he ascended through this tube. If he reached the top, he received gifts from one of a group of gods there who conferred regular powers for war, long life, and hunting."

6. *Occasional Aberrant Dreams.* One man dreamt that the spirits of the dead pitied him. If he was in danger, a ghost always came and stood between him and the source of his trouble to ward off any attack. A few have dreamed of Manabus.

There is also a class of dreams which give the faster the right to own a sacred bundle.

7. *An Aberrant Potowatomi Dream.* This is a dream reflecting the myth about a wandering being supposed like the wandering Jew to ramble for ever through the forest in punishment for his offence against the Gods. Old Kanasot dreamed of Petcicunan Naiota (" sacred bundle on his back," the Menomini name), whose abode is among the greatest rock ledges. He promised Kanasot the power of clairvoyance and safety by both day and night. The dreamer was obliged to make and keep a crooked knife whose handle was carved to represent the wandering man and to sacrifice tobacco and liquor to him at intervals.

8. Among the Menomini all of the above dreams are also common to girls. One class is peculiar to them, those of social preferment, or of brave sons, or of many children. " One may dream of a tall pole with a flag at the top. This is a sign that she will marry a chief's son. She may also dream of one of the sacred families of sky sisters."

9. No male or female is eligible to dream who is long past puberty or who has ever had sexual intercourse.

10. *Regular Night Dreams.* These are also regarded as important. For instance a man may dream of drowning or being saved from drowning, in which case he makes and always carries about with him a small canoe as a talisman. It is not clear if the canoe is made in accordance with injunctions received in a puberty dream, but he thinks not.

11. Many Potawatomi visions might be Menomini. The thunder staff is peculiar to the Potawatomi, but is never found among the Menomini.

269

12. Those who dreamt of the sun used to roach the hair and wore a brass collar or a beaded rope about the neck to symbolize its rays, or a figure of the sun suspended over the chest. (*Note.*— The sun is the supreme God among the Ojibway.)

13. The sacred bundles of the Menomini for war, hunting, witchcraft, etc., are all the private property of individuals who have derived them from the gods by means of dreams.

14. The Society of Dreamers, and the Dream Dance originated in the vision of a little girl, according to the myth.

15. *How the Sauk War Began.* " A young man had just received his sacred dream. In it he had been told by the powers above that he must go and visit a white man and this man would give him a rifle and plenty of ammunition." The boy was pleased and gave a feast.[1]

The Ojibway Indians.[2]

The following are some of the different types of dreams, linguistically distinguished by these Indians :

    Dream
    Bad dream
    Beautiful dream
    Good dream
    Impure dream
    Ominous unlucky dream
    Painful dream
    Dreamer
    Great dreamer
    Vision

The Winnebago Indians.

During the fasting experiences of this tribe the attitude of the faster varies from childish playfulness to religious intensity. Both boys and girls fast and seek a vision or dream before reaching the adolescent stage. These experiences conform to a stereotyped expression of life. The youth's fasting experience is

[1] Alanson Skinner, " Social Life and Ceremonial Bundles of the Menomini Indians," *Amer. Mus. of Nat. Hist. Anthro. Papers*, Vol. 13, 1915, pp. 49, 50, 532–9. (Reprinted by permission of Amer. Mus. of Nat. Hist.)

[2] Frederic Baraga, *Grammar of Otchipwe Language*, p. 79.

tested by the elders and if found wanting the youth must try again or give up. The guardian spirit is only called into aid during crises in life.[1]

Old Pattern Dreams.

Ottawa and Ojibway Puberty Fasting Experiences.[2]

1. *Obtained at Hiawatha, Rice Lake.*

In the olden days Indians used to fast for the purpose of revealing their future. When a young Indian began fasting he was given very little to eat in the morning and at night, with nothing at all at noon for two days. Then the older people would build him a scaffold on top of a hill near some big tree, an iron-wood preferred. There he would stay both day and night. His father and mother would come in the morning to inquire about his dreams. If he had dreamt of a snake or some kind of serpent, he would have to give up fasting entirely ; but if he dreamt of other animals, he received a blessing. If he was blessed by land animals, he became a hunter, and if he dreamt of birds, he became a great man among his people.

When a faster starts to dream, a man or woman appears to him with a blessing. If he accepts the blessing offered the spirits will take him away and show him the nature of the blessing that he is to use in years to come. After this the spirits take him back to his fasting place. Here he sees the spirits disappear and he can then identify the spirit who has blessed him.

2. *Obtained at Sarnia.*

" When I was a boy of eleven my mother told me that it was time for me to find out about my future. I was told to fast. First I was told not to eat or drink anything except at supper-time. This I kept up for five days. On the sixth day a wigwam was built on the bank of a little creek, running through the woods. There I was left on the evening of the sixth day and there my mother came to see me the next morning to find out if I had had a dream. But I had not slept that night, for I went

[1] Paul Radin, " The Winnebago Tribe," *37th Annual Report of B.A.E.*, 1915–16, p. 290. (*Note.*—For account of fasting experiences see also pp. 291, 293, 299–309.)

[2] Paul Radin, unpub. Notes collected 1927.

to a creek for a drink of water. It was early in the fall of the year and the nights were quite warm. My people saw the tracks along the creek the next morning and immediately realized that I must have left my sleeping-place.

" They asked me where I had been and I told them that I had gone to the creek for water. Then I was told to go home.

" After about two weeks I had to start all over again. This time I was placed together with another lad. On the fourth day they changed my wigwam to another part of the woods far away from the creek. On the evening of the fourth day, I went to the place they had built for me. That night the other boy had a bad dream and when our mothers came the next morning he told his mother what he had dreamt. He had had a vision in which a snake appeared to him and made him sick and that he finally died. He was told to go home. After that I was all alone in the wigwam. My people visited me quite often, about three or four times a day. I stayed there five days and on the fifth night I had a dream.

" I dreamt that I was alongside a lake and had not had anything to eat for some time. I was wandering in search of food for quite a time when I saw a big bird (*majg*). This bird came over to where I was staying and spoke to me, telling me that I was lost and that a party was out searching for me ; and that they really intended to shoot me instead of rescuing me. Then the bird flew out into the lake and brought me a fish to eat and told me that I would have good luck in hunting and fishing ; that I would live to a good old age ; and that I would never be wounded by a shot-gun or rifle. This bird who had blessed me was the kind that one rarely has a chance of shooting. From that time on the *majg* (loon) was my guardian spirit."

3. *Obtained at Sarnia.*

When a boy gets to be ten years old, his grandmother always wishes him to fast, so that he may know what blessing he is going to receive. Such a boy will start to fast in the autumn, getting very little to eat in the beginning, either for breakfast or supper. Of course, not everyone is very strict about eating during the daytime.

In the spring a little scaffold is made and on it is built a little wigwam for the fasting boy. Here he is to stay for ten days and nights, getting a little to eat twice a day. He is warned by his grandmother not to believe every spirit that comes to bless him, for some like to deceive people. She tells him to accept only that spirit who came with a great noise and with mighty force.[1]

" On the first and second nights, I didn't dream of anything, but on the third night a very rich man came to me and told me to go with him, and that I would become rich. I went with him but I refused to accept his gift. Then I returned to my wigwam and looked around, for the man had told me that I would be able to recognize his identity when he went away. He was an owl, and the big house was a hollow tree with holes all around it.

" The next night another rich man came, dressed in red. He offered me the same thing as the first one and, in addition, he told me that I would be able to buy two suits of clothes a year. Then he told me to turn around. I did so and saw nothing but oak trees with dry and green leaves.

" The next night, another man came and offered me boxes of sugar, but although I went with him I refused his gift. I went with all of them, even after I had decided to refuse. The last man, like the others, told me to turn around to see who he was, and when I turned I saw a big maple tree.

" Twice a day my grandmother came to feed me and to ask what I had dreamt of. I told her of what I had already dreamt. She then warned me not to accept any spirit until one with noise and strength came ; and that before the tenth night was up I would surely be blessed, if I had observed carefully all that I had been told. Surely enough, on the night of the tenth day I heard a gust of wind above me, and when I looked up I saw a very stout man. I went with him towards the north and came to a place where nine old men were sitting in a circle, with a very old man in the centre. The man in the centre was the one who had blessed me. He told me that he had just been sent from above.

" Then the one who had been sent after me took me back to my wigwam and told me to turn around as soon as he had gone some distance. I did so and saw ten big white stones in a circle and another one in the middle.

[1] Here the narrator suddenly changes from an impersonal to a personal description (Radin).

"In the morning, when my grandmother came to feed me and inquired about my dreams, I told her of what had happened. That was the end of my fasting.

"Some fasters are fooled by a bird called the chickadee. This bird also comes with a gust of wind."

4. *Obtained at Sarnia.*

"When I was a boy of ten years, my father told me to fast, so that I might know in what manner I was to be blessed. My father told me to blacken my face with charcoal in the morning, and to leave it on all day till evening. Then I could wash it off. During the day I did not eat much. The next day I again blackened my face, and I kept this up for four days. On the fifth day, when I got up, my father told me not to blacken my face any more and that I was to eat. However, I was to eat only my breakfast and to drink a little water at night. For two days I kept this up. On the eighth day, my father built me a little hut on top of four poles, in which I was to live and in which my *maneto* was to visit me.

"The first night I spent there I did not sleep a wink. I was up all of the next day. In the evening my father brought me something to eat and inquired if I had dreamt of anything or if anyone had come to bless me. I told him that I hadn't slept a wink. In this fashion a few days passed and I became very hungry. On the night of the ninth day, I lay down with the hope that I would dream of something. The next morning my father came to bring me some food and inquired again whether I had dreamt of anything, and when I told him that I hadn't dreamt of anything, he got angry and told me that I had better give up. However, I told him that I would try once more and if then I had not dreamt of anything, I would stop.

"On the tenth night I went to sleep early, and after a while I dreamt that I heard a great noise. Then I jumped up and ran to the north until I came over a river. There was no way in which I could get across and there a man caught me and took me back to my wigwam. From there he took me to a place where another man waited for me.

"This is my fasting experience, but I won't tell the exact details of how I was blessed, for I would never tell that to anyone."

5. *Obtained at Sarnia.*

" When I fasted I was about ten years old, that being the age at which grandparents generally desire their grandchildren to fast. My parents never bothered me at all about fasting, and I don't suppose I should have fasted at all if I hadn't a grandparent at that time.

" About the middle of the little bear month, that is, February, my grandmother came to our house to fetch me. I did not know what she wanted of me. After two days she told me why she had come. So the next morning I received very little to eat and drink. At noon I didn't get anything to eat at all, and at night I only got a bit of bread and water.

" There were about seven of us fasting at the same time. All day we would play together, watching each other lest anyone eat during the day. We were to keep this up for ten days. However, at the end of the fifth day I became so hungry that, after my grandmother had gone to sleep, I got up and had a good meal. In the morning, she found out that I had eaten during the night and I had to start all over again. This time I was very careful to keep the fast, for I didn't want to begin on another ten days.

" After a while, they built me a little wigwam. It was standing on four poles and about three to four feet from the ground. This was my sleeping-place. My little wigwam was built quite a distance from the house, under an oak tree. I don't know whether it was the custom to have the young boy fast under a particular tree or not. I believe that the wigwam was built in the most convenient place for the old folks to watch it during the day.

" The first morning my grandmother told me not to accept the first one that came, for there are many spirits who will try to deceive you, and if one accepts their blessings he will surely be led on to destruction.

" The first four nights I slept very soundly and did not dream of anything. On the fifth night, however, I dreamt that a large bird came to me. It was very beautiful and promised me many things. However, I made up my mind not to accept the gift of the first one who appeared. So I refused, and when it disappeared from view, I saw that it was only a chickadee.

" The next morning, when my grandmother came to visit

275

me, I told her that a chickadee had appeared in my dream and that it had offered me many things. She assured me that the chickadee had deceived many people who had been led to accept this offering.

" Then a few nights passed and I did not dream of anything. On the eighth night, another big bird appeared to me and I determined to accept its gift, for I was tired of waiting and of being confined in my little fasting-wigwam. In my dream of this bird, he took me far to the north where everything was covered with ice. There I saw many of the same kind of birds. Some were very old. They offered me long life and immunity from disease. It was quite a different blessing from that which the chickadee had offered, so I accepted. Then the bird who had come after me, brought me to my fasting-wigwam again. When he left me, he told me to watch him before he was out of sight. I did so and I saw that he was a white loon.

" In the morning when my grandmother came to me, I told her of my experience with the white loons and she was very happy about it, for the white loons are supposed to bless very few people. Since then, I have been called White Loon." [1]

MODERN INDIVIDUAL OTTAWA DREAMS.

Dreams of J. P. [2]

1. " I dreamed I was a woman and had a little girl. I was laughing as I woke up."
Comment. " This is a good dream. I was very much amused at this dream."

2. " I dreamed that somebody was chasing me. He never caught me. I have dreamt this often."
Comment. " This is a good dream. J. S., another Indian who was present, volunteered the following interpretation :—" J. P., this is a good dream. What was pursuing you was disease. Disease can never catch your life. You will live to be an old man."

---

[1] Other old-time pattern dreams are recorded in H. R. Schoolcraft, *Oneota*, pp. 430–2, and George Copway, pp. 38, 39, 154–63, and in P. Radin, unpub. Field Notes.

[2] Paul Radin, Field Notes told in 1927 (Unpub.). " J. P. is an Ottawa Indian about 73–75 years old. The comments are by him and were freely given without any specific questioning on my part."

3. " I dreamed that a small black bear ran after me. I tried to climb a tree to escape him, but the bark was slippery and in addition would always come off as soon as I attempted to climb. When I woke up I had an erect penis."

Comment. None given.

4. " I dreamt I was very rich. I saw a large round hotel and in it I saw many large sacks full of money, all of which belonged to me."

Comment. " This is a bad dream. I got sick soon after dreaming it."

5. " I dreamt I was lousy. When I walked I could see myself covered with lice. Then I went to the bush to get rid of these lice."

Comment. " This is a lucky dream. The year in which I dreamt it I was very lucky. I made $500."

6. " I dreamt of honey-bees."

Comment. " This is a lucky dream."

7. " I dreamt that I ran away from three people. I ran towards the south-east. These three people, however, ran after me in order to kill me. I was alone and there were three of the others. I finally came to a lake about half a mile from where I lived. I intended to swim across this lake and thus get away from them. As I reached the lake there was one man in front of me and two behind. I jumped into the water and turned around immediately to watch the man. When I was about half way across I saw two of the men in the water following me. One fellow was pretty close to me. I had nothing in my hand with which to defend myself. This fellow soon got so close that I could almost reach him. Then I struck him and knocked out one of his eyes. The second man behind me then came along but I got to the other side before he reached me. I thought then that I had gotten away from all three. I walked towards the west, towards a river, but when I had walked about half a mile, I found two of the men in front of me again. One of them said, ' This is the man who almost killed my brother.' He was a very big fellow. Then he again spoke to his partner and said, ' If you can kill him do so ! ' Then I thought to myself, ' I am going to fight him and the best man will live.' We all walked a little farther together along the shore. I felt I was as mad as the devil and thought to myself, ' I'm going to kill him (the man

who had spoken) if I can.' Then this one stopped and went back. He told his partner that he wouldn't fight. 'This Indian is going to kill us,' he said. 'We had better run away.'

"Then I went to the river to see what kind of a boat these people had. As they paddled back I saw the occupants. They were the muskrat, mink and otter."

Comment. "This is the first dream I have ever had. Everything was going along nicely when I dreamt it. That winter I made $200."

8. "I dreamt that a person I had known very well, in fact a girl who had been my sweetheart, and who had been dead about ten years, came to me. Smiling, she put her hand on my chest and gradually brought it down lower and lower. I knew she was going to touch my penis, but just before she got there I shrieked out and awoke."

Comment. None.

9. "I dreamt that I saw two logs and between them a naked girl who wanted to cohabit with me. I got on top of the logs and tried to get into a position for copulation but couldn't succeed."

Comment. None given.

10. "Some time after my mother's death I dreamt I was home. I saw my mother's footprints and although I knew she wasn't there, yet I looked for her everywhere.

"On another occasion I dreamt that she was home."

Comment. "This is a bad dream."

11. "I dreamt I saw a well and that there were two women living in it. They were then outside of the well. They were my sweethearts and they were called women-living-in-water. They spoke to me and wanted to take me down into the well with them, but I told them that I couldn't go down. Then they said, 'Don't be afraid ; you won't die for we will help you to get out afterwards. Do come with us for we have a nice home.' I at first refused because I was afraid that if I went with them I would die. So I played with them on the outside of the well. They urged me to go with them and tried to entice me to live with them in the well. I again said, 'No I don't want to go there for if I do, I'll die.' Finally, however, I did go there with them. I entered the well and felt nothing in particular nor did I die. They had a very nice home in the water. How-

ever, I knew I was a prisoner and that I wouldn't be able to get away again. Indeed, I tried to get out, but there was a high fence around me. I felt as one does toward people whom you don't like yet who are very good to you. Finally I got out just as I woke up."

Comment. " This is a good dream. I felt unhappy when I woke up for I wanted, in my dream, to get out of the well and yet I also wanted to stay because these women were so good to me. I asked an old man what the dream meant and he said that it meant life for me. That I would overcome every sickness that came to me and that I would live long. He said that if I hadn't succeeded in getting out of the well, I would have died."

12. " I was sleeping with my wife. At that time we had two children and this is the dream I had. I stood on top of a platform and as I looked around I saw lots and lots of people. Everyone was looking at me. Some of these people motioned to me with their hands. Everyone was laughing and feeling good. Then I left the platform. All the people—white, red, black— wanted to see me. After that I went to another place, to a big church. On this journey a woman went along with me. I wore a long coat. Just before I got to the place I saw a large number of people standing around the church. I knew some of them. I had nothing in my hand. As I began to walk up the steps of the entrance I suddenly felt that I had a black book in my hand. A man standing at the door—bell-ringer—began to toll the bell, and as I entered everyone bowed their heads and didn't look at me. I tried to smile and look at them but no one would look at me. I was still holding the big black book. I knew that I was to be the preacher in the church. I went up to the pulpit and just as I was to open the book, my wife woke me up and asked me what was the matter. Apparently, I had been talking in my sleep."

Comment. " I asked an Indian about this dream (this was twenty-five years ago) and he said, ' Soon every white man will look at you and help you out. So this is true, for white people have helped me out and now you have come to ask me all these things. This is a good dream."

13. " I dreamt I was standing near a lake and there in the water, I saw my brother drowning. I tried as hard as I could

to drag him out of the water before he drowned. I could see him moving under the water. However I couldn't reach him in any way. When I woke up I left him still drowning in the water."

Comment. " I was told that this was a good dream and that my brother was going to live long. He is still living and is ninety-two years old."

14. " I dreamt a dream that my wife was going to leave me and that a white woman was going to help me out with my children. I didn't want her to go and I didn't want the white woman to come. I thought to myself, ' I can help myself out.' My wife was already in the train ready to leave. I was outside. My wife was going away alone and I didn't know where. Then my wife left and the white woman came to take care of the children. I didn't want her. She was very good to the children. Then I woke up."

Comment. " I was told that when a man dreams that he is dreaming, it means that he has almost died.

" My wife told me that this dream meant that I was going to get another wife after she died. She died shortly after."

15. " I dreamt after my wife's death, that I was with my wife and that she was still sick. She didn't speak much to me. We were living together in the house and taking care of the children. Soon after the huckleberry season began and we went away to pick huckleberries. There I dreamt that I saw an old friend of mine who was also picking berries. My wife was sick all the time. Then she left me, and I didn't know what became of her. I looked everywhere but I couldn't find her. Then I woke up."

Comment. " I have dreamed this dream very often. It is always the same, my wife is always sick."

16. " I dreamt that the end of the world had come and that a few Indians were standing around me. As I stood on the ground I could almost hear the fire burning under the ground. West of this place there was a hill. There also I found a road and at the end of it a large house, low on one side and high on the other side. Everyone was supposed to enter the house and get a yellow permit. Then when the end of the world came the possessor would not have to go to hell. I didn't have one of these yellow slips and I asked a man, ' Can't you go in and get

this permit for me?' 'No, you have to get it yourself.' So I didn't get it. I was ready to go in and was quite frightened, but I woke up before I went in.'

Comment. "This is not a good dream."

17. "I dreamt that there were many people around me. All of them—white, red, black—were good to me and talked to me kindly. Some of them really wanted to hurt me, yet spoke to me kindly. Some of them wanted to hurt me but I got away. They were drunk. I ran away and got into some mud and hid myself there, just with my nose sticking out.

Comment. "I have dreamt this dream repeatedly during the last two years."

18. "I dreamt that as I was walking alongside of a river I saw all kinds of snakes lying on the ground. They were all quiet. I killed most of them and then walked on."

Comment. "This is a bad dream."

19. "I dreamt I saw two big snakes of a green-like colour like an applesnake. These snakes were going to fight me but I killed them all."

Comment. "This is a bad dream. Snake dreams mean you have an enemy. If you kill the snake it means you have good luck."

20. "I dreamt I was naked and in an empty house in a city. I hid myself there. Then I asked for clothes from some of the people who were passing and they were just about to give it to me when I woke up."

Comment. "Some people say this is a good dream."

21. "I dreamt that I saw two suns shining in the sky together and that the world was going to end. That was what all the people were saying. Everybody was looking at the sun, hollering and crying. I saw many goats running towards the west telling everyone that the world was going to end."

Comment. "This dream is neither good nor bad."

22. "I dreamt of Pharaoh's little wood idols. They came after me and began jumping on the pit of my stomach tickling me. I laughed and cried out and my wife woke me up."

Comment. "This dream is neither good nor bad." [1]

---

[1] Not an indication of the "collective unconscious." He had been reading recently in the newspapers about excavations of the Pharaohs' tombs. (Radin.)

23. " I dreamt that I was walking along and came to a river. There along the bank I saw lots of people. They were all washing and talking, laughing and feeling good at the same time. As soon as they finished washing their clothes they all jumped into the water. I looked at them and they all turned into musk-rats. Then I dreamt that I was going to set the trap for them and kill them. I fixed my traps and was preparing to go after the muskrats. When I was finished blackening the traps I woke up."

Comment. " This is a good dream."

24. " I dreamt that my dead uncle was alive and that I was talking to him. He wanted to show me how to hunt and to help me as much as he could."

Comment. None given.

25. " I dreamt that I was still at school. I was at Carlisle and was just beginning to start all over again. I had some books in my hand. I dreamt that I was going to study another five years. This seemed a very long time to me. I was feeling very lonesome and wanted to go home. Yet there I stayed for five years. Then I came home. Then I woke up."

Comment. " This is a good dream."

26. " I dreamt of an old abandoned log road. There I met a young boy smaller than myself. He looked kind of negro-like. Now this boy who was three feet high was not a human being. He really was the devil. He had a tail. He was very good-natured but yet he was the devil. He laughed at me and wanted always to shove me in fun. He didn't want to hurt me very much but his shoving me all the time got me mad and I thought to myself that I would knock him down. But I couldn't do it ; I couldn't lick him. He was too quick for me. All the time that he was shoving me in play, he laughed. He really was very good-natured. Thus we fought for a long time. Then I woke up. Neither of us got licked."

Comment. " This is a good dream. Just thought the young boy was the devil because he had a tail."

27. " My wife dreamt that a woman wearing a white dress came into the house and that this woman was going to have a race with her. She was an old woman. This woman said, ' The winner of this race is going to live.' My wife looked at the woman. She was very smart and could jump well. Then

they started to race and my wife in spite of her illness beat the old woman. The old woman said, ' Well you beat me, you can go.' "

Comment. " My wife lived another two years. She asked an old woman what it meant and this one told her that it was death. If the old woman had beaten her she would have died."

28. " I dreamt that I saw a road about two feet wide. It was straight. I dreamt this last April before my boy died. Under the road was water. The road was four feet high. If you fell in the water you would die. I had to cross this road. The water was about as large as Lake Michigan. I went across without trouble and then came to a high hill on the other side of the lake, covered with snow. I went on top of the hill to look around. I could see far in the distance. I don't know what I was doing there. I was just walking and looking around. Then I went back to the place I had started from. I did not go the same way back. Then I was to cross again in the same way, so I went across and saw a lot of Indians who were not able to cross. No one could go more than fifty rods and then they would fall into the water and die. I looked at them and I couldn't help them in any way. I could only look after myself. I didn't cross again for I was waiting for them to get ready and to gain strength. Then I awoke."

Comment. " This is a good dream. This is life. I guess I am going to be an old man."

29. " I dreamt I was going to take a ride with a crow. I sat on its back just below its neck. The crow flew up with me on him. It got to the top of a tree and took a rest there. I held on to him tightly. The tree was a beech and there were many other crows there. My crow could talk Indian and said to me, ' Let's go over there.' ' All right,' I said. ' Well, hang on.' The other tree was lower and he flew in a big curve and left me there. Then I thought to myself, ' How am I going to get down? ' Then I woke."

No comment.

30. " Twenty years ago I dreamt that I was going to get married. The woman was young and very rich. Her hair almost reached to her feet. She didn't talk much but liked me all the same. Before I was to be married, I saw everything, food and presents on a table. One of the presents was a small

table made of diamonds. Then the woman and myself walked out and got ready to meet the preacher. My mother-in-law to be was there and she liked me too. I felt fine. Then I got married. My sister was there and helped me out. Then I woke up."

Comment. " Bad dream. My wife left me that fall for two months. She got angry at me."

31. " I dreamt that I killed a man. I was going to be arrested and so I ran away. Then the ' murdered ' man came to life again and I was excused."

32. " I dreamt that I had killed an otter and that the game-warden was chasing me. I ran with the otter strapped to my shoulder. I had really killed the otter merely out of deviltry. I ran into the bush, but the game-warden followed my tracks. Finally he caught me, talked to me and then let me go."

Comment. " This dream means good luck for the winter's hunting."

Dreams of J. S.[1]

1. " I dreamt that I was married to a half-breed coloured girl. She was prettier than Indian girls. After marriage we owned a home. We had a big nice house. After we got to the house we gave a wedding-feast. There were lots of girls there, also Indian girls. Soon many coloured people came, dark as a stove. I felt very bad at seeing them. Indeed I didn't like them at all although they were nice and happy. In the house I saw many tables lavishly decorated with silver. Outside of the hall I saw my nice big car. I knew I had everything nice. We didn't eat at all and I woke up."

Comment. " A man told me that this means that my son is going to marry a rich girl."

2. " When I was a child and before my father died, I dreamt that my father and myself went to a certain place together. We entered a funny-looking house. The floor was very shiny. We walked through the house and in the second room we saw that the floor was slightly curved and this curved trough was covered with nice sheep-skins. Both of us knelt down and as we looked up we saw a place like a Catholic church in front of us. God sat at one side. He had long whiskers. Jesus sat on the other

---

[1] J. S. is a man about forty-five years of age (Radin).

side and there was a little white bird in the middle. Jesus held a ball in his palm. God, Jesus and the bird sat on something raised high from the floor. Christ made the sign of the Cross to us and we did the same."

Comment. " This is my life. I am very good natured."

3. " After I got married (I was then nineteen years old), I dreamt that my wife and I were living on a farm. We had crops planted on this farm, corn, beans, etc. I was hoeing corn when my wife came over to me. Suddenly I seemed to see my home and I started to dig graves there. I dug them in such a fashion that one grave cut across the other at right angles. I didn't know who was going to be buried there. Everything was ripe at the time. Then I awoke."

Comment. " This is a bad dream. By next summer both my wife and child were dead : they died when everything was ripe."

4. " I dreamt that I saw a great big snake lying in the road. It was about one-fourth of a mile long. I had to go in the direction the snake was lying and so I started running on its back. Its head was sticking up.

" When I reached the head of the snake I saw another snake twenty inches in diameter lying there. It was one hundred and fifty feet long and bloody and cut to pieces. I was so scared that I jumped off the bank of the road on which I was standing. Then I woke up."

Comment. " Bad dream. About Christmas time a cousin, my stepbrother and myself had a fight with another Indian. We were going away from him but we again came across him unexpectedly. He grabbed hold of my stepbrother and threw him on the ground. I got mad, turned on him and struck him till he was quite bloody. I didn't know I could fight like that."

5. " I dreamt early in the spring of my mother-in-law, after she was dead. My wife said, ' Let's go and see my mother's grave.' ' All right, let's go.' As we entered the cemetery, it looked like a house. We went inside the house and I saw many coffins lined up, my mother-in-law's coffin was in the centre. We looked at it and saw that the lid was slightly opened. My mother-in-law's eyes were open too and seemed to be looking at us. I told my wife, ' Your mother's eyes are open.' We didn't go near but turned around and went back home. A few

days after my wife said, ' Let's go to my mother's grave. Let's go nearer this time.' We went again. Everything was as before. I stood at the door and stopped. I saw my mother-in-law's arm moving and I said to my wife, ' Your mother's arm is moving. Can you see it ? ' ' Yes.' ' Well I'll go nearer and look at it.' I went closer with my wife near me and I saw my mother-in-law move. I lifted up the cover and talked to her, ' What's the matter ? ' said she. ' Why, you've come back to life. You've been dead.' ' Am I dead ? ' ' Yes, indeed, you've been dead for quite a while.' ' I didn't know I was dead. I thought I just woke up.' ' Oh my, you've been dead for quite a while.' ' Well,' said she, ' I'm going to get up. Bring my clothes.' I looked around and saw all her clothes. She put them on and I helped her get out of the coffin. She said, ' I'm in a hurry to get home.' ' Good, we'll go right away.' We walked out and I held her by her arm, afraid she might fall down. My wife said, ' You go ahead. I can't walk so fast.' When we started out, there were streets just as in a town. We went around the corner and I looked back and saw my wife quite some distance back. We went one block and turned again. Then we came to a place with woods on all sides. We walked one and a half blocks further and found our home. It looked quite different from our home, however.

" I went towards the house and saw my horses on fresh ground recently dragged. I said to my mother-in-law, ' I'm going to take care of these horses. You go into the house.' Then I started towards the horses. They ran towards the corner of the field. I looked around and saw potatoes, corn, beans, all of different sizes from the ground. Everything looked poor. I started to chase the horses and caught them. Just before I got there I saw a man running towards me yelling, ' Leave my horses alone.' ' These horses belong to me,' I said. Words led to words and then we started to fight. I licked him. I took the horses towards home but before I got there I woke up."

Comment. " In dreams one of course always whips the other fellow. You never get licked yourself. I don't know what this dream means. My brother told me that it meant that crops would be good for the coming year and that I had better plant them. Perhaps the spirit told you to plant these things, perhaps the coming winter will be hard. My brother-in-law said, ' I think that it means that it isn't time to plant crops this year. I guess it will be a pretty poor crop. When the corn is a foot high you may die.' Long dreams always mean something.

6. " I dreamt that I saw my mother coming. I knew that she was dead. I was very glad to see her coming. As she passed she didn't look at me at all, but she spoke and said to me, ' So you are going to leave to-day. Be careful, take good care of yourself and don't be foolish. I don't want you to get hurt or to get into jail.' Then I went away towards the woods where I found some camps. I entered one hut and saw a lot of groceries piled on the table. I also saw the tablecloth and the dishes. Then I went away and saw a woman there who asked me, ' Are you looking for work.' ' Yes,' I answered. ' Well, I think you can get a job right here,' she said. I didn't see anybody else and I started to walk away from the camp. I hadn't gone very far when I woke up."

Comment. " Every time I dream of my mother I have a quarrel with my wife. All the groceries meant that I was going away. Indeed I did go away. I went to Indianapolis and I left my wife for a long time."

7. " I dreamt that I was standing on top of a high rock. I jumped down and as I was jumping I had the feeling that I was really flying down. I saw the world just as a bird does. Then I fell into some deep blue water and almost got drowned. There was no place to save myself for the rock from which I had jumped was very steep and the water was very close to it. Then I thought I would save myself by hollering and someone woke me up."

Comment. " I don't know the meaning of this dream."

8. " I dreamt that I was in a room and that I had to get to this room by passing through a number of rooms in which there were many women and men. Then I dreamt that I left my pants on the other side of the house and that I had to go through all these rooms to get them. I walked through just with my shirt on. I felt very much ashamed but I had to do it. As I crossed through one of these rooms somebody stopped to talk to me. I didn't like it at all, because I felt that somebody was looking at me. Finally I got away and just as I had put on my clothes, I woke up."

Comment. " I don't know what this dream means."

9. "I dreamt that I was walking in the woods and came upon a lake that had no outlet. Logs were lying all over this lake and there were trees standing in it too. There were just a few clear places where a person could take a boat and paddle around. Then I saw a boat and I got into it and paddled off. Suddenly I hit a log without seeing it. I pushed back because I didn't want to get stuck. Then I saw a snake killed against the log. I had killed it as I hit the log. I got so frightened that I went back."

Comment. "This is a bad dream." [1]

10. "I dreamt when I was a child that two boys about eight to fourteen years old, one of them four feet high, and the other five feet high, coaxed me to play with them. I consented and they then took me towards a big hill. Then one of them said, 'Let's go into my house.' I went in. There was very little room. Whenever these boys laugh, they laughed in a very funny way. I stayed inside with them for quite a while and then I decided to come out. I came out and they said to me, 'Now, remember, whenever you want to go and play somewhere just let us know and we'll go with you.' I went out of the hole inside of the hill. Then as I looked back I saw that the places I had left were really graves. These people were dead people."

Comment. "An old man told me that this dream of mine was an old time dream. He said, 'Spirits have come to you, you will be a scout and will have the power of being invisible. If you think of these spirits no one will be able to see you when you are on the warpath.' 'And you know, Paul, he was right. I really have this power and I have frequently thought of my dream."

11. "I dreamt that I saw a road, first going down the hill and then going up. The ground on top of the hill was level and from the top of it one could see another hill in the distance. In the centre of the road I saw a rope. I walked along the road until I came up to the rope, and I saw that it was all knotted up. Along the road I also saw a number of boxes. As I stood on top of the hill, I saw many of these boxes, many knotted-up ropes and a number of other things. After I had ascended the first hill and got to the top I looked behind me and I saw my

[1] An " Œdipus " dream?

wife coming with a little boy. She was just coming down one hill as I came to the top of the other. I waited for her at the top of the hill but she never came. The road as it wound up and down the various hills took on a bluish look in the distance."

Comment. "An old man told me that this dream was my life. I dreamt this before I had married. This old man told me, ' One of these days you are going to be married and you will lose both your wife and your child. The knotted-up rope means sickness. When you come to the box that will mean that you have a good job and that you own property. The hills mean that you will live many years and the blue means long life. You are going to live to be an old man. Whenever you are sick you must think of this dream and it will help you.' "

12. " I dreamt that a bull ran after me. I ran but I didn't make much progress. Just when the bull was about to catch me I woke up."

Comment. " The bull means sickness. Something is going to happen to me."

13. " I dreamt that I went across a lake in the sail-boat. We had started from a place Harbour Spring. We sailed nicely around the point, but we didn't go very fast. Then I woke up."

Comment. " It is dangerous to dream of water, and to leave for somewhere means that you are going to get sick."

14. " I dreamt that I was going across the ice and suddenly I saw a railroad track on the ice. I decided to wait till the train came for I knew that my mother was coming on that train. I waited and soon I saw the train coming very fast. I stepped back in order to see my mother because I knew that the train would not stop. Then the train passed and I saw my mother in the train and I waved to her and she waved back to me. The train was going in a straight line towards the east. Then I awoke."

Comment. " This was the train of the dead and it meant that somebody was going to die."

15. " I dreamt that I went across the ice and saw the railroad track on the ice. I knew that a train was coming and that my mother would come on the train. Soon the train came and this time it stopped. A number of people got on. I, too, was

to go on, but somehow I got left. I didn't see my mother although I knew she was on the train. Then I saw the train leave."

Comment. "This was the train of the dead and it meant that somebody was going to die."

16. "I dreamt that my body was in a coffin and that I walked around and saw my body in the coffin in the house. I tried to talk to my people but they wouldn't talk to me. I didn't know that I was dead. Then I woke up."

Comment. "When I woke up I found myself pressed in somewhere and for a moment I really thought I was dead. I kicked and yelled and putting out my hand I felt something that was real hard. Then I knew that I was under the bed. Apparently in my dream I had got out of my bed and crept under it."

17. "I dreamt that I went to war. I was pretty close to the battlefield and I could hear the guns. Then I had to go across the place where they were shooting. I told someone, 'I have come here to go across.' Then I took my gun with me and walked across on knees and hands. I was terribly scared and I could hear the bullets whistling past me all the time. I didn't know where the American soldiers were. When I got across I ran into the bush thinking that the Americans were there but they were Germans. As soon as I found this out, I rushed into the raspberry bushes and walked on my knees and hands. My purpose was to go back to where I had come from but by a round-about way. The German soldiers did not see me. Finally I returned and told the general that there were Germans on that side. The Americans then brought their big cannon around and shot them. The jar of the shot woke me up."

Comment. "A man told me that this dream meant that I was never to go to the war and that I never would smell powder."

18. "I dreamt that I was in a small boat all alone. Near me was a steep rock against which the spray was dashing continually. I was pretty close to the rock when the waves rushed back. I was frightened and thought that the boat would surely tip over. Finally I landed at some place or other and found a woman there. She said, 'I have been waiting for you to come. I'll give you something to eat.' She gave me a very small dish full of meat and some other food in small plates. I thought it was a pretty small meal for me. She said, 'Don't think so.' I

had not said a word as a matter of fact but she knew my thoughts. She said, ' You can't eat all of that. You'll never get hungry if you taste it.' Then I began eating it and I couldn't finish it. I got up from the table and I saw her. She looked like an Indian half-breed. She took me into the house to look around. I saw many horses there in what looked like a barn. After I had eaten she came back and she saw the food I had left on the table. There were many big plates and lots of food. She said ' Your table will always be like this.' Then I woke up."

Comment. " The work that I do is of such a kind that I never find myself hungry.

" I often dream of this woman. She looks very much like my wife. The Indians believe that if a man dreams of such a woman he will get power from her and that she will help him. I did not tell these dreams to my wife because she wouldn't like it."

19. " I dreamt that a man told me, ' You take this road.' Then I followed along that road. It was pretty wide. I could see tracks where I was going but none were coming back. When I got to my destination a man stopped me. He had a big sword and he said, ' Now you have to pick out which road you wish to take. There is one to the left, one in the centre, and one to the right. Here is the box from which you must pick out a number. The number will tell you in which direction you are to go.' I picked out a number and got the road to the left. Then I started. Before I got to the place I saw a wall of rock but I could see right through it. There were no windows yet everything inside was very clear to me. I saw a man. He said, ' Wait a minute, here is your name-card with all the particulars as to where you have to go.' Then he handed me the card. He turned around and told me, ' Pick out a place where you wish to sit until something comes.' I went over there and found a number of seats. They looked like pews in a church. I sat there but I saw nobody. Then I tried to get up, but I couldn't and someone said to me, ' You can't get up. That is your seat.' Soon I heard a wind coming. The wind came like a fire and I felt myself to be burning. I couldn't move as it passed through me. I looked at myself and saw that I wasn't in the least burned. I tried again to get up but I couldn't. Then another gust of fire came. Again I tried to get up. This time I felt as though

291

I were burning a little bit longer. Then from above I heard the voice of the man whom I couldn't see talking, ' You come on, I'll show you something.' So I got up, turned around and saw some steps. I went up a little way and there I saw the man. He was dressed like a priest in garments of gold. He opened the door and said, ' Look down there.' I looked and there I saw some people who were still living. What I saw was something like burning syrup and people in it. Then he shut up the door and opened another. I looked and I saw a nice green field full of flowers. Then the man said, ' You are not ready to come here yet ; I am just showing you this. Tell your father and mother.' ' Now step over here and I'll show you something else.' I stepped over and I saw my father sitting there playing the organ. There were people looking like women standing near him singing. I couldn't make out who they were. Then the man said, ' Which one of these three do you like best ? ' I said ' This last one.' Then I turned around and came back. On the road a man stopped me and asked, ' Did you see all the things down there ? Did you see your father ? Your father used to do that work in this world and he has taken the same position there.' Then I woke up."

Comment. " An old man told me, ' You will have two burnings. This dream means that your heart is going to burn twice before you die.' And indeed my heart did get two burnings."

20. " I dreamt that I was walking along a road and finally got to a hill which I ascended. I saw my uncle ahead of me and behind me I saw my stepfather coming. I didn't know what to do, wait for my stepfather or catch up with my uncle. Finally I waved my hat to tell my stepfather to come faster and I went over the hill. My uncle had preceded me over the hill and when I was going down the hill I saw my stepfather coming up and walking fast. I motioned to him to come still faster. When I got to the top of the next hill, my uncle had already crossed it. There I suddenly saw my mother standing and she asked me, ' Where are you going ? ' ' I don't know. I am trying to catch my uncle and also wait for my stepfather.' Then she said, ' You had better go home with me.' She was sick in bed at the time. I turned around to go with her and woke up."

Comment. " Before I told my mother this story, she told me, ' I dreamt of you last night. I dreamt that your uncle passed over this road. I saw you pass too and I tried to grab hold of you but missed you. I also saw your stepfather coming behind you.' My mother had had a bad boil that night. She motioned to me to come, saying, ' Come here.' I told her that I had had the same dream. The boil burst then and she became well. This is the way my mother interpreted the dream. She said, ' My uncle would die first, then I would die and then my stepfather.' However, my stepfather died first, my uncle afterwards, and I am still alive."

CORRELATION OF WOODLAND DREAMS TO
THE CULTURE

1. CULTURE PATTERN DREAMS.

The great majority of the dreams and visions of the Menomini and all the puberty fasting experiences of the Ottawa and Ojibway are culture pattern phenomena in form and manifest content. They reflect the old religious cultures in full force. Many of the fasters' comments are of interest, because they show specifically how the dream or vision is induced and how the quest of a supernatural guardian to guide the youthful visionary throughout life is the motive for which the dream or vision is sought. Again we have proof that in an area where the culture imposes a rigorous dreaming requirement the form of the dreams is determined by the culture, and the manifest contents reflect the religious culture in its relation to the supernatural.

2. INDIVIDUAL DREAMS.

Among the Menomini and all the woodland tribes the regular night dream or individual dream was also regarded as important even when the culture was in force, but from the data it would seem not as important as the puberty fasting or culture pattern dream. The only one of the former here recorded (Part I, No. 10) is an individual dream, with no culture traits in the manifest content. The regular night dreams of the two modern Ottawa Indians are all individual dreams. The contents of Woodland Dreams reflect the following :

Out of fifty-two dreams of two individuals, twenty-six show no culture items at all and reflect only personal psychology

(Nos. 1, 2, 3, 5, 6, 8, 9, 11, 17, 18, 19, 21, 23, 26, 27, 29, 31, 32 of J. P. and 4, 7, 8, 9, 10, 12, 13, 16 of J. S.).

Twelve reflect in their manifest content personal psychology in relation to parents or the family (Nos. 10, 13, 24, 14, 15, 30 of J. P. and 3, 5, 6, 14, 15, 20 of J. S.).

Eleven reflect besides personal psychology some influence of white or American negro culture (Nos. 4, 16, 20, 22, 25 of J. P. and 1, 2, 6, 11, 14, 17 of J. S.).

Three reflect Christian religious influence besides personal psychology (Nos. 12 of J. P. and 2, 19 of J. S.).

Two of the same individual reflect a personal conflict and an effort to escape from the bonds of the old culture. This interpretation is assumed in the case of dream No. 7 of J. P., in which is portrayed a conflict and an escape from the muskrat, the mink and the otter, the only items of the old culture mentioned in the dream. It is also assumed for dream No. 28, where is mentioned an escape to where many other Indians could not follow.

Some of these same dreams take the following forms : eight persecution dreams, J. P. Nos. 1, 2, 7, 17, 22, 31, 32 and J. S. No. 12.

Seven death dreams, J. P. Nos. 15, 24, 27 ; J. S. Nos. 5, 6, 10, 16.

Two prophetic dreams, J. P. No. 27 ; J. S. No. 11.

One falling dream, J. S. No. 7.

Here we have data from another area in which the Indian culture formerly had a rigorous dreaming requirement. When this old culture was at its height all the dreams with religious and social significance were culture pattern dreams induced by the culture,[1] and the individual dreams though they were regarded as important, played a comparatively minor and personal rôle in the life of the tribe. As the old culture broke down, however, the individual dreams became increasingly important to the Indian and no longer reflected items of Indian culture. The dreams of J. P., who was about seventy-five years old in 1927, are all personal psychology dreams, yet he must have been born

[1] See examples, pp. 271-6.

when the old culture was still in existence but on the wane.

Hence in the Eastern Woodlands area,[1] as well as in the Lower Colorado area,[2] we find ample proof that when a culture breaks down, the pattern dream formerly produced by the culture disappears, and the individual dream reflecting no Indian culture at all gradually takes its place.

[1] See Chap. I for further discussion.   [2] See pp. 195–206.

6. THE NORTH-WEST PACIFIC COAST CULTURE AREA

The Kwakiutl Indians

Their direct approach to the supernatural (*here regarded as identical with the vision*), the customs, secret societies and ceremonialism resulting from this approach. Beliefs and customs relative to the dream.[1]

Visionary Acquisition of Guardian Spirits.

1. In order to gain the help of the spirits to endow him with supernatural powers, the youth must prepare himself by fasting and washing because only the pure find favour with them, while they kill the impure. Every young man endeavours to find a protector of this kind.

2. The guardian spirit is hereditary. When a youth prepares to meet a guardian spirit, he does not expect to find any but those of his clan.

3. There are a relatively small number of guardian spirits, namely,

    (I) Wina'lagilis or making war all over the earth. The youth obtaining his protection may acquire one of the following powers. He may become a—

        (*a*) T'o'X'uit, who is invulnerable. He assists the youth and his friends in war.

        (*b*) Ma'maq'a. He has the power to catch the invisible disease spirit which is constantly flying through the air in the form of a worm. He is able to throw it into his enemies, who die from its effects at once.

[1] Franz Boas, *The Social Organization and the Secret Societies of the Kwakiutl Indians*, extract from the Report of the United States National Museum for 1895, pp. 311–737.

> (c) Hawi'nalaL, or war dancer, who is insensible to the pain of wounds and cannot be killed.

(II) BaxbakualanuXsi'wae or the " first one to eat man at the mouth of the river in the north." (The ocean is considered a stream running northward.) He is a cannibal living on the mountains who is always in pursuit of man. A person who meets him or one of his suite may become a—

> (a) Ha'mats'a, a cannibal, into whom he instils the desire of eating human flesh, and who devours whomsoever he can lay his hands upon.
>
> (b) Ha'mshamtsEs, a cannibal of less violent character.
>
> (c) No'ntsistalaL, who is able to devour and touch fire with impunity.
>
> (d) The grizzly bear of the cannibal spirit who delights in killing people with his strong paws.
>
> (e) Ki'nqalaLala, who procures human flesh for the ha'mats'a.
>
> (f) Ho'Xhok, who breaks the skulls of men.
>
> (g) and (h) Two other kinds.

(III) MatEm, who lives on the top of steep mountains. It is a bird, and bestows the faculty of flying.

(IV) The ghosts who bestow the power of returning to life after the person has been killed.

(V) *Other Hereditary Spirits.* Their principal gifts according to the legends are the magic harpoon which insures success in sea-otter hunting ; the death bringer which kills enemies ; the water of life which resuscitates the dead ; the burning fire ; and a dance, a song, and cries peculiar to the spirit.

4. When nowadays a spirit appears to a young man, he is given a dance, and the youth also returns from the initiation filled with the powers and desires of the spirit. He authenticates his initiation by his dance in the same way as his mythical ancestor did. The dances of the initiates are known as the Winter Ceremonial.

5. *Organization of the Tribe during the Winter Ceremonial Season.*
> (a) The same spirits which appeared to the mythical

ancestors of the clan continue to appear to their present-day descendants.

(b) Each name of the nobility have a separate tradition of the acquisition of supernatural powers, and these have descended on the bearers of the name.

(c) *The Spirits give New Names* to the men to whom they appear but these names are in use only in winter when the spirits are supposed to be present. All the summer names are dropped at this season. Hence, at this period the whole social system is altered and the place of the clans is taken by a number of secret societies, who are the groups of all these individuals upon whom the same power or secret has been bestowed by a spirit.

6. *The Purpose of the whole Winter Ceremonial* is " to bring back the youth who is supposed to stay with the supernatural being who is the protector of his society, and then, when he has returned in a state of ecstasy, to exorcise the spirit which possesses him and to restore him from his holy madness."

These objects are attained by songs and dances in which members of all the secret societies join.[1]

BELIEFS ABOUT INDIVIDUAL NIGHT DREAMS.

Boas does not mention whether the regular night dreams of the Kwakiutl here recorded are regarded as having any significance to the Indian or not,[2] but the comments of some of the dreamers of regular night dreams throw some light on the subject. For instance :

Some hunting dreams are regarded as good (26, 27 [3]).

A dream of being overpowered sexually is regarded as foreboding pregnancy (29).

A dream is interpreted as indicating fishing conditions (5).

A dream of the dead and the ghost house is regarded as a great bad dream, that will cause an epidemic in which many will die (31).

[1] Franz Boas, for detailed description of the winter ceremonial see *ibid.*, pp. 431–544.

[2] Boas and Hunt, " Contributions to the Ethnology of the Kwakiutl," *Columbia Univ. Cont. to Anthrop.*, Vol. III, pp. 3–54.

[3] Numbers refer to numbers of individual dreams recorded on pp. 304–21.

A dream of the dead grandfather is regarded as bad (36).

A dream is believed to prophesy length of life for certain people (39).

Certain men are known as dreamers, who dream prophetic dreams which are regarded as good (68).

Many dreams are interpreted.

A dream of a man's late father in poor condition in the next world is followed by the ceremony of burning two pairs of blankets and food for the soul of his late father (38).

Two of these night dreams are partially pattern dreams similar to initiation dreams (41, 42).

Not following out the commands of a supernatural being about a baby in a dream is regarded as having caused the death of the baby (57).

A dream of a woman in which her late husband has sexual intercourse with her and then declares he will enter her womb so that she can become his mother is interpreted as meaning that she will have a son and that her living husband will die shortly after the birth of the child (63).

OTHER KWAKIUTL BELIEFS ABOUT DREAMS.[1]

When a chief's son dreams of ghosts his father will protect him by various actions (17).

Nightmare indicates the death of a near relative. If in a nightmare the sleeper does not cry, but if he merely hears or utters indistinct sounds, it means that a person not a member of the dreamer's family is going to die (393).

Dreams are considered as signs of approaching events ; but it is believed that generally the significance of the coming event is distorted ; for instance when a person dreams that his own child has died, it means that the child of another person will die (395).

To dream of snakes is an evil omen (396).

To dream of lice forbodes sickness (397).

A louse on the eyebrows (not only in a dream) indicates the speedy death of a near relative (398).

---

[1] Franz Boas, " Current Beliefs of the Kwakiutl Indians," *J. of Amer. Folklore*, April–June 1932, Vol. 45. The numbers are the paragraph numbers given in this citation.

When the shaman dreams that the sick person has his hair hanging down over his face, the patient will die (400).

To dream of ascending a mountain which suddenly tilts presages death (401).

Shamans are guided in their cures by dreams (402).

If the owner of a trap dreams of a woman who refused his love, his trap will fall without killing anything. If he dreams that the woman accepts him his trap will have killed game (403).

Sleeping with the head towards the sea causes bad dreams (483).

When the hunter dreams of cohabiting with a woman still alive, it means good luck ; when he dreams of cohabiting with a woman already dead, it signifies bad luck (576 (b)).

To meet the double-headed serpent is fraught with danger. An unexpected meeting will cause death, paralysis, or insanity (11).

KWAKIUTL DREAMS

(a) PATTERN DREAMS.

1. *An initiation legend.*[1]   (*Belonging to the clan* Ge'xsEm *of the* T'Ena'xtax.)

" The first of the TEnaxtax lived at Lēkwadē. Their chief was Lāwag.is. He was in love with a girl. Once upon a time she went up the river to pick berries, and Lāwag.is followed her. He walked along the bank of the river, while she had gone up in her canoe. When it grew dark, he heard cries in the woods. Then he jumped into a pond and rubbed his body with hemlock branches. He went on. He heard cries all the time and bathed in another pond. He walked on. Now the cries were close to him. He bathed again. Now the cries came quite close to him. He bathed the fourth time. As soon as he had finished he saw a woman with a large head and matted hair and with a face which was full of scratches. Lāwag.is went up to her and put his arm around her waist. As soon as he had done so they both fainted. He recovered first, but he put his arms around her waist even tighter. Then the woman

---

[1] F. Boas, *Social Organization and Secret Societies of the Kwakiutl, op. cit.* Boas says that the legendary experience is identical with those of the youths of to-day.—*Ibid.*, p. 396. (Reprinted by permission of the Smithsonian Institute.)

with the great head recovered and spoke : ' I am the crier of
the woods. Now let me go and I will help you to obtain everything easily. I will be your magical helper. You shall obtain
easily all kinds of property.' Lāwag.is only held her more
tightly. Then she spoke again : ' I will raise property for you.'
But he held her still tighter. Then she spoke again : ' I will
give you the water of life. Let me go.' But he held her still
tighter. She spoke again : ' Let me go. Take my name, it
shall be yours. You will be Qoādasgamāls. I will give you
the apron that burns everything.' Then he let her go. She
disappeared at once. She only left the four gifts, which she
had given him, on the ground. Then Lāwag.is took his magical
treasures. He went on and tried his apron against the trees of
a mountain. Immediately they were burnt and you can see
even now that the mountains of Tsawatē are burnt. Now he
was glad. He hid his magical treasures under a cedar tree and
went on. He arrived at the village where his sweetheart was
living. She asked him : ' Why did you not come sooner ? '
He replied, ' I lost my way.' That night they went to bed and
played together. After a short time he was poked in the side
through a hole which was in the boards of the house. He arose
and went to look. As soon as he went out his face was covered
and he was led away by a man. He did not dare to speak and
to ask, but he knew that he was led three times up a mountain
and three times down. During all this time his face was not
uncovered. Then he knew that they were going up a mountain
again, and he heard a cry, ' hāp, hāp, hāp ; haó, haó ; gaó,
gaó ' (the cries of the hāmatsa, the hōXhok, and of the raven).
Then the man spoke : ' My dear, do not be afraid. I want to
give you magical power. This is my house. I am BaxbakuālanuXsīwaē. You shall have everything in my house.' They
entered, and he uncovered the face of Lāwag.is. ' Now look,
friend,' said BaxbakuālanuXsīwaē. ' You shall have my name,
Wilgasālag.ilîs, and your name shall be Hāmatsa. Now watch
the dance of the hāmatsa.' Then he heard the cries, ' hāp,
hāp, hāp ; haō, haō ; gaō, gaō.' Then the raven that was
painted on the front of the hāmatsa's secret room opened its
mouth and the hāmatsa came out, vomited by the raven.
Then he danced. Lāwag.is did not see the singers. After the
first song the hāmatsa went back and the hōXhok came out

and danced. After one dance he went back and the raven came out and danced. With the next song the hāmatsa came out carrying a corpse in his arms, which he ate. When he had eaten it, he danced again, and went back. He had four songs. BaxbakuālanuXsīwaē spoke : 'This shall be your hāmatsa, your name shall be Wilgasālag.ilîs and Hamigālagalitsaku and Naxnawisālag.ilîs. Don't forget the head masks of the hōXhoku and of the raven and the painting of the secret room.' He called Lāwag.is to see a ditch that was in the rear of the house. Then he went and saw it. Something like a rainbow was standing in the hole. Lāwag.is looked down and saw all kinds of animals and fishes in the hole. BaxbakuālanuXsīwaē spoke : 'This is the cannibal post of the dancing house. This shall be your magical treasure ! '

" Then he taught him his song :

" 1. You are the great BaxbakuālanuXsīwaē, aho, o,o,o, hem, aem.
2. This is the way of the true BaxbakuālanuXsīwaē, ahō, ō,ō,ō, hēm, aēm.
3. O, nobody can live before the great BaxbakuālanuXsīwaē, ahō, ō, ō, ō, hēm, aēm.
4. Who came out of the woods to me, ahō, ō, ō, ō, hēm, aēm.

" Now he had learned the one song and BaxbakuālanuXsīwaē taught him the second song :

" 1. You are looking for food, you great magician, mahamai, hama, hamamai ; yi hama ma mai hama.
2. You are looking for men whom you want to eat, great magician ; mahamai, hama, hamamai ; yi hama ma mai hama.
3. You tear men's skins, great magician, mahamai. You try to eat many men, great magician, mahamai, hama, hamamai ; yi hama ma mai hama.
4. Everybody trembles before you, you great magician. You who have been to the end of the world, mahamai, hama hama mai ; yi hama ma mai hama.

" After the song BaxbakuālanuXsīwaē called Lāwag.is and asked him : 'Don't you want this harpoon shaft ? It kills everything. Now it is yours, and also this red cedar bark and the fire with which you may burn everything, the water of life, and the quartz for killing your enemies.' Then Lāwag.is went home. That is the end." [1]

[1] For deeper analysis of this legend-vision, see Chap. IV, pp. 151-2.

The following dreamed as night dreams [1] :

2. " I dreamed I was going sealing near MāpEGEM. There I got many seals. I came home here to Fort Rupert. Immediately I singed the seals. After I was through singeing I butchered them. Then I found a quartz crystal in the stomach of a large seal. Then I had a treasure. Then I hid it in the woods. Then I gave a feast to the Kwāg.ue tribes with the seals. After I had given the feast I lay down. Then I dreamed that I was asleep. A man came and sat down by my side, towards the middle of the house. Then he said, ' You must not lie down with your wife for four years else you will be unlucky, for you have received your treasure, the quartz crystal from me.' Thus the man spoke to me. Then I awoke."

3. " I dreamed I travelled across the water in a small canoe. I was not half way across when a north-westerly gale began to blow. I steered towards Nexagad. Then my small travelling canoe capsized. I climbed out of the small canoe and was drifting upside down on the water. I lay on it with my chest down. Then a gull came flying and alighted on the bow of the small canoe that was drifting on the water. It took my hand and told me to walk on top of the water. Thus I arrived at Blunden Harbour. Then he taught me what to do when a great epidemic should come in summer. He said so and spit out a quartz crystal. Then he put the quartz crystal into my body at the lower end of my sternum and pressed it in. Then he said, ' Now make a rattle in my form (imitate me). Then you will be a great Shaman,' thus said the gull. ' Now you shall have the name Q!uelEnts!esEmega from now on.' Then I awoke." [2]

(b) INDIVIDUAL DREAMS. [3]

1. " I went to look after my mink and otter traps. Then the otter trap was looked after by me first. Then I saw that it had

[1] Partial Pattern Dreams.

[2] " This dream is typical for the initiation of a shaman. The novice dreams in this way of dying persons, of the War-spirit, or of other supernatural beings." These partial pattern dreams 2 and 3 from Boas and Hunt, *ibid.*, Nos. 41 and 42. See (b).

[3] Reprinted from Boas, *Contributions to the Ethnology of the Kwakiutl*, by permission of the Columbia University Press. (Boas and Hunt— *Columbia University Cont. to Anthrop.*, Vol. III, pp. 3–54.)

fallen. Then I saw that a silver salmon was in it. Then I awoke."

2. " I dreamt that I was asked by a handsome man to go hunting with him in the woods. I followed him and we had not gone far into the woods when I saw a deer. I was about to shoot it when my gun burst. Then I awoke."

3. " I dreamt I was going mountain goat hunting in Knight Inlet. Then I saw two mountain goats. Then I shot them. I hit both and I butchered them. I took out the kidney fat and put the kidney fat down on the rock. Then I heard the noise of walking up the river from me. Then I looked there and saw two grizzly bears quite near to me. Then I just had time to take up my guns and I hit the one. Then it was dead. Then I shot the other one. Unfortunately, my shot missed it. Then it took hold of me. After that I awoke."

4. " I dreamed that I went aboard a steamer and I went to River's Inlet. Then I arrived at G.ip'a. Then I was given a drift net. Immediately I went fishing. Oh there were many sockeye salmon in my net. Then my heart was glad because I had at once caught many sockeye salmon. Threw net back —got more. I had not reached the middle of the extent of my net when a whale went into it. Then the whale swam away. I had no time to throw into the water the other half of the net which was in my boat that contained the net. Then the boat capsized and the whale pulled out the whole net. I awoke after this."

5. " I dreamed that there were many olachen in Knight Inlet. We caught them in bag nets. We had not been fishing with bag nets for a long time before the canoe containing the bag net was full of olachen. Then we went home. As soon as we arrived we carried up the olachen and put them on the ground. Then the hole in the ground was full. Then the olachen which had been in the hole disappeared. Then I awoke." (" This dream signifies there were many olachen in the river but that the water was so high that the fishermen could not use their bag nets.")

6. " I dreamed I went to pick many salmon berries in the woods and also many blueberries. I obtained many. Then I asked four men to help me carry them out of the woods. That was the time when I gave feast to the four Kwag.ut tribes. Then

I went again to pick salmon berries and I hurt myself. After that I awoke."

7. " I dreamed last night of a pretty woman who came to call me to pick cranberries. We went inland. Then we saw many cranberry and blueberry bushes which were hanging down and shook them into baskets. Then our berry-picking baskets were full. I awoke after that. Then Haelalas knew that she was going to keep alive until the season of cranberry picking."

8. " I dreamed I was going to pick dogwood berries inland, together with Mawitsu. Then we went inland and I saw a snake. Then we were afraid of it and I awoke."

9. " I dreamed that I went to pick many salal berries at G.iox. Then I saw many hump-backed salmon spawning in the river of G.iox. Then I struck the salmon with my cane. Then I got many salal berries. Then I went home. Before I arrived at home I woke up." (" This dream signifies that the woman who dreams will live until the salal berries are ripe, but that she will be sick before that time.")

10. " I dreamed that I was going to dig clams on the beach here. Then I was digging. I had not been digging long before my digging stick struck something soft. Then there came out and showed itself a large squid which had buried itself on the beach. Then I woke because I was very much afraid of it."

11. " I dreamed I was going seawards to Shell Island. Then I was digging. I had obtained many clams by digging. Then I stopped digging. Then I intended to go to my canoe to get the clam basket which was in the little clam-digging canoe. Then I saw that my little clam-digging canoe was drifting about north of Shell Island. It was drifting away. Then I shouted in vain. That was the reason why my husband called me and I awoke. My heart was beating violently."

12. " Much herring-spawn spawned the herrings. This was my dream in the morning when day was almost breaking." (Explained as meaning spirits would come and that a bad epidemic would break out. When a sick person eats herring-spawn—his sickness increases.)

13. " I dreamed I fell into the water while we were paddling at the foot of the mountain in deep water. I was frightened very much, and that was the moment when I awoke."

14. " I dreamt I fell from a tree here (behind the houses)

inland. Then I knew that I had broken all my bones. Then I was dug up by my tribe, the Kwag.ut. Then I had not yet reached my house when I awoke."

15. " I dreamt I was out paddling with my four children. Then we were going to Xumdasbe. When we were opposite P'ELEMS it became very thick and foggy. Then we were lost in the fog. I was just sitting still in our travelling canoe. Then I stopped paddling. In my dream we were drifting about on the water.

" Then it became night and I went to sleep. When I awoke our travelling canoe was being rolled against the rocks. It was still foggy. I did not know the rocks. Then it cleared up and I knew that this was Yut'E. Then I awoke."

16. " I dreamed that a steamer had been wrecked here at Le'lad and that many men and women had perished and that they were found drifting about. Then I was paid by the whites ten dollars for every man found by me. Many pieces of clothing were found by me. Then I was very glad on account of the large amount that I received. Then I awoke."

17. " I dreamed that I was paddling with my wife to Rivers Inlet to go fishing. When we reached Cape Caution a south-easterly gale began to blow but we were unable to enter Gwalg-wal'alatis. Then I tried to reach Geyaxsta'ye. Then the sea was boiling on account of the south-easterly gale. My wife tried to bail out the canoe but she could not cope with the sea water which was thrown into my boat. Then we cried, I and my wife. Then I awoke."

18. " I dreamed of LE'LENdzo' that she was going in the boat of her father Xaxelg'ayogwi'lak, and that she was travelling in his gasoline launch. Then I went out in my little canoe. A long log was drifting on the water and so I was on one end of the drifting log in my canoe, and Xaxelg'ayogwi'lak was in his launch on the other end. Then LE'LENdzo' stepped on the end of the log and walked across it towards me. Before she reached me she fell into the water and sank. Then I jumped into the water and looked in vain for her down below. I did not find her. Then I came up and saw Guyodedzas carrying LE'LENdzo' in his arms. She was dead. Then I awoke."

19. " I dreamed our house in G.iox was on fire. Then all our property burned up and we were very poor and I woke up."

20. " In my dream all the tribe came invited by AwaxElag'lis. Then AwaxElag'lis invited the people to a feast, and they were to eat in his house after their journey. Then LAbid and Neg.a a chief of the Mamaletegala quarrelled. Then LAbid promised to give a potlatch and then Neg.a broke a copper and gave the pieces to LAbid. Then LAbid broke a copper and gave the pieces to Neg.a. Then the Mamaletegala and the Kwag.ut quarrelled and I was really afraid. That must have been the reason why I awoke."

21. " In my dream I paddled to the Mamaletegala who were living in Nox'dem. Then I arrived there. Then I asked at once payment for that which they had received from me, for I was intending to buy the exclusive copper K.ints'!egum. Then they paid me many dollars and I was glad on account of the five thousand dollars which the Mamaletegala had paid me. Then I bought the copper K.ints'!egum with it. Then I was the owner of the copper. After that I awoke."

22. " I dreamed that many tribes came invited by the late NEgah'.EnkEM. Then the late chief became ecstatic in his quality of fool dancer. Then he broke a copper and gave the pieces to the late Agwi'la. Then the late Agwi'la broke a copper and gave the pieces to the late NEgah'.EnkEM."

23. " I dreamed that I had been invited by the DZawad-EONox. Then I saw how the chiefs broke coppers against one another. Then SEsaxalas gave a piece to me. Then I broke the Long Killer whale, an expensive copper and gave it to SEsaxalas. Thus he was vanquished by me. Then I awoke."

24. " I dreamed I had twins last night with my late wife Kunxalayngwa. One was a boy, the other a girl. Then the Kwag.ut followed the twin customs. I and my late wife painted our faces with ochre. The twins each wore wing feathers of gulls. Then we were led around four houses, and when we and the Kwag.ut finished walking around four houses, we went into my house. Then I awoke."

25. " I dreamed last night that a bull followed me. Then he overtook me and overpowered me. At that time I awoke from my sleep."

26. " *Good Dream of a Hunter*."

" I dreamed that I met my sweetheart last night and I lay

with her behind the village and it seemed true. Then I woke up."

27. "*Good Dream of the Hunter Omx.td.*"

" I dreamed that I made ready to bathe in the river here for I intended to go hunting. Then I went inland to the upper part of the river. Before I came to the place where I am accustomed to bathe I saw my sweetheart coming through the salal bushes. I went to her and immediately we lay down. After that we went bathing, I and my sweetheart. After we had finished, I and she, she went home first. Then I awoke from this dream which seemed as if it had really happened." (" This dream corresponds to the procedure of the hunter who tries to secure good fortune.")

28. " In my dream I and many women who were singing love songs in our house. After we had been singing for a long time, my husband came into my house and beat me. Then I awoke."

29. *Dream of Abayaa.*

" I dreamed I was going to pick crab-apples in a patch of crab-apple trees which were growing on a pretty level place. Then I recognized that it was Knight Inlet where I was picking crab-apples. Then I saw four grizzly bears. I tried to run away for one of the bears pursued me. It took hold of me. I looked at it, and what should it be but this man Tsanis here. Then he said he would overpower me. Then we took hold of each other and I succumbed and he embraced me. Then I wanted to go home. On the way I was weeping. Then I awoke." (" This means that Abayaa will be with child.")

30. " In my dream my late child came to invite me to go from here to the place which they call the beautiful country, the place where all those go who are no more. I got ready at once. Then I was awakened by a noise."

31. *Bad Dream of Enemokuyahs.*

" It was this way that I and my wife were in a large house with many platforms. Then we were asked by a man to sit down in the house. Then I saw all those who were dead, many men, some of the late chiefs of the Mamaletegala, that is the late Guyotelas, and the late Neg.E, who were sitting in the rear of the house, and also many old men. And on the platform made of boards placed over the door of the house, the late

T.Egwap was sitting with his late friends. Then Guyotelas spoke and T.Egwap ridiculed the speech of Guyotelas. Then he killed T.Egwap and T.Egwap was dead. That was the moment that the late X.iltx'it asked me and my wife to leave the house of the ghosts.

"We went to the door led by X.iltx'it. Then he said, ' If you do not go out of this house immediately you will stay here for ever.' Then we went home while the ghosts were fighting."

" *This is a great bad dream.* It announces that a bad epidemic is going to come and that many Indians will die."

32. " I dreamed of my late lover who came to call me to go paddling with him, and then it occurred to me that he had been dead for a long time. I said to him that I did not care to go. Then he became angry and took hold of me. Then I cried out. Then I awoke."

33. " I dreamed last night that I was dead and I was taken away by a pretty woman who was unknown to me to a nice beach to a village in which there were only women, not a single man among them. Then one of them asked me, ' How do you like this beach? ' I felt depressed there and I told her so. Then she chased me away. Then I awoke."

34. " In my dream my late father came to see me in my house here. Then he invited me to go to his village, and so I made ready to follow him. Then it occurred to me that my late father had died long ago. I became very angry because he had come on behalf of the ghosts to invite me. Then I awoke."

35. " I dreamed that I was going digging clams on the island ALanodza'ye. And so I approached the beach where there are clams. I saw many women sitting around a fire on the beach. There were your late mother and her late friend L'.agwait, and the sick Gaaxstalas was sitting with the spirits for that is the way we call the ghosts. They were roasting clams and eating them. Then your mother called me to eat clams with them. I went ashore and sat down. I did not know the other women but they probably died long ago. Then L'.agwait wanted that I should eat roasted clams with them. Your mother did not permit me to eat clams with them, ' for I do not wish her to come to us. She shall remain with my son, her husband,' thus she said. Then your late mother sent me away home. Then

I left them and went aboard my little travelling canoe. Then I awoke."

36. *Bad Dream of Gwuyodedzas.*

" I dreamed I was being paddled about by my late grandfather. I only recollected that he had died long ago after we were far away. Then we landed on a sandy point. I left him and went along the beach and came home. I came to G.iox. Then I could not get across the river of G.iox. I began to swim and I was almost drowned. At that moment I awoke."

37. " In my dream I was paddling to Gwadze at night. As soon as I arrived at Shell Island I heard the voices of many young men who were singing love songs and they said these words :

" I give it up to win my love in this world ; ha ha yi ya ha ha.
　Oh in another way will go down my crying on account of my love ;
　　ha ha yi ya ha ha.

" I learned two lines of the words of the love song of the young men of the ghosts. Then I went right on to Gwadze and I arrived there when the day broke. Then I awoke." [1]

38. " In my dream I was called by my late father to a place which he called the Nice Country. Then I followed him. We came to his house. I entered his house. Then he asked me to sit down on the floor. Then he told me it was a very poor place where he was. He said, ' Look at my bed. I have no cover, nothing to maintain myself.' Thus he said to me. Then I arose and went home. Then I awoke." (" After this Tx'wid burned two pairs of blankets and food for the soul of his late father.")

39. *Koskimo.*

" At night I dreamed of many dead women, of the late Ak.ilayugwa, the late Ada, the late L'.agwait, and the late L'.aL. . . . They had all been dead a long time. They came ashore at Xates. Then Ak'.ilayugwa called Hex.hae . . . and L'.agwaga to come aboard the canoe. They went aboard the canoe of the supernatural ones. They steered away from shore. After they had been under way for some time I saw many salmon jumping on the beach seaward from the village Xates. They were speared by the spearsmen of the Koskimo, and the spearsmen's canoes were full. After this I awoke."

---

[1] See Ch. II, pp. 75–7, for songs originating in dreams.

" This is the meaning of the beginning of the dream for Hex.hae
. . . and L'.agwaga—for they were still alive—whose souls went
aboard the canoe of those who had died long ago. Then the
dreamer knew that these two were almost dead. At the end
of the dream about the many salmon, she knew that she would
live until the salmon run."

40. " I dreamed I was invited by my late father to Ts'.ade.
I had forgotten that he was dead long ago. I entered his house
and sat on the floor of his house. Then he spoke and said, ' I
wish to cure you of your ways and to remove those sicknesses
which cause you pain for I see you are always ill.' This said
my late father. Then with both his hands he squeezed both
sides of my head downwards to the lower end of my back.
Then he closed both hands and drew up the disease. Four times
he did so. After he did so he sent me home. Then I awoke."

41. *Dream of Qeldedzem.* (As a shaman this man had the name
Qu'lad.)

" It was at the time that many chiefs of all the tribes died
of the great epidemic, influenza. Then we all saw Qu'lad was
really sick for he was coughing all the time and yellow fluid
was running all the time from his nose. His breath was short
and he was not able to walk. Then he was informed of the
death of many people. For seven days he was in bed. I mean
Qu'lad. Then he slept for a short time. Then it is said he
had a dream of a wolf which came into his house. Then it is
said the wolf spoke to him and said, ' Do not act like this Qu'lad,
good friend, but go into the water of this river morning and
evening. For four days do this if you want to get well, and
take a bucket and dip water out of this river while you are
sitting in the water, and pour the water in the bucket over both
sides of your neck. Two buckets full of water in the bucket
pour over the right side of your neck, and in the same way two
buckets full over the left side of your neck.' Thus said the wolf
in the dream of Qu'lad. Then the wolf left."

He follows out instructions in reality and is cured. All those
who acted according to his words recovered. Only AwalosElat
died.—Shaman. Too many witnesses.[1]

42. This was also the dream of the shaman Togumalis as he
was dreaming. " A squirrel came here and asked me to go into

---

[1] See Chap. II, pp. 68–75, for cures originating in dreams.

the water of the pond behind the village of Fort Rupert, for he was very sick of the influenza. Then I was asked to sit down in the water early in the morning when day broke, and to spray myself with cold water also late in the evening. And I obeyed the squirrel. Then it showed to me what I was to do, and I went into the water. Therefore I do this when I begin to cough. Then I go immediately into the water in this pond behind our house. Therefore, I am never sick." It was a squirrel that made Togumalis a shaman and it was a wolf that made Qu'lad a shaman.

43. " I dreamed of my late mother who asked me to rub my body always with branches of hemlock trees in the river behind our village in the morning and in the evening, ' And if you do this you will never be sick,' thus said my late mother to me. After that I went immediately into the water." (This is the usual method of ceremonial purification.)

44. " I dreamed of many men who were sitting in a house. I entered but I was not welcome to the chief who was very angry against me. Then I was addressed by another man who said to me : ' We are the diseases, every one of us men who are assembled here, and we are discussing where we shall go next summer. Now go out ! ' said the man to me. When I was about to go out of the door of the large house, the man who had talked to me came and pinched me with his right hand in my right side saying, ' You are going to die of the sickness which has taken hold of you now.' And I awoke."

45. *Bad Dream of Lekasa.*

" I dreamed that the late LagEyos came and sat down on the floor of my house and he asked my whole tribe to go into the water of a river which I did not know on account of a great epidemic which was to come this summer. Thus he said to me and those would not be infected in the epidemic who would go into the river. Thus he said to me. Then I went into the water of this river. Then I awoke."

46. " I dreamed I saw my late father who advised me not to be careless and to behave well and that he was going to take something on account of witchcraft practised against me in order to kill me. That was the end of his speech to me and I awoke." (" When a person is bewitched by bringing into contact some excretion of his body with some part of a human skeleton, the

witchcraft may be counteracted by 'taking' some analogous material and repeating the action of witchcraft.")

Dreamer Emaxulag.Ilis.

47. "In my dream I was at anchor at Dals. There were many canoes on both sides on the water and they were known not to me. Then I discovered in his canoe close to me at the place where I was at anchor 'nEmogwis, the Nak'.wax.da'x'. He said, 'Oh, son-in-law, take care for these who are at anchor here are the spirits who are referred to by the people of ancient times as War-spirits,' thus he said to me and hauled in his anchor. Before he had pulled up his anchor a strong tide began to run. Big waves were breaking. Then I and 'nEmogwis went ashore and to the house in Dals. Then the spirits came along paddling and stopped on the water near the place where we had gotten out of our canoes. After that I awoke. Then I went to sleep again and a man came and said, 'You did well to go ashore quickly for the spirits were ready to take you,' thus he said to me. Then I awoke."

48. "I dreamed I had gone sealing on Xwegats'.e. I arrived at the point lying towards the mouth and stepped out of my small travelling canoe in order to place the anchor line on shore. Then I went to the sea side of Xwegats'.e. There I saw two large seals lying on a seal rock and I was about to shoot them. Then I saw that their heads had long hair and they had human faces. I discovered that they were what is called Sea-men. Then I was afraid to shoot them. I went away from them. Now I was afraid of them. I had not arrived at my small travelling canoe when I awoke."

49. *Dream of Omx.td.*

"I dreamed I was taking a walk with my friend YaxLEN. We were passing through a door in a wide wall which was standing on the ground. Its upper end was invisible. As soon as we had passed through I saw the late wife of YaxLEN, L——. Then I saw that this was the house of the ghosts. L—— called her husband YaxLEN to come to her and to lie down. Then my friend YaxLEN went and lay down with her. Then L—— asked me to go home, 'for my husband is going to stay away,' thus she said. Then I awoke."

50. "In my dream I went inland to a place which I did not

know. I saw a house at the foot of a mountain. I entered the house. I did not sit down on the floor. I looked about in the house. Then I saw human bones, many in boxes. I was frightened. Then I awoke."

51. " In my dream many spirits came to get Chief EMaxwa. He, however, did not want to go along. Then he was left by them. When the spirits went away they took along a boy. Then our tribe discovered that the spirits had taken along a boy. He was not found. Then I awoke."

52. " I dreamed I was walking along the river of Made. There I saw many men walking about and also a woman. They were going up to the river of Made. The last one (of the people) saw me and spoke to me. He said, ' Do not walk on the ground that belongs to these spirits who are walking along this river and they intend to bathe in this river.' Thus the man spoke to me. Then I awoke."

53. " In my dream I was much afraid last night when I dreamed I was out paddling and steered towards Xwegats'.E. I had almost arrived there when a strong tide began to run. Then I paddled hard but I could not make any headway against the tide. I was steering towards Xwegats'.E but it was as though Xwegats'.E was pushing me away. Then many gulls came. Now I knew that the sea monster of Xwegats'.E was about to come up. Then I was very much afraid. Then I was awakened by my wife." (" This dream signifies that a relative of the dreamer is going to drown ".)

54. " In my dream, I was walking along the beach to get cockles. Then I came to Dzodzad looking for cockles. When I found four cockles a thick fog came up. Then a very beautiful man came. He spoke and said, ' Come, K'.wamaxalas, let us go where there are many cockles,' thus he said to me. I followed him at once. I did not know the man, and I did not see where we were going, because the fog was very thick. Then we entered a large house, and the man said, " This is my house. I am L'.agwag.ila, the prince of Q'.omogwa. Now I shall have you for my wife, K—— and these carved posts I shall give to your father." Thus said L'.agwag.ila to me. I agreed to his words and I had L'.agwag.ila for my husband. He was very kind to me. L'.agwag.ila said to me, ' Now take care. You are going to stay with me all the time.' And so I awoke."

55. " I dreamed I had gone out and met a large grizzly bear in Knight Inlet. That is where I live. And so I shot at it, and it stood up and spoke to me and said, ' Do not do that, child, I am your late father. I was killed by that which looks the way I look now. Go up the river and there is a place where you are going to see grizzly bears.' Thus said the large grizzly bear. Then I went and in my dream I saw many grizzly bears walking about. I woke up, evidently because I was very much afraid."

56. *Kwakiutl. Dream of one of Twins.*[1]

" I was lying in our house in Knight Inlet with my husband, WaLed," said HayosdesElas. And then she told me her dream, for HayosdesElas was one of twins, and her husband, WaLed, was also one of twins. She said :

" I dreamed that we were sitting on the floor of our house, I and WaLed, in the morning at the time when the olachens were running. We heard the sound of a song at the mouth of the river of Knight Inlet. It was coming up the river. Then we began to understand the words of the song which was being sung. And these are the words of the song heard by Hayosdes-Elas and her husband.

' The treasure of the salmon is coming to you, the great treasure. Ha'yo, ha'yo ha'yo. Beautifully he is coming, the treasure of the salmon, this Mamenla'ya of the salmon.'

" Then the singing in front of the house of HayosdesElas stopped and in her dream HayosdesElas saw a small woman coming from the place where the sound of the singing had been. In her arms she carried something that was like a new-born child, and she placed the child in the lap of HayosdesElas. Then the child disappeared in the body of HayosdesElas. Then the salmon woman said to HayosdesElas, ' You will call this treasure which you receive from me Mamenla ya,' thus she said and disappeared. ' From that time on my wife was pregnant with this child,' said WaLed when he was telling me his dream. Now that is the end of this.

" When HayosdesElas had been pregnant the right length of time she gave birth to a boy. As soon as night came she dreamed

---

[1] A Kwakiutl belief is that twins of the same sex are salmon that have taken the forms of men (Boas, " Current Beliefs of the Kwakiutl Indians," *J. of Am. Folklore*, Vol. 45, April–June 1932, Par. 232).

again of the little salmon woman. " She came and sat down on the floor of the house at my right side. She was carrying this little child Mamenla ya in her arms and she spoke. She said to me, ' Now be careful, friend, of this your treasure, and your husband. Always paint yourself with ochre, you and your husband, and also this Mamenla ya, and also put on the sides of the head two feathers of a gull, and the painting on the cradle shall be a whale. And furthermore, if you do not obey what I tell you, I am going to come and take back this child.' 'Thus she said to me in my dream,' said HayosdesElas to me as she was telling me her dream."

" Then a cradle with a notched head-piece was made and gull feathers were placed on each side of the head of HayosdesElas and her husband WaLed. They were not able to get any ochre. Now the child of HayosdesElas was four months old. Then WaLed the husband of HayosdesElas came into my house and said, ' Oh friend, last night I had an evil dream relating to this child.' And so he told me his dream. He said, ' All kinds of salmon came to me in canoes here to Fort Rupert in the morning when day was dawning. Then she of whom my wife spoke, the salmon woman, came into my house. She was very angry with us, particularly with my wife HayosdesElas.' She said, ' We have come to take away Mamenla ya, according to what I told HayosdesElas, namely, if you did not follow all my instructions relating to the dress which Mamenla ya should wear (which I gave you at the time) when he came to you.' Thus said the salmon woman, and she took the child in her arms and went out of the door. Then the salmon woman went aboard the canoe from the side of the canoe which was towards the shore. Then the many canoes of the salmon went away.

" As soon as I awoke I looked at Mamenla ya. I saw he was lying in the house. Then I called HayosdesElas and told her my dream. As soon as I had told my dream to her Hayosdes-Elas spoke and said, ' Right from the beginning I was afraid on account of what she said in the beginning when she brought Mamenla ya to us. For the salmon woman said, " If you do not do everything I tell you, if any of these is not taken for the dress of Mamenla ya, I shall come back and take him," as she said this. Now it seems the salmon woman means that we never got ochre for him.'

317

" Three days after this the child died. I have got the notched cradle with the painting of the whale. That is all."

57. " I dreamed last night about all the tribes that had been invited by the late Chief NEG.adZe. He gave a winter ceremonial and all the men and women were very happy. Then I was taken and I was to disappear, and so I disappeared. Then I saw the supernatural beings, the givers of the Winter Ceremonial. They flew and took me to the house of the magical powers, the givers of the Winter Ceremonial. That was the place where I was taught the war-dance, all the ways of the war-dance. Then my head was cut off and I walked with my head around the fire in the middle of a large house. Then my head was put back. After that I awoke."

58. *Dream of the Shaman Q'walENts'es.*

" I dreamed I had gone to the other side of our world, the sky, I went up and saw a house. Then I approached the house. Before I was close to it a very beautiful woman came up to me. Then the woman spoke first to me. She said, ' Thank you, lord. You are the one to whom I refer as my husband ! Come, let us go into the house of this my father,' thus the woman said to me. Then we entered the beautiful house. Then the woman told her father that she had me for her husband. He became very angry, the one who was a very old man, on account of the speech of his daughter. The man would not permit me to have his child as my wife. Then the man said he was going to knock me down. Then I was very much afraid of him. This was evidently the cause why I awoke.

" Then I went to sleep again, for it was not yet morning. Then the dream about the woman came again. She said, ' Go into the water in the river so that you may be successful this summer. My father is the one who takes care of the world,' thus she said to me. Immediately I went into the water of the river, into this river of Fort Rupert. After I finished bathing I woke up. As soon as I began to be awake, I went into the water of this river of Fort Rupert."

59. " I dreamed I had been called by a man to go with him to the upper side of our world, the sky. He took my right hand. Then he went up holding my hand while we were going straight up. Then we passed through the door in the middle of the upper side of our world. The man showed me everything that

was in the house there. Then he said to me that we should go on. We went along.

" Then we went to the hole in the edge of the world. Then he said, ' Through this (hole) pass the children when they are born when they come from the upper side of the world. Now pass through it and go home. I am going to help you that it may not be hard for you to pass through.' Then I went on, but before I arrived I awoke."

60. εmaxulag.Ilis.

" In my dream I flew upwards. It was as though I was going to the place where the stars are for the stars were showing in the daytime. I saw all around our world. Then I wished in vain to go down again. I was not able to do so. I was very afraid. Then I awoke."

61. " I dreamed I was going to the house of the Master of the Salmon on the sea side of our world. I do not know why I was going there. There I saw my late father. Then he scolded me because I had gone to the place where he was. He asked me to go back home. Then I remembered that my late father had died long ago. Then I went home. Then I awoke."

62. " I dreamed I had been taken by a man unknown to me to a distant place. We were travelling in a strange-looking canoe. I thought I would ask the man where he came from. Then he spoke to me and said, ' I know your thoughts. You wish to ask me where I came from. I will tell you. I am the great star which comes down twice and which you see in the evening,' said the man. Then I was afraid on account of his speech. I awoke and I went to sleep again."

63. " In my dream I went into the woods to fell cedar bark, together with my late husband LELeLEwek. We were going inland. Then my late husband asked me to lie down with him. Then we lay down. Then it occurred to me that he had died long ago. Then he said, ' Oh mistress, I am in great trouble for your sake. I long for you very much, mistress. You do not think of me at all since you have NoIbe for your husband. So I am going to enter your womb that you may become my mother,' thus he said and disappeared. Then in my dream I went to a cedar grove and peeled a good many cedar trees. I had a great deal of cedar bark which I had peeled. Then I tied it up and

put it on my back. In my dream I came to my house and in my dream I told my husband.

"Then my husband became jealous on account of the one who had died long ago. In my dream my husband said he would beat me. Then I was afraid and therefore I awoke." [1]

64. "I dreamed that the moon came down to our world. As soon as she reached the ground a man stepped out of the side door of the Moon. Then he told Kwag.ut not to hate one another, not to steal the property of their fellow-men and also this, that they should pray to the Creator of man, ' that he may pity you and help you,' said the Moon man. Then I awoke."

65. "I dreamed that I was going to the upper world, which was very beautiful. Then I saw many people and all of them seemed to be women. One of them came to me and spoke to me and advised me to never speak a lie, ' For I know that you always lie when you talk about the feasts that you give to your tribe in the country down below. If you go on talking this way you will fare ill with our chief here when he judges you. And you shall not steal your brother's property, and you shall not hate your fellow-men. If you obey what I tell you, you will have no reason to fear,' thus she said to me. Then she asked me to go home. She opened the rear door of the house and I went out and when I looked up and saw my house. Then I awoke."

66. ɛmaxu.lag.Ilis.

"I dreamed this night of Mr. Hall," said ɛmaxu.lag.Ilis to me. It may be two years since he told me this dream. He said, "I dreamed I was sitting in a house, not mine, and I thought in my mind who might be the owner of the bad house in which I was sitting. Then a man behind me spoke and said, ' Oh brother ɛmaxu.lag.Ilis, what are you doing in this house? ' I turned around and looked at him and recognized Mr. Hall, the former missionary at Alert Bay. He wore a long coat and a black hat covered his head. His black cap was embroidered all around with gold. On his forehead he wore gold which shone like the sun. Then I arose and stretched out my hand, intending to take his hand. Then he said, ' Oh no ! I am now different, for as I used to preach to you at Fort Rupert I am

---

[1] " This dream means that the dreamer will have a son, but also that her husband will die after the birth of the child."

dressed thus because I am now in the world above. I can not take your hand because you did not obey what I preached to you,' thus he said and disappeared. That was the end of the dream of ɛmaxu.lag.Ilis on the twenty-eighth of February.[1]

" When the month of April was almost gone a letter came from England telling of Mr. Hall's death on the twenty-seventh day of the month of February. The only point that makes me believe the dream of ɛmaxu.lag.Ilis is that he came at once and told me about his dream in the morning, he had dreamed about Mr. Hall dressed up in this way. That is what is called by the Indians a true dreamer, and a good dream."

[1] " This man is known as a dreamer. He belongs to the SenL'.EM."

CORRELATION OF THE DREAMS TO THE CULTURE

The initiation legend which is similar in form and content to actual initiation experiences of the young initiates follows a period of fasting and isolation, and is an example of another stereotyped culture pattern vision, which reveals the usual tribal approach to the supernatural and the gifts and powers which result from the experience. Among these people this type of experience is of immense importance in the cultural life of the tribe. Dreams two and three (p. 304) are only partial pattern dreams. The form and content of a part of the dream is identical with the typical pattern reflecting the relation to the supernatural as just outlined. (A supernatural being who presents a sacred gift such as the quartz crystal, or a name.) The other portion of the two dreams are individual dreams in content, reflecting sealing, and canoeing, the usual occupations of this tribe. These two dreams are regular night dreams, and are not induced by a prior period of fasting and concentration to bring about a supernatural experience. They are each one examples of mixed culture pattern and individual dreams.

The other regular night dreams are practically all individual dreams reflecting very clearly and definitely different aspects of the highly individualized social and religious culture of these people, besides a rather distinct personal psychology.[1]

For instance :

Out of sixty-three dreams (number of individuals unknown),

---

[1] See Chap. IV, pp. 150–4.

Seventeen reflect occupations such as hunting, fishing, berry picking, clam digging, canoeing (1–11, 13, 15, 17, 48, 53, 29).

Five reflect the very specialized attitudes towards property such as the potlatch, and the destruction of coppers and property (19, 20, 21, 22, 23).

Eleven reflect special social customs ; about hunting (27), about twins (24), singing love songs (28, 37), ceremonial for a new-born baby (56), about curing (41, 42, 45), burial custom (50), Winter Ceremonial (57), witchcraft custom (46).

Twenty-eight reflect belief in supernatural beings, ghosts, spirits, the return of the dead, the next world, etc. (30, 31, 32, 33, 34, 35, 36, 37, 38, 39, 40, 43, 46, 47, 48, 49, 51, 52, 53, 55, 56, 58, 59, 61, 62, 63, 64, 65).

Three reflect white influence (18, 65, 66).

Nineteen reflect personal psychology, the majority in relation to deceased relatives :

The dead father or grandfather (34, 36, 38, 40, 46, 55, 61).

(These often appear in the dream in cultural form such as the late father, as the Grizzly Bear or Master of the Salmon.)

The dead mother (43).

Other dead relatives (35, 63).

Other personal psychology dreams with absence of culture items (13, 14, 26, 32, 33, 44, 54, 60).

Some of the dreams are in the following form :

Seventeen death dreams.

Two falling dreams (13, 14).

Two persecution dreams (25, 29).

Two prophetic dreams (56, 66).

Five undisguised sexual dreams (26, 27, 29, 49, 63).

Boas points out that in this area where the arts, industries, customs and beliefs differ so much from those of all other Indians, the culture is one of the best defined on the North American continent, in spite of the peculiarities of the individual tribes which prove that the culture has developed slowly and from a number of distinct centres. The Kwakiutl are a highly individualized people with their complex social organization, their methods of acquiring rank through potlatch, their secret societies and initiations and their cannibalistic ceremonialism and tradition.[1] All of this organization is reflected in the individual dreams.

Hence, here in an area where the culture induces important pattern visions and also lays emphasis on individual dreams, there is found mixed individual and pattern dreams, reflecting all aspects of the culture. The individual dreams, as elsewhere, differ from the pattern dreams in form, and reflect besides the religious beliefs and personal psychology, those aspects of objective social culture which are not shown in the pattern dreams, which in turn deal only with the personal approach to the supernatural in a rigidly formalized manner.

It is interesting to note that many of the pattern dreams (initiation myths) deal with the youth's winning favour with a supernatural cannibalistic being whose chief desire is to kill and eat men, and that most of the individual dreams that reflect personal psychology in their manifest content deal with the appeasing or propitiating of the late father.[2]

[1] F. Boas, *Social Org. and Secret Societies of the Kwakiutl,* pp. 317, 328, 341.
[2] See Chap. IV, pp. 150–4.

7. REGIONAL TABLES OF DREAM VARIATIONS

Although it is evident that the data for each of the areas presented in this study is not complete, yet there seems to be ample to make certain general conclusions with a reasonable amount of accuracy. Further detailed study of the dreams of many individuals and tribes in the field, over long periods of time will be necessary in order to form any really comprehensive theory of the relationship of individuals and cultures based on dreams, and to further the deeper study of the latent contents of the dreams of American Indians.

For instance the following tables show the variations of pattern dreaming and individual dreaming in the areas covered as well as the different methods of inducing dreams and a comparison of the forms of different dreams. These suffer from the defect of trying to classify living processes which are changing over a period of time.

I. There are found :

   A. *In areas where the old Indian culture exists or existed.*[1]

      (1) Pattern dreaming and individual dreaming both regarded as important by the native, with the cultural emphasis on pattern dreaming. (In the Woodlands among the Ottawa, Ojibway, Menomini. In the North-West Coast, among the Kwakiutl. In the Plateau area, among the Thompson Indians.)

      (2) Pattern dreaming exclusively regarded as important.

[1] See also Part II, Chap. IV, pp. 169–75, for Analysis of Omaha visions, especially p. 172 ; and Chap. II, pp. 71–3, especially p. 73, note 2, for Paviotso shamanistic dreams. In both groups are found individual dreams, dreamed spontaneously, yet in form and contact are identical with the induced culture pattern dreams which occur in both groups.

(In the Plains, among the Crow, the Blackfoot. In the Lower Colorado area among the Yuma.)

(3) Individual dreams reflecting culture exclusively emphasized, and no pattern dreams at all. (Among the Navajo.) [1]

(4) Individual dreams reflecting no culture in their manifest contents of individuals who have lost contact with the culture either temporarily or permanently because of peculiarities of individual psychology. (Among the Navajo, and the Kwakiutl.)

B. *In areas where the old Indian culture has broken or is breaking down.*

(1) Individual dreams reflecting mixed Indian-white or not reflecting any cultural phenomena, hence largely personal psychology. (Among the modern Yuma of the Colorado Area, Ottawa of the Woodlands Area, and Wintu of the California Area.)

II. INDUCTION OF DREAMS.

A. *Pattern Dreams.* These are all induced by the cultures in the following manner :

(1) Induced by conscious auto-suggestion usually preceded by a period of fasting, isolation, or torture. The individual seeking a vision has his mind concentrated on a limited culturally determined field. Occur in the Plains (Crow, Blackfoot), the North-West Coast (Kwakiutl), and the Plateau (Thompson River). (The Crow sometimes dream without a prior period of fasting and torture, in sleep, but always after concentrated auto-suggestion.)

(2) Induced by formal suggestion or instruction of medicine men. Occur among the Lower Colorado tribes (Yuma, Mohave).

(3) Induced by formal parental suggestion with instruction to the child vision seeker to keep dreaming until he dreams right. Occur in the Woodlands (Ottawa, Menomini, Ojibway).

[1] The exceptions among the Navajo to this general rule are the stargazing visions of diagnosticians. These are culture pattern visions, but are confined to this profession. See p. 217, ref. 1.

B. *Individual Dreams.* These are not formally induced. They occur spontaneously in sleep and are primarily phenomena of individual psychology. The culture reflections in the manifest contents of many are probably caused, in large part, by random collective suggestion of the culture on the varying psychology of the individual.

III. THE FORMS OF DREAMS.

(1) The cultural forms of the pattern dreams are obviously all laid down by the culture, and determined by the different methods of induction.[1]

(2) The forms of individual dreams are not consciously induced by the culture even if the manifest contents reflect culture items. Types taking such forms as undisguised sex dreams, falling dreams, prophetic dreams, death dreams, and persecution dreams are phenomena of individual psychology, determined by the unconscious processes occurring in sleep. How these in turn are primarily determined by the culture is another problem not discussed here.[2]

[1] See S. Freud, on influencing the manifest content of the dream, and O. Pfister, p. 173, Ref. 4.
[2] See Chaps. III and IV.

APPENDIX

" SEVERAL instances of dreams apparently involving something of the nature of thought transference came to my notice.[1] Unfortunately, I did not check any of them by questioning the other people concerned, so I cannot offer corroborative evidence. They seem, however, to be sufficiently interesting to record at their face value.

" A man may dream of having connection with a woman and the woman with the man. The next day the man will say to the woman : ' I dreamed about you last night. My skin wants you.' Then if the woman is willing they go to the bush (implying that they have sexual intercourse there).[1]

" It was made clear in subsequent conversation that the speaker had in mind the occurrence of ' reciprocal dreams,' in which both parties dreamed simultaneously of the other. But the account was given as a generalized statement, not as an actual dream. The following appears to have been an actual dream, though not of the night before :

' Sometimes my dreams come true. Once I dreamed that a certain man went to the house of a certain girl and they walked about together with his arm round her neck. Afterwards I went to the man and told him the dream, and he said : ' True, I did walk about with my arm round the girl's neck.' He was very much ashamed that I had dreamed such a thing.' "
Comment by the recorder. " Etiquette forbids any show of affection between lovers in public. The couple in question were shortly afterwards married by the missionary."

" On one occasion, after my return from a trip during which

---

[1] From Blackwood, B., *Both Sides of Buka Passage*, chapter on Dreams of the Coastal Solomon Islanders (unpub.).

I had left my native servant in charge of my house at Kurtatchi, he told me that during my absence the following incident had occurred :

'No. 24. Ross. (Adult male.) One night I thought I heard some-one knocking on the wall of the house, and I got the torch to look, but there was no one to be seen. Then I went to sleep and dreamed a woman came under the house and knocked on the floor, and asked me to have intercourse with her, but I would not. Next day I found that the people in the village were talking about me, and saying that women came to me at night. But that is not true, I do nothing but sleep at night.'

" The belief in the efficacy of certain ' prescriptions ' involving dreams may be due to their use having been coincident with success explicable along similar lines. The two which are here given were told to me in the course of my inquiries after plants powerful as ' medicine,' and had no connection whatever with any of our discussions on dreams."

" To make a Woman desire You

Rarakot (a grass with numbers of small sticky seeds)

Take the roots and some of the seeds when they are ripe. Chew them with the betel-mixture, go to the woman with this in your mouth and talk with her. When she has answered you, go away. At night the woman will dream of you. In the morning she will come and ask you : ' What have you done to me ? I dreamed about you.' You say : ' No, I did nothing to you, but you and I talked together while I chewed something.' The woman dreams about you every night, and if she sleeps during the day she dreams about you again. By and by you two get married.

" To Make a Woman Visit You

Wadodowu (a small plant)

If you dream in the night that you have connection with a woman, you get up at earliest dawn and get a leaf of this plant, rub it in your hands and wash with it in a river, then go back to the village and the woman will come to you.

" As independent corroboration of the possibility that some form of thought transference is associated with these incidents, I may add the testimony of Mr. Gordon Thomas, a resident on the island of Pororan, West Buka, who, without my ever having mentioned the subject to him, wrote to me : ' After nearly twenty years of association with the Buka native I am convinced that he is remarkably susceptible to thought transference,' citing several instances which had come under his personal observation. One experience of my own is possibly relevant. I was once sitting on the verandah of a native hut chatting with my host about nothing in particular. There was a silence, and I was just about to ask him if he knew of the death of a native of a neighbouring village, who had recently been taken to the Government hospital at Kieta, when he said : ' Wanawatch is dead, isn't he ? ' It must be admitted that it was probable that he had heard the news, but it is at least an odd coincidence that he should have mentioned at the moment when I was about to do so, since nothing in our previous conversation had led up to it. This episode, however, differs from those recorded in connection with dreams, in that it took place while the two people concerned were together, while the occurrences related above, if accepted, would involve the ' transference ' of the idea to someone at a distance, or, at least not at the time in the company of the other individual."[1]

From the Melanesians of British New Guinea is recorded the following [2] :

" Romilly records that a party of Tubetube men started on a trading voyage to a village in Milne Bay . . . They had often traded there before and anticipated no danger ; they had started at an auspicious

---

[1] After the paragraphs dealing with " thought-transference " were written, I accidentally came across a passage in which Rivers discusses incidents involving apparently unplanned concerted action, noted by him among the natives of the Western Solomons during his travels in 1908. These he is inclined to explain as due to suggestion, comparing them with thought-reading among ourselves. He uses the term " thought-reading " " as a name for the unwitting transmission of ideas from person to person in the presence of one another as distinguished from the problematical telepathy or distant thought-transference " (*Instinct and the Unconscious*, pp. 94–96, 1922). Since, however, this latter phenomenon has not, so far as I am aware, been entirely discredited (I have personal knowledge of instances among ourselves which it is difficult to explain otherwise), the foregoing material is presented for what it may be worth (Miss Blackwood's note).

[2] C. G. Seligman in *Melanesians of British New Guinea*, p. 654.

time, however, as an old woman the night previous to their departure had dreamed a dream and warned them against going. On their arrival in Milne Bay they were received in an apparently friendly manner, but at a given signal the whole party with the exception of one young man and a little boy were treacherously tomahawked."

From the Basuto Bantu, among other cases, the following is recorded :

" A final illustration I will give, upon which I confess my inability to comment in the very least. I was on trek in the heart of the Drakensberg, and by chance called for twenty-four hours at a village which I had never visited before, and as a matter of fact, have never visited since. Towards the afternoon of the day that I was there, a native rode into the village, on a dead-beat horse, inquiring for the white priest. On his being brought to me, he exclaimed : ' Thou art the man, my father ! ' and forthwith asked me to go into the hut. Within he told me that he was a Mosuto from the far south, naming a distant district that I knew although I did not know the village. He said he had dreamed that he was to seek out this village, and finally myself ; that he had been told that he had but six days in which to make the journey ; and that he was to give me this. Thereupon he placed in my hand a golden sovereign.

" That is the end of it. He did not want to become a Christian, and could not see that he had been ' called ' to be converted. I had not good work particularly languishing for want of a sovereign, and I did not give him a Bible. No one in the place knew him, and he said he had not been there before. Certainly I had not been near his village, and I had not even come along any part of his road. Also, if he had been a day late, he would not have found me there ; and he made nothing out of his journey save only that he shared my evening meal. We went our several ways in the dawn. Maybe we shall meet again in the dusk and understand a little better. In the meantime I confess that this remains the most curious, the most unexplained, the most trivial, and the most bewildering incident that I have known even amongst a people of dreams." [1]

Without completely committing himself to thought transference and telepathy, Freud in his recent work [2] cites experiences occurring during his analytic practice that give the appearance of both these processes in dreams. He tells of a man who

[1] R. Keable, " A People of Dreams," *Hibbert Journal,* April 1921, pp. 522–31.

[2] S. Freud, *New Introductory Lectures on Psychoanalysis,* p. 50.

dreamed on a certain night that his wife had had twins, and the next morning he received a telegram saying that his daughter had had twins on that night.[1] He says

" that in occultism there is a core of facts which have hitherto not been recognized, and round which fraud and phantasy have woven a veil which it is hard to penetrate. . . . It is here, it seems to me, that the dream comes to our aid by suggesting to us that we should pick out the theme of telepathy from all the confused material that surrounds it." [2]

He points out that telepathy is not confined to dreams, and " The only ground for mentioning the connections between dreams and telepathy is that the condition of sleep seems to be especially suitable for the reception of telepathic communications." [3] He also suggests that telepathy in spite of the difficulty of proof occurs particularly in the mental life of children.[4] He presents the case recorded by a reliable observer in which a mother and child are being analysed at the same time [5] :

" One day in her analytic hour the mother was talking about a gold coin which had figured in one of her childhood's experiences. Immediately afterwards, when she had returned home, her little ten-year-old boy came into her room and brought her a gold coin to keep for him. She was astonished and asked him where he had got it from. He had been given it on his birthday, but that was several months ago, and there was no reason why the child should have remembered the gold coin just then. The mother told the analyst about the coincidence, and asked her to try to find out from the child why he had behaved in this way. But the analysis of the child elicited nothing ; the action had made its way into the child's life that day like a foreign body. A few weeks later the mother was sitting at her writing-table, in order to make a note of the occurrence as she had been asked to do. At that moment the boy came in and asked for the gold coin back, saying that he wanted to take it to show his analyst. Once more the child's analysis disclosed nothing that led up to the wish."

---

[1] *Ibid.*, p. 53.   [2] *Ibid.*, p. 51.   [3] *Ibid.*, p. 52.
[4] *Ibid.*, p. 76.   [5] *Ibid.*, p. 77.

BIBLIOGRAPHY AND SOURCES[1]

PART I

*BLAND, N. . . . . "On the Muhammedan Science of Tabir or Interpretation of Dreams," *J. of Royal Asiatic Soc.*, Vol. XVI, 1856.

FLÜGEL, J. C. . . . . *The Psychoanalytic Study of the Family*, 1931.

*FOUCART, GEORGE . . Hastings' *Encyclopedia of Religion and Ethics*, Vol. 5, p. 33.

FREUD, SIGMUND . . . *The Interpretation of Dreams*, 3rd ed., 1927. *New Introductory Lectures On Psychoanalysis*, 1933.

*GARDINER, ALAN . . . See Part II.

GOODWIN, PHILIP . . . "*The Mystery of Dreams Historically Considered,*" in Seafield (see below), Vol. 1, pp. 145–7, 154.

JUNG, C. G. . . . . Seminar Notes, Zurich, 1928 (unpub.).

*PHILLPOTTS, B. S. . . Hastings' *Encyclopedia of Religion and Ethics*, Vol. 5, pp. 37–8.

RANK, O. . . . . . "Modern Psychology and Social Change," *Action et Pensée*, May–July 1934. 10e année, Nos. 5–6, pp. 96–9, 97 (Geneva).

*SAYCE, A. H. . . . . Hastings' *Encyclopedia of Religion and Ethics*, Vol. 5, p. 33.

SEAFIELD, F. . . . . *Literature and Curiosities of Dreams*, London, 1865 (Chapman & Hall).

PART II

ABRAHAM, KARL . . . "Dreams and Myths," *Nervous and Mental Disease Monograph Series*, No. 15, N.Y., 1913.

---

[1] An asterisk denotes all primary historical sources, as well as works based on anthropological field work, as differentiated from theoretical or reconstructed treatments of cultures, however valuable the latter may be, and from purely psychological works. *B.A.E.* means Bureau of American Ethnology.

BAUDOUIN, C. . . . . "La Mentalité Primitive," *Action et Pensée*, Nov. 1931 (Geneva).

*BEST, ELSDON . . . . "Omens and Superstitious Beliefs of the Maori," *J. of the Polynesian Soc.*, Vol. VII, No. 27, Sept. 1898, p. 124 *seq.*

BOAS, FRANZ . . . . *The Mind of Primitive Man*, 1911.
The Social Organization and Secret Societies of the Kwakiutl Indians, 1895.

*BLACKWOOD, B. . . *Both Sides of Buka Passage*, chapter on Dreams of Solomon Islanders. Unpublished. 1935.

*CARDINALL, A. W. . . "Dreams among the Dagomba and Moshi," *Man*, May 1927, p. 87 *seq.* No. 59.

*CHARLEVOIX, P. F. X. DE *Journal d'un voyage dans l'Amérique septentrionale*, III, pp. 369–70, 1744.

DÄNGEL, R. . . . . *Siamesische Traümdeütüngskünst*, Leipzig, Vol. VII, p. 3, 1931 ; *Imago*, Vol. 17, Heft 1, 1931, pp. 126–9.

*DENSMORE, F. . . . . *Chippewar Music*, *Bul.* 45—*B.A.E.*, 1910 (Smithsonian).

*DRIBERG, J. H. . . . "Dreams among the Lango and Didinga," *Man*, Aug. 1927, pp. 141–3.

*FIRTH, RAYMOND . . . "Meaning of Dreams in Tikopia," in *Essays Presented to C. G. Seligman*, 1934.

*FLETCHER AND LA FLÈCHE "The Omaha Tribe," *27th Ann. Rep.* *B.A.E.*, 1905–6, pp. 325, 459.

*FORTUNE, R. F. . . . "Omaha Secret Societies," *Columbia Univ. Cont. to Anthropology*, Vol. XIV, 1932.

FRAZER, SIR JAMES . . *Belief in Immortality*, Vols. I, II, III. See Index for "Dreams," and Vol. I, p. 139 ; Vol. II, p. 92.
The Golden Bough, "The Magic Art," Vol. I, pp. 172–3 ; Vol. III, pp. 368, 404 ; Vol. IV, pp. 14–28, 219 ; Vol. VI, pp. 162, 255.
Totemism and Exogamy, Vol. I, p. 497 ; Vol. II, pp. 455, 442 ; Vol. III, pp. 380, 395, 497.

FREUD, SIGMUND . . . *The Interpretation of Dreams*, 1927 Ed.
New Introductory Lectures on Psychoanalysis (1933), Lecture XXX.
Totem and Taboo.

*GARDINER, ALAN . . . *Hieratic Papyri in the British Museum*, 3rd series, Chester Beatty Gift, Papyrus No. III, The Dream Book. 1935.

*GILL, W. W. . . . . "Mangaia" (Harvey Islands), *Australasian Assoc. for Adv. of Science*, Vol. II, 1890.

*GOLDENWEISER, A. . . *History, Psychology and Culture*, 1934.

*GRINELL, J. B. . . . *Blackfoot Lodge Tales*, 1893.

HANDY, E. S. C. . . . *Polynesian Religion*, Bishop Museum, Bul. 34, 1927.

*HERSKOVITS, M. J. . . " Freudian Mechanism in Negro Psychology," in *Essays Presented to C. G. Seligman*, London, 1934.

*HILL-TOUT, C. . . . "Totemism : Its Origin and Import," *Transactions of the Royal Society of Canada*, 2nd series, Vol. IX, 1903, pp. 64-7.

*HODGSON, A. G. O. . . " Dreams in Central Africa," *Man*, April 1926, pp. 66-8.

*HOSE AND McDOUGALL . *Pagan Tribes of Borneo*, 1912.

*IVENS, W. G. . . . . *Melanesians of the South-East Solomon Islands*, 1927.

**Jesuites dans la Nouvelle France, Relations des.* Quebec 1858, LVXI, pp. 236-8 ; Relation, 1648, Vol. 2, Chap. XII, pp. 70-1 ; Relation X, 1636, p. 170 ; Relation LIV, 1669-70, p. 96.

JONES, E. . . . . . " Theory of Symbolism," *Papers on Psychoanalysis*, 3rd ed.
On the Nightmare, 1933.

JUNG, C. G. . . . . Zurich Seminar Notes 1928 (unpub.).

*KEABLE, ROBERT . . . " A People of Dreams," *The Hibbert Journal*, April 1921, pp. 522-31 (Basuto Bantu).

*KOHL, J. G. . . . . *Kitchi-Gami—Wanderings Around Lake Superior*, London, 1860 (Chapman & Hall).

KROEBER, A. L. . . . Review of Jung's Collected Papers, *American Anthropologist*, Vol. 20, July–Sept. 1918, pp. 323-4.
" Totem and Taboo : An Ethnologic Psychoanalysis," *American Anthropologist*, Vol. 22, 1920, pp. 48-55.

*LANDTMAN, G. . . . *Folk Tales of the Kiwai Papuans* (Helsingfors), 1917, p. 196, and Nos. 63, 64, 94-101, 104, 125, 128, 201, 263, 268, 275, 284, 287, 366, 385, 386, 390, 391, 395, 398, 441.
The Kiwai Papuans of British New Guinea, 1927.

BIBLIOGRAPHY

*Laufer, B. . . . . "Inspirational Dreams in Eastern Asia," *J. of American Folklore*, Vol. 44, 1931.

Lévy-Bruhl, L. . . . *La Mentalité Primitive*, Chap. III, "Les Rêves," 1922.

*Lincoln, J. S. . . . Navajo Field Notes (unpub.), 1930, 1932. "A Dream Interpretation and Curing Ceremony of a Navajo Medicine Man," *Action et Pensée*, Nov. and Dec. 1932 (Geneva).

*Lowes, John Livingston *The Road to Xanadu* (Constable & Co.).

*Lowie, R. H. . . . . "Religious Ideas and Practices," in *Essays Presented to C. G. Seligman*, pp. 183–6 (1934).

*MacDonald, Rev. J. . *Africana*, Vol. II, 1882.

*Malinowski, B. . . . *Sex and Repression in Savage Society*, 1927. *The Father in Primitive Psychology*, 1927.

Melland, F. H. . . . *In Witchbound Africa*, 1923

Money-Kyrle, R. . . *The Meaning of Sacrifice*, 1930.

*Mooney, J. . . . . "The Ghost Dance Religion," *14th An. Report B.A.E.*, 1892–3, pp. 716, 771, 772, 928–52, 970.

Oldham, C. F. . . . *The Sun and the Serpent*, 1905.

*Park, Willard Z. . . "Paviotso Shamanism"—*Amer. Anthropologist*, Vol. 36, No. 1, Jan.–March 1934, pp. 99–103.

Parkman, Francis . . *Pioneers of France in the New World*, p. 347, note.

*Persian Dream Book (Eighth Century) Translation, *Islamic Culture*, Vol. VI, 1932, pp. 569–85.

Pfister, O. . . . . . *Psyche and Eros*, Vol. II, Jan.–Feb. 1921, pp. 1–11 ; March–April 1921, pp. 90–9.

*Radcliffe-Brown, A. R. *The Andaman Islanders*, 1933.

*Radin, Paul . . . . *Primitive Man as Philosopher*, 1927. Dreams from Eastern Woodlands (unpub.), 1927.

Rank, O. . . . . . "The Myth of the Birth of the Hero," *Nervous and Mental Disease Monograph Series*, No. 18, 1914, p. 70 and note 66.

*Rattray, R. S. . . . *Religion and Art in Ashanti*, Chap. XXI, pp. 192–204. 1927.

Reik, Theodore . . . *Ritual*.

*Rivers, W. H. . . . *Dreams and Primitive Culture*, Bulletin of John Rylands Library, Vol. 4, Nos. 3–4, Feb.–July 1918. *Instinct and the Unconscious*, 1922.

*Roheim, Geza . . . "Primitive High Gods," *The Psychoanalytic Quarterly*, N.Y., Vol. III, No. 1, Part 2, Jan. 1934, pp. 120–3.
"Psychoanalysis of Primitive Cultural Types," *Int. J. of Psychoanalysis*, Vol. XIII, Parts 1 and 2, Jan.–April 1932.
Social Anthropology, pp. 95, 96, 77, 83, 135 (Amer. ed.).
"Women and their Life in Central Australia," *J. of Royal Anthrop. Instit.*, Vol. LXIII, 1933, Jan.–June.
The Riddle of the Sphinx, 1934.

*Rose, H. J. . . . . "Central Africa and Artemidorus," *Man*, 1926, p. 211.

*Roth, W. E. . . . . "Superstition, Magic and Medicine," *N. Queensland Ethnography*, Bul. 5. No. 106.

Sauer, E. . . . . . "Das Wesen des Traumes in der Talmudischen Literatur," *Zt. f. Psychoanalyse*, I, 465.

Seafield, F. . . . . *Literature and Curiosities of Dreams*, London, Chapman & Hall, 1865.

*Seligman, Brenda Z. . "The Part of the Unconscious in Social Heritage," in *Essays Presented to C. G. Seligman*, pp. 307–17. 1934.
"The Incest Barrier : Its Rôle in Social Organization," *British J. of Psychology*, Genl. Section, Vol. XXII, Part 3, Jan. 1932.

*Seligman, C. G.
  and Brenda Z. . . *Pagan Tribes of the Nilotic Sudan*, 1932.

*Seligman, C. G. . . . Appendix to Chap. XXI of R. S. Rattray's *Religion and Art in Ashanti*, 1927.
Melanesians of British New Guinea.
"Anthropology and Psychology," *J. of Royal Anth. Inst.*, Vol. 54, 1924, pp. 13–46.
"Anthropological Perspective and Psychological Theory," Huxley Memorial Lecture, 1932, *J. of Royal Anthrop. Inst.*, Vol. LXII, July–Dec., pp. 193–228.
"The Unconscious in Relation to Anthropology," *British J. of Psychology*, Vol. XVIII, Part 4, 1928, pp. 374–87.

*SKEAT AND BLAGDEN . . *Malay Races*, Vol. 1, p. 365.
Pagan Races of the Malay Peninsula,
Vol. III, pp. 201, 367. 1906.

*SKINNER, A. . . . . . " Social Life and Ceremonial Bundles of
the Menomini Indians," *Amer. Mus. of
Nat. History Anthropological Papers*, Vol.
13, 1915, pp. 532–9.

SPENCER AND GILLEN. . *Native Tribes of Central Australia*, 1899.

*SPIER, LESLIE . . . . *Yuman Tribes of the Gila River* (Univ. of
Chicago Press, 1933).

TALBOT, P. A. . . . *The Peoples of S. Nigeria*, Vol. II, 1926.

*THOMSON, DONALD F. . " The Hero Cult Initiation and Totemism
on Cape York," *J. of Roy. Anthrop. Inst.*,
Vol. LXIII, July–Dec. 1933, pp. 493,
497, 498, 499, 501, 506 *seq.*, 585.

*TRILLES, R. P. H. . . " Le Totemisme chez les Fân," *Collection
Internationale de Monographies Ethno-
logiques*, Bibliothéque Anthropos, Tome
I, Fasc. 4, 1912, pp. 176–247.

TYLOR, SIR E. . . . *Primitive Culture*, 4th ed., Vol. I, pp. 121
seq., 440–5, 478 ; Vol. II, pp. 24, 49,
75, 410, 416. 1903.

*WHEELWRIGHT, MARY . *Navajo Myth of Sontso* (unpub.), 1933.

*Unpublished Letters to C. G. Seligman—from J. H. Hutton, A. G. O.
Hodgson, C. K. Meek, J. P. Mills, Mc-
Ilwraith, Margaret Meade, E. Wester-
marck.

PART III

*AITKEN, BARBARA . . " Temperament in Native American
Religion " (reprint from *Journal of
Royal Anthropological Institute*, Vol. LX,
July–Sept. 1930, pp. 370–1).

*BARAGA, FREDERIC . . *Grammar of Otchipwe Language*, p. 79.

*BENEDICT, R. . . . " The Vision in Plains Culture," *American
Anthropologist*, New Series, Vol. 24, 1922.

*BOAS, FRANZ . . . . *The Social Organization and Secret Societies
of the Kwakiutl Indians* (report of United
States National Museum, 1895, pp.
311–737).

*BOAS AND HUNT . . . " Contributions to the Ethnology of the
Kwakiutl," *Columbia University Contri-
butions to Anthropology*, Vol. III, 1925.

*Dorsey, J. O. . . . . "A Study of Siouan Cults," *Eleventh Annual Report of B.A.E.*, 1889–90.

*Fletcher, A. C. . . . *Handbook of American Indians*, United States *B.A.E. Bulletin*, No. 30, Part I, p. 400. 1907.
"Ogallala Sioux," *Reports of Peabody Museum*, Vol. III, 1882.

*Forde, C. Daryll . . "Ethnography of Yuma Indians," *University of California Publications in American Archæology and Ethnology*, Vol. 28, No. 4, Dec. 1931, pp. 201–3, 272.

*Franciscan Fathers, The *A Vocabulary of the Navajo Language.*
An Ethnologic Dictionary of the Navajo Language, pp. 346, 350, 379, 501.

*Gifford, E. W. . . . "Yuma Dreams and Omens," *Journal of American Folklore*, Vol. 39, 1926, pp. 59–66.
"The Kamia of Imperial Valley," *B.A.E. Bulletin*, No. 97, 1931.

*Harrington, J. Peabody "A Yuma Account of Origins," *Journal of American Folklore*, Vol. 21, 1908, pp. 326–7.

*Kroeber, A. . . . . "The Mohave Indians," *American Anthropologist*, No. 4, 1902, pp. 279–85.
"Handbook of Indians of California," *B.A.E. Bulletin*, No. 78, pp. 754, 755, 783, 784. 1925.

*Lincoln, J. S. . . . Navajo Field Notes, 1930, 1932 (unpub.).

*Lowie, R. H. . . . "The Religion of the Crow Indians," *American Museum of Natural History Anthropological Papers*, 1918–22, Vol. 25, pp. 317–24.

*Morgan, William . . "Navajo Diagnosticians," *American Anthropologist*, Vol. 33, No. 3, July–Sept. 1931, pp. 390–402.
"Navajo Dreams," *American Anthropologist*, Vol. 34, No. 3, pp. 390–405. 1932.

Pfister, Oskar . . . "Instinktive Psychoanalyse unter den Navaho Indianern," *Imago*, Vol. XVIII, No. 1, pp. 108–9. 1933.

*Radin, Paul . . . . Ottawa Field Notes (unpublished) and Ottawa and Ojibway Puberty Fasting Experiences (from older sources), 1927.

*Radin, Paul . . . "The Winnebago Tribe" (*Thirty-seventh Annual Report of the B.A.E.,* 1916–17, p. 290).

*Reichard, Gladys A. . "Social Life of the Navajo Indians," *Columbia Univ. Cont. to Anthrop.,* Vol. VII, 1928.

*Riggs, S. R. . . . . "Dakota Grammar, Texts and Ethnography," *United States Geographical and Geological Survey of the Rocky Mountain Region,* Vol. IX, p. 166. 1893.

*Skinner, Alanson . . "Social Life and Ceremonial Bundles of the Menomini Indians," *American Museum of Natural History Anthropological Papers,* Vol. 13, 1915, pp. 42, 51, 79, 80, 95, 434, 486.

*Teit, James . . . . *The Thompson Indians of British Columbia,* pp. 354–72.

*Wissler, Clark . . . "Ceremonial Bundles of the Blackfoot Indians," *American Museum of Natural History Anthropological Papers,* Vol. 7, Part II, pp. 72–85. 1912.
The American Indian, Chap. XIV, 1922.

INDEX

A CATALOG OF SELECTED
DOVER BOOKS
IN ALL FIELDS OF INTEREST

A CATALOG OF SELECTED DOVER
BOOKS IN ALL FIELDS OF INTEREST

CONCERNING THE SPIRITUAL IN ART, Wassily Kandinsky. Pioneering work by father of abstract art. Thoughts on color theory, nature of art. Analysis of earlier masters. 12 illustrations. 80pp. of text. 5⅜ x 8½. 23411-8

ANIMALS: 1,419 Copyright-Free Illustrations of Mammals, Birds, Fish, Insects, etc., Jim Harter (ed.). Clear wood engravings present, in extremely lifelike poses, over 1,000 species of animals. One of the most extensive pictorial sourcebooks of its kind. Captions. Index. 284pp. 9 x 12. 23766-4

CELTIC ART: The Methods of Construction, George Bain. Simple geometric techniques for making Celtic interlacements, spirals, Kells-type initials, animals, humans, etc. Over 500 illustrations. 160pp. 9 x 12. (Available in U.S. only.) 22923-8

AN ATLAS OF ANATOMY FOR ARTISTS, Fritz Schider. Most thorough reference work on art anatomy in the world. Hundreds of illustrations, including selections from works by Vesalius, Leonardo, Goya, Ingres, Michelangelo, others. 593 illustrations. 192pp. 7⅛ x 10¼. 20241-0

CELTIC HAND STROKE-BY-STROKE (Irish Half-Uncial from "The Book of Kells"): An Arthur Baker Calligraphy Manual, Arthur Baker. Complete guide to creating each letter of the alphabet in distinctive Celtic manner. Covers hand position, strokes, pens, inks, paper, more. Illustrated. 48pp. 8¼ x 11. 24336-2

EASY ORIGAMI, John Montroll. Charming collection of 32 projects (hat, cup, pelican, piano, swan, many more) specially designed for the novice origami hobbyist. Clearly illustrated easy-to-follow instructions insure that even beginning papercrafters will achieve successful results. 48pp. 8¼ x 11. 27298-2

THE COMPLETE BOOK OF BIRDHOUSE CONSTRUCTION FOR WOODWORKERS, Scott D. Campbell. Detailed instructions, illustrations, tables. Also data on bird habitat and instinct patterns. Bibliography. 3 tables. 63 illustrations in 15 figures. 48pp. 5¼ x 8½. 24407-5

BLOOMINGDALE'S ILLUSTRATED 1886 CATALOG: Fashions, Dry Goods and Housewares, Bloomingdale Brothers. Famed merchants' extremely rare catalog depicting about 1,700 products: clothing, housewares, firearms, dry goods, jewelry, more. Invaluable for dating, identifying vintage items. Also, copyright-free graphics for artists, designers. Co-published with Henry Ford Museum & Greenfield Village. 160pp. 8¼ x 11. 25780-0

HISTORIC COSTUME IN PICTURES, Braun & Schneider. Over 1,450 costumed figures in clearly detailed engravings–from dawn of civilization to end of 19th century. Captions. Many folk costumes. 256pp. 8⅜ x 11¾. 23150-X

FRANK LLOYD WRIGHT'S DANA HOUSE, Donald Hoffmann. Pictorial essay of residential masterpiece with over 160 interior and exterior photos, plans, elevations, sketches and studies. 128pp. 9¹/₄ x 10¾.   29120-0

THE MALE AND FEMALE FIGURE IN MOTION: 60 Classic Photographic Sequences, Eadweard Muybridge. 60 true-action photographs of men and women walking, running, climbing, bending, turning, etc., reproduced from rare 19th-century masterpiece. vi + 121pp. 9 x 12.   24745-7

1001 QUESTIONS ANSWERED ABOUT THE SEASHORE, N. J. Berrill and Jacquelyn Berrill. Queries answered about dolphins, sea snails, sponges, starfish, fishes, shore birds, many others. Covers appearance, breeding, growth, feeding, much more. 305pp. 5¼ x 8¼.   23366-9

ATTRACTING BIRDS TO YOUR YARD, William J. Weber. Easy-to-follow guide offers advice on how to attract the greatest diversity of birds: birdhouses, feeders, water and waterers, much more. 96pp. 5³/₁₆ x 8¼.   28927-3

MEDICINAL AND OTHER USES OF NORTH AMERICAN PLANTS: A Historical Survey with Special Reference to the Eastern Indian Tribes, Charlotte Erichsen-Brown. Chronological historical citations document 500 years of usage of plants, trees, shrubs native to eastern Canada, northeastern U.S. Also complete identifying information. 343 illustrations. 544pp. 6½ x 9¼.   25951-X

STORYBOOK MAZES, Dave Phillips. 23 stories and mazes on two-page spreads: Wizard of Oz, Treasure Island, Robin Hood, etc. Solutions. 64pp. 8¼ x 11. 23628-5

AMERICAN NEGRO SONGS: 230 Folk Songs and Spirituals, Religious and Secular, John W. Work. This authoritative study traces the African influences of songs sung and played by black Americans at work, in church, and as entertainment. The author discusses the lyric significance of such songs as "Swing Low, Sweet Chariot," "John Henry," and others and offers the words and music for 230 songs. Bibliography. Index of Song Titles. 272pp. 6½ x 9¼.   40271-1

MOVIE-STAR PORTRAITS OF THE FORTIES, John Kobal (ed.). 163 glamor, studio photos of 106 stars of the 1940s: Rita Hayworth, Ava Gardner, Marlon Brando, Clark Gable, many more. 176pp. 8⅜ x 11¼.   23546-7

BENCHLEY LOST AND FOUND, Robert Benchley. Finest humor from early 30s, about pet peeves, child psychologists, post office and others. Mostly unavailable elsewhere. 73 illustrations by Peter Arno and others. 183pp. 5⅜ x 8½.   22410-4

YEKL and THE IMPORTED BRIDEGROOM AND OTHER STORIES OF YIDDISH NEW YORK, Abraham Cahan. Film Hester Street based on *Yekl* (1896). Novel, other stories among first about Jewish immigrants on N.Y.'s East Side. 240pp. 5⅜ x 8½.   22427-9

SELECTED POEMS, Walt Whitman. Generous sampling from *Leaves of Grass*. Twenty-four poems include "I Hear America Singing," "Song of the Open Road," "I Sing the Body Electric," "When Lilacs Last in the Dooryard Bloom'd," "O Captain! My Captain!"–all reprinted from an authoritative edition. Lists of titles and first lines. 128pp. 5³/₁₆ x 8¼.   26878-0

MY BONDAGE AND MY FREEDOM, Frederick Douglass. Born a slave, Douglass became outspoken force in antislavery movement. The best of Douglass' autobiographies. Graphic description of slave life. 464pp. 5⅜ x 8½.   22457-0

FOLLOWING THE EQUATOR: A Journey Around the World, Mark Twain. Fascinating humorous account of 1897 voyage to Hawaii, Australia, India, New Zealand, etc. Ironic, bemused reports on peoples, customs, climate, flora and fauna, politics, much more. 197 illustrations. 720pp. 5⅜ x 8½.   26113-1

THE PEOPLE CALLED SHAKERS, Edward D. Andrews. Definitive study of Shakers: origins, beliefs, practices, dances, social organization, furniture and crafts, etc. 33 illustrations. 351pp. 5⅜ x 8½.   21081-2

THE MYTHS OF GREECE AND ROME, H. A. Guerber. A classic of mythology, generously illustrated, long prized for its simple, graphic, accurate retelling of the principal myths of Greece and Rome, and for its commentary on their origins and significance. With 64 illustrations by Michelangelo, Raphael, Titian, Rubens, Canova, Bernini and others. 480pp. 5⅜ x 8½.   27584-1

PSYCHOLOGY OF MUSIC, Carl E. Seashore. Classic work discusses music as a medium from psychological viewpoint. Clear treatment of physical acoustics, auditory apparatus, sound perception, development of musical skills, nature of musical feeling, host of other topics. 88 figures. 408pp. 5⅜ x 8½.   21851-1

THE PHILOSOPHY OF HISTORY, Georg W. Hegel. Great classic of Western thought develops concept that history is not chance but rational process, the evolution of freedom. 457pp. 5⅜ x 8½.   20112-0

THE BOOK OF TEA, Kakuzo Okakura. Minor classic of the Orient: entertaining, charming explanation, interpretation of traditional Japanese culture in terms of tea ceremony. 94pp. 5⅜ x 8½.   20070-1

LIFE IN ANCIENT EGYPT, Adolf Erman. Fullest, most thorough, detailed older account with much not in more recent books, domestic life, religion, magic, medicine, commerce, much more. Many illustrations reproduce tomb paintings, carvings, hieroglyphs, etc. 597pp. 5⅜ x 8½.   22632-8

SUNDIALS, Their Theory and Construction, Albert Waugh. Far and away the best, most thorough coverage of ideas, mathematics concerned, types, construction, adjusting anywhere. Simple, nontechnical treatment allows even children to build several of these dials. Over 100 illustrations. 230pp. 5⅜ x 8½.   22947-5

THEORETICAL HYDRODYNAMICS, L. M. Milne-Thomson. Classic exposition of the mathematical theory of fluid motion, applicable to both hydrodynamics and aerodynamics. Over 600 exercises. 768pp. 6⅛ x 9¼.   68970-0

SONGS OF EXPERIENCE: Facsimile Reproduction with 26 Plates in Full Color, William Blake. 26 full-color plates from a rare 1826 edition. Includes "The Tyger," "London," "Holy Thursday," and other poems. Printed text of poems. 48pp. 5¼ x 7.
24636-1

OLD-TIME VIGNETTES IN FULL COLOR, Carol Belanger Grafton (ed.). Over 390 charming, often sentimental illustrations, selected from archives of Victorian graphics—pretty women posing, children playing, food, flowers, kittens and puppies, smiling cherubs, birds and butterflies, much more. All copyright-free. 48pp. 9¼ x 12¼.
27269-9

LITTLE BOOK OF EARLY AMERICAN CRAFTS AND TRADES, Peter Stockham (ed.). 1807 children's book explains crafts and trades: baker, hatter, cooper, potter, and many others. 23 copperplate illustrations. 140pp. 4⅝ x 6.   23336-7

VICTORIAN FASHIONS AND COSTUMES FROM HARPER'S BAZAR, 1867–1898, Stella Blum (ed.). Day costumes, evening wear, sports clothes, shoes, hats, other accessories in over 1,000 detailed engravings. 320pp. 9⅜ x 12¼.   22990-4

GUSTAV STICKLEY, THE CRAFTSMAN, Mary Ann Smith. Superb study surveys broad scope of Stickley's achievement, especially in architecture. Design philosophy, rise and fall of the Craftsman empire, descriptions and floor plans for many Craftsman houses, more. 86 black-and-white halftones. 31 line illustrations. Introduction 208pp. 6½ x 9¼.   27210-9

THE LONG ISLAND RAIL ROAD IN EARLY PHOTOGRAPHS, Ron Ziel. Over 220 rare photos, informative text document origin (1844) and development of rail service on Long Island. Vintage views of early trains, locomotives, stations, passengers, crews, much more. Captions. 8⅞ x 11¾.   26301-0

VOYAGE OF THE LIBERDADE, Joshua Slocum. Great 19th-century mariner's thrilling, first-hand account of the wreck of his ship off South America, the 35-foot boat he built from the wreckage, and its remarkable voyage home. 128pp. 5⅜ x 8½.
40022-0

TEN BOOKS ON ARCHITECTURE, Vitruvius. The most important book ever written on architecture. Early Roman aesthetics, technology, classical orders, site selection, all other aspects. Morgan translation. 331pp. 5⅜ x 8½.   20645-9

THE HUMAN FIGURE IN MOTION, Eadweard Muybridge. More than 4,500 stopped-action photos, in action series, showing undraped men, women, children jumping, lying down, throwing, sitting, wrestling, carrying, etc. 390pp. 7⅞ x 10⅝.
20204-6 Clothbd.

TREES OF THE EASTERN AND CENTRAL UNITED STATES AND CANADA, William M. Harlow. Best one-volume guide to 140 trees. Full descriptions, woodlore, range, etc. Over 600 illustrations. Handy size. 288pp. 4½ x 6⅜.   20395-6

SONGS OF WESTERN BIRDS, Dr. Donald J. Borror. Complete song and call repertoire of 60 western species, including flycatchers, juncoes, cactus wrens, many more–includes fully illustrated booklet.   Cassette and manual 99913-0

GROWING AND USING HERBS AND SPICES, Milo Miloradovich. Versatile handbook provides all the information needed for cultivation and use of all the herbs and spices available in North America. 4 illustrations. Index. Glossary. 236pp. 5⅜ x 8½.
25058-X

BIG BOOK OF MAZES AND LABYRINTHS, Walter Shepherd. 50 mazes and labyrinths in all–classical, solid, ripple, and more–in one great volume. Perfect inexpensive puzzler for clever youngsters. Full solutions. 112pp. 8⅛ x 11.   22951-3

CATALOG OF DOVER BOOKS

ANATOMY: A Complete Guide for Artists, Joseph Sheppard. A master of figure drawing shows artists how to render human anatomy convincingly. Over 460 illustrations. 224pp. 8⅜ x 11¼. 27279-6

MEDIEVAL CALLIGRAPHY: Its History and Technique, Marc Drogin. Spirited history, comprehensive instruction manual covers 13 styles (ca. 4th century through 15th). Excellent photographs; directions for duplicating medieval techniques with modern tools. 224pp. 8⅜ x 11¼. 26142-5

DRIED FLOWERS: How to Prepare Them, Sarah Whitlock and Martha Rankin. Complete instructions on how to use silica gel, meal and borax, perlite aggregate, sand and borax, glycerine and water to create attractive permanent flower arrangements. 12 illustrations. 32pp. 5⅜ x 8½. 21802-3

EASY-TO-MAKE BIRD FEEDERS FOR WOODWORKERS, Scott D. Campbell. Detailed, simple-to-use guide for designing, constructing, caring for and using feeders. Text, illustrations for 12 classic and contemporary designs. 96pp. 5⅜ x 8½. 25847-5

SCOTTISH WONDER TALES FROM MYTH AND LEGEND, Donald A. Mackenzie. 16 lively tales tell of giants rumbling down mountainsides, of a magic wand that turns stone pillars into warriors, of gods and goddesses, evil hags, powerful forces and more. 240pp. 5⅜ x 8½. 29677-6

THE HISTORY OF UNDERCLOTHES, C. Willett Cunnington and Phyllis Cunnington. Fascinating, well-documented survey covering six centuries of English undergarments, enhanced with over 100 illustrations: 12th-century laced-up bodice, footed long drawers (1795), 19th-century bustles, 19th-century corsets for men, Victorian "bust improvers," much more. 272pp. 5⅜ x 8¼. 27124-2

ARTS AND CRAFTS FURNITURE: The Complete Brooks Catalog of 1912, Brooks Manufacturing Co. Photos and detailed descriptions of more than 150 now very collectible furniture designs from the Arts and Crafts movement depict davenports, settees, buffets, desks, tables, chairs, bedsteads, dressers and more, all built of solid, quarter-sawed oak. Invaluable for students and enthusiasts of antiques, Americana and the decorative arts. 80pp. 6½ x 9¼. 27471-3

WILBUR AND ORVILLE: A Biography of the Wright Brothers, Fred Howard. Definitive, crisply written study tells the full story of the brothers' lives and work. A vividly written biography, unparalleled in scope and color, that also captures the spirit of an extraordinary era. 560pp. 6⅛ x 9¼. 40297-5

THE ARTS OF THE SAILOR: Knotting, Splicing and Ropework, Hervey Garrett Smith. Indispensable shipboard reference covers tools, basic knots and useful hitches; handsewing and canvas work, more. Over 100 illustrations. Delightful reading for sea lovers. 256pp. 5⅜ x 8½. 26440-8

FRANK LLOYD WRIGHT'S FALLINGWATER: The House and Its History, Second, Revised Edition, Donald Hoffmann. A total revision–both in text and illustrations–of the standard document on Fallingwater, the boldest, most personal architectural statement of Wright's mature years, updated with valuable new material from the recently opened Frank Lloyd Wright Archives. "Fascinating"–*The New York Times*. 116 illustrations. 128pp. 9¼ x 10¾. 27430-6

CATALOG OF DOVER BOOKS

THE STORY OF THE TITANIC AS TOLD BY ITS SURVIVORS, Jack Winocour (ed.). What it was really like. Panic, despair, shocking inefficiency, and a little heroism. More thrilling than any fictional account. 26 illustrations. 320pp. 5⅜ x 8½.
20610-6

FAIRY AND FOLK TALES OF THE IRISH PEASANTRY, William Butler Yeats (ed.). Treasury of 64 tales from the twilight world of Celtic myth and legend: "The Soul Cages," "The Kildare Pooka," "King O'Toole and his Goose," many more. Introduction and Notes by W. B. Yeats. 352pp. 5⅜ x 8½.
26941-8

BUDDHIST MAHAYANA TEXTS, E. B. Cowell and others (eds.). Superb, accurate translations of basic documents in Mahayana Buddhism, highly important in history of religions. The Buddha-karita of Asvaghosha, Larger Sukhavativyuha, more. 448pp. 5⅜ x 8½.
25552-2

ONE TWO THREE . . . INFINITY: Facts and Speculations of Science, George Gamow. Great physicist's fascinating, readable overview of contemporary science: number theory, relativity, fourth dimension, entropy, genes, atomic structure, much more. 128 illustrations. Index. 352pp. 5⅜ x 8½.
25664-2

EXPERIMENTATION AND MEASUREMENT, W. J. Youden. Introductory manual explains laws of measurement in simple terms and offers tips for achieving accuracy and minimizing errors. Mathematics of measurement, use of instruments, experimenting with machines. 1994 edition. Foreword. Preface. Introduction. Epilogue. Selected Readings. Glossary. Index. Tables and figures. 128pp. 5⅜ x 8½.   40451-X

DALÍ ON MODERN ART: The Cuckolds of Antiquated Modern Art, Salvador Dalí. Influential painter skewers modern art and its practitioners. Outrageous evaluations of Picasso, Cézanne, Turner, more. 15 renderings of paintings discussed. 44 calligraphic decorations by Dalí. 96pp. 5⅜ x 8½. (Available in U.S. only.)   29220-7

ANTIQUE PLAYING CARDS: A Pictorial History, Henry René D'Allemagne. Over 900 elaborate, decorative images from rare playing cards (14th–20th centuries): Bacchus, death, dancing dogs, hunting scenes, royal coats of arms, players cheating, much more. 96pp. 9¼ x 12¼.
29265-7

MAKING FURNITURE MASTERPIECES: 30 Projects with Measured Drawings, Franklin H. Gottshall. Step-by-step instructions, illustrations for constructing handsome, useful pieces, among them a Sheraton desk, Chippendale chair, Spanish desk, Queen Anne table and a William and Mary dressing mirror. 224pp. 8⅛ x 11¼.
29338-6

THE FOSSIL BOOK: A Record of Prehistoric Life, Patricia V. Rich et al. Profusely illustrated definitive guide covers everything from single-celled organisms and dinosaurs to birds and mammals and the interplay between climate and man. Over 1,500 illustrations. 760pp. 7½ x 10⅛.
29371-8